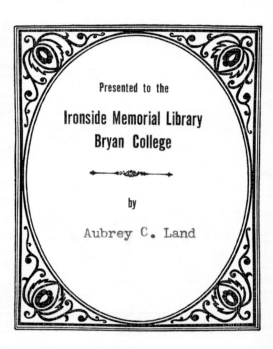

ROBERT S. KERR: THE SENATE YEARS

A characteristic pose of the "uncrowned King of the Senate."
Source: Robert S. Kerr Collection, University of Oklahoma.

ROBERT S. KERR: THE SENATE YEARS

by Anne Hodges Morgan

UNIVERSITY OF OKLAHOMA PRESS

Library of Congress Cataloging in Publication Data

Morgan, Anne Hodges, 1940–
    Robert S. Kerr.

    Bibliography: p. 307
    Includes index.
    1. Kerr, Robert Samuel, 1896–1963. 2. Legislators—United States—
Biography. 3. Oklahoma—Governors—Biography. 4. United States—
Politics and government—20th century. 5. Oklahoma—Politics and gov-
ernment—1907–
E748.K42M67   328.73'092'4 [B]   76–62514

This study is dedicated to my parents,
Velvon and J. G. Hodges

PREFACE

Robert S. Kerr was one of the most important and influential members of the twentieth-century United States Senate. This book is not a full-scale biography but rather an attempt to identify the reasons for Kerr's prominence and to assess his contributions to Oklahoma, the Democratic party, and national politics.

A successful oilman and the founder of Kerr-McGee Oil Industries, Kerr served as the governor of Oklahoma from 1943 to 1947. Elected to the Senate in 1948, his tenure in Washington was relatively brief. But after his death on New Year's Day, 1963, senators of both parties, allies and antagonists, mourned him as the "uncrowned King of the Senate."

He achieved prominence and influence in the Senate because of his legislative work on public works questions, such as the development of the Arkansas River Navigation System, the regulation of gas and oil production, expansion of the Social Security program, the development of medical care programs for the aged, and establishment of the manned space program. In the course of dealing with these issues—and partially as a result of his overlapping membership on such strategic Senate committees as Finance, Public Works, Appropriations, and Aeronautics and Space Sciences—Kerr worked closely with major national leaders—Lyndon Johnson, Richard Russell, and John Kennedy. Developing a masterful understanding of how to secure legislation, he became

a major figure in a southern-dominated Senate during the fifties
and early sixties.

Adept in the tradition of the southern, border-state style of
political activity, Kerr was effective with the electorates of the
small towns and emerging cities of Oklahoma alike. He was a
transitional leader who helped take his state from an essentially
agrarian, small-town society into the modern industrial, techno-
logically oriented society that followed World War II.

As a view of national politics from within the legislative
process, this book examines the complexities and subtleties of
Senate-Executive relationships. Since historians have begun to look
more closely at the Truman, Eisenhower, and Kennedy Administrations, this emphasis on legislative politics is offered as a corrective to the idea that little of consequence was accomplished
during those years. And despite their importance in the total
governmental process, there are few scholarly studies of southern
and southwestern national legislative leaders of this period. This
book attempts to help fill in that gap.

I wish to thank the children of Senator Kerr—Robert S. Kerr,
Jr., Breene M. Kerr, Kay Kerr Clark, and William G. Kerr—for
their courteous assistance. At no time did they attempt to shape
my judgments or to influence my conclusions. They gave me considerable insight into the Senator's personality, as well as helpful
information concerning his political career.

During the research and writing of this book, I had the good
fortune and pleasure to live in Oklahoma, where memories of
Robert S. Kerr are still vivid. Most Oklahomans over forty have
sharp recollections of Kerr; and, like all people still close to a
rural past, they love to recount the myths, as well as the facts,
about their local heroes. Despite the frequent exaggerations and
the understandable biases that a powerful and colorful political
figure always provokes, the scores of conversations I had with
Oklahomans helped me to understand the man and his times in
a way that the documents of his past can only partially illuminate.

Many of the people who worked closely with Kerr as governor and senator graciously shared their recollections with me.
Although I was hesitant in the beginning about the scholarly value

of such interviews, Rex Hawks' remark that Kerr's memory could best be served when "the whole story is known" was typical of the attitude I encountered. I am particularly grateful to Mr. Hawks, Burl Hays, William R. Reynolds, Don McBride, and former Senator J. Allen Frear for their candor and their encouragement.

I am also indebted to the librarians who assisted me. Jack Haley and the staff of the Western History Collection at the University of Oklahoma's Bizzell Memorial Library did everything possible to facilitate my work in the Kerr Papers and related manuscript collections. Mae Warburg's excellent guide to the Kerr Papers was especially useful. Vicki Withers at the Oklahoma State University Library, Sylvie Turner at the John F. Kennedy Presidential Library, and Charles Colley at the Arizona State University Library deftly guided me through their collections. And the staffs of the University of Virginia Library, the Chicago Historical Society, the Harry S Truman Library, the Sam Rayburn Library, and the Manuscripts Division of the Library of Congress also helped in countless ways.

I owe special thanks to Professor William L. Settle, Jr., of the History Department at Tulsa University. Dr. Settle shared not only his own research on the Arkansas River Navigation Project with me, but his office, his typewriter, and his friendship. I am also in his debt for his careful review and critique of several portions of this study.

Professor John S. Ezell, curator of the Western History Collection at the University of Oklahoma, was of inestimable help to me in researching Senator Kerr's business career. He generously provided intricate and elusive details from his own research on the Kerr-McGee Corporation.

Professor Louise Welsh of the University of Oklahoma's History Department was very kind to read and criticize the early chapters on Kerr in Oklahoma. Mrs. Amy Moorhead, who cheerfully reviewed every version of this study, was far more than a proofreader. Her genuine interest and enthusiasm for the subject was a constant encouragement. Mrs. Irene Ferrar of the Congressional Research Service of the Library of Congress generously helped in arranging the bothersome details of several research ventures. She was a welcome companion on two research trips, and her insights into congressional politics frequently slipped past her modest demeanor to stimulate my thinking. I am also grateful to Alexis Rodgers, who typed the manuscript with good humor augmented by good judgment.

Mrs. Robert Hasskarl of Ada, Oklahoma gave me considerable information on the Kerr family in Missouri and her inventory of the Rosedale Cemetery for the Pontotoc County Historical and Genealogical Society was also useful. I am especially grateful to Mrs. Mattie Logsdon for her generous help in securing several early photos. The faculty of the University of Texas at Austin History Department offered many constructive suggestions. Robert A. Divine was particularly helpful on the 1952 election. Thomas McCraw, Clarence Lasby, and Robert Cotner also made useful and corrective comments which strengthened the study.

But Lewis L. Gould merits separate recognition. Although his enthusiasm and interest in this project were always helpful and encouraging, the example of his own scholarship and his professional commitment to excellence provided the most compelling standard.

I am also indebted to my husband, H. Wayne Morgan, for four years of seemingly endless conversations about this book. His observations have helped broaden my historical perspective, and his insights into American political history have stimulated my own thinking.

I, of course, accept full responsibility for the imperfections of this work.

Norman, Oklahoma   Anne Hodges Morgan
August, 1976

CONTENTS

ILLUSTRATIONS

ROBERT S. KERR:
THE SENATE YEARS

CHAPTER I
The Oklahoma Years

Robert Samuel Kerr began life with all the trappings of an American folk hero. He was born on September 11, 1896, in a fourteen-square-foot, windowless log cabin in Indian Territory southeast of what is now Ada, Oklahoma. His parents, William Samuel and Margaret Wright Kerr, were early pioneers on the Oklahoma frontier, and the family's struggle to survive produced strong traits of self-reliance and independence in all their children.

William Samuel Kerr was born near Bakersfield, Missouri, on January 13, 1868. Violent hatreds growing out of the Civil War plagued this border country. When Sam was only nine months old, Quantrill's raiders, a guerilla band of former Confederate soldiers, murdered his father in the family's front yard. The raiders continued to terrorize southwestern Missouri, and after an invalid uncle was killed and his home burned, Sam's mother fled with him to a relative's farm near the Arkansas border. His mother died when Sam was five and an uncle, Peter Mitchell, raised the orphaned boy. Mitchell realized that the code of the hills required that Sam avenge his father's and uncle's murders. Several of the raiders still lived in the area, and the young man knew who they were. Sam's choice was a bleak one—kill or be killed.

But Mitchell persuaded his nephew to forego revenge and make a new life. In 1885, wearing a suit purchased with the profits from two barrels of molasses made from sugar cane he had raised on Mitchell's farm, Sam Kerr left Missouri. He settled in Texas because he found work as a farm hand near Milford in Ellis County. Determined to improve himself, Kerr attended subscription schools between cotton-picking seasons and earned the equivalent of a high school diploma. Soon he began teaching school in addition to his farm job. In December 1893, Sam married Margaret Wright, the daughter of a former Confederate soldier. Like her new husband, Margaret had learned self-reliance early. When she was very young her father, a Texas peace officer, had been killed while rounding up horse thieves.

In 1895 Sam Kerr leased 169 acres in Pecan Grove Valley in the Chickasaw Nation and moved his wife and baby daughter, Lois, in a covered wagon to their new home. Six more children were born there, and Robert Samuel Kerr, a robust twelve pounds at birth, was the eldest of five sons.[1]

All the Kerrs worked hard to support this large family. Sam supervised the cotton and corn while his sons tended the fruit orchard. As the territory's population grew, nearby Ada "on the tank town-oprey circuit"[2] offered more diversified employment. Robert's most vivid childhood memory was of his father's struggle to support the family. "I would see him leave home and walk down the railroad track on Sunday evening, and then come back on Friday."[3] Sam taught school in Ada and worked at the lumber yard in the winter months. When the Oklahoma Portland Cement Company opened in 1907, he worked there while also serving as a bookkeeper for the First National Bank. Sam Kerr's efforts to provide for his family soon paralleled a concern for civic matters. As a member of the Ada city council, he helped organize the town's public school system and the public water system. After statehood he served as county clerk. The elder Kerr "was in every progressive move of the citizens of Ada,"[4] and he instilled a sense of public service and civic responsibility in his children. As he grew to manhood, Robert resembled both his parents. His father's tenacity and determination to succeed leavened the salty wit and cheerful disposition inherited from his mother.

Sam Kerr's passion for work and his ambition to better himself flowered in his eldest son, and his religious and political convictions passed to Robert with the consistency of Mendelian genetics. Robert joined the Baptist church in 1905 and taught a Sunday School class regularly while governor and senator. He held both state and national office in the Southern Baptist Convention and was the single largest contributor to Baptist causes in Oklahoma, reportedly giving 30 per cent of his income to the church throughout his career.[5] Robert Kerr's religious convictions were undoubtedly genuine. He kept the boyhood pledge not to drink alcoholic beverages, and his command of Scripture was legendary. But being a Baptist also enhanced his political possibilities later in life. The Baptist church wielded enormous political power in Oklahoma, and membership in, or endorsement from, the church was important for political advancement.[6]

Robert attended public school in Ada through the eighth grade. He then transferred to Ada's East Central Normal for the four years of high school, except for the eleventh grade at the new Oklahoma Baptist University in Shawnee. His mother hoped he would decide to study for the ministry while at O.B.U., but Robert already had other plans. A twelfth-grade diploma qualified him to teach; and, eager to be on his own, Kerr found a teaching job at a small, country school in Beebee, Oklahoma. He used the meager salary to finance a two-year correspondence degree from East Central State College. During this time he became friends with Ernest McFarland, who later served with him in the United States Senate.[7]

Although rudimentary, Robert's education was the best Oklahoma offered at the time. He mastered the basic skills easily, exhibiting a quick mind and an enormous capacity to absorb and recall information. Never seriously interested in scholarship, the son, like his father, saw an education as the foundation for social and financial success. Growing up during Oklahoma's transition from territory to statehood, Robert developed a keen interest in politics. Although he had no aversion to hard work—he once picked 396 pounds of cotton in a single day at the age of fifteen— Robert saw no intrinsic merit in physical labor. He recalled his father's advice that "the practice of law was the quickest route to public life,"[8] borrowed $350, and enrolled at the University of Oklahoma in the fall of 1915 to study law.

Though only nineteen at the time, Robert was a tall, husky farm boy restless from teaching school in an isolated community and eager to prove his ability on the football field. He wrote his father for permission to join the team. But Sam Kerr was cool toward athletics, which he considered a waste of time. The elder Kerr, ambitious for his son to develop skills that would enhance his chances for a career in public life, had other contests in mind when he replied, "I would rather have made Bryan's cross-of-gold speech in 1896 than to have won every athletic contest which has taken place since Cain and Abel ran their first footrace on the banks of the Euphrates."[9] That ended football, and Robert joined the debating team.

The borrowed money ran out in 1916, and with it Robert's formal education. Instead of returning to a rural teaching post or his father's farm, he found a job as a magazine salesman for the Curtis Publishing Company. Selling magazine subscriptions was neither as easy nor as glamorous as Robert had imagined, but he "got new inspiration everytime he thought about chopping cotton."[10] His travels took him to Webb County, Missouri, where he met Robert Elliott, a prominent attorney. Elliott was so impressed with Kerr's sales talk that he suggested Robert work as a clerk and errand boy in his office while continuing to read law. He promised a monthly salary of $100. Though eager to earn such a large sum and to finish his education, Kerr refused to accept until Elliott agreed to subscribe to a magazine.[11]

When the United States entered World War I, Kerr was commissioned a second lieutenant in army field artillery. He served nine months in France, but the armistice came before he experienced combat.[12] Although Kerr played down his military service in later years, saying, "The only powder I smelled was face powder,"[13] he recognized the value of maintaining contacts with other veterans for both business and politics. He served in the Officer's Reserve Corps after the war and rose to the rank of major in the Oklahoma National Guard. Active in forming the American Legion Post in Ada, Kerr was elected state commander in 1925—the youngest in the nation. In this capacity he traveled throughout Oklahoma making speeches and friends.[14]

For Kerr the early 1920's were years of personal tragedy and private anguish. After the war, he returned to Ada. With borrowed money he and two partners established a wholesale grocery business. Samuel Kerr had been in the produce business since 1902, and it seemed natural for Robert to follow. On December 5, 1919, he married Reba Shelton of Ada and settled down to life as a young merchant. The following year twin daughters died at birth. In November 1921 fire destroyed the produce warehouse leaving Kerr $10,000 in debt. Reba Kerr taught school so that her husband could resume studying law in the office of Judge J. F. McKeel. In addition to his studies, he worked as captain for Battery F of the 160th Field Artillery National Guard Unit at Ada for $60 a month.[15] Kerr passed the bar examination in 1922 and entered a partnership with Judge McKeel that lasted five years. The young family's hardships seemed almost behind them when both Reba and a baby son died in childbirth in February, 1924. Alone, grieving, and deeply in debt, Robert Kerr turned to the solace of his pioneer heritage—all-consuming work.[16]

Kerr early told his father that he wanted three things in life: a family, a million dollars, and the governorship of Oklahoma, in that order. The elder Kerr was not surprised at Robert's ambition and offered some practical advice. "First establish yourself in some kind of business or profession, so that you will have something substantial besides the salary of your office to fall back on, and thus be able to increase your opportunity for service."[17] With his family dead and his business in ashes, Robert Kerr started over. Soon the new law practice and his duties as the American Legion commander the following year provided escape from private griefs. Making only $125 a month from his practice and still over $10,000 in debt, Kerr decided to begin a new family. On December 26, 1925, after a brief courtship begun at a tennis match, Kerr married Grayce Breene, a tall, soft-spoken, graceful blonde from Tulsa.

The youngest daughter of a well-to-do Tulsa drilling contractor, Harry Hooker Breene, Grayce Kerr had studied music as a girl and had hoped for a career as a singer. Although her interest in politics did not develop until after her marriage, the Breene family connections helped to launch Kerr's business and nourished his ambition for public office.[18] The marriage was the harbinger of good fortune. In later years Kerr mused, "The day I met her was the turning point in my life."[19] Over the next dozen years the Kerrs had three sons and a daughter. Although he never spoke of his sadness, the lingering grief Kerr had experienced in losing his first family made him very protective and solicitous of his new brood.

Earning his first million—Kerr's second goal—took a little longer than acquiring a handsome family. In 1926 Kerr's law firm did some legal work for Dixon Brothers, a small contract-drilling firm in Anadarko, Oklahoma. Dixon Brothers' chief fieldman was Kerr's brother-in-law, James L. Anderson. Kerr was paid for his legal services and also was given a chance to work out a 20 per cent share of stock worth $10,000. In less than three years he had acquired the share, and the company had expanded by adding one large drilling rig. In 1929 Kerr gave up his law practice. He and Anderson, each owning 20 per cent of the stock, borrowed $5,000 in cash from Lew Wentz, a Republican millionaire from Ponca City and close associate of his father-in-law, Harry Breene; and, with two $25,000 mortgages, the pair bought the business, calling it the Anderson-Kerr Drilling Company.[20] This readiness to take a risk when he saw a chance for future success characterized Kerr's business ventures, as well as his political career.

In 1932 the Kerr family moved to Oklahoma City, where the new company had already established headquarters. Here the talents of its owners flourished. "Anderson had a nose for oil, and an ability to drill cheaper than his competitors; and Kerr had a talent for finding investment capital and separating it from its owners."[21] There were extensive oil reserves within the limits of Oklahoma City, but "town lot" drilling was dangerous and expensive. The possibility of accidents and serious damage to property frightened many companies. The city also discouraged drilling with the requirement of a $200,000 bond for each well. In spite of the Depression, Anderson-Kerr raised enough money to buy four leases in 1932 and obtained two more in partnership with Continental Oil Company. Anderson-Kerr lacked the money to post bond, so Kerr devised a way for Continental Oil to assist.

Continental paid $360,000 for a half-interest in the six wells and agreed to advance another $15,000 apiece when they were drilled —a total investment of $450,000. Anderson-Kerr kept the other half-interest but pledged *one-half* of any revenues from their interest to paying off the $15,000 advances. The complicated scheme worked. All the wells came in, Continental was reimbursed, and Robert Kerr was on his way to the first million.[22]

In 1935 Kerr began a long and profitable collaboration with Phillips Petroleum Company. Phillips Petroleum had a large number of potentially valuable oil leases in Oklahoma City. But the city had passed an ordinance requiring voter approval of any extension of the drilling done within the city limits in an attempt to ensure against future drilling accidents. K. S. "Boots" Adams, assistant to President Frank Phillips, consulted Kerr about a campaign to win a drilling zone extension. Adams went to Kerr not only because he was one of the best-known civic leaders in Oklahoma City, but he also recognized that Kerr's obvious ambition would ensure a successful campaign.[23]

Kerr eagerly undertook the job for Adams, but not for the traditional fee. Instead of cash, Kerr required that his firm be given preferential treatment when Phillips awarded drilling contracts in the Oklahoma City field. Adams agreed to this rather unorthodox proposal, and Kerr began the campaign. He went from house to house persuading residents that a vote for expanded drilling would mean a share of the oil profits for the entire city and for many residents individually.[24] The vote for extension was overwhelming, and in 1936 Kerr managed another successful campaign for Phillips.

Anderson-Kerr made a small fortune drilling for Phillips Petroleum.[25] But this venture paid greater dividends to Kerr than mere cash. When Anderson decided to retire in 1937, Kerr persuaded two Phillips executives to join him, R. B. Lynn and Dean McGee, and formed the Kerlyn Oil Company. Although Kerr got along well with Lynn, other officers in the company, particularly Kerr's brother Travis and Dean Terrill, the firm's counsel, "heartily detested him."[26] Lynn eventually left the firm, probably because of political differences. In 1946 McGee became the executive vice-

president, and the company's name was changed to Kerr-McGee
Oil Industries, Inc. His partnership with Dean McGee was Kerr's
master stroke but a serious loss to Phillips Petroleum. McGee
was regarded correctly as one of the greatest geologists in the
oil industry's history. In 1943 Frank Phillips was anxious to renew
his association with his former geologist Dean McGee. Under
McGee's direction, Kerlyn had recently opened a large oil field
in Magnolia, Arkansas—a field Phillips Petroleum had refused
to explore earlier. Aware of Kerlyn's need for capital, Frank Phillips offered Kerr a five-year arrangement that gave Phillips Petroleum a one-half interest in all acreage acquired under McGee's
supervision. In exchange, Phillips agreed to pay three-fourths of
the cost of McGee's explorations, lease acquisitions, and initial
exploratory drilling costs. The arrangement, which lasted about
ten years, was enormously successful. And as a result, Phillips
Petroleum and Kerr-McGee participated in oil drilling throughout
the world.[27] Kerr's association with Dean McGee indicated his
unerring ability to spot a winning combination.

Kerr-McGee Oil Industries prospered on Kerr's original policy
of "aggressive borrowing." The partners were fervent expansion-
ists. They diluted their own original equity in several public stock
offerings to increase liquidity and enlarged certain parts of the
business, such as refining, that offered both tax depreciation as
well as profits. The company quickly diversified its operations
from oil drilling to fuels and minerals. By the late fifties Kerr-
McGee owned or controlled one-quarter of all known United
States uranium deposits, operated a uranium concentrating mill,
and had contracts with the Atomic Energy Commission to sell
over $300 million in uranium ore.[28] Instead of reducing their $70
million long-term debt in the 1960's, Kerr-McGee expanded into
new fuels such as boron and beryllium used in the space industry.
They acquired a one-half interest in 165 million tons of potash in
New Mexico and planned helium extraction plants.[29] At his death
in 1963, Robert Kerr's personal wealth was estimated conserva-
tively at $35 million before taxes.[30]

From the 1930's onward Kerr became identified as a spokesman for the oil and gas industry. After his successful campaign

for Phillips Petroleum in the drilling zone extension, the Kansas-Oklahoma division of the Mid-Continent Oil and Gas Association elected Kerr president. He had been a member less than an hour. The organization had been deadlocked over the leadership question when Kerr brashly offered his services as "a sort of dark horse like we have in politics."[31] As president, he organized an aggressive campaign to curb rising state expenditures, which he believed inevitably resulted in "increased and discriminating taxes levied on petroleum."[32] Kerr never apologized for his efforts on behalf of the oil and gas industry—second only to agriculture in Oklahoma. When the association asked him to accept a fifth term in 1941, he declined because of his plan to run for governor. Chuckling, he said if he lost the election, they would not want him, and if he won, they would not need a man in the industry post.[33]

Concurrent with his business ventures, Kerr had built up his ties with the Oklahoma Democratic party during the preceding decade. His business experience had taught him the value of knowing every level of an organization's activity in order to discover new talent and to appraise performance. At various times from 1919 onward he served as a delegate to precinct, county, and state conventions, as well as precinct chairman and inspector of elections.[34] He also used his position as American Legion state commander to make scores of public speeches across the state. Believing that "money talks," he contributed generously to the Democratic party once his own fortunes prospered.

His first political appointment came in 1931 when Governor Holloway named him special justice on the Oklahoma Supreme Court to hear the Shawnee-Tecumseh county seat case.[35] But Kerr's rise in state politics started in 1934 when he secured the active support of Ernest Marland, former oil millionaire and New Deal congressman. As governor, Marland selected Kerr to serve on the unofficial pardon and parole board.[36] Marland failed in his promise to bring the New Deal to Oklahoma primarily because of opposition from Leon Phillips, speaker of the Oklahoma House of Representatives. Under Phillips' leadership, the legislature refused the increases in state spending for welfare, education, and employment that Marland wanted.[37] But his stillborn proposals to reduce the state's indebtedness, to achieve comprehensive development of Oklahoma's resources, and to attract industry impressed Kerr. These precepts would form the basis of his own governorship several years later.[38]

Association with Marland did not prevent Kerr from backing Leon C. "Red" Phillips in the 1938 gubernatorial election, but he refrained from becoming embroiled in the controversy in the Democratic party over the New Deal. While he favored programs like Social Security and believed in the merits of planning, as an oil man Kerr feared that higher taxes would be imposed on the oil industry to finance deficit spending. When Phillips emerged as the economy candidate and the leading contender, Kerr was eager to work for him. The two had been classmates at the University of Oklahoma, and Kerr was primarily responsible for persuading businessmen that Phillips meant what he said about an economic administration and stopping waste. Kerr also campaigned extensively for Phillips throughout the state.[39]

But the ballots had scarcely been counted when the relationship cooled. Governor Phillips had no intention of becoming the pawn of any interest group. Cynical, skeptical and suspicious, Phillips kept everyone at arm's length. To demonstrate his independence and to avoid pressure on appointees, Phillips boycotted a "fishing party" at Kerr's Pelican Lake, Minnesota, retreat shortly after the 1938 primary. Instead, the wily Phillips turned up in Colorado vacationing with legislative leaders.[40]

Although irritated at Governor Phillips' aloofness, Kerr was not ready to break with him. He wanted and needed Phillips' support for election as Democratic national committeeman in 1940. In November 1939, when the Dies Committee charged Oklahoma Democratic national committeeman Scott Ferris had been paid $32,000 for assistance in a proposed Russian munitions deal, Kerr was acknowledged his most likely successor.[41] Kerr did not announce his candidacy but undertook the responsibility of raising the money to pay Oklahoma's $12,500 assessment from the national Democratic party for the 1940 campaign. So successful were his efforts with the Jefferson-Jackson Day dinners that he earned Democratic National Chairman Jim Farley's quiet endorsement.[42]

In canvassing the Democratic precinct and county conventions during the spring of 1940, Kerr discovered so much sentiment for a third term for Roosevelt that he decided, against Governor Phillips' wishes, to push for an instructed delegation to the national convention. A pragmatic appraisal of his own future in the national Democratic party, not any particular enthusiasm for FDR or the New Deal, dictated Kerr's break with Phillips. But he shrewdly delayed the final breach until the state convention had ratified his election to the Democratic National Committee.[43]

The weakness in the Oklahoma Republican party made the rift between Kerr and Phillips inevitable. In 1940 the GOP was virtually dormant in the Sooner State. The specter of the Hoover depression and Roosevelt's landslides in the thirties left the Republicans unable to exploit the growing anti-New Deal, anti-Roosevelt sentiment. Opposition to the national administration then naturally erupted within Democratic party ranks with Governor Phillips at the helm. At the 1940 Democratic convention in Chicago, Phillips opposed FDR's try for a third term. He threatened Kerr, "If you support Roosevelt, I'll break your back."[44] But Phillips' career, not Kerr's, ended. As national committeeman, Kerr stumped for Roosevelt in every county in Oklahoma. The split with Phillips was the beginning of Kerr's own campaign for the governor's office.[45]

Kerr's campaign for the governorship was the most difficult of his entire political career. Following the 1940 presidential election in which he did nothing to promote the Democratic candidate in Oklahoma, Governor Phillips concentrated on discrediting Kerr for the 1942 gubernatorial race. Phillips charged Kerr with improper conduct in lobbying for a secondary oil recovery bill, and warned Oklahomans not to repeat the experience of the Marland Administration by electing "a rich oil man for governor."[46] The Governor also tried to persuade Kerr's good friend Henry G. Bennett to enter the race. President of Oklahoma A & M College at Stillwater, Bennett had widespread support among teachers, the Baptist church, and farm groups. Allied with Governor Phillips' supporters, he probably could have defeated Kerr for the Democratic gubernatorial nomination.[47] But Phillips' support of Bennett revealed the depths of the governor's animosity for Robert Kerr. Phillips' motives were more personal than political. Bennett, a friend of Vice-President Henry A. Wallace, had helped set up various New Deal agencies in Oklahoma and had worked for Roosevelt's reelection in 1940. There were also indications that the Roosevelt Administration might concur in Bennett's candidacy. The President had told Oklahoma Congressman Jed Johnson, "We would like to see a governor elected [in Oklahoma] without a fight between the national and state Administrations."[48]

Bennett wavered, unwilling to resign his college presidency for the uncertainties of a political campaign but reluctant to decline for fear of alienating the Governor. As the election year approached, Phillips, determined to crush Kerr, resorted to firing known Kerr backers in the state administration. Although he claimed economic necessity to reduce the state payroll, all the vacancies were soon filled with new appointees.[49] Political purges were not new to Oklahoma politics, but they illustrated the extent of factionalism growing within the state Democratic party.

No part of the party organization was immune from this internecine struggle. Kerr "had to win his race in spite of his own headquarters, and that was about the worst I ever saw," an aide recalled.[50] Governor Phillips boycotted the 1942 state Democratic convention; and a month before the election, he bolted to the Republicans. The Democratic primary became a brutal contest among six contenders.

But Kerr enjoyed campaigning, and Oklahomans liked Robert Kerr. They shared his pride in a rise from humble beginnings to substantial wealth. He was fond of saying to crowds during his campaign, "I'm just like you, only I struck oil." He appealed to the indestructable dream that with hard work and a little luck every man can make it big. A curious combination of tycoon and common man, Kerr had a sense of humor that included the rare ability to laugh at himself. Gomer Smith, a former congressman and perennial Democratic candidate,[51] tried to discredit Kerr in rural areas where he was strongest. He said that Kerr had a "drinking problem" and that he was campaigning with "a couple of blondes." Kerr responded good naturedly with an advertisement that he would visit Seminole in southeastern Oklahoma with the blondes. He did so to the delight of a large crowd and introduced his wife and his ten-year-old daughter, Kay.[52]

The Oklahoma political scene into which Robert Kerr made his way in 1942 reflected the state's complex heritage. The rapid movement of white men into Oklahoma after 1889 transplanted economic, political, and religious patterns that changed little in the decades following the land run. Methodist wheat farmers from the Jayhawker State contributed heavily to settlement north and west of the Canadian River; while Baptist Texans led members of the old "Cotton Kingdom" in settling the south and east. Partisan politics followed these patterns of settlement, with Republicans strong in the northwest and Democrats entrenched in the southern counties known as "Little Dixie."[53] With the discovery of rich petroleum fields in the early 1900's, industrial development provided fortunes for some and jobs for many more. Although almost one-half of all Oklahoma voters still struggled to make a crop on wind- and sun-ravaged land in 1942, the great exodus to the urban centers of Oklahoma City, Tulsa, Lawton, and Enid had begun, adding another dimension to the state's political complexity. Suspended between the last days of the Depression and the postwar boom, Oklahoma was a state where the physical geography seemed to exaggerate the extremes of poverty and wealth. Entering public life in this crucial period of transition, Robert Kerr's style embodied the past and his ideas forecast the future.

Life magazine satirized the 1942 Democratic race in Oklahoma as "the corniest primary in the United States," but cowboy bands and candidates warbling "Take Me Back To Tulsy, I'm Too Young To Marry" were standard fare in Sooner election gatherings.[54] And candidate Kerr quickly revealed a talent for this kind of showmanship accented with broadly humorous anecdotes. Although his folksiness repelled some voters, "Smilin' Bob" appealed to the masses of Oklahomans for whom daily life was already grim enough. Kerr ran as a Roosevelt Democrat in 1942, but he emphasized war themes rather than New Deal reforms. It was already clear to him that the war would have enormous impact on the Sooner State. Munitions factories and military air fields dotted

Oklahoma prairies; Royal Air Force fliers trained for the attack
on Berlin on land near Ponca City, which had been an Indian
campground a few years earlier. And columns of army vehicles
thundered along highways once crowded with Okies straggling
west.

As a businessman and a politician, Kerr knew that a state
administration friendly to the White House would get roads, dams,
military installations, and industrial projects. He constantly stressed
his access in Washington because of his work on the Democratic
National Committee. Although he avoided any mention of Governor Phillips' name, Kerr pledged to change the direction of state
government. Assailing the isolationists within the state, he promised "no bickering, no balking and no bellowing in providing
straightforward and efficient cooperation" in the war effort.[55]

Despite an extensive campaign organization and ample funds,
Kerr narrowly won the primary runoff over Gomer Smith, and
defeated Republican William J. Otjen in the general election by
a mere 16,202 votes.[56] That was the slimmest margin for any
Democrat since 1914.[57] The narrow Democratic victory reflected
the strength of anti-New Deal and isolationist sentiment in Oklahoma and presaged the reawakening of the GOP in the Sooner
State.

The small turnout in November 1942, less than 30 per cent
of the potential voters, hurt the Democrats. When Gomer Smith
defected to the Republicans after his Democratic primary runoff
defeat, Kerr had to make a crucial choice. The southern and southeastern Oklahoma counties known as "Little Dixie" were heavily
Democratic and favorable to Smith. "Little Dixie's" residents embodied the traditional American's innate suspicion of government
when it takes either taxes or freedom and a grudging willingness
to accept largesse at someone else's expense. The chief beneficiaries
of the New Deal in Oklahoma, they were the most vocal anti-New
Dealers because it seemed to threaten social change. Kerr feared
if he campaigned extensively there to bring out the vote, a large
portion of it might follow Smith into the Otjen camp. If he failed
to campaign in "Little Dixie," the voting would be light since

local contests had been settled in the primary. He chose the latter strategy and concentrated on increasing his margin in the urban centers. It was a wise strategic retreat.[58]

Kerr's victory was the result of seventeen years of careful planning. He had woven the winning mosaic from the friendships and associations of diverse groups who identified the new Governor as one of themselves. His support came from all the facets of public life he had entered: party organization, New Deal followers, Baptists, the American Legion, Negroes, and small-town merchants.[59] But Kerr's personality was an important ingredient in his election. A zest for hard work, an enormous vitality, an earthy and subtle sense of humor, and an obvious pride in being a native son reflected Oklahoma's aspirations at the end of the bitter years of dust bowl and Depression.

Barely able to retain the statehouse, the Democrats lost the Senate seat of Josh Lee, a New Dealer. Senator Lee had stayed in Washington to press an amendment to the youth draft bill, an illusory attempt to ban alcoholic beverages from army and naval installations.[60] Leon Phillips still had enough influence to crystallize sentiment among disgruntled Democrats into victory for Tulsa oil millionaire E. H. Moore, the seventy-one-year-old Republican candidate. At first glance, Moore's election seemed an unfavorable omen for the Kerr Administration. But it was actually a fortunate development for Kerr's future ambitions. Elmer Thomas, veteran senator and powerful chairman of the Senate Agriculture Committee, safeguarded Oklahoma's interests in Washington. And Kerr's own increasing prominence in the national Democratic party gave him access to the White House. The election of a Republican to a historically Democratic seat was an aberration, and Governor-elect Kerr decided in 1942 that he would restore the seat to the Democratic party.

The Kerr Administration marked the beginning of a new epoch in Oklahoma political history. Turbulent, often violent politics had characterized the early years of statehood. The Phillips Administration ended "an era of self-interest and locally dominated frontier-type politics."[61] By 1943 Oklahoma politics and politicians had matured. The Depression was the background for a growing awareness of the need for change and acceptance of government as the instrument for change.

Governor Kerr had painful personal memories of the turmoil and disorder in Oklahoma at the end of World War I. A postwar recession developed into a major depression, primarily because the state's economy was dependent on agriculture and oil production. Farmers went into debt to expand their production and profit from wartime inflated prices. When prices declined after the war, extensive foreclosures and bank failures swept the state. Kerr had lived through the dust bowl years in Oklahoma when first ponds, then springs, then wells, then hope dried up. He hated the name "Okie," spat out like brackish water, and was determined to remove the pall that had settled over Oklahoma's image from John Steinbeck's *Grapes of Wrath.*

Kerr's tenure as the Sooner State's twelfth governor was a success. He maintained remarkably good relations with the legislature and the voters in general. Unlike many public figures, Kerr did not mind appearing foolish for a good cause. During his term the newspapers were full of pictures of Kerr peddling sorghum to advertise Oklahoma products. He earned the picturesque nickname, "Sorghum Bob" during World War II. An elderly Brooklyn woman read news stories about Governor Kerr wagering Oklahoma sorghum and pecans against Nebraska hogs in a contest to see which state could sell the most war bonds. The woman wrote Kerr that she had lived in Oklahoma as a girl and loved the taste of sorghum. Could the Governor help her get some? On his next trip to New York, Kerr took her a gallon of sorghum and won an incredible amount of national publicity in return.[62] During those years his work table in the governor's office was always covered with cans of grease for the "Save Fats" campaign of the war. He cheerfully played a tuba or heaved bowling balls to launch charity drives.

He deliberately cultivated harmony with the legislature and squelched vendettas when they threatened to weaken his administration. Kerr pledged in his inaugural address to end the practice of "smearing the reputations of persons who did not agree with the administration"—an obvious swipe at former Governor Phillips.[63] Kerr's brothers, Aubrey and B. B., served in the legislature in the thirties and forties, and their friendships helped create an initial nucleus of support.[64] Instead of denouncing opponents as his predecessor had done, Kerr won them over with reason, a great deal of personal attention, and some well-placed patronage.

Oklahoma was an economic paradox when Kerr took office in January 1943.[65] The state debt, $37 million, was growing. But the war boom and increased taxes from incomes and gasoline swelled the revenues. Kerr believed that private borrowing could foster private business growth but argued that only a solvent state could attract new industry. To achieve this, he stuck to Phillips' policy of economy in government expenditures. He then proposed to commit the surplus revenue at the end of each month to a sinking fund to retire the state's bonded indebtedness. The plan succeeded and Kerr freed Oklahoma of debt.

Kerr also worked against the personalism that characterized the administration of the state's penal system and educational institutions. He pushed an amendment to curb the governor's power in clemency matters. A scandal in the Phillips Administration had resulted in the conviction of the governor's clemency aide for dealing in parole payoffs. Phillips was later tried, but acquitted. The new system created an official pardon and parole board, restricted reprieves and leaves of absence to sixty days, and required that the governor report all acts of clemency to the legislature. Kerr also secured a constitutional amendment to lengthen the educational regents' term to seven years with dismissal only for "cause." Although neither reform completely insulated these groups from politics, they minimized favoritism and corruption.

During the first legislative session of his term, Kerr resisted any tampering with the tax structure and attempts to increase spending until he won provisions for debt retirement. He reversed the policy in the next legislature and supported increased taxes to enlarge schools, build roads, and expand other necessary government services. The legislature responded to Kerr's lead with a generous program for improved public-school financing, including a special levy to upgrade Negro schools and to provide free textbooks.

Education was one of the highlights of Kerr's record as governor. It also was the background for his most serious political mistake, the so-called textbook scandals. The trouble had started in the Marland Administration. At Governor Phillips' instruction the state filed a suit alleging conspiracy to fix prices on state-adopted textbooks, but it was dismissed. Kerr supported a routine but inconclusive legislative inquiry. He then quarreled with a Tulsa prosecuting attorney, Dixie Gilmer, who won indictments in new proceedings against A. L. Crable, state school superintendent, and Dr. Henry G. Bennett, president of Oklahoma A & M. Kerr recognized the Tulsa County suit was crucial: if the charges were proved, jurisdiction properly belonged to the state. The Governor ignored Gilmer's summons to testify on the grounds of executive immunity but refused to invoke the doctrine of executive silence. He openly defended Dr. Bennett and accepted the presidency of the Oklahoma Baptist Convention with Bennett as vice-president that year.

Meanwhile the scandal festered. In 1945 Kerr wrapped the executive mantle around Bennett and Crable again. He opposed the legislature's impeachment proceedings against the superintendent and insisted that the action be dropped because it would only aggravate factional strife and wreck his legislative program. John Davis Hill, representative from Tulsa and Kerr's hand-picked speaker, resigned in protest at the Governor's meddling; and Crable escaped impeachment by only four votes.[66]

The reasons for Kerr's involvement in the textbook controversy were vague, but the affair was crucial to understanding him as a politician. Since the scandals started long before his term, he could have easily escaped involvement. The public suspected more corruption than was alleged; and the Governor seemed to be on the wrong side, as indeed, he was. He was unwise to take any side. But Kerr's private code of loyalty would not permit him to abandon Henry Bennett, even though his friend endangered his own effectiveness as governor. Kerr may have been too grateful to Bennett for not entering the governor's race in 1942, but he always returned a favor in kind.[67]

As chief executive, Kerr worked to develop the resources Oklahoma could use as an industrial base. Previous governors had been suspicious of federal assistance, but Kerr sought it. His quick mobilization of federal agencies to help eastern Oklahoma flood victims in 1943 dramatically illustrated the value of constant liaison with Washington.

The flood of 1943 awakened Kerr to the need not only for flood prevention, but also to the opportunity to control water for irrigation, municipal and industrial use, hydroelectric power, recreation, and even the possibility of navigation. Working with an engineer from the Planning and Resources Board, Don McBride, and a Tulsa banker, Newton R. Graham, the Governor began to contact federal agencies, legislators, and key Roosevelt Administration officials to involve the federal government.[68] He toured river development sites, studied TVA, and absorbed as much information on water resources as possible.

He also prepared Oklahoma to handle postwar problems. Wartime had disrupted normal state activities. Highways, schools, and industries showed the effects of neglect. Kerr foresaw new demands for state services and the possibilities that a bitter intraparty struggle could result over allocation of funds. The Governor, as usual, had a plan to prepare for postwar reconstruction and expansion while sidetracking factional bickering. He created a Joint Legislative Council, which agreed upon state goals and established priorities for required projects.[69]

Kerr also anticipated the need for diversified industrial activity if Oklahoma were to avoid repeating her post–World War I experience. He traveled over four hundred thousand miles outside the state while governor, extolling Oklahoma products and resources and urging businessmen to investigate the potential of the Southwest. Kerr avoided any question of conflict of interest, paying his own expenses on most of these trips.[70] The work of the executive office was so well integrated that not even political opponents seriously suggested that his frequent absences handicapped state business.[71]

While advertising Oklahoma, he also advertised Robert S. Kerr. He received more recognition from the Democratic party nationally than any previous Oklahoma governor. As a member of the Democratic National Committee from 1940, Kerr was a major fund raiser for the party. In 1944 he attracted attention with his handling of a special election in Oklahoma's second congressional district. Most observers saw the election as a test of the prestige of the Roosevelt Administration, and Democrat William Stigler's victory in Oklahoma further elevated Kerr's prestige in Washington. The President—impressed with the Oklahoman's ability, loyalty, and talent for stem-winding oratory— picked him as keynote speaker for the 1944 Democratic National Convention. Kerr instantly grasped the potential of such an appearance, although he tartly rejected the national committee's forty-page draft. "I saved one sentence from the ghost job they gave me. It was a good sentence." In the quiet of his Lake Pelican, Minnesota, retreat, he and Henry Bennett wrote a new address. Shortly before the convention, when Paul A. Porter of the national committee tried to persuade the Governor to make a few changes in the text, he countered, "All right, Paul, *you* make the speech."[72] Kerr's keynote address revitalized a drowsy, routine convention. It was a rafter-ringing endorsement of the New Deal and a scathing disparagement of Hooverism and Republican philosophy. "Its highly favorable reception won Kerr greater influence with the party."[73]

Kerr was interested in more in 1944 than speechmaking. As a result, the vice-presidential candidate, Harry Truman, was in his debt after the convention. Before Chicago, Kerr's detractors said he would use the keynote address to vault to the number two spot on the ticket. While he would not have refused a draft, he had no hope of being selected.[74] Representative William Stigler (D., Okla.), in a rush of gratitude for Kerr's help in his election, actually nominated him, but the Governor declined. He knew he had no chance of winning and had already assured Robert Hannegan, Democratic National Committee chairman, that he could deliver Oklahoma's votes to Truman. During the first vice-presidential ballot, Hannegan called a conference under the speakers' platform with Kerr and Maryland's Governor O'Conor and Senator Millard Tydings. He told Kerr that the Marylanders would go for Truman on the next ballot if Oklahoma would join them. The only condition was that Tydings should lead the move and get credit for it. Kerr agreed. The strategy was successful, and Truman was nominated.[75] In the 1944 campaign and during the years that followed, Kerr filled more speaking engagements for the national ticket than any Democrat except the presidential candidate.

When Kerr stepped from the governor's office in 1947, he left impressive achievements. But his administration had been favored from the beginning. He had no Depression to combat; instead he enjoyed the lush prosperity of the war years. He was also relatively free of most problems that ensnarl governors. The demands of war production siphoned off many of those usually seeking state jobs, and he was free to hire capable personnel. Military requirements for materials expanded the economy, and soaring revenues allowed the Governor to experience the politician's dream—to spend lavishly and to pay off debts.

Unlike other Oklahoma governors, Robert Kerr was not remembered as an eccentric personality or as the champion of a specific issue. His chief contribution was to preside over the end of the Wild West era of politics. One editorial writer noted, "He was the first Governor of Oklahoma who gave the state an adult administration, . . . to act like a grown man instead of like a little boy."[76]

Although Kerr's administration was less colorful and less spectacular than his predecessors', it was far more important. As governor, he relinquished the traditional role of lawmaker and judge and established the chief executive. He brought a sense of dignity and maturity to state government. And he stressed Oklahoma's full co-operation in winning the war with the knowledge that there were unlimited possibilities for the Sooner State to develop and modernize through federal war programs. He prepared Oklahoma to develop both economically and industrially and to meet the postwar conditions. He also restored Oklahomans' pride and gave them a sense of involvement in national affairs.

Robert Kerr was fifty-one years old when he left the statehouse for private life. He had achieved his boyhood goals of a family, wealth, and the governor's office. But long before his term as governor ended, Kerr was looking toward a seat in the United States Senate. He approached the 1948 campaign with careful and extensive preparation. The opposition outside his party did not seem formidable. Republican E. H. Moore was seventy-one when elected in 1942, and within four years already appeared too ill to seek reelection.[77] Popular with the voters, a happy contrast to several previous governors who had suffered impeachment,[78] Kerr seemed likely to overpower any candidate the Republicans could recruit if he could unite the always factious Democrats.

Kerr anticipated that Gomer Smith, his 1942 primary opponent, would be the strongest challenger.[79] But Smith was a bolter as well as a loser. He had sided with Leon Phillips in 1942 and endorsed the Republican candidates. Despite the stigma of party infidelity, Smith was an effective speaker with a considerable following among rural and small-town voters.[80] He also had significant support in southeastern Oklahoma, the state's former Socialist stronghold, and among low-income whites.[81] His supporters were a curious mix of those who hated Roosevelt and the New Deal and those who were recipients of federal relief programs but did not know Smith had repudiated the New Deal. Governor Kerr also correctly assumed that the Republicans would offer Smith some financial help to defeat him in the primary.[82] Then, with a weaker opponent, the GOP's chances of repeating the 1942 victory would be much greater.

While governor, Kerr began to thwart Smith's ambitions for 1948. When Oklahoma's Twentieth Legislature increased public works appropriations, Kerr's pet projects for paving U.S. Highway 70 in "Little Dixie" and constructing Roosevelt Bridge over Lake Texhoma were included. These programs helped to undermine Smith's political base in southeastern Oklahoma.[83] And Kerr's attentiveness to rural needs and his businesslike administration endeared him to small-town residents as well as farmers.[84]

During his final year in office, the Governor traveled to every county to evaluate the prospects for the Senate race. His staff identified those who came to hear him and corresponded with those who expressed interest in his candidacy. He quietly established campaign headquarters in the Kerr-McGee Oil Industries offices in Oklahoma City. Under Aubrey Kerr's watchful eye, Burl Hays, the Governor's assistant at the capitol, recruited and directed other professionals. After Robert went to Washington, Aubrey, who had set up the local organization for the successful gubernatorial campaign, became his brother's political right arm in Oklahoma. Although he continued to live in Ada, Aubrey traveled to Oklahoma City several times a week to keep in touch with activities in the Oklahoma legislature. The brothers had an unspoken arrangement that all good news would come from Robert, while Aubrey would quietly handle anything unpleasant.[85]

By the summer of 1947 the campaign was underway. With the political environment of the community always uppermost in his mind, Kerr and his staff selected county chairmen and provided them with lists of supporters in each precinct.[86] The Kerr campaign organization looked for votes beyond the state boundaries too. Howard Payne, former secretary to Representative Will Rogers (D., Okla.), and Don McBride, then a lobbyist with the National Reclamation Association, organized a registration and absentee ballot campaign among Oklahomans in Washington, D.C.[87] When Kerr officially announced his candidacy on April 14, 1948, the campaign organization was functioning smoothly.

Throughout 1947 and early 1948, Kerr used his position as Democratic national committeeman to solidify friendly relations with President Truman.[88] Prior to leaving the governor's office there had been rumors that Kerr would succeed Harold Ickes as Truman's secretary of the interior, but nothing happened.[89] The Governor did consider the possibility of following Robert E. Hannegan as national party chairman but concluded that the race in 1948 would take all his time and energies.[90] But he kept the national party in his debt by continuing his speaking engagements. He also continued to advise Truman on federal appointments and retained influence over patronage in the state.[91]

Kerr's strategy in the 1948 primary race dictated the exhaustive preparations. With nine opponents, a runoff was likely. Although several polls Kerr commissioned indicated the possibility of his winning initially,[92] his staff assumed the worst and worked to get every Kerr backer identified, registered, and to the ballot box. Kerr's plan in the primary was threefold: to avoid factionalism, to increase his urban vote, and to win the rural vote from Smith.[93] Because of lingering anti-New Deal sentiment in Oklahoma, Kerr wisely did not call for Truman's renomination during the primary. However, he did not deny "the record that I have supported him," when asked.[94]

Although he hesitated to call attention to his close relationship with the President, Kerr followed a strategy to win the farm vote that had been suggested at a meeting with Truman.[95] His approach to the farmers' grievances was economically unsound, but politically appealing. Although Kerr realized that the nation's farm problem in 1948 was surplus, not scarcity, he also knew that Oklahoma farmers chafed under the New Deal production restrictions, even though increased production would only worsen their lot. For the immediate future, he endorsed parity price supports to maintain farm prosperity. He then predicted long-range world food shortages because of increasing population, soil fertility depletion, and water shortage.[96]

To combine rural and urban interests, Kerr offered an imaginative program. Hearing him talk about it was reminiscent of a refrain from the musical "Oklahoma!"—that "the farmer and the cowman should be friends."[97] It harmonized the interests of farmer and industrialist, cattle grower and oilman. Using the theme of "a stronger America and a more prosperous Oklahoma," he argued that agriculture was the state's greatest asset. Industrial growth and increased prosperity would depend on greater agricultural production. To bring about this increase, Kerr outlined the multipurpose development of the Arkansas, White and Red River basins. The completed project would prevent floods, slow soil erosion, produce cheap electrical power, retain water for irrigation, make navigation an alternative to high freight rates, and furnish chemical fertilizer at economical prices. Kerr even speculated about the day when revenues from water-related recreation would surpass those from oil. Water would attract industries, create jobs, and relieve the plight of the farmer in an arid state.[98] From anyone but Robert Kerr such a plan would have sounded like daydreams. But from the man who had made a fortune during the Depression and had revitalized state finances, it sounded modern and possible. Supersalesman Kerr made the problems of obtaining federal money and interstate co-operation seem relatively simple. As Oklahoma's senator in Washington and as a friend of the President, Robert S. Kerr promised to implement the dream.

The primary contests were a colorful mixture of entertainment and professional political management. Each of Kerr's appearances began with the Daughters of the Pioneers, a cowgirl quartet, "singing the songs you like best."[99] To attract Smith's voters in the first primary, Kerr's managers staged two huge Gene Autry-Bob Kerr Day parades and rallies in the southeastern towns of McAlester and Seminole. Local politicians were invited to share the platform and prizes were offered to lure the apolitical from the surrounding farms and ranches. About twenty thousand people attended each celebration, perhaps because, as one local wag said, it was such a novelty to see a whole horse in an Oklahoma political campaign.[100] But Kerr was always the main attraction. He appeared with shirt sleeves rolled to the elbows, collar open, and red galluses holding up his ample trousers. The crowds loved Kerr's quips about himself and his opponents. At a rally in Guymon before the primary, a dog in front began howling when a train whistle sounded. Kerr shooed him away with the remark that "one Kerr around here is enough."[101] Despite his picturesque entourage and ability to attract a crowd, Kerr never equated the size of any rally with eventual votes. He understood the subtlety that eludes the disappointed politician, namely that all stump speakers attract almost the same individuals in every town.

The Democratic primary, as usual, failed to produce a nominee. Kerr received 135,878 votes, twelve per cent short of the majority needed for nomination.[102] His campaign organization feared a light vote in the runoff and used bandwagon appeals advertising Kerr as "the man who can win in November" to create new interest.[103] They quietly concentrated on counties lacking heated local contests to get known Kerr backers to the polls without attracting attention to Smith. To give local people a financial stake in the outcome, local funds were always used when available. Advertising contracts were let in the town where Kerr would appear, and his speeches always ended with an emphasis on his gubernatorial achievements that had affected the community.[104]

Gomer Smith's success in the runoff hinged on his ability to consolidate the defeated candidates' votes. But it was a losing effort. In "Little Dixie," where he should have garnered O. J. Fox's support, he spent his time fighting the "bolter" tag and foolishly ignored the Oklahoma Dixiecrat party.[105] Smith abandoned all talk of issues for attacks on personalities and preached racial prejudice. He made irresponsible claims that the "Democratic Party's civil rights plank was lifted from the Communist Party credo," and gambled on Kerr's overconfident supporters staying home.[106]

But Kerr took no chances. He deliberately ignored Smith's remarks, never mentioning his name. At the last minute he also decided against attending the Democratic National Convention because he did not want to sacrifice one of the remaining three weeks of campaigning before the runoff.[107] He reiterated his program for a stronger America and a more prosperous Oklahoma. With this theme he forged the political coalition of urban and rural interests that kept him in office until the Arkansas River Navigation Project was a near reality. Kerr won the runoff with 57.5 per cent of the vote in a light turnout.[108]

Kerr's opponent in the general election was Republican Congressman Ross Rizley, an attorney from Guymon. When Senator Moore decided not to run, Republican leaders convinced Rizley it was his duty to be the candidate. The promise of a $1 million campaign fund from party financiers and oil millionaires W. G. Skelly of Tulsa and Lew Wentz of Ponca City made the task more palatable. In exchange for his candidacy, Rizley forced acceptance of a plan to try to build a coalition party with state anti-New Deal Democrats based on the experience of Moore's victory.[109] Convention endorsement was tantamount to primary victory for a Republican, and Rizley won 68.4 per cent of the vote in a field of five.[110]

Had Kerr followed his original plan, he would have campaigned in the general election independent of the national ticket. He expected to win regardless of Truman's fate and did not wish to complicate the issues. This aloof attitude angered some in the state party hierarchy, as did Kerr's refusal to endorse the national platform's civil rights plank. There were rumors that Kerr feared Truman could not win and was looking for a way to build ties to the GOP.[111] His sudden purchase of a newspaper in Enid, the citadel of high Republicanism in Oklahoma, fanned this speculation. The purchase was interpreted as a stratagem "to make friends rather . . . than money."[112] But Governor Roy J. Turner and Democratic State Party Chairman J. H. Arrington, insisted that the senatorial candidate join a unified campaign for the entire Democratic ticket, and Kerr wisely relented.[113]

Harry Truman's campaign train arrived in Oklahoma on September 28 with an agenda of seventeen scheduled stops. Since neither the Dixiecrats nor the Wallace Progressives would be on the ballot in Oklahoma,[114] Truman's strategy was to create as much interest as possible in his candidacy and heighten the bandwagon effect. The President did not mention those parts of his platform such as civil rights and the repeal of Taft-Hartley that were unpopular in Oklahoma. Instead he warned "the entire farm program will stand in danger of being junked," if Republicans were elected.[115] Then he instructed the crowds to "send Bob Kerr to the Senate to take Old Man Moore's place—he never was any good anyway."[116] Truman made twenty-one speeches in two days in the Sooner State—an indication of how necessary he felt it was to get out the vote in Oklahoma.[117]

Kerr quickly picked up the President's fighting style and his theme of the Democratic party as the guardian of the common man against the special interests. His attack on Rizley was bitterly partisan, designed to put the Republican on the defensive. He interpreted Rizley's voting record in Congress as opposition to public power and federal aid to develop the Southwest. He accused him of military and economic isolationism. He condemned the Congressman as a "tool of the special interests" because he had sponsored a bill to remove the independent natural gas companies from the Federal Power Commission's regulatory jurisdiction. Kerr said the legislation would raise the consumer's gas bills by $56 million, with all the profits going to the gas companies. He also accused Rizley of conflict of interest because many of the gas companies affected were clients of Rizley's law firm.[118] This attack haunted Kerr throughout his long career in the Senate, when he was accused of the same thing. Kerr clinched his case against the Republican with the revelation that, two days before Pearl Harbor, Rizley had committed the ultimate heresy—he had criticized the Democratic President. "The war scare," he had declared, "is a fantastic creature of Roosevelt's disordered mind."[119]

Kerr, like the President, failed to mention Taft-Hartley, although labor groups openly supported him and contributed to his campaign.[120] And he also deliberately omitted appeals to oil producers and Baptists as groups. Both were so dependable in their loyalty, yet so sensitive, that openly requesting their votes was unwise.[121] Truman's charge that a Republican president and Congress would mean disaster for farm prosperity was very effective in Oklahoma. He promised price supports and increased conservation programs and even mentioned the Arkansas Basin Development Project, with a bit of prompting from Kerr.[122] Democratic nominee for the vice-presidency, Alben Barkley, and House Speaker Sam Rayburn (D., Tex.) also endorsed the idea of river development on their campaign tours in Oklahoma.[123]

The Democratic party's proposed civil rights program was the most difficult issue for Kerr. In the primary runoff with Smith, Kerr got virtually all of Oklahoma's seventy thousand black votes. They may have supplied the margin of victory.[124] He could not openly repudiate the Democratic platform, but neither could he champion it. Rizley made no rabble-rousing appeal to "Little Dixie" as Smith had done. He merely asked the residents of southern Oklahoma to vote for a Republican who believed that the State of Oklahoma, not the federal government, could protect the civil rights of Negroes. Rizley defended state's rights claiming that under such a system "in a single generation, the Negro has risen from abject slavery to the pinnacle of fame and fortune."[125]

Kerr tried to minimize the race issue with ambiguous statements. He sent a letter to his friend, J. W. Sanford, a black he had appointed state High School Inspector while governor, asking his black supporters not to campaign publicly. He presented his qualifications to the black voters through a form letter which Sanford signed and distributed.[126] When pressed, Kerr responded as Rizley had done. If such matters came to the Senate, he would vote in accord with the laws of Oklahoma.[127]

Kerr's campaign exploited Rizley's major weakness as a candidate—the inability to ignore his opponent's charges. Rizley spent most of the time explaining his record. And the appearance of the Republican presidential nominee, New York's Governor Thomas E. Dewey, did Rizley no good. Kerr ridiculed Dewey as "Oklahoma's favorite son-in-law who married a Tulsa girl and came to see her folks 12 years later," while Oklahoma editors ridiculed Dewey's "station-wagon type mustache," diminutive stature, and aloofness.[128]

Shortly before the general election, a controversy over campaign spending erupted. L. G. Burt of Tulsa, the candidate who finished last in the Democratic primary in June, charged that Kerr violated the election code by exceeding the $3,000 limit allowed for primary campaign expenditures.[129] The Senate Subcommittee on Privileges and Elections investigated but "failed to develop any evidence in support of the charges. . . ."[130] The subcommittee accepted Kerr's argument that he was not accountable for expenditures of the "Kerr for Senate Clubs."[131] But few Oklahomans were inflamed over campaign expenditures, and neither party was immune from suspicion of excessive spending. It was common knowledge that a campaign was as helpful to Oklahoma's economy as a "good calf crop." Kerr's supporters manipulated the controversy to stir up old animosities toward the Republicans. They implied that Rizley's money came from nefarious eastern financial interests, but Kerr's was strictly homemade. The Purcell *Register* summed up the general suspicion: "If money can buy an election, the Republican ticket will do well in Oklahoma."[132]

The election results proved that a unified campaign had been the correct strategy. The Democratic party won every contest for federal office in Oklahoma in 1948. But Kerr, who expected to lead the ticket, was disappointed. Truman carried 67 of the 77

counties and received 453,000 votes, 62.7 per cent of all ballots
cast. The President won a startling 11,000 vote margin over Kerr.
However, Kerr's percentage of the senatorial vote, 62.2 per cent,
almost equaled Truman's percentage of the presidential vote, so
theoretically he avoided the embarrassment of being labeled a
"coattails senator."[133]

Kerr's enormous popularity helped him to become the first
Oklahoma governor ever to win a Senate seat.[134] But not even
the combination of popularity, wealth or organization could have
achieved this victory without the President. Truman's insistence
that prosperity depended on a Democratic Administration kept
"Little Dixie" faithful to the Democratic party. And in the eighth
congressional district, traditionally a Republican stronghold, Truman ran better than Kerr. Oklahomans, like other Americans in
1948, feared depression and Dewey far more than they mistrusted
Truman on civil rights. Robert Kerr learned a very important
lesson from the 1948 election that shaped his career in the 1950's.
Postwar Americans, and especially Oklahomans, were only superficially concerned with the issues of civil rights, mutual security,
and labor problems. They wanted more jobs, better schools, and
improved housing—their share of the new prosperity following
World War II.

Kerr was better prepared than most newly elected senators
for the responsibilities that awaited him in Washington. His term
as governor had given him executive political experience to complement his background in industry. And after two statewide
campaigns and thirty years of extensive travel around the state,
he understood what Oklahomans expected of their representatives
in Washington, and was ready to comply. The techniques he used
to mollify recalcitrant legislators in the Oklahoma capitol—a little
personal attention, some public expenditure in their district, and
appropriate help at election time—were equally effective in the
United States Congress. But the fatherly, protective attitude for
the welfare of the Sooner State which Kerr acquired as governor
became his consuming political interest in the fifties and the key
to understanding his political stature in the sixties.

CHAPTER II
Freshman Senator

When the United States Senate convened January 3, 1949, the scene resembled a Renaissance painting. The sun, filtered through the intricate, stained-glass skylight, suffused the oval chamber with an amber glow.[1] All the cherished mementos were in place—the handleless ivory gavel, the bottles of blotting sand, the ornate match and snuff boxes, and the gleaming brass spittoons. Pages flanked either side of the rostrum ready to respond to a summons from this member's lifted finger or that member's cocked eye. Among the antique desks arranged in a graceful arc, senators rose to address one another through the elaborate courtesy of the third person. The scene was like a pantomime: the participants deliberate, the gestures exaggerated, the sound pianissimo. To the untrained eye, the Senate looked more like a ballet than a law-making body. Both impressions were accurate, because the Senate was a place of mixed values and purposes. Yet, despite its apparent contradictions, the United States Senate was undeniably the most powerful and independent legislative chamber in the world.

That power stemmed from two unique situations. Senators represented states, not numbers of people as did congressmen in the House. Men from states small in terms of resources, population, or electoral votes often became very powerful. The Senate's power also rested on the tenure of its members. Elected for six-

year terms, senators had leisure to devote to the institution. In
the Senate there was time to master rules and parliamentary
stratagems, to understand the established leaders and their ec-
centricities, to develop expertise in a legislative area. There was
time enough between campaigns to acquire the aura of permanence
which distinguished the Senate from the hurly-burly of the House.
Once reelected, a senator acquired seniority. And seniority meant
chairmanships—the basis of influence and respect in the upper
chamber. Only the prerogatives of a president exceeded the exalted
position of a secure senator who held a critical chairmanship—
such as Appropriations, Finance, or Armed Services. Harry Byrd
of Virginia, Patrick McCarran of Nevada, and Richard Russell
of Georgia saw presidents come and go; but their legislative powers
were diminished only at retirement or death. In the nineteenth
century the most distinguished men in public life often served in
the Senate, not the White House. And in the era after World War
II, many a president watched an unyielding Senate batter or ignore
his legislative program.

Tom Reed, the legendary, corrosive Speaker of the House in
the 1890's, dismissed the Senate as "a place where good representatives went when they died."[2] Although some men still got
to the Senate accidentally in the fifties, most worked a hard passage that required more than luck or money, family connections
or political position. The Senate was an exclusive group. First,
there was the exclusiveness of success, of being one among a select
ninety-six.[3] Then, as test succeeded test, for a few there was the
exclusiveness of the Inner Club—"a distinct minority within this
place of the minority."[4] The Inner Club was southern in spirit,
although its membership was not necessarily limited by geography.
And those who belonged to this unofficial, unchartered body were
easily identified as "Senate types"—"for whom the Institution is
a career in itself, a life in itself and an end in itself."[5]

Despite all its traditions and formality, the Senate retained
a certain unfettered quality of the frontier. It allowed men and
issues to be out of proportion. Senators could achieve greatness,
and they could abuse power. And this atmosphere suited a wildcatter like Robert Kerr. When he stepped forward to take the oath

of office, he was already recognized as an uncommon politician. A mere fourteen years later, his colleagues would acknowledge him as the "uncrowned King of the Senate."[6]

The freshmen Democratic senators who joined Kerr in the swearing-in ceremony were a colorful and exceptional group, the Class of '48. In fewer than twenty years that group would produce a president and two vice-presidents and would influence virtually every national issue of the fifties and sixties.[7] To the casual observer, Paul Douglas, Estes Kefauver, and Hubert Humphrey appeared to be the most promising Democratic newcomers. But seen from within the Senate, those most likely to succeed were Clinton Anderson, Lyndon Johnson, and Robert Kerr.

Clinton Presba Anderson was elected Senator after a six-year stint as New Mexico's representative in the House and three years as Truman's secretary of agriculture. Born in South Dakota in 1895, Anderson went to New Mexico in 1917 to die of tuberculosis. He became a news reporter and made a fortune in the insurance business instead. Anderson's paranoia about his health earned him the title "fabulous invalid"[8] and doubtless accounted for a perpetual crankiness. His brusque, no-nonsense manner gave his opinions an edge of authority.[9]

Before his election to the Senate with a majority of only eighty-seven votes, Lyndon Baines Johnson had served for a decade in the House of Representatives.[10] Known as a Roosevelt man on Capitol Hill and as a protégé of Speaker Sam Rayburn, Representative Johnson was on "intimate terms with a coterie of top level and middle level New Dealers."[11] Yet with legislative experience and important friends, he was the man least confident of success. The Majority Leader, Scott Lucas (D., Ill.), tagged him "Landslide Lyndon" when he introduced the freshmen senators. And to Johnson's dismay, the nickname stuck with both politicians and the press. To him it symbolized personal and political insecurity. Entering the Senate was a difficult transition for Johnson. He was leaving the familiar House and Rayburn's protection: he had a new constituency, the richest of whom distrusted him as Roosevelt's lackey. Also, his personal fortune had not yet been made. But Johnson was already preoccupied with the art of politics to the exclusion of all else. Beginning a quest for national prominence, he was both "ebullient and elaborately deferential to his Senate elders."[12] The Texan patiently courted the ruling Senate coalition and the so-called Southern Caucus. From the Senate grandees he won a seat on the Armed Services and Interstate and Foreign Commerce committees. These assignments enabled him to capitalize on his House legislative specialty, defense preparedness, and to oversee matters affecting the oil and gas industry.

Johnson took great pains to avoid being labeled a typical southerner. In a very risky maneuver, he declined to attend the Southern Caucus, where Richard Russell (D., Ga.) outlined strategy to defeat civil rights legislation. But he voted with the southerners to quash the biennial attempt to revise Rule XXII to facilitate cloture. His alliance with the South was a "common law union" easily forsaken in 1957 when he wanted to shed regional identification and pursue national ambition.[13]

Anderson and Kerr had known one another since the first Truman Administration, and the Oklahoman had taken time off from his own difficult 1948 primary to help Anderson to victory in New Mexico. Anderson did not learn until after the election that Kerr had canceled an important rally in Tulsa, where he needed votes, to accommodate his friend.[14] But Lyndon Johnson and Kerr did not meet until their mutual friend, Sam Rayburn, introduced them in his office just off the House floor shortly after the 1948 election. The three Senators became fast friends. They shared an aversion to ideological politics. As political adventurers, they were interested in power and became skilled in acquiring and using it. During the fifties they joined in several business ventures, and their southwestern heritage of cattle and horses was a strong common bond.[15] Harry McPherson, an aide to Johnson in the Senate, retained vivid memories of the three. "Near the cloakroom door they sat and complained about the spavined horses and impotent bulls the others had sold them — taking time off from legislation to act out a Faulknerian comedy of abuse and outrage. Urban liberals and Chamber of Commerce conservatives did not share or appreciate their country humor."[16]

Among the Class of '48, Robert Samuel Kerr looked least like a senator. He definitely bore no resemblance to old Senator Tom Connally (D., Tex.) who, at least in appearance, was quintessentially the embodiment of a United States Senator. Six feet three inches tall, Kerr had starved down to two hundred pounds when he entered the Senate. He struggled constantly to keep weight off. He never drank or smoked, but he was unable to pass up a Dairy Queen, even at 7:00 A.M., without indulging in a butter-pecan sundae.[17] He wore a baggy suit that looked as if it had been ordered from a Montgomery Ward catalog and then slept in. A "feedsack blue" shirt with an exclusive Park Avenue men's store tie, suspenders, and a gold Kerr-McGee lapel pin completed the ensemble. Kerr looked more like a small-town prosecuting attorney or a frontier evangelist than the junior senator from Oklahoma.

But a presence about him commanded attention. Walking down the Capitol's corridors, he resembled a "Sherman tank in search of a target."[18] And when he appeared on the Senate floor, he seemed to fill the chamber. Kerr often used his size to overwhelm opposition. Once in a debate he backed the fiery but diminutive John Pastore (D., R.I.) "up the center aisle of the chamber like d'Artagnan feuding with a dwarf."[19]

Kerr was not merely a big man physically. He had a self-assurance characteristic of men of strong religious beliefs and great wealth. A teetotaler, Kerr shocked official Washington when he declared to a startled dinner partner, "Alcohol has cost more money, destroyed more property, killed more people and created more illhealth and human suffering than all of the wars . . . in the entire history of the human race."[20] His aversion to alcohol denied Kerr one of a politician's favorite routes to power—the cocktail circuit. But he never lacked the kind of inside information or private understandings reputedly gleaned at Washington watering holes.[21]

The Senator's self-confidence was coupled with a massive self-reliance. At the height of his power, Kerr did many things which other men in his position delegated to assistants. Remembering his triumph as keynoter at the 1944 Democratic National

Convention, he continued to write many of his own speeches. He also drove his own car, an inconspicuous black sedan, in Washington and loved to slip away from the Senate for a quick lunch at the nearest Dairy Queen with "Mr. Ling," his eighty-five-pound, black German Rottweiler riding in the passenger's seat.[22]

Kerr also liked being in charge. While he relished the authority that came with seniority and a committee chairmanship, no decision was too trivial. On the Kerr-McGee plane he told guests where to sit, "then assigned them places in the waiting car, and then supervised . . . stowing . . . the luggage."[23] Dining out with his staff or with other senators, Kerr always checked the addition on the bill and paid in exact change.[24] Despite his wealth, he retained some of the simple tastes of his early life. His remark about the bed in his $375,000 home in Poteau, Oklahoma, revealed his view of Mrs. Kerr's preference for antiques and elegant surroundings. The bed had belonged to Napoleon I, but to Kerr it was just a place to sleep. "All I know is that it sleeps good and I bought it secondhand."[25]

While his physical requirements for comfort were few, "his emotional requirements were the most of any man I have ever been around," an aide recalled. "He had various people around him that fulfilled a certain emotional requirement that he had to have."[26] Kerr assumed patriarchal duties, overseeing the welfare of one sister's son, caring for his elderly mother, and giving financial help to scores of people. William A. Underhill, the Senator's personal attorney, was never able to persuade Kerr to make a new will after 1939 although his financial status changed dramatically. The Senator was always too busy with everyone else's business. "He was a soft touch. He always carried a lot of cash, and he gave it away in $100 chunks."[27] He never turned down the requests for help from old people or people down on their luck. But Kerr could be "plenty touchy if somebody was trying to take him."[28]

Kerr cared little for relaxation. He was too competitive, too driven to slow his pace. He was often contemptuous of President Eisenhower's leisure activities. With tongue in cheek, Kerr suggested that the State Department exhibit the President's paintings, rather than those of modern American artists, in a show for Europe and the Soviet Union. He thought that they were not only superior to the canvases of Jackson Pollock, but also that "they would prove that Ike doesn't play golf all the time."[29] Except for brief fishing trips to his Minnesota retreat, where political cronies usually joined him, Kerr seldom traveled for pleasure. He had little curiosity about the Old World. The only sightseeing that interested him was the inspection of dams and power facilities which helped in his plans for the Arkansas navigation project. A trip was for business, for speechmaking, for striking political bargains.[30] He had enormous energy and in the business of politics was tireless.

Kerr had almost no social life, particularly after the children left home and Mrs. Kerr became involved with her antique business in Washington and building the family home in Poteau.[31] Although he had little time to read anything that was not primarily connected with his legislative work, Kerr enjoyed historical works —primarily those on the Civil War and the Jeffersonian and Jacksonian periods—as well as the short stories of O. Henry. The only game he liked was gin rummy, and when Senate debate became tedious he usually retired to the cloakroom for a few hands with Clinton Anderson, Warren Magnuson (D., Wash.), or Styles Bridges (R., N.H.). Kerr played cards for money and with all the concentration and intensity he used when considering a business investment, and he almost always won.[32]

Senator Kerr's thunderous voice matched his body and confidence. Kenneth Wherry (R., Neb.), whose profession as an undertaker caused Kerr to dub him "the merry mortician," praised the Oklahoman as "the only man I ever met I could not outshout."[33] Having patterned his speaking style on William Jennings Bryan's, Kerr sprinkled his speeches with passages from the Bible and folksy stories. He even kept a list of government departments and agencies with a scriptural reference for each. The list was appropriately titled "It is Written."[34] An indexed Bible was always within easy reach of the two telephones on his desk for impromptu quoting.[35] The Senator's repertory of "stories my father used to tell me" seemed to rival that of Will Rogers. Kerr could produce a frontier anecdote for almost any situation, and he often resolved an argument that days of debating had obscured with a simple story.[36]

Although Kerr was a gifted extemporaneous speaker, most of his Senate speeches were as carefully researched, organized, and written as any business prospectus he prepared.[37] His well-deserved reputation as the most skillful debater in the Senate was the result of this exhaustive preparation and his quick mind. "Every other senator knew that the Senator from Oklahoma had done his homework."[38] Kerr could be charming in light banter, but in serious debate "one could only let the dialogue stray from the issue at one's peril."[39] Especially when managing a bill, he tried "to know more about it than anyone in the place."[40] Senator Douglas, a brilliant economist and Kerr's long-time opponent, actually feared a debate with the Oklahoman and would spend long hours preparing for the encounter.[41] He acknowledged Kerr "as probably having the highest I.Q. in the U.S. Senate."[42] Clinton Anderson once confessed to a desire to "take a knife and open up [Kerr's] skull to examine the convolutions of his brain."[43] When asked the secret of Kerr's legislative success, Senator George Smathers (D., Fla.) replied, "Brains."[44]

As a successful businessman Kerr valued facts and was an avid note-taker. He constantly scribbled figures on bits of paper and stuffed them into pockets, seemingly forgotten. Later, he fished them out during debates to confound his colleagues with the exact cost of a billion cubic feet of natural gas or the actuarial probability of a man's contribution to the Social Security system over thirty years.[45] Albert Gore (D., Tenn.) paid Kerr a dubious compliment when he remarked that "the distinguished Senior Senator from Oklahoma can take the least amount of information and look and act more authoritative than any man in the world."[46]

Kerr was a powerful and effective debater, but he frequently fractured the Senate's traditions of elaborate courtesy. Often caustic and bruising in debate, he could be utterly careless of his colleagues' sensibilities.[47] And Republican Senator Homer Capehart of Indiana enraged Kerr more than any other member. At times he was almost sadistic in his verbal assaults on the Indianian.[48] On one occasion Kerr contemptuously dismissed Capehart as a "rancid tub of ignorance." When Capehart protested being called a "cup of ignorance," Kerr thundered that anyone in his right mind would know he never used such an expression. The *Congressional Record* would clearly show that he had called Capehart a "tub," not a "cup," of ignorance.[49]

Kerr's instinct for the jugular was a two-edged talent. While no other member of the Senate questioned his brilliance or skill in debate, his occasional vindictiveness hurt him.[50] Some of his legislative feats were more the result of cowardice than co-operation. "He was more feared than liked, and the vast majority not caring to tangle with him, preferred to go along, lest they excite his anger."[51]

The new Senator from Oklahoma steadily attracted national attention. The *Saturday Evening Post* portrayed him in stereotypes that lasted throughout his career.[52] He was "the big boom from Oklahoma: the richest — and loudest — man in the Senate . . . a multimillionaire teetotaler . . . an aggressive optimist. . . ." The legends about Kerr flourished because the stuff of which legends are made was there. Robert Kerr never smiled, he grinned; he never walked, he strode; he never stood, he loomed up; he never talked, he roared. And the Senator undoubtedly fostered the mythology. He relished the dual role of the "good ole boy" talking in Will Rogers' aphorisms and Bible-Belt homilies and the shrewd, calculating business tycoon miraculously pyramiding information and influence into new empires. It was a good performance, but never an accurate portrayal. As an Oklahoma newspaper noted after Kerr's death, "He was a locomotive. He was ruthless, and he was human. He was acquisitive, and he was generous. He was partisan and he was also patriotic. He was a complex and amazing man."[53]

Neither a liberal nor a conservative in traditional Senate parlance, Kerr remained an anathema to his enemies and an enigma to his friends. So diverse and seemingly contradictory were his views that he appeared to be fighting off ideology the way a healthy body fights disease. At a Tulsa Chamber of Commerce dinner shortly after his election to the Senate, Kerr remarked that he thought he was an oil man when he ran for governor. Although a few oil men supported him, most opposed him because they believed he was a New Dealer. "And then, the New

Dealers found out I was an oil man and I almost lost the election."[54]
Among Senate New Dealers and Fair Dealers, many critics saw
Kerr as merely a wheeler-dealer. They felt that "no one could be
quite so brazen as Kerr and get away with it every time."[55] But
Kerr relished the freedom this ambiguity afforded and joked about
it. "My worst enemies think I'm too liberal and my second worst
enemies think I'm too conservative."[56]

Kerr had little interest in most questions that preoccupied
Senate liberals in the fifties and early sixties. His avoidance of
civil rights, labor reform, civil liberties, and McCarthyism was
deliberate. The Senator knew such issues were not important in
Oklahoma, and he did not think the nation ready to grapple with
them. But there were also other reasons for his avoiding the "larger
issues." He did not want to repeat the mistake of many senators
who spent their influence on hopeless causes, however noble. As
a businessman, he knew the dangers of dispersing energies or
resources too widely. As a legislator he tried never to dissipate
his effectiveness by dabbling in too many things. Early in his first
term he told an aide, "I don't want to be a splatter gun; you've
got to concentrate."[57] As an oilman he wanted no dry holes; and
as a senator he wanted to avoid an "Armageddon of convictions."
Kerr knew precisely what was important to him and learned to
achieve it within the limits of the Senate's tolerance.

However contradictory or ambiguous his actions seemed to
others, the Senator had a political philosophy. When a serious
young man asked Kerr to define his political creed, he replied,
"Son, my philosophy is that I'm ag'in any combination I ain't
in on."[58] Stated in frontier terms, Kerr's philosophy was the "how
to" technique for the American phenomenon of "upward mobil-
ity." Uninspiring in intellectual terms, the philosophy explained
his success as oilman, cattle baron, and politician.

Although not essentially introspective, at some point between
the log cabin in Ada and his election to the Senate, Robert Kerr
began to identify with Oklahoma. Its growth, reputation, and
future became a part of his personal quest for recognition and
achievement. Concern for Oklahoma governed his public career.
Those who said Kerr thought only of himself were mistaken, for

the interests of Robert S. Kerr and the State of Oklahoma were inseparable. When asked if he would ever retire to private life, he always replied, "But who will do it for Oklahoma if we don't?"[59]

Kerr had chafed at the economic stagnation in the Sooner State long before he entered politics. Careless farming, ignorance of soil conservation, shortage of facilities and water for irrigation, and high transportation costs wasted the state's wealth and depleted the citizens' energies. In a public commitment to his conviction that the proper use of wood, land, and water resources could revitalize the state's economy, Kerr invested thousands of his personal fortune in coal and pasture land in eastern Oklahoma, an area in decline for forty years. Throughout his Senate career he would use his influence to help reverse that situation.[60]

Kerr was unabashed when others charged that his approach to politics was "provincial." He might even have volunteered the term. Although he seldom belabored the subject, from his first day in the Senate he applied strict criteria to all legislation. "In my voting on any measure before the Senate, I have three criteria which I keep in mind," Kerr wrote to a constituent. "Is the expenditure necessary; will we get value received; and what will be the effect upon the State of Oklahoma?"[61] Kerr was a "swashbuckling Southwestern entrepreneur," in the Senate "to do a certain job for Oklahoma."[62] He believed literally in representative government. "If a man doesn't represent the views of his constituency, they'll get rid of him and send somebody who will."[63] Kerr never forgot that senators represented states and their specific interests. He could only hope to make those interests coincide with national progress.

Kerr's devotion to Oklahoma's best interests merged with the sectionalism still powerful in the Senate in the 1950's. The struggle among the various sections of the country for money and programs was as old as the Senate. Southern and western members dominated the strategic spending committees. They were a majority on the Democratic Steering Committee, which determined committee assignments, and on the Appropriations Committee.[64] Like the youngest son arguing for his part of the family inheritance, Kerr saw matching grants as a device to equalize the inequities among the states. "Those other [New England, Middle Atlantic, and Upper Midwest] states have had many many years in which to build up, say, a good school system. Oklahoma has had but fifty. We can't compete with New York City with its own resources or the State of New York. I think the people in Oklahoma are as deserving of a good education as the people of New York. And in order for us to match up with them, we're going to have to have government matching funds."[65]

Most of Kerr's sectional appeals were made away from the Senate floor, sometimes privately to sympathetic listeners.[66] He reserved his bluster against the North and East for home consumption. He was too cunning a legislator to think he could accomplish all he sought for Oklahoma without the help of the Midwest's Michael Kirwan (D., Ohio) and Clarence Cannon (D., Mo.) or such influential New England Republicans as Styles Bridges and George Aiken (R., Vt.).[67]

Robert Kerr was a complex individual, difficult to fathom. While a man of vision, he was not a visionary.[68] A realist in the best sense of the word, his dreams were not idle. The Senator believed in planning carefully and working hard. He preferred some kind of progress and advancement to the "perfection of an issue without any achievement."[69] Kerr probably never stopped to examine his political philosophy, for he was not concerned with ideological consistency, only with consistent achievement. As he began his first term, he was as sure of his proper role in the Senate as he was of his religious convictions. "When I can no longer be of service to the people of Oklahoma, I do not care to serve in the Senate."[70]

Midway through the twentieth century, the folkways of the United States Senate still prescribed the ritual of an apprenticeship for all new members.[71] The freshman senator was admonished to "be a work horse, not a show horse," to learn from senior members, and to keep quiet on the Senate floor. One observer noted, "All the newcomer needs, . . . is the passage of time—but this he needs indispensably, save in those rare cases where the authentic genius among Senate types are involved."[72]

Kerr was one of those rare cases. In 1949 he was neither a

neophyte in national politics nor unknown to House and Senate Democrats. His activities as the major fund raiser for the Democratic National Committee in the 1940's had directly benefited scores of his new congressional colleagues. He was also well known to fellow legislators because he had appeared frequently at committee hearings on water resource development while governor of Oklahoma. The friendships he made with other governors during the war and as the chairman of the Southern Governors' Conference for 1945–1946 had enlarged his circle of acquaintances as a new senator. Before the 1948 election, Spessard Holland (D., Fla.) wrote Kerr that he would be quite at home in the Senate with fourteen other war governors from the Roosevelt years.[73]

While these friendships and associations were useful during Kerr's early years in the Senate, he still had to make the transition from an executive role to that of a legislator. His experience as a business and political executive had accustomed him to the type of power and perquisites not found in the legislative life. The difference between being governor of a state and being one of ninety-six senators, all equal in theory, was enormous. As governor of Oklahoma, Kerr had a grander office, a larger staff, and more publicity than he merited as a junior senator. The pace of legislative life was also slower, more deliberative, and often more frustrating. Men comfortable in the even rhythm of the legislative body often hesitated to welcome those with experience in the more turbulent executive affairs. Many senators complained that former governors "come down here expecting to be big shots and they often are unwilling to realize that they are just one of the boys."[74]

Kerr was aware that this judgment applied to him. With characteristic thoroughness he tried to counter any suspicions among the powerful Democratic leadership. Immediately after the election he sent his principal aides, Ben Dwight and Burl Hays, to Washington to prepare for his arrival. They spent several days with Secretary to the Minority Felton Johnston, learning the intricacies of running a Senate office. On Kerr's specific instructions, they hired two staff members who had worked for influential former senators. Kerr knew the value of hiring a staff person familiar

with daily routines, and who had established contacts with other
Senate staff. The choices were fortunate. Marjorie Banner, secretary to former Senator Tom Stewart (D., Tenn.) was hired as a
stenographer. When the Senator's long-time personal secretary,
Ralph Trask, died in 1955, she assumed that position. The other
recruit, Peggy McCormack of New Mexico Senator Carl Hatch's
staff, was a specialist in veterans' problems. In the 1950's she
handled the military service-related matters which made up the
major caseload of a Senate office.[75]

Most of the people in the Washington office had served Kerr
as governor and remained until his death in 1963.[76] Staff longev-
ity was rare on Capitol Hill and a tribute to Senator Kerr as an
employer. Unlike his close friend Lyndon Johnson, who used "the
bear pit school of personnel management,"[77] Kerr was tolerant
of human foibles and easy to work for. "He gave you a job and
didn't look over your shoulder. All he wanted was the job done.
He liked to be kept apprised of the progress you were making. . . .
The only mistake he wouldn't tolerate was the mistake of doing
nothing."[78] Senator Kerr knew from experience that "a staff is
the best part of a Senator."[79]

Don McBride, chairman of the Planning and Resources Board
in Kerr's gubernatorial administration and in 1949 the Washington
representative for the National Reclamation Association, was already in the nation's capital. Kerr liked to boast of McBride's
expertise in water resource development. "He's good enough to
be Secretary of the Interior in any administration."[80] Kerr often
referred to McBride as "the third Senator from Oklahoma," and
when the Senator was away from Washington, other senators
accepted McBride's word as Kerr's own. On occasion, Kerr would
loan McBride to a colleague who needed expertise on water matters
with the understanding that this favor would be returned when
Oklahoma water projects were funded.[81]

Since the Oklahoman insisted on bringing his top personal
assistants from the governor's office—Ralph Trask, Ben Dwight,
and Burl Hays—there was not enough money for four large salaries. McBride did not officially join Kerr's Senate staff until the
mid-1950's because of the limit on clerk hire funds.[82] The Okla-

homa Water Development Association, a citizens' group seeking federal funds to make the Arkansas River navigable, paid McBride's salary as their Washington representative.[83] Despite the financial arrangement, he was Kerr's legislative assistant. During the years 1949–1950 McBride divided his time between problems concerning the natural gas industry and water development.[84] Kerr's insistence on this special arrangement to acquire Don McBride's expertise without sacrificing other equally able individuals was characteristic of his belief that a staff "can make or break a politician."[85]

In addition to the Capitol Hill staff and a small staff in Oklahoma City, Kerr retained former White House advisor and attorney Clark Clifford for advice on how to get quick results from the Washington bureaucracy. Kerr never economized on staff salaries as some senators did and paid well to obtain and hold talent.[86]

He realized that the path to influence in the Senate was committee work, not oratory. New members eager to attract national press coverage to advertise their talents for higher office usually sought the prestige committee assignments, such as Foreign Relations, Appropriations, Finance, and Armed Services.[87] In response to the formal letter from Alben Barkley (D., Ky.), chairman of the Democratic Conference, asking his committee preferences, Kerr requested Appropriations and Finance, the two most powerful and influential committees within the Senate.[88] Kerr knew that both parties traditionally reserved seats on these committees for conservative members with seniority, but thought it worth a try. He noted in his reply that he was sure his chances of assignment to Appropriations were negligible since Oklahoma's senior senator, Elmer Thomas, was the third-ranking Democrat. "However, I would like to be on record with this preference so that my appointment to this committee may be given consideration at such future time as it might be appropriate."[89] Kerr had campaigned on the need for federal projects such as the Arkansas River Navigation Project to develop Oklahoma's economy, and membership on the Appropriations Committee seemed the most advantageous place to influence the financing of federal projects.[90]

Neither preference materialized.[91] Kerr was appointed to Public Works, his third choice, and Interior and Insular Affairs, fifth among his six preferences.[92] He was not disappointed though, because he knew that both Appropriations and Finance were considered inappropriate for a freshman.

His apparent satisfaction with Public Works, however, was not so readily understood. In the thirties and early forties, senators had coveted assignment to the Public Works Committee. But by 1949, interest had waned. Most senators believed the committee's usefulness was exhausted after the hectic activity of the New Deal. The anticipated post–World War II boom in private industry convinced them that the federal largesse of the Roosevelt era was unlikely to continue. But Kerr reasoned that prosperity following the war would require the extension, not the contraction, of federal activity to develop natural resources and power to fuel industrial expansion.[93] The Oklahoman predicted that one of the most significant problems of the postwar period would be the growing demand for water and the inadequacy of existing resources. He believed that Oklahoma's industrial development, as well as the expansion of her agricultural base, depended on federal development of national water resources. In an October 1947 speech to the National Reclamation Association meeting in Phoenix, Arizona, Kerr had talked of the need to develop water for industrial use. "Time and again our Oklahoma Planning and Resources Board has reported the grim fact that our state has lost out on the establishment of new industries where thousands of men could find employment. Why? Because we would not furnish ample and cheap industrial water. There is water in our rivers, but we need reservoirs to conserve it and make it available when and where it is needed."[94] The authorization for Corps of Engineers and Bureau of Reclamation projects was the province of the Public Works Committee. As a member of the committee, and after 1955 as chairman of its Subcommittee on Rivers and Harbors and Flood Control, Kerr became the pivotal figure in the "golden era of federal construction" of water and power facilities.[95]

Kerr turned the failure to be assigned to Appropriations into a triumph, and Public Works became his power base in the Senate.

He used his position there the way other senators used Appropriations. Every authorization for reclamation or dam site preparation in Oklahoma, regardless of size, appeared in his newsletter to show what Kerr was doing for his state.[96] But more significantly, Kerr expanded a narrow concern for Oklahoma's water development into a broad policy position that touched the interests of almost every other senator and large numbers of congressmen. "After he took effective control of the Public Works Committee, . . . he never approved a single dam or road or river dredging without trading it off for something he might want in return."[97]

Although Kerr respected the traditions of the Senate, he deliberately chose not to conform to the traditional behavior expected of a freshman senator. An apprenticeship, "being seen but not heard," was unthinkable for such a vigorous and aggressive man. And unlike most senators, he actually looked forward to the prospect of making his first formal speech.

The choice of subject matter was as crucial and difficult as the timing. Most members opted for a noncontroversial topic of interest to their own constituents to ensure a few lines in the local press. The more timid chose an elevated, bipartisan, rhetorically pleasing topic calculated to offend no other senator at the risk of interesting no one. But Kerr ignored all these precautions and traditions in planning his maiden speech.

The occasion was the debate on the Interior Department appropriations bill, H.R. 3838, one of the most heated and protracted disputes of the Eighty-first Congress. It reflected the fervor of the friends and foes of public power development, an important issue in the 1948 campaign, particularly in the West. The question of federal construction of transmission lines to carry electricity from federal dams to the user sparked the controversy. The House bill granted funds for erecting transmission lines from the Bonneville Power Administration, the Southwestern Power Administration, and the Reclamation Bureau's power marketing systems.[98] The Senate Appropriations Committee deleted most of the funds for federal transmission lines, the largest cut being two-thirds of the House-approved funds ($2,383,885) for the Southwestern Power Administration (SPA). Because of vigorous opposition during the Senate hearings from eleven private utilities operating in Texas, Oklahoma, Arkansas, and Missouri, only three of the forty-four House-approved SPA projects survived. Instead, the committee instructed the Interior Department to negotiate "wheeling arrangements"—contracts with private firms to move electricity in lieu of building additional government transmission lines—whenever possible. They cited a contract between the SPA and the Texas Power and Light Company as a model.

Elmer Thomas, Oklahoma's senior senator, was the chief spokesman for the committee's amendment to delete SPA funds. But Thomas was not as concerned with the question of appropriations as with the need to legislate. He opposed spending any additional money. "The trouble has been that the Congress has not yet developed . . . a public power policy," he argued.[99] Congress was forcing the Appropriations Committee to write a policy bit by bit.[100]

The appropriate role of the federal government in developing public power was a divisive philosophical issue, and party affiliation was not necessarily a key to a man's position. In several instances during the debate, western senators of the same party disagreed. While Senator Kerr was a known advocate of greater federal involvement in natural resources development, no one expected him to take issue with his own senior senator in his maiden speech. But Kerr plunged into the debate with the ferocity he ordinarily reserved for attacks on Republicans. Not only did he accuse Thomas of wanting to abandon the public to "control by the private utilities," but he also questioned the wisdom of the bill's manager, Carl Hayden (D., Ariz.), who virtually invented public power. In discussing the history of the wheeling contracts the committee had directed the Interior Department to negotiate, Hayden said he hoped other companies would follow the example of the "farseeing" Texas Power and Light Company.[101] Kerr disagreed. "If such contracts were made general the utilities would have a profitable monopoly granted and protected by the Federal Government, and that should never be tolerated."[102]

This unprecedented maiden speech was startling enough, but Kerr compounded the effect when he won approval for an amendment to prohibit using the SPA continuing fund to rent power-generating facilities.[103] Don McBride was rapturous as he described the event in a private letter. "Senator Thomas spoke for three and one-half hours prior to our man's taking the floor and confidentially, our rooster won the fight to the extent that the gizzard of the opponent was emptied of its contents—sand, gall and all."[104]

After a mere seven and one-half months in the Senate, it was clear that Robert Kerr was no ordinary freshman. He was fearless, confident, and capable of defending his views. But there was also a glimpse of another side of his character—he could be merciless. Although a respected twenty-three-year veteran of the Senate and chairman of the Agriculture Committee, Elmer Thomas was a spent force in Oklahoma politics. A. S. "Mike" Monroney, a Democratic Sooner congressman and former news reporter, was threatening to wrest the Democratic nomination from the seventy-three-year-old Thomas in 1950. With Thomas probably on the way out, Kerr saw no reason to indulge in the usual amenities. His attack on Senator Thomas must have caused many a member to shudder. Kerr purposely played this "bear at the children's picnic" role, confident that the meaning was clear. And it was. No senator of either party who witnessed Kerr's attack on Elmer Thomas ever felt completely safe from his sudden verbal maulings.

Nor did he hesitate to clash with Carl Hayden. Kerr genuinely feared that the utilities' new approach "constituted a change in tactics rather than in objective."[105] He believed that the leathery Arizonan was a natural ally on the power question and gambled that Hayden would forgive this apparent affront as a minor disagreement between honest men. Kerr knew instinctively that this single performance would do more to launch his Senate career than would years of patient, quiet work. He was an ambitious politician and saw no reason to feign otherwise.

Kerr's maiden speech was also the key to understanding his approach to all major policy issues for the remainder of his career. While he tolerated discussion of broad philosophical questions, he was primarily interested in legislative details. He had little patience with colleagues who used the Senate chamber as a "bully pulpit." Kerr knew that the policy debate could only be resolved in favor of public power if the federal government became so extensively committed through financing and building projects throughout the country that there could be no turning back. Once enough funds were appropriated, the momentum of incremental commitments would assure success for the public power advocates. Kerr grasped what few of his colleagues ever fathomed: Congress made policy in spending money, not in talking.

Kerr's tenure on the Interior and Insular Affairs Committee was brief. In August 1949 J. Howard McGrath (D., R.I.) resigned to become Truman's attorney general, leaving a vacancy on the Finance Committee. Two Democratic senators senior to Kerr applied, Pennsylvania's Francis J. Myers, the democratic whip, and John Stennis (D., Miss.). But Walter George (D., Ga.), chairman of Finance and the most-respected member of the Democratic Steering Committee, which made the committee assignments, refused to accept any senator but freshman Robert Kerr.[106] The southerners were expressing their gratitude for Kerr's quiet role early in the session to defeat proposed changes in the Senate rules.

Early in the Eighty-first Congress the Truman Administration attempted to liberalize Rule XXII to facilitate scheduling civil rights legislation.[107] After a lengthy and bitter floor fight, the only change the southerners countenanced was to make cloture more difficult to invoke. A coalition composed mainly of southern Democrats and Republicans agreed on a compromise permitting cloture by a vote of two-thirds of the membership of the Senate, not merely those present. Known as the Hayden-Russell-Wherry compromise, the amended rule applied to all questions, substantive as well as procedural, except any motion to change the rules. This ensured unlimited debate on any attempt to change the cloture rule in the future.

Kerr considered the annual furor over rules and precedents as dry as writing a will. But he knew "that a command of the rules was one of the most powerful weapons in the conservative arsenal."[108] Anything he could do to augment that arsenal would benefit him in the future. He rarely dabbled in internal Senate business, but 1949 was the exception. Kerr devised a plan based on the 1944 Democratic National Convention experience to ensure victory for the coalition's compromise and to ingratiate himself with the southern leadership.

The Oklahoman had a keen sense of other men's needs and weaknesses. He knew Millard Tydings (D., Md.) was easily flattered and liked attention. When the Hayden-Russell-Wherry compromise was drafted, the Maryland patrician was still uncommitted.[109] Kerr asked if he would lead a maneuver to end the filibuster, in return for full credit for his role. Never shy of headlines, Tydings readily agreed to vote with the conservatives if he could "be the difference in determining the issue."[110] All Tydings had to do was circulate the compromise petition among northern and western Democrats. Kerr promised to help, which meant he would round up the extra votes needed. The Oklahoman approached two other undecided freshmen, Lester Hunt (D., Wyo.) and Andrew Schoeppel (R., Kans.). The three had worked together as governors during the war and had been elected to the Senate in 1948. With Hunt, Kerr probably stressed the so-called Hayden reasoning.[111] Since the western states were small in population and had relatively few members in the House of Representatives, they could exercise real power in the Senate. Any attempt to liberalize cloture would diminish their power. The approach to Schoeppel, an old friend, was more personal. The two states' interests were similar, as were their constituencies. Kerr probably reminded the Kansan of his own pledge in Oklahoma. "I . . . told my people . . . that I wanted the right to debate their cause just as long as I had the strength to do so."[112] With very little persuasion, both Hunt and Schoeppel agreed to go along.

Later in the office of Les Biffle, secretary of the Senate, they all signed a "Tydings-dictated" pledge to vote as a unit for a cloture rule requiring two-thirds of the Senate membership. Kerr immediately took the pledge to the southern Democrats, who were waiting in conference. With these votes, the compromise passed.[113] In its account of the compromise, the *Congressional Quarterly Almanac* reported, "Tydings, who had supported Barkley's ruling, was the coalition's major recruit."[114] Kerr did not even participate in the debate except to heckle Paul Douglas on one occasion.[115]

In appreciation for his maneuvering in the cloture fight, the

Democratic Steering Committee passed over one of their own, John Stennis, to award McGrath's seat on Finance to Kerr. Although this "promotion" was not reported in the Oklahoma press at the time, other senators noticed. The appointment was significant for reasons other than the surprising disregard of the seniority rule. The leadership recognized the Oklahoman's potential talent for "producing shifting bi-partisan majorities on a variety of issues."[116] They also approved of his loyalty to the institution and his indifference to public credit for the job he had done. While Kerr was not self-effacing, he was careful never to seem to subordinate devotion to the Senate to a desire for power within the organization and popularity outside. The move up to the Finance Committee signaled the end of Kerr's brief apprenticeship and his acceptance as an intimate among the "Sanhedrin at the heart of the so-called 'Senate Establishment'."[117]

CHAPTER III
The Leland Olds Affair

During his first year in the Senate, Kerr assumed leadership of a cause that brought him national prominence. Ironically, the events of late 1949 and 1950 that earned him recognition as a possible presidential contender for 1952 eventually explained a major part of his failure to receive the Democratic nomination.

The legislative controversy was over attempts to clarify the meaning of the Natural Gas Act of 1938. With the exception of monetary laws on gold and silver, natural gas was the only mineral subject to direct federal controls. Regulation of other minerals was indirect and operated through import controls, enforcement of state proration laws, or regulation of transportation rates.

The 1938 act authorized the Federal Power Commission (FPC) to regulate the construction of facilities such as pipelines for interstate transportation and sale of natural gas. The commission also regulated the wholesale rates charged for natural gas in interstate Commerce. Section 1(b) exempted only two areas from federal regulation: (1) intrastate sales and distribution and (2) the "production and gathering" of natural gas.[1] Independent producers and gatherers, who did not own pipelines or were not affiliated with interstate pipeline firms, could set the price of gas sold "at the wellhead." Since state utility commissions set rates at the final stage of the production-distribution process—the prices local gas distributors charged the consuming public—the FPC's regulatory role was strictly circumscribed. The law gave the FPC jurisdiction only over the rates pipeline companies charged local distributors. The commission was required to set these rates high enough to cover the cost of gas at the wellhead, plus all other costs, and allow for a reasonable rate of profit, usually 6 to 6½ per cent. The crucial factor in determining the rate was what the pipeline company paid for gas.

In the early years the FPC adhered to a strict interpretation of the law.[2] But in a decision in the Interstate Natural Gas Company case in 1943,[3] the commission's opinion implied a broad jurisdiction over all sales, even those of independent producers and gatherers, if those sales eventually moved in interstate commerce. While the Interstate case was being appealed, another development indicated the FPC might attempt to extend jurisdiction to the previously exempt independents.

In 1944 the FPC began a comprehensive inquiry into the "complex and difficult problems of the natural gas industry."[4] Hearings were held throughout the country in 1945 and 1946 to determine if additional legislation would be helpful in administering the Natural Gas Act of 1938. The status of independent producers and gatherers was the most frequently mentioned topic during the hearings. The natural gas investigation aroused fears that the commission was trying to establish control over all producers and gatherers as "public utilities" and provided a catalyst for industry-sponsored bills to confirm the exempt status.[5] No amount of reassurance from the commission was sufficient to dispel the widespread alarm among gas industry officials that regulation of independent producers' sales was imminent.[6]

Early in the Eightieth Congress, Oklahoma Republicans, Representative Ross Rizley and Senator E. H. Moore, introduced identical legislation to limit FPC jurisdiction over independent producers and gatherers.[7] In the House hearings, the FPC unanimously opposed the Rizley bill. H.R. 2185 not only reaffirmed the exempt status of the independents but also modified the FPC's rate-making formula, restricted the commission's jurisdiction over the interstate transportation of natural gas, imposed detailed accounting procedures in FPC rate-fixing activities, and transferred jurisdiction over pipeline companies who were neither owners nor sellers of natural gas to the Interstate Commerce Commission. The FPC asked the House to defer action until the natural gas investigation findings were complete and the Supreme Court had ruled in the pending Interstate case.[8] President Truman also endorsed the idea of suspending legislation until the natural gas investigation was completed.[9] While the commission argued that it was unwise to legislate in an atmosphere of urgency, they did not suggest that all of the amendatory proposals lacked merit.[10]

Following the hearings, Representative Rizley introduced a revised bill, H.R. 4051.[11] The House committee reported the substitute bill and urged immediate passage, remarking, "The Commission is doubtful, the courts divided, and the industry is at sea."[12]

While the Senate and House were considering amendatory legislation, the Supreme Court ruled on the appeal in the Interstate case. The Court unanimously upheld the 1943 FPC ruling but "found it unnecessary to resolve" the question of FPC jurisdiction over independent producers and gatherers, since the particular case involved a natural gas pipeline company rather than an independent producer or gatherer.[13]

The Court's broad language alarmed industry representatives. Wishing to avoid further confusion and industrywide chaos, the FPC advised Congress of the need for immediate amendatory legislation to clarify and reaffirm the independents' exempt status. The commission accompanied this recommendation with draft legislation that Representative James Percy Priest (D., Tenn.) introduced. The commission unanimously endorsed the Priest bill to "dispel the uncertainty regarding the status of such independent producers and gatherers which has been created following the recent decision of the Supreme Court in the Interstate case. Such action by Congress now should dispose of this important and noncontroversial matter." FPC Chairman Nelson Smith assured the House committee that the Priest bill was "fully in accord with the legislative program of the President."[14]

The House rejected two attempts to substitute the Priest bill for the more stringent Rizley proposal, H.R. 4051, and the latter

passed on a voice vote. In late July 1947 the Senate Interstate
and Foreign Commerce Committee voted 6–5 not to report the
Rizley bill, and the first session of the Eightieth Congress adjourned without taking any further action to exempt independent
gas producers from FPC regulation.[15]

When Congress failed to clarify the situation, the FPC assumed the initiative. The commissioners issued Administrative
Order No. 139, assuring independent nontransporting producers
and gatherers that the commission would not assert jurisdiction
over arm's-length sales to interstate pipeline companies. The order
concluded, "It is also our intention . . . to continue to recommend
to the Congress that it take appropriate clarifying legislative action
regarding this matter."[16] In a brief dissent to the order, Commissioner Claude Draper cautioned that the "Commission should
hesitate to do by rule what the Congress had failed to do by law."[17]

By 1948 the issue was very confused. The Senate Committee
on Interstate and Foreign Commerce held hearings on the House-
passed Rizley bill early that year. Only six months after their
endorsement of the Priest bill and the issuance of Administrative
Order No. 139, FPC Commissioners Leland Olds and Claude
Draper abruptly announced they had changed their minds. Olds
and Draper presented a separate report on the natural gas investigation as part of their testimony. They concluded that the study
established strong grounds for recommending regulation of all
sales of natural gas in interstate commerce "whether made in the
field or at the conclusion of the interstate journey."[18] Olds, in
particular, was adamant that "the Natural Gas Act . . . should not
be amended in any fundamental way."[19]

The two remaining commissioners (there was one vacancy
on the FPC), Nelson Lee Smith and Harrington Wimberly, said
their study of the investigation findings had not changed their
view that Congress should clarify the exempt status of the independents.[20] Although most committee members favored exemp-
tion, other proposed amendments dominated the hearings and the
issue was postponed until the Eighty-first Congress.[21]

In his campaign that fall for election to the Senate, Kerr
attacked his Republican opponent, Ross Rizley, for sponsoring

the natural gas bill—legislation which favored "the interests."
He even accused Rizley of conflict of interest because several of
the major independent gas producers were clients of Rizley's Guymon law firm.[22] It was effective campaign rhetoric, but nothing
more than rhetoric. Less than four months after his swearing-in,
Kerr was learning the cardinal lesson of Senate political life: "What
a Senator had to do who wanted both to do good and to be elected,
was first to bow before the prevailing icons in his state, and having
made obeisance, to turn to more promising endeavors."[23]

Every senator faced the same requirement. The southern
Democratic liberals, Lister Hill and John Sparkman of Alabama,
took part in every filibuster against civil rights. "Proxmire paid
his fee of support to the dairy farmers of Wisconsin, Douglas,
his to the corn growers of Illinois."[24] Capitol Hill tolerated these
concessions to special interests as a necessary part of being reelected. Unfortunately for Senator Kerr, Oklahoma's household
gods were the oil and gas industry. As a multibillion-dollar enterprise, the oil industry had acquired a reputation for power and
rapacity in the late 1800's which a half-century of trust-busting,
taxation, and philanthropic penance had done little to dim. When
natural gas, a byproduct of oil exploration, was recognized as a
valuable commodity in the late 1930's, the old robber baron image
reappeared. And Kerr's efforts on behalf of the industry were
always suspect, no matter how much of the non-gas and oil economy those efforts helped. The total regional economy of the Southwest was so dependent on oil and gas and the ancillary industries
it fostered that even the slightest alteration could profoundly af-
fect the livelihood of millions of people. Had he not owned considerable oil holdings and been associated in business with Phillips
Petroleum, Kerr's defense of the industry would probably have
attracted no more attention than Ralph Yarborough's (D., Tex.).
Yarborough, "Texas' version of La Follette," was more orthodox
on oil and gas matters than his colleague, Lyndon Johnson. But
Johnson and Kerr shared opprobrium as the Senate's spokesmen
for the "oil and gas crowd." Had Kerr not defended the industry,
he would undoubtedly have been a one-term senator. Had his
defense been less evangelical, he would not have been Robert Kerr.

The controversy over natural gas regulation intensified in the Eighty-first Congress. In addition to the legislative struggle, there was an equally important conflict over naming a new member to the vacancy on the Federal Power Commission. This appointment was decisive because the commission had split 2–2 as a result of the natural gas investigation. There were hints that Kerr was trying to pack the commission as early as 1947. These rumors stemmed from the knowledge that Harrington Wimberly, appointed to the FPC in 1945, was "Kerr's man on the Commission."[25] Wimberly was an Altus, Oklahoma, newspaper publisher who had worked hard for Kerr in his 1942 governor's race. A consistent contributor to Democratic campaign chests, Wimberly readily acknowledged that his appointment to the FPC "was a straight piece of patronage."[26]

Truman nominated Burton N. Behling, staff director of the FPC's natural gas investigation, to fill the vacancy in 1947. Since Behling was sympathetic to the gas industry, the press assumed he was Kerr's henchman and referred to him as "the gas lobbyist."[27] The Senate failed to act on Behling's nomination in 1947, so Truman sent it up again in early 1948. Under pressure from senators from the natural gas-consuming states, the President withdrew the nomination and proposed Thomas C. Buchanan of Pennsylvania.[28] Buchanan was acceptable to those who favored FPC regulation of independent gas producers and gatherers because of his record as a member of the Pennsylvania Public Utilities Commission from 1937 to 1945. As a presidential hopeful, Truman was in no position to offend senators from the populous urban states in 1948. Gas industry spokesmen opposed Buchanan, and when Pennsylvania's senators, Edward Martin (R.) and Francis J. Myers failed to agree, the Senate refused to act. Buchanan served quietly under an interim appointment from June 1948 until his confirmation on June 6, 1949.[29]

While the Buchanan appointment was stalled in the first session of the Eighty-first Congress, southwestern members renewed attempts to amend the Natural Gas Act. Kerr had begun preparations for his role shortly after the election. Don Emery, vice-president and general counsel of Phillips Petroleum, wrote the

Senator-elect about a strategy meeting with representatives from the concerned branches of the natural gas industry. There had been some rash talk of an effort to overturn all federal regulation, but common sense had prevailed. Emery reported that the "pipeline companies are willing now to give the independent producers and gatherers a chance, as a first step, to importune the Congress to amend the act as it applies to them only."[30] He promised to forward a draft proposal in a few days. Emery's draft became the basis for S. 1498 which Senators Kerr and Thomas introduced April 5, 1949.[31] Similar legislation had already been introduced in the House.[32]

The Kerr bill provided that the Federal Power Commission should not have the power to regulate prices of arm's-length sales by one producer and gatherer to another, nor of transactions between an independent producer and an interstate pipeline operator provided neither had a controlling interest in the other.[33] In April a subcommittee of House Interstate and Foreign Commerce held extensive hearings on H.R. 79 and H.R. 1758, legislation similar to the Kerr bill.[34] As in the 1948 hearings, the FPC split on the issue of regulation, but this time a majority opposed the legislation, fearing it would probably increase prices to consumers. Speaking on behalf of Draper and Buchanan, Leland Olds said, "The bills under consideration would benefit—primarily large enterprises."[35] FPC Chairman Smith and Commissioner Wimberly held to their view expressed in the 1948 hearings, that it would not be "adverse to the public interest to amend the Act so as to clarify the status of the independent producers and gatherers."[36]

The House committee reported a modified version of H.R. 1758 on July 28, 1949.[37] Six Democrats from gas-consuming states appended a minority report charging that a few big oil companies fostered the drive for the amendment.[38] They suggested that the only independents exempted should be small firms whose annual production did not exceed two billion cubic feet of natural gas.[39] Two other reports, one calling for a delay of H.R. 1758 until a national fuel policy was enacted and one recommending a new valuation procedure for the FPC, were filed.[40]

The complexities of the subject, which caused the committee

to present four separate reports, threatened to stymie House action before members could even vote on the rule to consider the bill.[41] The House debate was spirited but not rancorous, and the bill passed August 5 on a roll-call vote of 183–131. The Democratic vote was 93–97; the Republican vote, 90–34.[42] This was no simple partisan issue. With the exception of George A. Dondero (R., Mich.), Republicans and Democrats from the major eastern and midwestern cities voted against the bill. Kansas City's delegation split along the state and party lines: Richard Bolling (D., Mo.) voted against it, while Errett P. Scrivner (R., Kans.) voted for it. Representatives from the southwestern gas-producing states— Arkansas, Texas, Louisiana, Mississippi, Kansas, and Oklahoma— reinforced with solid votes from Tennessee and Virginia, were unanimous in their support. The lines were drawn for the Senate debate, the producing states against the consuming states.

By May 1949 the Senate Interstate and Foreign Commerce Committee was ready to begin hearings on the Kerr bill. Chairman Edwin C. Johnson (D., Colo.) designated freshman Lyndon Johnson to chair a subcommittee composed of Ernest McFarland (D., Ariz.), Francis Myers, John Bricker (R., Ohio), and Clyde M. Reed (R., Kans.) to conduct the hearings.[43] Selecting the Texan was the first tactical error the pro-industry forces made. Although Lyndon Johnson was still a suspect New Dealer to most of the influential oil and gas people in Texas, he had important connections with the industry which justified many of the accusations made later regarding the biased handling of the hearings. Johnson was a protégé of Alvin Wirtz, a lawyer from Austin, Texas. In the thirties, Wirtz' firm was assigned receivership over part of Samuel Insull's public utilities empire, including the unfinished Colorado River dam in Johnson's congressional district. Wirtz became Johnson's closest adviser and "showed him how to translate Washington influences into political dividends back home."[44] Congressman Johnson and Wirtz had worked together to obtain federal funds to finish the dam and helped a rising pair of Texas contractors, George and Herman Brown, secure the contract.[45] In 1949 Wirtz was attorney for the Brown brothers' construction firm, Brown and Root, owners of the famed Big and Little Inch pipelines that transported southwestern natural gas to the East Coast markets.[46] Shepherding the Kerr bill through the hearings helped Johnson solidify his shaky political position at home, and it also lent credence to charges that the hearings were stacked in favor of the gas industry.

The Senate hearings on the Kerr bill were a dress rehearsal for the episode that denied Leland Olds reappointment to the Federal Power Commission later in the year. Olds was an economic consultant and labor writer who had served as head of the New York State Power Authority for eight years when President Roosevelt appointed him to the FPC in 1939. "A mild-mannered, tough minded, zealous old New Dealer,"[47] Olds was the commission's most outspoken advocate of government regulation of private utility rate-making. During the first day's testimony, it was clear that the proponents of the gas industry felt Olds was the cause of the uncertain future of regulation. In his opening statement, Lyndon Johnson left no doubt that Leland Olds was the target of the hearings. "The reversal of the Commission opinion has not been solely the project of changing membership. Individual members . . . have felt compelled to reverse their own thinking on this question within the space of six months or less."[48]

Although not a member of Interstate and Foreign Commerce, Senator Kerr dominated the hearings on S. 1498. He appeared as a witness for his bill, and he was also free to cross-examine any other witness. Whenever there was opposition to S. 1498, Subcommittee Chairman Johnson would defer to Kerr in questioning the speaker.

In his prepared testimony, Senator Kerr focused on Olds' record as a commissioner in an attempt to discredit his judgment. Kerr pointed out that until he testified in the Senate hearings on the Rizley bill in 1948, Olds had held that the FPC had no jurisdiction over the sales of independent natural gas producers and gatherers. Olds had signed Order No. 139 disclaiming any intention to exercise such jurisdiction. After the Interstate decision, he had joined the other commissioners in endorsing the Priest bill to clarify the exempt status. However, six months later, when he felt changed conditions in the industry warranted extended regulation, he had used the Interstate decision to justify this new jurisdiction. Kerr recited event after event, date upon date, to illustrate that Olds "has been on both issues and in the middle."[49]

Olds, of course, was not alone in opposing the Kerr bill, although the committee, and Senator Kerr in particular, tried to give that impression. Commissioners Draper and Buchanan supported Olds' testimony that "the contention that the natural gas production business is conducted by thousands of small independent producers in keen competition with each other to sell natural gas to pipelines . . . does not present a true picture of the regulatory problem in the industry."[50] But there was a subtle difference. Claude Draper had been consistent in his views although they were very complicated. He had always held that the law *might* give the FPC authority to control field prices but that the authority would invade the rights and functions of the states. At the same time, he had argued that Congress should not deprive the FPC of the authority, in case it was needed sometime. Draper had dissented from Order No. 139 following the Interstate decision because "it is now too late for the Commission to issue any order which might be interpreted to constitute a legal limitation upon its power."[51] He had not opposed the Priest bill since he believed Congress had the power to define or alter the authority of the Federal Power Commission. But once convinced that the situation in the gas industry required regulation, he was in a stronger position. Unlike his colleague Olds, Draper had always argued that the FPC had the authority to regulate sales under the 1938 law. Draper's cautiousness before and after 1947 spared him the animosity that Olds attracted. Thomas Buchanan's position, favoring regulation, like Draper's, was predictable because of his record on the Pennsylvania Utilities Commission.

Leland Olds was the only member of the FPC to alter his interpretation of the law. Olds testified that he had simply changed his mind about the nature of the natural gas industry. From 1939 to 1947, he had not believed that the industry required public regulation of producers' prices.[52] After the natural gas investigation report in 1947, he concluded it did. He was not concerned solely with possible monopolization and consequent price-fixing, but as an ardent conservationist Olds feared that the supply of natural gas would soon be exhausted without stringent federal controls.[53] With utter frankness, Olds said he had decided that the 1938 law permitted the degree of regulation he believed necessary. In his opinion the law should be interpreted as its administrators wished. "The question of whether you get effective or ineffective regulation depends on who is appointed to commissions. . . ."[54]

This assertion of the administrator's right to read the law as he saw fit was too much for Senator Kerr, who noted, "Commissioner Olds seems to suggest that independent producers and gatherers should be left in his custody in a kind of indefinite probation, but without specific legislative authority from Congress."[55] This view of the law was more traditional and less surprising than Olds'.

In addition to the findings of the natural gas investigation, there was a personal element involved in the commissioner's changed views. A Roosevelt appointee to the first Federal Power Commission, Olds "came to view himself as the guardian of the consumer's interests arrayed against a dark and sinister conspiracy of producers."[56] Olds tended to see public questions in stark relief—opposites of good and evil. And the question of natural gas regulation became his personal crusade.

Olds' entire testimony seemed like a deliberate attempt to antagonize an already unfriendly subcommittee. His opening remarks set the tone. "I am the same Leland Olds who has been referred to on numerous occasions in these hearings. Some, if not many, of the references to my views are erroneous and misleading. . . ."[57] Senators were accustomed to more humility, and as Olds' testimony developed, his position deteriorated. At every opportunity he seemed eager to provoke the subcommittee, especially Johnson and Kerr. In response to a question concerning the commission's recommendation to exempt small natural gas producers, Olds responded, "In order to maintain effective regulation, that regulation need only run to about 10 percent of the

producers." Then he added, "the producers of the seven southwestern producing states, yes sir."[58] As he concluded his prepared
testimony, Olds seemed deliberately to taunt the senators. "I
would remind you gentlemen of the oft quoted adage that a wise
man changes his mind, but a fool never."[59] The gauntlet was down.
When Johnson and Kerr picked it up in September, Leland Olds'
career on the Federal Power Commission was over.

The Senate hearings on S. 1498 served only to entrench and
embitter both sides in the controversy. Kerr and Johnson were as
guilty as Leland Olds of arrogant and provocative conduct. And
the arguments from both sides were full of logical contradictions
that passed unnoticed in the press coverage that capitalized on
personalities and slogans of the controversy, obscuring the real
issues. During the hearings, Kerr appeared unable to decide if
Olds' changed interpretation of the law or his social philosophy
was the major threat to the gas industry. "While I cannot reconcile
the different positions of Commissioner Olds . . . his positions
are consistent with a long-range purpose to oust the states from
the control of their own resources."[60] The commission majority
argued an equally contradictory case. To support the changed
interpretation of the Natural Gas Act, they cited the Supreme
Court Interstate decision and claimed that if Congress amended
the 1938 law it would "overrule the Court decision, which dealt
squarely with the intent of Congress in passing the Natural Gas
Act."[61] In view of their remaining testimony, this was, at best,
a contorted position. All the commissioners agreed that the FPC
had never attempted to assert jurisdiction over an independent
producer's or gatherer's arm's-length sale of natural gas during
the ten years since the adoption of the law.[62] It followed then that
the Supreme Court had never had a case in which the question was
"squarely decided," as the commission majority sought Congress
to believe. The Interstate case did not concern an independent
producer or gatherer, but rather an integrated company engaged
in both transportation and production operations. In their brief
to the Court, the FPC specifically and repeatedly disclaimed jurisdiction over the independents. They pointed out that the Interstate Company was not in the exempt category.[63]

In misrepresenting the significance of the Interstate decision, the commission majority laid the basis for the most serious distortion of the entire debate. They argued that instead of reaffirming Congress' intent in the 1938 Act, the Kerr bill would strip the FPC of its established powers. Then they predicted that this removal of the alleged authority to control the field price of gas would result in large increases in consumer prices. During his analysis of S. 1498, Olds skillfully led Kerr to an admission that became the death knell in the controversy. In response to Olds' assertion that "the chief proponents of S. 1498 are interested in higher prices for natural gas," Kerr replied, "That will be admitted."[64] Kerr's response was candid and disastrous. No producer of natural gas, or of any other fuel or product, was in business to lose money. If Kerr had responded otherwise, his motives would have been equally suspect. The opponents of the Kerr bill seized upon this response as proof of their charge that "the Kerr bill is certain to increase the price of natural gas more than $200,000,000 a year on a nationwide basis . . . and this increase assures Kerr of at least $50,000,000 in profits before taxes."[65]

The subcommittee on S. 1498 rewrote the Kerr bill, and on June 24, 1949, reported a committee version very similar to the House bill, H.R. 1758.[66] The only significant change was the deletion of the Kerr bill's provisions which would have removed the FPC's jurisdiction over any segment of the integrated pipeline companies.[67] The report urged the necessity of legislation because of the "threat" that the majority of the FPC would assume authority where "Congress has authorized no such jurisdiction."[68] The Senate was preoccupied with legislation to extend the Marshall Plan and debate on the North Atlantic Treaty, so the session slipped past with no further action on the Kerr bill.

Although the Senate Democratic leadership planned no consideration of the Kerr bill in 1949, they began to prepare for the eventual debate in the next session. In July, the Democratic Policy Committee asked the Bureau of the Budget for an endorsement of S. 1498.[69] Since the administration had favored the Priest bill in 1947, the leadership anticipated a similar endorsement.[70] But the assumption was unfounded in light of President Truman's

recent appointment of Thomas Buchanan and his renaming of
Leland Olds to a third term on the FPC. While Truman might have
succumbed to pressure from northern urban interests when he
made the Buchanan appointment in 1948, he was securely elected
and very popular when he renamed Olds in 1949. If he had disagreed with Olds' new interpretation of the Natural Gas Act, he
could easily have named a commissioner with views similar to
Smith's and Wimberly's. Truman's reappointment of Olds after
Olds' public repudiation of his earlier views indicated at least
the President's acquiescence to extended regulation, if not his full
endorsement. But the gas industry proponents seemed oblivious
to the significance of these two appointments.

The Bureau of the Budget advised Truman to endorse the
Olds-Draper-Buchanan view as "compatible with the Administration's position for strong anti-monopoly programs."[71] The President followed the advice.[72] On August 1, 1949, the Budget Bureau
informed the chairman of the Senate Interstate and Foreign Commerce Committee that S. 1498 was "not in accord with the President's program."[73] If the Senate committee felt some legislation
was necessary, the President did not object to FPC-proposed legislation to exempt the small producers and gatherers. Also during
the House debate on H.R. 1758 in August, the President authorized
his aide, Charles S. Murphy, to inform the House leadership and
the chairman of the Rules Committee that he did not want the
bill.[74]

Senator Kerr seemed unwilling to believe he was at odds
with the President so soon. And he tried to persuade Truman in
person on August 8. The discussion turned on the President's
concern that the Kerr bill would allow the rates charged for natural
gas to domestic consumers to rise unchecked. Although the meeting was inconclusive, the President asked Kerr to respond to the
rate question in a brief memo. The Senator's analysis was a suc-
cinct answer to the assumption that rates charged domestic gas
consumers were dependent on federal regulation of independent
producers and gatherers. The response was threefold: (1) state
and municipal regulatory agencies, not the Federal Power Com-

mission, controlled the rates distributing companies charged consumers; (2) since there was no testimony from consumers for relief or protection, state and municipal agencies were doing an effective job; and (3) even if the FPC had the power to reduce the field price of gas, there was no assurance the saving would pass on to the consumer since federal authority did not extend to the burner-tip price of natural gas. Kerr concluded that "opposition to these bills (H.R. 1758 and S. 1498) is tantamount to endorsement of regulation for regulation's sake alone."[75]

Something in the August 8 meeting with Truman unsettled Kerr, and he decided that the President was not personally aware of the complete development of the controversy. He wrote the President on August 12, 1949, that despite Elmer Staats' letter to Chairman Edwin Johnson, he did not believe that Truman agreed with the FPC majority who favored additional regulation.[76] Along with the memo on the rate question, Kerr attached a lengthy review of the legislative and administrative history of the Natural Gas Act. He also warned Truman of the undesirable effects of the proposed regulation.[77] The best Kerr hoped for was that Truman would not now actively oppose his bill.

When it became apparent in late 1948 that the Senate would not act, the industry proponents had changed their tactics. Thwarted in efforts to clarify the law, they decided to change the Federal Power Commission. Leland Olds' term was expiring when the Eighty-first Congress convened. Although Truman renominated Olds in June 1949, Senate Interstate and Foreign Commerce Committee Chairman Edwin Johnson delayed hearings until his committee completed action on the Kerr bill. After the acrimonious hearings, it seemed inevitable that the committee would never vote to confirm Olds. Given the circumstances, it was unlikely that the full Senate would override the committee's unfavorable recommendation without enormous pressure from the President. Majority Leader Scott Lucas pleaded with Truman not to renominate Olds, but the President seemed impervious to defeats in Congress. Undoubtedly, his preoccupation with the Korean invasion caused him to underestimate the Senate's hostility to Olds

and distorted his judgment. Truman renominated Olds and promptly left him "to shift for himself."[78] Finally a combination of newspaper criticism and prodding from the President spurred Chairman
Johnson to act.[79]

Lyndon Johnson sought the job of chairing the subcommittee
on the Olds nomination.[80] Kerr had found him an effective ally
in hearings on S. 1498 and the Oklahoman probably encouraged
him to seek the assignment. Since he was not a member of the
Senate Interstate and Foreign Commerce Committee, Kerr did
not participate in the hearings. But he made no secret of his antipathy for the commissioner. The day the hearings opened, Kerr
announced he would fight "to the finish on Olds' appointment."[81]

The subcommittee, enlarged for the confirmation inquiry,[82]
was unanimously hostile to the commissioner. Four members—
Chairman Lyndon Johnson, Ernest McFarland, John Bricker, and
Clyde Reed—still smarted from Olds' arrogance during the Kerr
bill hearings. Homer Capehart and Edwin C. Johnson were suspicious of Olds' leftist leanings, and Herbert O'Conor (D., Md.)
silently endorsed the proceedings. Representative John Lyle (D.,
Tex.), a decorated World War II veteran elected while serving
overseas, set the tone of the hearing when he tried to portray
Olds as a communist or, at least, a "fellow traveler." He introduced fifty-four photostats of articles Olds had written as an
employee for the *Federated Press,* a labor news service. Written
between 1922 and 1929, some of the articles had appeared in
publications associated with the Communist party. The charge
that Olds was an enemy of capitalism were neither new nor surprising. Senator E. H. Moore had opposed Olds' nomination to
a second term on the FPC in 1944 claiming that his writings
proved, "He was a communist then [in the 1920's] and he is still
a communist."[83] Using the same articles which Congressman Lyle
introduced, Senator Styles Bridges had accused Olds of communist
associations in 1943.[84] The charges were dismissed as unfounded
in the 1944 hearings, but the subcommittee found them impressive
in the atmosphere of 1949.[85]

Even though Congressman Lyle misrepresented many of Olds'
writings and quoted freely without regard to context, there was

enough evidence of sympathies with the left to cause some members to change their minds in the floor debate.[86] Olds' defense was ineffective; although, given such a hostile subcommittee, any defense would have been difficult. But in September, Leland Olds was no longer the bluff, self-confident witness he had been in June. He surely anticipated the communist smear, but his defense was listless. He denied ever having been a communist, but he would not repudiate his writings. He defended them as necessary to arouse the American public and as the work of his youth.[87] It was an unfortunate explanation, and Representative Lyle pounced on it like an animal scenting the kill. He observed that Olds became industrial editor of the *Federated Press* in 1922 at age thirty-two and continued until 1929 at age thirty-nine. Elected to the House at age thirty-two,[88] the Congressman was then thirty-nine years old. "Throughout my years here, I have been held responsible for my philosophy and for that which I write and speak. I think Mr. Olds can and should be held responsible also."[89] Had Olds' vanity permitted, other witnesses might have been able to answer the charges or at least direct the hearings toward his career on the FPC.

Early in October, while the nomination was before the full committee, President Truman's interest in Leland Olds suddenly revived. He sent a letter to the Senate committee saying that if they failed to approve Mr. Olds they would be serving "the powerful corporations."[90] At Truman's instructions, Vice-President Barkley read a copy of the letter to the Senate.[91] In response, Chairman E. C. Johnson thundered that Truman was supporting a "crusader of foreign ideologies."[92] The senators ignored the President's plea and rejected the Olds nomination 7–0 in the subcommittee, 10–2 in the full committee.[93]

Truman now seemed determined to save Olds at any cost. He took the extraordinary step of instructing William Boyle, Jr., national chairman of the Democratic party, to wire all state chairmen asking them to let their senators know "the people want Olds confirmed."[94] Later the same day, Truman defended his action in making a party issue of the appointment saying that party discipline was essential to party responsibility.[95]

Truman had blundered. Senators were jealous of their role to "advise and consent" on presidential appointments and punctilious in observing the protocol of senatorial courtesy. Since the Republican senators Irving Ives and John Foster Dulles from Olds' native New York both opposed his appointment[96] and the Interstate and Foreign Commerce Committee recommended against his confirmation, the Senate had no inclination to act. Truman's insistence on Olds was difficult to understand. With the 1948 election safely behind him, there was no immediate need to placate the populous urban interests. And, as Senator Kerr observed in his August 12 letter, there had been no plea for redress from the consumer. While Truman had campaigned as the champion of the little man, he had so little to gain from this confrontation with the Senate that the only feasible explanation was sheer obstinacy. His threatened lash of party discipline cost him any effective support he might have gained through more discreet means. Senator Harry Byrd (D., Va.), in his familiar white suit and crêpe-sole shoes, said what many other Democratic senators were thinking. "By implication, at least, Chairman Boyle threatens every member of the U.S. Senate with the loss of patronage if the order in this telegram is not obeyed."[97]

Truman's handling of the Olds nomination was inept, particularly for a man who supposedly understood the Senate's balky and independent temperament. By the end of the hearings on the Kerr bill in June, Olds was clearly a marked man. Both Senators Richard Russell and Robert Taft (R., Ohio) opposed his reappointment.[98] But the President deliberately ignored the Majority Leader's warning that Olds could not be confirmed. The Boyle telegram had been a futile and destructive gesture because "99 % of the state party leaders had never heard of Leland Olds."[99] If Truman wanted to advocate extended regulation, he should have retreated and offered a less controversial nomination. But he seemed determined to assert his presidential power and to have Leland Olds at any cost. Senator Kerr was equally determined to be rid of him.

The Senate debate on Olds was intemperate, full of exaggerated accusations, and punctuated with verbal personal abuse.[100] The vote rejecting the nomination was 53–15, with virtually all

Republicans voting against confirmation.[101] Senator Kerr was credited with masterminding Olds' defeat, but the extent of his participation was unclear.[102] While he openly opposed Olds' views on regulation, he never indulged in the rhetoric of the witch hunt that drove the commissioner from office. Kerr was concerned with the consistent and predictable application of the law. He believed if the Natural Gas Act was so unclear that a man who had thought it meant one thing for ten years, could change his mind within six months, the law should be clarified. He believed that the Congress, not an administrator, should determine the law.

Paul Douglas' recollection of the hearings helped perpetuate the myth that Kerr singlehandedly ousted Leland Olds as "a warning to all the regulatory bodies not to enforce the laws to protect the public."[103] According to Douglas, "at the hearings, Kerr kept Lyndon Johnson by his side as he struck his threatened blow. The two read into the record Olds' writings of a quarter of a century previous."[104] The facts were otherwise. Senator Kerr did not appear as a witness against Olds. He was present only for a few hours on the first day to introduce testimony from Reford Bond, chairman of the Oklahoma Corporation Commission. Bond's statement, which the press interpreted as Kerr's,[105] was confined to Olds' record on the FPC. There was no mention of Representative Lyle's charges, no insinuations about Olds' loyalty.[106] During the Senate debate, Kerr's only contribution was to clarify some technical points about the natural gas industry.[107] Kerr took no part in the red-baiting, "although Homer Capehart and Ed Johnson were firing at will."[108] Given Olds' early career and the anxiety in the late forties over questions of spy scandals and loyalty problems, his early writings were bound to cause concern. Alvin Wirtz, Lyndon Johnson's and John Lyle's Texas patron, inspired and directed the strategy used to defeat Olds.[109] Johnson was also close to Harold Ickes, Roosevelt's secretary of the interior, who may have used the confirmation hearing as a personal vendetta against Olds. "Ickes believed that Olds had poisoned President Roosevelt's mind against him, thereby ruining Ickes' chance to become chairman of a new federal Water-Power Commission."[110] Abe Fortas, Johnson's private counsel for the hearings, had been Ickes' undersecretary during the Ickes-Olds feud. Still close to the "Old Curmudgeon," Fortas supplied Johnson daily with material and arguments against Olds.[111]

Kerr always confined his opposition to Olds' record as commissioner. Lowell Mellett, a Washington columnist who was a major contributor to the confusion and misinformation surrounding the gas controversy, was scrupulously correct in reporting Kerr's position on Leland Olds. After an hour-and-a-quarter interview with Kerr, Mellett wrote, "The Senator offered documentary evidence to show that this changed interpretation of law represented a change of viewpoint on the part of Mr. Olds, one that rendered him unacceptable to any producer or gatherer of natural gas."[112] In explaining his opposition to Olds in an interview with Marquis Childs, the Oklahoman stated, "I opposed him after he declared on the witness stand that unless stopped by Congress he would impose a control program upon a great American non-utility industry which . . . would not be regulation but confiscation."[113] Although Kerr was not alone in his silence on the communist issue, it was interpreted as an endorsement of the charges.[114]

Leland Olds, more than any other individual, was responsible for his own defeat. He was politically unwise to insist that only the southwestern gas producers needed regulation.[115] This response heightened sectional animosity and reinforced the oil and gas industry's conviction that they were being treated unfairly while other fuels, such as coal, continued to be unregulated. Olds' conduct during hearings on the Kerr bill was also harmful. Senators reserve the right to be arrogant; witnesses are expected to be above or without petty feelings. And those who act otherwise are punished. Had Olds been less of a dogmatist, he would have welcomed a congressional amendment clarifying the legislative intent, but he unwisely maintained that Congress could have no future voice in the matter since the Court had ruled that regulation was permissible under the 1938 law. If the Court had made such a ruling, which they did not do in the Interstate case, Congress could still have legislated otherwise. From May to October of 1949, there was a growing sense that Olds would have to go. But the loyalty question was not decisive. The large majority that failed to confirm him was voting against the rigidity he embodied. Olds was "a man whose assumptions of exclusiveness were incompatible with the processes of government as the senators saw them."[116]

By the end of 1949, the cliché about "private versus public interest" began to reemerge. Journalists repeated the conspiracy interpretation of Senator Kerr and the greedy gas industry ready to bilk the helpless consumer now bereft of his protector, Leland Olds. Like all clichés, it obscured the important issue that able and honorable men can, and often do, disagree. Before the matter was resolved, both sides were guilty of ascribing evil motives to anyone who differed on the question of the proper philosophy and extent of public utilities regulation.

Senator Kerr retained his objectivity throughout 1949. His refusal to become emotionally involved in the altercation over Leland Olds was proof of his growing maturity as a politician. But in the year that followed Kerr seemed a changed man. The struggle over the Kerr bill so consumed him that he lost all perspective. He allowed the outer emotionalism which always characterized his speeches to become an inner emotionalism that paralyzed his judgment while it spurred his ambition.

CHAPTER IV
The Natural Gas Controversy

The Senate began debate on the Kerr gas bill early in the second session of the Eighty-first Congress.[1] Since 1950 was an election year, the Democratic leadership was anxious to adjourn early. They anticipated a fierce campaign from Republicans seeking to reverse the liberal trend apparent in President Truman's surprise 1948 victory.

The House companion to S. 1498, the so-called Harris bill, passed on August 5, 1949, with little controversy preceding the 183–131 vote. A large number of Democratic congressmen voted for the Harris bill because they understood that the Senate sponsors had President Truman's personal assurance that he would accept the legislation.[2] But smooth House passage was no guarantee of quick acceptance in the Senate. In fact, the easy success of the measure in the House alarmed the bill's opponents in the Senate and sparked rumors in northern and eastern cities that the legislation would result in higher gas prices to the consumer. Articles began to appear in trade journals, labor publications, and the urban press warning of "a new crop of strutting millionaires," hinting at an astronomical price rise in gas, and predicting that the Senate debate would be "a sordid, unblushing grab for money. . . ."[3] The Senate debate would be bitter, lengthy, and divisive with faint echoes of the rhetoric of nineteenth-century European class struggles. Clearly, it would be a conflict between "people born in the shadow of the gas stove and people born in the shadow of the gas well."[4]

Although the Senate debate on the Kerr bill was essentially a reenactment of all the arguments made since the 1947 Interstate case, both sides participated with opening-night enthusiasm. Senator Kerr made two early miscalculations that profoundly affected the fate of the gas bill. He did not anticipate any well-organized opposition and thought a two- or three-day debate would suffice.[5] He knew that Senator Douglas was preparing a major speech with Leland Olds' help[6] but relished any confrontation with the Illinoisan. The Oklahoman never underestimated Douglas' brilliance, but he was so secure in his own intimate knowledge of the natural gas industry that he dismissed the likelihood of any other member possessing the competence to discuss the technicalities. This presumption of privileged knowledge and anticipation of a technician's colloquy, not a layman's debate, was an incorrect prediction of how the struggle would develop. And Kerr's own familiarity and preoccupation with the details of the gas industry severely hampered the effectiveness of his case.

The Oklahoman was reasonably sure of a majority of Democratic votes as debate began. The seven southwestern gas-producing states, plus most of the southern bloc and a few scattered western Democrats, totaled a possible thirty-two votes—a probable twenty-eight firm votes.[7] A sizeable group of GOP senators seemed ready to support the Kerr bill. The Republican leader, Robert A. Taft, and Colorado's influential Eugene Millikin (R.) were outspoken in favoring the bill. Although both represented gas-consuming states, they supported the legislation because they opposed the general principle of government price-fixing.[8] Kerr calculated that as many as twenty Republicans might follow this lead, certainly no fewer than fifteen.[9] Even his most conservative estimate, carefully checked with Richard Russell and Lyndon Johnson, who was beginning to show a knack for voting predictions, promised victory.[10]

With this cushion of votes, Kerr decided to withhold his own presentation until late in the debate.[11] Meanwhile his staff ornamented the chamber with billboard-size charts and graphs portraying the natural gas industry from every possible statistical view. He intended to use the exhibits to answer technical inquiries and to correct misconceptions about the bill. He also planned to give a memorable curtain speech to sweep away all confusion and clinch final passage. Kerr was not so naïve as to believe a Senate speech changed anyone's mind, but his self-confidence deceived him into believing that Senate debate was meaningless.

Edwin C. Johnson, as chairman of the Senate Interstate and Foreign Commerce Committee, gave the traditional introductory speech outlining the bill's legislative history. But he was hardly into the perfunctory discussion of the original intent of the 1938 Natural Gas Act when Missouri Republican James P. Kem began to probe the chairman's familiarity with the technical aspects of the legislation. Johnson immediately floundered, answering with the obliqueness of a deaf man who has not heard the question. Lyndon Johnson, as chairman of the subcommittee that held the hearings, tried to rescue the Coloradan, but also blundered. Kem had asked whether the Supreme Court interpreted the 1938 Act as giving the FPC authority "to fix the price of those who sell at wholesale."[12] The Texan tried to shrug off the question as a mere restatement of the "Olds plan" to subject the gas industry to regulation that Congress never intended. Johnson's reference to Leland Olds was unfortunate because it revived the hostility of the confirmation debate. It also reinforced the opposition's belief that the Kerr bill was the dénouement of the gas industry's vendetta against the martyred Olds.

Sensing that the bill's defenders were vulnerable, other Republicans quickly joined Senator Kem. All afternoon they kept up such a drumfire of questions that Kerr finally intervened to save Edwin Johnson from additional embarrassment. The nature of the questions and the diversity of the questioners suggested that a number of Republicans saw the makings of a good political issue.

The Missouri Republicans, Kem and Donnell, had obviously prepared with great care and relieved one another throughout the two weeks of debate that followed. But Senator Kem was clearly the leader of the Republican opposition. Although unknown in the country, Kem was the President's most persistent Republican critic on Capitol Hill. He was one of thirteen senators who had voted against the NATO alliance calling it "a sinkhole for untold billions of the money of American taxpayers."[13] As a highly successful corporation lawyer, Kem was no stranger to the natural gas industry. Anticipating a primary challenge in 1952 from Truman's secretary of the Air Force, Stuart Symington, the Missouri Republican redeemed his image as James "Petroleum" Kem.[14]

The white-haired, white-moustached Senator was as tenacious and fearless as the other Missourian in the White House. Kerr failed to intimidate Kem although he badgered him with countless questions and then haggled over the accuracy of the responses. This was one of Kerr's proven techniques to shatter an opponent and was so effective that many senators avoided any exchange with him on the floor. But Kem was not rattled. He finally silenced Kerr with the firm declaration, "I shall answer any questions the Senator puts to me in my own way, in my own words, in my own time, and at such lengths as I see fit."[15] Nor did he blink when Kerr threatened *argumentum ad hominem*, the most devastating part of his repertoire. Kem actually welcomed the challenge, "If the Senator wants to indulge in personalities, let the bar go down."[16] A bit surprised, Kerr retreated.

The Republican strategy was simple—beat the Democrats at their own game. Harry Truman had ravaged the GOP in 1948 by claiming that the Democratic party was the protector of the little man against the "special interests." In the natural gas bill, some Republicans saw an opportunity to steal the mantle of public protector and a majority of them rushed under its ample folds. Republican Alexander Wiley of Wisconsin scoffed at the administration's sanction of the Kerr bill. "It belies the phony, highsounding claims that have been made through the years as to the alleged love by that party of the great masses."[17] Senator Kem maintained that the concern for the southwestern independent producer was a smokescreen behind which Wall Street bankers were "attempting to hold up the American people for at least one hundred million dollars a year."[18]

But the most brutal attack was from Maine's Republican Owen Brewster, known in Washington circles as the "Pan American Airways Senator."[19] Brewster delivered an angry speech selecting the most partisan passages from Kerr's keynote address to the 1944 convention and applying them to the Democratic party. In an interview afterwards, he said Republicans were disgusted with Kerr's vote to make millions available for co-operative housing. "I'm somewhat allergic to being instructed in the virtues of free enterprise by a gentleman who has voted to put $1,000,000 into a program that certainly won't help free enterprise along."[20]

The Republican opposition also led Kerr to a frank admission which they later represented as a direct threat to cut off gas supplies to families on the East Coast. Early in the debate the genial New England patrician, Leverett Saltonstall (R., Mass.) asked Edwin Johnson if he felt gas supplies to the East would "be retarded" if the Kerr bill failed. Johnson speculated that they would surely be diminished and that the "price would go up."[21] At this point Senator Kerr intervened with several charts to demonstrate that because of the confusion over the FPC's regulatory powers, most gas contracts negotiated over the preceding two years contained automatic termination clauses if the FPC attempted to fix the independents' prices. Several of those contracts were between Tennessee Gas Transmission Company and the New England states. Kerr said the purpose of those clauses was to "prevent the confiscation of his [independent gas producer's] property by the Federal Power Commission."[22]

The New England Republicans feigned confusion and continued to repeat the same question. Near exasperation trying to convey his meaning to Senator Charles Tobey (R., N.H.), Kerr snapped, "If we are permitted to do so, we will continue to produce gas and make it available for New England."[23] Kerr startled the senators present when he rashly suggested that New England manufacturing interests might become aware "that they can come to the Southwest and get their fuel for one-fourth or one-fifth or one-sixth of what they now pay. . . ."[24] Even the plodding Tobey understood the implications of this response.

It was a serious mistake. Kerr probably did not intend to threaten the New England consumer with the chilling prospect of cold furnaces and industrial ghost towns. But the words and tone precluded any other interpretation. He was trying to explain the complex economic problems the industry faced and the difficulties that uncertainty about regulation had caused. But he became irritable at the New Englanders, whom he suspected of being dupes of the coal interests who opposed the legislation. Did not they understand that not only was natural gas cheaper and cleaner than coal, but also that the gas industry was virtually free of the turbulent labor relations that frequently disrupted coal supplies and raised prices? The coal strike settled in mid-March had raised the price of coal to a new high. On the first day of the debate Lyndon Johnson tried to anticipate coal-inspired opposition. He charged that John L. Lewis and the United Mine Workers (UMW) were working covertly to defeat the Kerr bill. As a senator from a conservative, right-to-work state, Johnson had all the traditional suspicions about the conspiratorial and subterranean methods of organized labor. Obsessed with Leland Olds, Johnson now believed that he was the coal industry's secret weapon against competition from cheap gas. "It was Mr. Olds who came to the fore with a proposal which serves coal's purposes as clearly and as directly and as effectively as any argument advanced by coal's lawyers. Mr. Olds struck with the rapier where the Coal Trust failed with its broadsword."[25] The Texan said the UMW wanted to defeat the Kerr bill so the FPC would fix gas prices at the wellhead. To avoid regulation, producers would then invoke the escape clauses in their contracts with the pipeline companies, and the result would be a happy one for coal: "No gas, or less gas at higher prices."[26]

Kerr's intemperate threat to New Englanders was also probably a result of his pique with Francis J. Myers' unexpected opposition to S. 1498. In the 1949 hearings of the Senate Interstate and Foreign Commerce Committee, Senator Myers had disavowed the FPC's authority to regulate the independent producers and gatherers.[27] Kerr believed that Democratic Whip Myers was obligated to support the bill. If the Pennsylvanian had to vote against it, Kerr thought he should have done so quietly. Majority Leader Scott Lucas was already occupied with his campaign against Republican Representative Everett Dirksen and had done nothing to facilitate the debate. Now Myers recanted his earlier support.

The elected leadership seemed ineffective and, perhaps, unreliable.

The Kerr forces learned of Myers' defection early enough to coach Garrett Withers (D., Ky.) and Tom Connally to cross-examine him. So many of the questions put to Myers actually anticipated his remarks that he accused the Press Gallery, which had the only other copy of his undelivered speech, of leaking the text to "a number of persons."[28] Kerr was visibly angry about the speech, and that anger prevented him from appreciating the political difficulties in Pennsylvania that had occasioned Myers' reversal. Myers was facing a serious challenge from the amiable Republican governor, James H. Duff. Elected in 1944 by a narrow margin of 23,000 votes—compared to Roosevelt's margin of 105,000—Myers was fearful about November 1950. Pennsylvania was traditionally a Republican state and had been in the GOP column in every bi-election except 1934. Governor Duff, elected in 1946 with a hearty 557,000 votes to spare, had gained popularity.[29] 1950 was no year to discount the votes of Pennsylvania coal miners.

The *New York Times* reported that Myers had decided to oppose S. 1498 because he disagreed with some coal operators' views that passage of the Kerr bill was a panacea for Pennsylvania's sluggish coal industry. They reasoned that the Kerr bill would permit gas prices to rise unchecked. Coal would become more competitive as gas prices soared, and the Keystone State's economy would benefit.[30] It seemed more plausible that coal industry spokesmen, who hoped that the bill's defeat would follow the lines of Johnson's predicted scenario, had influenced Myers. Whatever the particular reasoning, one fact was overwhelming. National party obligations and personal loyalties were secondary. Pennsylvania was a coal-producing, gas-consuming state. Francis Myers' political future dictated his public switch on Kerr's gas bill.

The Republican opposition's most devastating argument against the Kerr bill was, ironically, incapable of either proof or refutation. And it was effective because it evoked irrational fears. William Langer (R., S. Dak.), who often roamed the chamber chewing cigars still in their wrappers,[31] resorted to the debater's favorite ploy of trapping an opponent with his own words. Senators were still trying to absorb the implications of Kerr's implied threat to New England, and, in effect, to all gas-consuming states, when Langer rose and began quoting from the 1949 hearings on S. 1498. "Leland Olds said, 'I believe the chief proponents of S. 1498 are interested in higher field prices for natural gas.' Kerr responded, 'That will be admitted.'"[32] Regardless of how Kerr tried to explain his meaning—that all businessmen were interested in higher prices for their products—Langer continued to bellow, "The proponents of this bill are interested in getting higher prices at the expense of the consumers. . . ; the average person, if he is interested in higher prices, if he is engaged in an honest business, does not object to regulation."[33] This accusation of certain higher prices to the consumer and the implied perfidy of all who opposed regulation became the opposition's litany for the remainder of the debate. As articles appeared in the press about the "ripper" gas bill, "the producers' gas grab," alleging that "householders and manufacturers have a stake amounting to hundreds of millions of dollars," the tempo quickened.[34] Opponents from both parties began to read letters into the *Congressional Record* from indignant housewives, frightened old people living on fixed incomes, union officials, and municipal employees all expressing fear about the "inevitable" gas price increase.[35]

In spite of evidence that the consumer price of natural gas was "12 percent less than 10 years ago,"[36] the argument stuck. In a colloquy about the inequity of regulating the gas industry while exempting coal, Kerr and William Fulbright (D., Ark.) implied that the independent gas producers were more responsible toward the public than the coal miners. Following the 1950 coal strike, miners' wages rose $105 million in one year, or "50 percent more than the gross amount received by all independent producers in the Nation for every cubic foot of gas which was sold in interstate commerce up through 1948."[37]

The southwestern senators never fully comprehended that the gas industry in the twentieth century had inherited the stigma applied to oil in the nineteenth. Coal miners were hard-working, God-fearing, family men who mowed their lawns on Saturday and paid bills on the first of the month. Independent gas producers were and, like their cousins the pipeline owners and the oilmen, always would be robber barons. In the imagination of many critics, they did not really work or risk like other men, but rather they profited from gas which automatically flowed from the ground.

It was unclear whether the Republican assault on the Kerr bill was a well-orchestrated stratagem or a lucky happenstance. Fortune had seldom smiled so sweetly on the Republicans after 1912, so it seemed more plausible that they had foreseen the political advantages and decided on concerted action. Senator Kem, who dominated the debate, was a relentless Truman critic. The prospect of stealing the President's thunder through appropriating the Democratic party's role as protector of the public interest must have been irresistible. And the role Saltonstall and Tobey played in gently provoking Kerr's threats about curtailing gas supplies to New England was gifted strategy. Other senators regarded both men as trustworthy—not brilliant or witty, but lacking artifice and vindictiveness. If Kerr's outburst had come after questioning from the volatile Wayne Morse (R., Ore.), it would have been attributed to bad temper. But made to those classic exemplars of New England Republicanism, it became sinister, quite in keeping with the stereotype of the "oil and gas crowd." Since neither Tobey nor Saltonstall made a formal speech opposing the bill or participated any further, their contribution must have been carefully and shrewdly contrived. Like all good actors in cameo roles, they played themselves to the hilt.

The press scarcely credited the Republicans' contribution to the ultimate defeat of the Kerr bill. Liberal columnists seemed mesmerized with their new Saint George, Paul Douglas, slaying the "vested interest dragon."[38] Stories began to appear hinting that Douglas w•uld be the ideal Democratic presidential candidate for 1952.[39]

Douglas, who was always extremely careful of his facts in debating Senator Kerr,[40] never seemed to enjoy these confrontations as did the Oklahoman. The Illinois Senator admitted that he feared Kerr's "unique capacity for brutal and casuistical argument."[41] But Douglas had expert advice. Leland Olds worked closely with him on the historical development of the controversy. And Mel Van Scoyoc, a specialist in gas rates for the Federal Power

Commission, helped Douglas' staff analyze over one hundred contracts to buttress the Senator's case concerning the concentration of ownership of gas reserves.[42] Douglas, who scrupulously avoided the appearance of being any group's spokesman, was apparently blind to the ethical question of employing the knowledge of a staff member of an impartial, regulatory agency to aid in a partisan attempt to augment the powers of that agency. The press also overlooked this questionable relationship.

Douglas originally intended to speak after Kerr defended the bill. As self-confident as the Oklahoman, he probably assumed that they would dominate the debate. The Republican opposition was a welcome and unexpected surprise. Douglas was apparently unaware of any plan for a concerted Republican attack. Being a loner within his own party, he would have been ill at ease in any strategy he could not dominate. While he preferred the role of solitary opponent and the exclusive press coverage this ensured, Douglas sincerely opposed the bill and was quick to exploit every opportunity to widen the opposition.

When the "steel-ribbed Iowa conservative," Democrat Guy Gillette, expressed shock at Kerr's "thinly veiled threat to withhold gas from New England,"[43] Douglas planted a notion that would be far more insulting to the New England members than implied reprisals. He suggested that Kerr's statement was merely a bluff intended to influence the twelve senators from New England. The Iowa Senator, who had withstood Roosevelt's attempt to purge him in 1938 only to be defeated in 1944 and then reelected with the largest majority in the state's history in 1948, was not easily intimidated or bluffed. Douglas' seemingly casual attitude enraged him. "When anyone asserts in good faith on the floor of the Senate that he can and will do such a thing, and in addition when he announces to the Senators from New England that it might be necessary to take action to deprive them of their fuel, so that their industries would be removed by some other section, I claim it is unfortunate, even if it is a bluff."[44] Douglas never returned to this argument; there was no need to. New England Senators accepted the traditional folklore that they were wily and shrewd, just as all southern members believed they were courtly and gracious. And to prove it, eleven New England Republicans did not fall for Kerr's bluff.[45]

On the fourth day of debate, fearing that the Kerr forces might have so large a majority that they would offer only a per- functory defense, Douglas decided to answer various arguments he expected Kerr to raise. He did not want to wait any longer and risk a sudden vote before he could be heard. He obtained the floor on March 20, saying that since the Kerr people seemed reluctant to present their own case, he would have to do it for them. "Mr. President, I am offering myself up as a votive sacrifice on the altar of fair play. . . ."[46]

Douglas monopolized the floor for three days and focused his attack on the changed conditions in the gas industry, which he believed made federal regulation of the independents' sales man- datory to protect the public interest. He refused to speak of the gas producers and gatherers as "independents"; he wanted to deny them the sympathy the term evoked.[47] These men were "nontrans- porting producers." They were not "men in overalls," but instead "giants, operating under near monopoly conditions."[48] Douglas produced Bureau of Mines statistics to illustrate that 3 per cent or sixty-nine of the twenty-three hundred nontransporting pro- ducers accounted for 70 per cent of all gas sales in interstate commerce in 1947.[49] He predicted that the 3 per cent would be re- ponsible for 80 per cent of the gas purchased in 1952. The location of the gas reserves in the seven southwestern states also com- pounded the problem of concentration of ownership.[50]

Douglas' strategy was to touch on every possible issue hoping to find a raw nerve. He was most successful in awakening sectional animosities, always barely dormant in any Senate debate over natural resources, and the Democratic party's traditional mistrust of big business. He claimed the Kerr bill would free the big oil and gas companies from regulation and "put the high prices paid by the consumer of the North, not into the pockets of the people of the Southwest, but into the pockets of the big oil and gas groups."[51]

The Illinoisan anticipated Kerr's argument that gas was the only fuel industry with long-term contracts between pipeline com- panies and producers that prevented producers from raising gas prices at the well. Douglas said the one hundred contracts he had

analyzed provided, at best, illusory protection. Most were studded
with provisions for periodic price increases through escalator
clauses, "most favored nation" provisions, and renegotiation terms
if the buyer wanted renewed or additional gas supplies.[52] Because
of contractual loopholes, Douglas claimed that the passage of the
Kerr bill would mean a minimum price increase to the consumer
states of $1,155,000,000 and a maximum of $4,620,000,000 over
the next thirty years based on 1947 sales.[53]

Only a few Democrats outside the southwestern bloc had
defended the Kerr bill. Douglas feared that, as in the earlier House
debate, many intended to vote for it on Kerr's personal assurance
that the President favored the legislation. Now there were cloakroom rumors that Truman was ready to abandon the Kerr bill,[54]
and Douglas decided to help them along. Despite his unfaltering
support of the Fair Deal, Paul Douglas had no entrée to the White
House. President Truman dismissed him as a "holier-than-thou-
reformer" and never forgave his impertinence in blocking presidential nominations for the federal bench in Illinois on the grounds
that the candidates were not qualified.[55] Douglas probably knew it
would be unwise to ask Truman directly about his support for
fear the President might stubbornly urge the bill to repay Douglas
for what Truman considered "irregular political behavior."[56]
Instead, his technique was to cast doubt on the President's support
of the Kerr bill. He quoted columnist George H. Hall, of the *St.
Louis Post-Dispatch*. "The nearest thing to an official word on
Truman's attitude is a letter dated August 1, 1949, sent by Elmer
B. Staats then acting Director of the Bureau of the Budget to
Senator Edwin C. Johnson, Democrat of Colorado, in which Staats
said the Bureau (and by implication the President) was opposed
to the measure [S. 1498] reported out by the Committee of which
Johnson is chairman."[57] The letter closed with the statement that
the President might approve an FPC recommendation to exempt
small producers but retain jurisdiction over large producers.[58]

The Kerr forces never openly responded to Douglas' insinua-
tion that Truman no longer supported the bill. They did not want
to force the President to make any public statement. It was unlikely that Kerr, Lyndon Johnson, and Sam Rayburn, all of whom

were close to Truman, would have pushed the legislation if they had had any indication that he would oppose it. Unlike Douglas, they were more sensitive to practical possibilities than to principles. But Douglas' innuendo may have encouraged a few Democrats to vote against the bill who otherwise would have favored it, fearing the President's tongue as much as his disfavor.

By the time Kerr began his formal speech, the issues were hopelessly entangled in factual misconceptions, sectional animosities, and fears of retaliatory measures. Kerr repeated the now familiar argument that the bill would not change the existing law. It would not free the independents from FPC control because they were not subject to any regulation of wellhead sales. Its purpose was to reaffirm the original intent of Congress in the 1938 Natural Gas Act and to alleviate the uncertainties that the FPC's altered interpretation of their own power to regulate had caused within the natural gas industry. He also tried to allay fears of astronomical consumer price jumps with a patient explanation about the protective features of long-term contracts. Should prices rise, he reassured the consumer that under the Kerr bill, the FPC retained full authority to reexamine and veto any contract for the purchase of gas in interstate commerce. He explained recent price increases as the result of producers withholding gas because of the uncertainty about regulation. Passage of the Kerr bill would resolve the question, producers would be eager to sell gas, and that increased volume of gas would be the principal deterrent to rising prices.

As he talked, Senator Kerr "ambled up and down the Senate chamber, haggling with opponents face to face, gesturing under their noses, pleading in whispers with the nearest senator when someone else had the floor."[59] Several times Majority Leader Scott Lucas had to urge Kerr to return to his seat because "it is . . . difficult for me to hear when the two Senators are so close together."[60] But for the most part, Kerr's manner was remarkably restrained.

His criticism was reserved for the press, whom he thought had not reported the debate correctly or without bias. He congratulated Lowell Mellett for abandoning his "beloved textbooks on socialism" but warned that too much Bible-reading might cause "that left wing to wither on his shoulder."[61] He interrupted the flow of his main speech for a crack at Drew Pearson. "No wonder American Broadcasting Company put Airwick on the air for fifteen minutes after he gets through. Boy, oh boy, do they need it."[62]

Predictably, not one senator murmured at this personal attack on two members of the press. Every national politician knew the sharp prick of a Washington columnist's pen, so Pearson and Mellett were fair game. Tradition in the Upper House reserved courteous treatment in debate only for fellow senators.

When Kerr concluded, Senator Fulbright praised the Oklahoman. "That is the most comprehensive statement of the issues made by anybody on the subject."[63] Even the rather cynical professional Senate staff recognized the significance of what they witnessed. Emery Frazier, chief clerk of the Senate, remarked to an assistant that he "had never seen a Senator gain such stature among his colleagues by a single speech."[64] And even Drew Pearson tipped his hat to Kerr as the Senate's "smoothest salesman."[65]

The speech was indeed a *tour de force* just as Douglas' had been. Each had presented a lucid and compelling analysis of differing interpretations of a complex legal and technical subject. The debate between Kerr and Douglas was a classic of Senate colloquy at its finest—two able and honorable men disagreeing about an issue where intellectual objectivity warred against emotional involvement. But both men maintained absolute fidelity to the facts they saw.

The speeches over, Douglas moved to send S. 1498 back to committee for further consideration, where he hoped it would die. The motion failed on a roll-call vote, 37–45.[66] The recommittal motion was the crucial test of Kerr's majority and ensured final passage. The Senate easily defeated three amendments to limit FPC jurisdiction before accepting a fourth. In an attempt to make the bill more palatable to the House of Representatives, and as protection against a possible White House veto if clamor about possible price increases grew, Kerr and White House attorney Charles Murphy had devised a watchdog provision.[67]

The amendment authorized the Federal Power Commission to oversee the gas industry's ability to maintain competition and reasonable prices. If the FPC found price-fixing or any restraint of trade, they would recommend remedial action to Congress and the President.[68] Murphy and Kerr believed that such an amendment would demonstrate the gas industry's good faith to support their claim that competition, not regulation, would keep prices reasonable. Although FPC attorneys drafted the proposal,[69] it was little more than window dressing since the gas industry was likely to oppose any remedial legislation. Douglas was correct in calling the added clause "pure surplusage."[70]

Despite its apparent shortcomings, the amendment passed on a voice vote 44–38. The final vote on the amended bill was identical; four votes more than Kerr predicted. Twenty-eight Democrats and sixteen Republicans voted for the bill. All the southwestern senators, except Dennis Chavez (D., N.M.), supported it. New Mexico was not a major gas producer in 1950, and Chavez feared the economic consequences of a price rise for consumers.[71] For Chavez politics was "strictly a cash-and-carry proposition," and although he was often touchy and extremely sentimental, the New Mexican was "an old Spanish American pol," hard-boiled and franker than most.[72] After large gas reserves were discovered in the Land of Enchantment in the early 1950's, Chavez consistently voted to exempt producers from federal regulation.

Harry F. Byrd was typical of Kerr's southern supporters, with Alabama's liberal Senator Lister Hill (D.) and Tennessee's Estes Kefauver voting no. Allen Frear (D., Del.), the only easterner to support the bill, and Styles Bridges, the solitary New England Republican, voted more out of loyalty to Kerr than out of any deep concern with the issues. Western and midwestern Republicans who voted for the bill generally followed Taft's position opposing government price-fixing.

The bulk of the opposition was an unstable alliance of New Deal-Fair Deal Democrats from the major gas-consuming states, New England Republicans, and a few scattered midwestern Republicans such as Kem and Donnell of Missouri. The West Virginia coal state Democrats Harley Kilgore and Matthew Neeley also voted for federal control of the gas industry.

Despite the bipartisan appearance of the vote, an editorial in the *Washington Post* concluded that "senatorial votes are influenced by sectional considerations and often result in approval of legislation not in the national interest."[73] The most significant aspect was the heavy Republican vote; the GOP was planning to accuse the Democrats of "coddling the special interests" in the fall elections.

The opponents of the Kerr bill were never certain of victory in the Senate. But Paul Douglas' leadership and the unexpected help of the Missouri/New England Republican coalition had narrowed Kerr's margin of victory to six votes. Regardless of strategy, they could not have expected more. Kerr simply had a mathematical edge with the combination of senators from gas-producing states, senators of both parties from northern states who were not immune to pressure from major oil companies, and a substantial group of senators "bound to Kerr for his support of their pet measures" and his financial assistance in their campaigns.[74] The anti-Kerr people also anticipated strong leadership from Speaker Sam Rayburn to ease the bill through the House. During the 1949 debate on H.R. 1758, Rayburn had relinquished the Speaker's Chair to plead for the bill.[75]

Concluding that they probably could not defeat the Kerr bill in Congress, the opponents decided to create such a furor in the country that President Truman would be forced to veto it. By March, a well-organized campaign in the press designed to alarm the public with predictions about gas price rises and to discredit Senator Kerr was apparent. Peter Edson, syndicated columnist for the Newspaper Enterprise Association, a press service catering to hundreds of small-town newspapers, wrote articles representative of the attack. In a series on the Kerr bill, Edson quoted Charles H. Rhyne, the Washington representative of the National Institute of Municipal Law Officers, who declared that the Kerr bill would "triple the price of natural gas in most parts of the United States. . . ." Rhyne estimated that the "total increase in dollars paid by the consumers will amount to more than $200,000,000 a year on a nationwide basis."[76] He also charged that the anticipated price increase would net Kerr personally "at least $50,000,000 in profits before taxes."[77] Malvina Stephenson, the *Tulsa Tribune*'s Washington correspondent who later became Kerr's press assistant, asked Rhyne for his source; but he refused saying only that he was presenting "data from unidentified experts."[78] In another column, Edson suggested that the Kerr bill was designed to punish Leland Olds, "a long-time battler for greater conservation of natural gas resources and greater regulation for lower prices."[79]

As the stories proliferated, the Kerr forces charged that Olds, not they, was conducting a vendetta. Lyndon Johnson said Olds was striking back at the Senate for failure to confirm him in 1949 "with a lot of phony figures . . . on which the price increase claims were made."[80] Kerr blamed Olds' followers in the Senate for "the propaganda of misinformation about the gas bill."[81]

There were also the usual rumors about "deals." One report said that Truman had agreed to the Kerr bill "in trade for enactment of the Columbia River Valley Authority."[82] Neither Kerr nor the President responded to the story. But Kerr's legislative assistant Don McBride wrote to Dan B. Noble, secretary manager of the Pacific Northwest Development Association, dismissing the rumor as inconsistent with Kerr's public record of opposing the concept of the valley authority to develop water resources.[83] The story attributed more influence on water matters than Kerr would have claimed at the time. He had transferred to the Public Works Committee from the Interior Committee only a few months earlier and, as the lowest-ranking Democrat and a freshman, had little leverage. It also seemed unlikely that Eugene Millikin, an unshakable foe of the Columbia Valley Authority, would have defended the Kerr bill so passionately if there had been such a swap.[84]

As Senate debate intensified so did the opponents' campaign. The Americans for Democratic Action (ADA) and the CIO joined the fight. Both organizations urged Majority Leader Scott Lucas to prevent Congress from giving the oil and gas industry "free license to rob the American consumer."[85] Senator Douglas asked influential publishers and editors to oppose the Kerr bill. He also sent them factual materials for editorial statements.[86] Robert Wallace, Douglas' legislative assistant, wrote an article for the *New Republic* that was little more than a thinly disguised polemic based on his boss' upcoming Senate speech. The article, "New Gouge for Consumers," was reprinted and widely circulated.[87]

Municipal officials, in Washington to attend the attorney general's conference on crime during the debate, joined the growing opposition. They issued a statement which claimed that the bill would exempt 80 per cent of the country's natural gas producers, thereby threatening a price increase of "200 million to 500 million [dollars] per year."[88] Hardly anyone noticed that Senator Douglas' thirty-year prediction had been telescoped to one year as the dire projections mounted. Many of the mayors used their stay in Washington to lobby personally with their congressmen, hoping to thwart the bill there if not in the Senate.[89]

The stories about Kerr's anticipated profits from the predicted price increase multiplied rapidly.[90] He responded explaining that he had introduced S. 1498 in response to a petition from the Oklahoma legislature.[91] Kerr also denied that he or his company would profit directly from the bill. "Every cubic foot of gas my company owns is and for many years has been contracted for for periods of twenty to fifty years at fixed prices. Under the contract, the price paid Kerr-McGee is already determined and would be unaffected by either an increase or a decrease in the price of natural gas."[92] Peter Edson, the NEA columnist, was the only one to print Kerr's response; the others were preoccupied with new evidence of conflict of interest.

Drew Pearson, always alert to the potential of political gossip, mined the rumors about "Bible-quoting Bob" to fill his daily columns. In addition to revenues from the gas bill, Pearson estimated that Kerr might "profit from an Oklahoma highway to be financed by the RFC by selling it 'blacktop' from the Kerr-McGee Company."[93] Kerr-McGee owned a refinery at Wynnewood, Oklahoma, that made blacktop from petroleum. L. G. May, an official at the Wynnewood refinery, confirmed that the company planned to bid on the highway contract as they did on all such contracts. Pearson also alleged that Kerr had inside control over granting the contract because his brother, Aubrey Kerr, was Truman's appointee as counsel for the RFC in Oklahoma.

Not content with stories of the profits from the gas bill and road construction, Pearson also reported that Kerr was pressuring the President to appoint to the federal bench W. R. "Bob" Wallace, an Oklahoma City attorney for Magnolia Oil Company, a subsidiary of Socony-Vacuum. The implication that an attorney was unfit to be a judge because he had been counsel to an oil company effectively barred every major corporate attorney in the Southwest from a career in the federal judiciary.

The columnists' skepticism about Kerr's motives in pushing the gas bill so vigorously was understandable and justifiable. Robert Kerr was a wealthy oilman, and his firm owned gas reserves. But their failure to acknowledge Kerr's response about personal profits and their apparent deliberate distortion of certain issues raised questions about their own motives. Only one major news commentator, Kenneth Banghart of WNBC, and *Time* magazine were faithful to the facts. Banghart tried to dispel the misconception that the Kerr bill would free the independents from FPC regulation and leave the gas consumer "to be victimized by the promoters and speculators" as some commentators charged.[94] He was correct in his statement that "there's been no such regulation of the so-called independent gas companies, but the FPC has intended—has indicated at times its plan to extend regulation to cover them."[95]

Time gave careful attention to the Supreme Court's role in the controversy. The bill's opponents created the impression that in the Interstate decision the Court had ruled that "under the 1938 law the FPC could . . . control the prices charged by producers before gas enters the pipeline. . . ."[96] The newsmagazine accurately reported that after the 1947 decision, "some members of the FPC thought that the FPC had the right to say what the natural gas producers could charge interstate pipeline operators for gas."[97]

There was little analytical reporting on the subject; the issue was so complex and so emotionally charged that both sides resorted to clichés for fear of complicating matters further. When several radio commentators joined Mellett's and Pearson's war on the "vicious, noxious Kerr bill,"[98] the Senator responded in kind. "The trouble with those noble knights of tongue and pen is that they have never furnished the American housewife a cubic foot of cooking gas. Ah, they have generated a lot of heat, but not for homes! They have produced an abundance of gas, but the kind . . . that will not burn."[99]

Although most of the Oklahoma press shared the *Tulsa World*'s xenophobia about the eastern press' misrepresentation of the purpose and probable result of the Kerr bill, there was some reservation about their Senator's motives. The Carmen (Okla.) *Headlight* summed up the local cynics' views. "For twenty years the federal government has been trying to acquire new power and Senator Kerr has gone along with all these demands for power . . . until now. Senator Kerr is in the oil and gas business."[100]

Opposition to the bill continued to build inside and beyond Congress. Kerr consulted with Speaker Rayburn and Oren Harris (D., Ark.), the House cosponsor, and decided to press for swift House action. Two days after the Senate vote, Harris tried to call up the bill on a unanimous consent procedure, but there were loud objections. Speaker Rayburn then requested a special session of the House Rules Committee to give the bill priority status and a special rule to bring it up for debate immediately. The ailing eighty-four-year-old chairman of House Rules, Adolph Sabath (D., Ill.) was absent, so Eugene E. Cox (D., Ga.), the acting chairman, quickly called the meeting. Ray Madden (D., Ind.) objected to this exceptional procedure and reminded the Republican-Dixiecrat bloc that dominated the committee that they had objected to "intemperate haste" on the FEPC bill under similar circumstances. He demanded that in fairness they should wait until the chairman returned and scheduled a regular meeting.[101] Acting Chairman Cox, "the most potent of the Southerners next to Speaker Rayburn,"[102] listened politely, then received testimony from Speaker Rayburn, and gaveled the bill through.[103]

Although the House had passed the Harris bill, H.R. 1758, the previous year with a fifty-two vote margin, Speaker Rayburn was uncertain of retaining that majority. He buttonholed every member within reach to vote for the bill as a personal favor to him.[104] Rayburn also apparently prodded Indiana Republican Charles Halleck to line up a few reluctant GOP votes if they were needed. Halleck had ties to the oil industry through the DuPont interests and was rumored to have received substantial campaign contributions from southwestern oil and gas concerns.[105] He made an impassioned floor speech and convinced three timid Republicans who had planned to vote against the bill to vote for it if they were needed.

Just before the roll call, Rayburn decided to reinforce his private lobbying. As in the 1949 debate, he relinquished the chair to make one of his rare speeches. He discounted critics who implied the bill was harmful to the public interest. "In my opinion—and I state this to you deliberately; I would not deceive you, you know that,—this bill will not raise the price of natural gas to any consumer in the United States one red penny."[106]

One critic labeled Rayburn's speech as an "assertion as bald as his own head,"[107] but the Speaker's liberal record did not justify such flippant judgments. His district in Texas was not petroleum country; he had never opposed the oil interests or helped them. Rayburn believed the bill acceptable to the President and was doing his job as Speaker to get it passed.[108] While friendship with Kerr may have sharpened the Speaker's enthusiasm for the task, it did not necessarily impugn his motives.

The Kerr bill failed on the first vote count, 178–172, but supporters quickly demanded a division. Halleck's three Republicans—Paul Shafer (Mich.), Earl Wilson (Ind.) and Henry Latham (N.Y.)—joined Missouri Democrat Morgan Moulder in switching their votes; and the bill passed, 176–174.[109] As the Representatives called out their changed votes someone from the Democratic side shouted, "How much did you get?"[110]

Senator Kerr was exuberant and expansive in victory. In a letter to his good friend Luther Bohanon, he wrote: "I think my friend Senator Johnson, of Texas, expressed it very well. You will recall that he was nominated by a majority of 82 votes. He became known as 'Landslide Johnson.' After the . . . House vote last Friday night of 176 yeas and 174 nays, he turned to me and said: 'Landslide Johnson' rides again."[111]

The Oklahoman immediately drafted a press release assuring the public that the independent gas producers would launch an intensive exploration program to find new gas reserves. He predicted that the increased volume of gas would flow to northern and eastern cities at lower rates than ever before.[112]

Although the bill had passed both Houses and Kerr was confident of the President's signature, he still rankled at the "campaign of misrepresentation and vilification" against the bill and himself personally.[113] Kerr intended for the press release to calm public fears about the gas bill, but it had the opposite effect. The opposition, their nerves raw and tempers strained from the long congressional debate, reacted to Kerr's statement as if doused with acid. Unable to defeat the bill in Congress, they concentrated a massive publicity effort on the White House.

Most liberals suspected that Truman had actually approved the Kerr bill in draft and feared he would sign it if they did not mount a strong campaign.[114] William Boyle, Jr., chairman of the Democratic National Committee, opposed the bill as a potentially "hot political issue."[115] The severity and effectiveness of the Republican assault on S. 1498 in the Senate and the preponderance of Republican votes against the legislation meant that if Truman signed it, the GOP would charge him with coddling his own favorite campaign target, "the special interests."

Truman was planning a swing through the country in May to launch Democratic candidates for the upcoming primaries. And Boyle must have cringed as he thought of the President's speech dedicating the Grand Coulee dam. If Truman signed the Kerr bill, he would look very foolish talking about his policy of regulation of public utilities in the public interest.[116] Working closely with Paul Douglas and the ADA, Boyle galvanized Fair Dealers to barrage the President with pleas for a veto.[117]

Truman was in Key West, Florida, when he finally received the Kerr bill.[118] With it was a letter from Sam Rayburn assuring the President that the bill was "in the form and language as prepared by Charley Murphy after he and Clark Clifford had talked to the group of us and then talked to you. I wanted you to know Mr. President that the bill enacted by both Houses is in the exact form in which you told us it would be acceptable to you."[119] Truman's reply hinted that he had reservations and was having the bill analyzed, but he concluded brightly that "things will work out in a satisfactory manner for all concerned."[120]

By the time he received the Kerr bill on April 5, the President had already felt the first wave of opposition. The ADA was in national convention just as the gas bill cleared Congress. They immediately passed a unanimous resolution calling for a veto and instructed their national director, Charles La Follette, to write the President condemning the measure as a blatant attempt to bilk the consumer. La Follette's letter implied that Kerr and his allies had practiced duplicity in gaining the President's backing. He closed with the warning that a presidential signature would mean disaster in the fall congressional elections.[121]

Tension continued to build as the election neared. Having failed to get action on the FEPC in the Eighty-first Congress, the liberals needed more seats on Capitol Hill to realize any of their goals. By the spring of 1950, they had abandoned any illusions about a major civil rights victory and had begun to work "not for a winning vote, but for a showing respectable enough to keep the Negro in the Fair Deal Coalition."[122] All their hopes for progress on civil rights in the Eighty-second Congress lay in electing as many like-minded Democrats as possible. If the Republicans could mock Truman with his own slogans about "catering to the interests," the liberals felt all chances for progressive legislation were dead.

Members of the President's own party, as well as Republicans, were already talking about his surrendering to the interests. Senator Gillette predicted that history would scorn Truman's "show of weakness" if he signed the gas bill.[123] House Democrats who opposed the bill also began to press Truman not to desert them as fall elections approached. The Minnesota Democratic congressional delegation and Orville Freeman, Democratic state party chairman, branded the bill a "clear violation of the principles of the Fair Deal."[124] The mayors of the nation's eighteen largest cities sent a petition demanding that the President veto the bill or be prepared to suffer the political consequences of alienating the urban vote on which the Democratic party depended.[125] Industrial labor groups allied with the National Farmers Union to fight the bill, and a CIO official charged that the Kerr bill would offset all the savings guaranteed to the consumer from the repeal of the federal tax on oleo.[126] Frank Edwards, radio commentator for the AFL, gave Paul Douglas air time every night to urge the public to write the President asking him to withhold his signature from the "ripper" gas bill.[127] So many letters and telegrams poured into 1600 Pennsylvania Avenue that the staff ordered a special teletype machine that printed in triplicate flown to Key West to keep the President informed.[128]

Senator Kerr never doubted that the President would sign the bill. And during the noisy campaign for a veto he stayed quietly in the background.[129] When the New York *Daily Compass* asked the Senator for eight hundred words on why the President should not veto the bill, the Oklahoman replied that he could not comply with the request in time to meet the paper's deadline.[130] Kerr obviously thought it unwise to make any statement that might embarrass or antagonize the President.

Lyndon Johnson was not so restrained. Still euphoric over his role in the defeat of Leland Olds and the passage of the Kerr bill, he boasted to friends that Truman would sign the bill. "Otherwise, he will have some very sore Democratic Senators on his neck and Harry Truman is just too smart to let that happen."[131]

Truman was being squeezed between his promise to cronies in Congress and his public commitment to the regulatory principle. And the Republicans were planning to make him eat his own words. The progressive Democrats were not helping fall election prospects by turning their opposition to the Kerr bill into a *cause célèbre*. Each side accused the other of misrepresenting the Kerr bill to the President.[132] The issue was so confused that the President was unable even to obtain consistent figures on the number of homes using natural gas transported through interstate pipelines.[133]

In addition to the Boyle-Douglas-ADA-inspired campaign, there was strong and effective opposition within the administration. Oscar Chapman, secretary of the interior, co-ordinated executive branch efforts to force a veto. In a memo to the President, he said that the Kerr bill "would benefit and enrich the relatively few . . . to the decided detriment of the consuming public." The President should not feel bound to his promise to sign the Kerr bill, Chapman argued, because the oil and gas people had

misrepresented the effects of the bill.[134] He also persuaded Charles
Sawyer, secretary of commerce, to counsel a veto because many
industries might suffer from a gas price increase. Finally, Chapman
convinced Monrad Wallgren, Truman's appointee to replace Leland Olds, to support a veto. This meant that a majority of the FPC
opposed the bill.[135]

In response to the Bureau of the Budget's customary practice
of surveying the departments concerned with pending legislation,
the Justice and Defense departments were the only two who did
not recommend a veto.[136] The Defense Department favored the bill
because it would remove uncertainties in the gas industry and increase the development of reserves vital to national security.[137]
The most interesting response came from Justice. While not urging
the President to sign the bill, they did not ask for a veto. The alleged
problem of monopoly control and the threat of price-fixing, which
worried Secretary Chapman and others, did not alarm the lawyers.
They indicated, as had the bill's supporters, that the Sherman Anti-
trust Act, the Robertson-Patman Fair Trade Act, and the Clayton
Act provided ample protection for the public interest.[138]

The veto issue appeared clear-cut to everyone but Truman,
and he alone had to make the decision. Charles Murphy, who had
been involved in drafting and securing the President's consent to
the original Kerr bill, was sympathetic. In a lengthy memo he summarized the possible alternatives. While Murphy was convinced
that the Kerr bill had "no merits whatever," he concluded that the
bad effects "have been greatly exaggerated by those who oppose
it." He thought it doubtful that the price of natural gas would rise
significantly within the next few years, so the economic consequences of the legislation were negligible.

The political consequences, however, would be a different
matter. Signing the bill "would take some of the shine off the New
Deal and confuse . . . our efforts to draw a clear distinction between measures that are in the public interest and those which are
for the special interests." The Republicans would exploit the issue,
but Murphy downgraded any significant effect on the fall elections
since the Republican leadership had supported the legislation. But
a veto "would seriously impair relations between the President and

the Speaker" and could jeopardize "the conduct of public business" —the Fair Deal legislative program.[139]

Murphy's only recommendation was that Truman send a letter to Kerr asking if he would support repeal of the gas bill in the event that gas prices rose unreasonably.[140] If Kerr agreed, the President would be justified in signing the bill with "a better chance of getting remedial legislation when and if . . . necessary." If he refused, the President "would be in a much better position to veto it." Murphy thought this complicated tactical maneuver would call Kerr's bluff about the bill's effect on prices, if it were bluff.

The suggestion was inappropriate. If Kerr refused to agree to the President's conditions, Truman would have to make the correspondence public to discredit the Oklahoman and his supporters. If Kerr agreed, the bargaining might become known, and Truman would be portrayed as having to placate a mere freshman senator. Either way it was not Truman's style. Politicians like Truman, Kerr, and Rayburn operated through verbal agreements and unspoken understandings. They disagreed in the same manner, but rarely committed really important bargaining to paper. Interested primarily in results, they were unconcerned if the story were garbled.

Ten days after receiving the gas bill, President Truman vetoed it with a firmly worded message. He justified the veto as necessary to prevent "unreasonable and excessive prices, which would give large windfall profits to gas producers at the expense of consumers." He felt to "withdraw from this field of regulation . . . would not be in the public interest."[141]

Senator Kerr, along with Rayburn and Johnson, believed to the last that Truman would sign the bill. On two occasions the President had informed the "big four"—Vice-President Alben Barkley, Speaker Rayburn, Senate Majority Leader Lucas and House Majority Leader McCormack—"that he approved the bill and would accept it if passed by Congress."[142] Kerr's immediate reaction was less anger than bewilderment. He was stunned. "The President made a mistake."[143] As if trying to untangle the President's reasoning, Kerr added, "The Kerr bill was identical in principle with the Priest bill. If the Priest bill was in the public interest in 1947 and 1948, the Kerr Bill would be in the public interest in 1950."[144]

Rayburn, who probably had more reason than Kerr to feel betrayed, refused to quibble with the President publicly. He told a *New York Times* reporter he was not "sore" at Truman. "The President and I are as friendly as ever. I exercise my judgment on legislation, and so does the President when a bill comes to his desk. He has his part and so do I."[145]

The liberals were jubilant, although most suspected that Truman would have signed the bill if they had not mounted a strong campaign against it.[146] "We suggest that Mr. Truman's instincts would have been on the side of a veto in any case; we think the liberal thunder gave him the courage of his convictions."[147] Douglas blessed the President as "the true defender of the common people," while the commentator Elmer Davis observed, "One man who can feel vindicated is Leland Olds."[148]

Truman's veto reflected his conviction about two political facts: that the future of the Democratic party lay in the nation's cities and that the southern wing had no place else to go. The southerners might form unofficial coalitions with Republicans in Congress to stall the Fair Deal. They might try to pick off administration favorites in primaries, such as Claude Pepper in Florida. They might struggle for control of state party machinery to purge progressives like Hill and Sparkman in Alabama. But their activities were not crucial. The Democratic party could stay in office nationally if it retained the urban vote, and Truman believed that vetoing the gas bill would help ensure that support.

The President was also more sensitive to the Senate Republicans' charges that the bill threatened the public interest than he was to the combined pressures from Douglas, union leaders, and the ADA. As a candidate in 1948, he had coined the phrase in his scathing attack on the Republican Eightieth Congress. He could not risk his campaign slogan becoming his political epitaph. He gambled that allies in Congress and supporters in the Southwest might rage and grumble for a time and that contributions might dry up for a while, but eventually the feeling of betrayal would fade. No matter how much the national party might need the financial patronage of the oil and gas industry at election time, in the final analysis Truman knew that politics depended more on votes than money. The Chicago *Daily News* summarized the veto as a political necessity. "It may alienate powerful leaders of his party, but they have nowhere else to go. The voters, who had been sold on the belief the bill would have meant higher gas rates, *would* have somewhere else to go, and the Republicans clearly meant to point the way."[149]

Kerr accepted the veto believing that the President had been "misled and misinformed."[150] But he privately acknowledged the enormous political pressures on Truman. From his experience as a governor, he was aware that a president's constituency was different from a senator's. Kerr rejected consideration of an attempt to override the veto because he felt it would be destructive to the Democratic party in Congress and disloyal to the man in the White House.[151] He also knew that Douglas and the liberals had won not only because of the veto, but also because his own majority was so slender.

The gas bill veto was Senator Kerr's first major reversal in public life, but he learned from it. He recognized that he was too personally involved to approach the issue objectively. His familiarity with the technical aspects of the gas industry actually had distorted his judgment about what issues were important. He had been so obsessed with the obscure questions of congressional intent and the precedents on regulation, that he failed to grasp the significance of his opponents' dismissal of these subjects as relatively unimportant. They had focused their attacks on the changed conditions in the industry, which they believed made federal regulation of all gas sales necessary. By the time Kerr realized the futility of his approach, the liberals had created a nationwide furor with their predictions about rising gas prices. While their quotations about prices had alternated between the irresponsible and the ridiculous, Kerr had argued that increased competition and new gas supplies would be the best check on prices. But his assurances were like plowing the sea.

The opposition had nourished fears about high costs and threats of no gas with a well-organized and apparently well-financed campaign to educate the public about the dangers of the Kerr bill. Their bombardment of the President with letters, telegrams, editorials, radio programs, and personal pleas through congressmen, senators, and high party officials was a model for any lobby group. Consumer groups, of course, do not engage in lobbying activities; they merely represent the public interest. Oil and gas companies lobby.

Senator Kerr never again assumed leadership of the fight to exempt independent producers and gatherers. Although Congress passed a similar bill in 1956, which Eisenhower vetoed,[152] and considered identical bills in every session until his death, Kerr recognized that anything he said would always be interpreted as a "conflict of interest." As a freshman senator from an oil and gas state, Kerr was obligated to lead the 1950 debate. He was also anxious to display his expertise and to impress colleagues with his access to the congressional leadership and the President. But the veto experience tempered his enthusiasm for the public struggle. After 1950 he found his colleagues were more amenable to persuasion in the privacy of Senate corridors and conference rooms than in the chamber.

The struggle over the natural gas bill matured Kerr as a legislator; he altered his tactics, not his goals. Truman's veto was not defeat, only delay. Three days after the veto Kerr wrote to his friend Earl Foster, the executive secretary of the Interstate Oil Compact Commission, "The firing has ceased; the peace has not been signed."[153]

The natural gas controversy typified one of the major social problems facing a democratic industrial society: Who was competent to make the difficult decisions about technical problems that determined future national development? Congress lacked the expertise to fathom the complexities or the unity to act. The unbiased, independent regulatory agency was an illusion. Kerr had firsthand technical knowledge and could translate the problem into understandable, if admittedly simple, concepts. Yet association with the gas industry made him liable to charges of conflict of interest. The cries from liberals about price increases drowned any hearing for the concept that expensive gas could be in the public interest as a conservation measure. They continued in the naïve nineteenth-century American belief that cheap and abundant goods were the American birthright.

Both sides reached an impasse in April 1950. After appearing to win in the congressional arena only to have Truman veto the law, Senator Kerr turned to the FPC, where he hoped to secure, through the appointment of agreeable men, decisions he had been unable to write into the statutes.

CHAPTER V
Seeking the Presidency

Senator Kerr never brooded over losses. The oil business had taught him that it was often necessary to drill a large number of wells before bringing in a gusher. The struggle to amend the Natural Gas Act was a dry hole, and the Oklahoman began to explore different terrain. He moved quietly and rapidly to consolidate his influence within the Senate. The working relationship he had established with Richard Russell during the 1949 cloture controversy deepened into a friendship which survived until Kerr's death in 1963. Russell, "by the force of his intellect, his hard work and his driving personality," was the unquestioned leader of the Senate Democratic power structure in the 1950's.[1] Although opposites in appearance and outward style, both the Georgian with his Roman bearing and unfeigned courtliness and the blustering Oklahoma millionaire had an intuitive approach to Senate politics. Russell said of Kerr, "He knew what I was thinking, without discussing it; and I knew the conclusions and the processes which led him to his positions. . . . We understood each other completely."[2] Unlike Lyndon Johnson, who would predicate his rise in the Senate on formal position, Kerr and Russell "operated outside or around the designated Senate Democratic leadership, wheeling and dealing with confidence."[3]

When the Senate Democratic majority caucused on January 2, 1951, to choose new leaders for the Eighty-second Congress, Kerr's influence was apparent. The 1950 congressional elections had taken a heavy toll on Senate Democrats. Both Scott Lucas, the majority leader, and Francis Myers, the democratic whip, had been defeated.[4] A sharp decline in Truman's popularity following his 1948 victory and the concern over America's intervention in Korea accounted for some of the casualties; many were simply caught in the traditional increase of the opposition party at mid-term elections.

The Lucas-Myers team had been Richard Russell's personal choice in 1949. Liberal Democrats who saw Truman's election as a mandate to enact the Fair Deal were so stunned that they were unable to organize any opposition. By May 1949 it was clear that Lucas was little more than "a kind of Burning Tree Club liberal" who would do nothing to move the Fair Deal legislative program against the Russell-Taft coalition.[5]

Although the Fair Deal was defunct by 1951, Lucas' successor would have to handle important legislation, particularly the funding of the Marshall Plan. As the conduct of the war took precedence over domestic concerns, Truman became more and more dependent on the Rayburn-Russell-Kerr forces in Congress. He needed every shred of support to salvage the coalition which had supported his foreign initiatives and quickly jettisoned Fair Deal policies that threatened the unity of congressional Democrats behind the war. Truman's desire to work with the powerful southern Democrats and their Republican allies prompted the rather clumsy overtures to Russell to assume the majority leadership in the Senate. Clinton Anderson persuaded Truman that since the civil rights portion of the Fair Deal legislative program was dead, Russell would be the ideal leader to guide the important appropriations through the Senate. Making Russell the majority leader would be a way to unite the northern and southern wings of the Democratic party.[6] Anderson's plan was audacious, and it might have succeeded if Truman had not been so preoccupied with events in Korea. Instead of asking Russell personally and publicly as Anderson hoped, the President sent Clark Clifford to Winder, Georgia. The meeting was private, and Russell declined.[7]

There was a brief flurry of activity as liberal Democrats tried to find a candidate acceptable to the southern leadership. Some thought Alabama's John Sparkman might be palatable to Russell because of his dependable opposition to civil rights. Although a southerner, Sparkman was "well outside the Senate's inner circle."[8] Unable to recruit a suitable southerner, some liberals decided to test their strength in a direct confrontation. Brien McMahon (D., Conn.) managed an abortive attempt to elect Joseph O'Mahoney (D., Wyo.), a staunch Fair Dealer.[9] But Russell prevailed as he had in 1949. Ernest William McFarland of Arizona became the new majority leader, and Lyndon Johnson was whip.

Senator Kerr was influential in selecting the new leadership team,[10] although little is known of the actual details. McFarland and Kerr had become boyhood friends when they attended East Central State Teachers College at Ada, Oklahoma, together. Although McFarland moved to Phoenix, Arizona, after World War I, they met again when Kerr was governor of Oklahoma and Mc-Farland a United States Senator, elected in 1940. McFarland faced a difficult reelection challenge in 1952 from conservative Phoenix city councilman and merchant, Republican Barry M. Goldwater. The Arizonan's friends advised him not to take the majority leader's job for fear his close identification with the Truman Administration would mean defeat for him as it had for Scott Lucas.[11] Kerr probably argued the positive merits of the job. As majority leader, McFarland would acquire national stature; Arizonans would be proud of the recognition accorded him; and the increased press coverage would heighten, not hinder, his reelection bid. Kerr was sincere in this appraisal. His loyalty to his old friends and his desire to help their careers prosper was well known. Just as he was always bringing friends into lucrative business deals and giving to their favorite charities, he believed that the leadership position would help, not harm, McFarland's career. And there would be benefits for Robert Kerr. McFarland would do a competent job, but he would be an accessible, perhaps manageable leader. Kerr and Russell probably both sensed that McFarland "was even less determined to shape a unified party position and even less capable of it" than Scott Lucas had been.[12] The Senate majority leadership was a mediocre job in the early 1950's; it seemed suitably tailored to McFarland's talents.

Johnson's selection as whip was more complex. Shortly after the November election, stories appeared in Oklahoma newspapers that Kerr was in line for the job.[13] Energetic, ambitious, intelligent, and well connected, he seemed a logical choice. But Kerr's aides quickly denied the story. They also said they had heard no mention of his name for majority leader.[14] Just as he had shied away from accepting the Democratic party chairmanship in 1946, Kerr refused all official Senate party leadership positions throughout his career. He had no interest in managerial duties. "He felt he could do more for his constituents by not being a part of the actual leadership but having influence and a close relationship with that leadership."[15]

Among friends, Kerr approached Anderson first about the whip's job. The New Mexican refused, pleading ill health as he always did when he wished to avoid responsibility. Kerr then turned to Johnson, who readily agreed. The task of persuading Russell that this geographically unbalanced team was acceptable was more difficult. Russell was suspicious of Johnson's New Deal background and still miffed at the Texan's secession from the Southern Caucus. But Kerr argued persuasively for Johnson. Kerr knew Russell's prejudices, and he probably appealed to the Georgian's grudging admiration for Johnson's energy, devotion to detail, reverence for the Senate, and his dependability as the hardest working member of Russell's Armed Services Committee.[16] Kerr may have intimated that a southwestern leadership team might attract oil and gas contributions to revitalize the party's finances for the 1952 election. Since Russell was already thinking of making a race for the nomination, he was sensitive to the needs for funds. Whatever the arguments, under Kerr's pleading, Russell eventually yielded.

These successes within the Senate, after only two years, showed that Kerr was on his way to becoming a powerful member. Despite his low seniority and lack of official position, he had worked his way into the inner circle of leadership. In 1951 Majority Leader McFarland gave him another boost, naming him to the Democratic Policy Committee. A product of the 1946 Legislative Reorganization Act, the policy committees were the political scientist's idea of how to introduce ideology into congressional politics. Each party policy committee defined party doctrine and took party positions on issues between presidential elections. "It was to be a kind of permanent floating party platform."[17] Despite these ideological pretensions, the Democratic Policy Committee became a screening committee to determine what bills would be called up for consideration in the Senate and what measures would be delayed or ignored. Under Johnson's leadership in the 1950's, the Democratic Policy Committee was a crucial traffic controller. Along with Johnson and Russell, Kerr took his duties on the policy committee seriously. They carefully scrutinized every bill in scheduling the calendar. "It was not for show. They were their only audience. Whether or not a bill fell within the usual scope of their interests, they fastened on it, shook it, questioned it, doubted or approved its wisdom, and rated its chance of passage. They were professional legislators."[18]

Events in the spring of 1951 further dramatized Truman's need for unity among Democrats in Congress. The furor resulting from his April dismissal of General Douglas MacArthur as the supreme commander of the United Nations forces in Korea gave Senator Kerr an unexpected opportunity to ingratiate himself with the President. For several days Kerr was the only Democrat to defend the commander-in-chief against the formidable attack from Republican senators Taft, Nixon, and Knowland. It was a gracious gesture from a proud senator whose pet legislative project had been unexpectedly jettisoned a year earlier.

Senator Kerr's motives in the MacArthur controversy were as complex as on any other important issue. He did not favor expanding the Korean War and killing more Americans. A month before the General's dismissal, Kerr had taunted Republicans to back up their support of MacArthur's strategy with the challenge that they introduce a resolution proposing that the U.S. declare war on China.[19] He feared MacArthur's strategy would risk "an all out struggle with Red China which would increase our casualties ten times, risking the intervention of Russia, which would increase them 100 times."[20] And he also knew that the only troops available for use on the Chinese mainland were semitrained National Guardsmen then en route to Japan. More than one-half of those men were from Oklahoma's 45th "Thunderbird" Division. On April 9 Kerr suggested that MacArthur be removed for open disregard of superior authority.[21] On April 10, the day prior to the President's decision, Kerr spent all day and part of the evening preparing a speech urging Truman to recall the General. He intended to give the speech when the Senate reconvened on the next day—April 11. The White House announced MacArthur's dismissal at 1:00 A.M. the following morning. Up early, the Senator heard the news on the radio and called his administrative assistant, Burl Hays. Relieved to hear of the President's action, Hays felt disappointed that their long hours of work on the speech had been wasted. "On the contrary," Kerr replied. He asked Hays to meet him at the office right away because he intended to use the heart of the speech in a new one defending the President.[22]

Oklahomans, like most Americans, were outraged at Truman's firing of MacArthur.[23] Kerr's defense of the President was unpopular in the Sooner State, where the issue was "hot as a depot stove."[24] In later years, Kerr wearied of trying to justify his defense of Truman on constitutional grounds. He seemed resigned to his critics' narrow view. In 1962, when asked if there had been no danger to Oklahoma troops would he still have thought MacArthur should have been dismissed, he replied yes. "But I wouldn't have gotten into the fight as I did otherwise."[25] The MacArthur episode taught Kerr the futility of trying to change people's minds about issues which became identified with patriotism, as was the case with MacArthur's dismissal.

The country was still preoccupied with the MacArthur firing as summer approached. In the swelter of Washington in July, hardly anyone noticed when the FPC ruled that the Phillips Petroleum Company, the country's largest independent producer and gatherer of natural gas, was not subject to regulation. The ruling, which directly reversed the effect of the President's veto of the Kerr bill, stunned the liberals. The five members of the Federal Power Commission who had recommended 3–2 that Truman veto the gas bill, now voted 4–1 to exempt the Phillips Company. Chairman Wallgren and Commissioner Draper had joined Commissioners Smith and Wimberly, leaving Commissioner Buchanan the sole dissenter.[26] The persistent fiction that regulatory commissioners were different from other men—nonpartisan, impartial, and incorruptible—was shattered.

Now the myth of the brazen Senator Kerr as hatchet man for the oil and gas industry grew even larger. Because Kerr made no secret of doing favors and expecting favors in return, Paul Douglas was sure his defense of the President's dismissal of MacArthur was Kerr's way of repaying Truman for the Wallgren appointment and the subsequent favorable decision in the Phillips Petroleum case.[27] And Joseph Alsop charged that Kerr had secured the FPC's vote in the Phillips case in exchange for lucrative gas leases from Phillips Petroleum.[28]

Kerr was now virtually impervious to charges of conflict of interest. Early in his career he had concluded that wealthy men in public life were not accorded the same foibles as poorer men, so he had ceased trying to explain his actions. An aggressive and willful man, Kerr was determined to have his own way. His frankness in acknowledging ties to the gas industry was more menacing than reassuring because Americans were traditionally suspicious of men of wealth. Kerr knew this but refused to dissemble, as a more adroit politician might. And this openness made him seem more threatening. Personal and corporate gain did not determine his role in the gas controversy at any stage, but a passion for political power surely did.

Kerr had embarked on his Senate career with his eyes on 1600 Pennsylvania Avenue. Some men aspired to a life-seat in the upper chamber as the pinnacle of public service, but Kerr was too active to remain content there. He had an executive, not a legislative, personality and was oriented toward initiating action. His successful maneuvering in the natural gas controversy and the national attention it attracted imbued him with a sense of political invulnerability. That and his restless ambition dictated his decision to seek the Democratic presidential nomination in 1952. His try for a spot on the national ticket was typical of Kerr's willingness to take calculated risks and to make financial investments to get what he wanted. Like exploring for oil, the 1952 probe was "wildcat" politics.

In the four years following the 1948 victory, events at home and abroad seriously eroded public confidence in the Democratic party. The fall of China, the Korean conflict, and the Soviet Union's development of an atomic weapon raised doubts about the viability of Democratic foreign policy. And revelations about scandals among the hierarchy of the Truman Administration reflected unfavorably on the President, as well as on the party.

Walter Lippman saw the Democrats' problem in 1952 as having to choose "new men to exercise the power which was organized by Roosevelt and inherited from him by Truman."[29] The problem of succession was compounded because, as the incumbent president, Truman dominated and, at the same time, divided the party. The successful nominee would need all of Truman's political assets without assuming any of his liabilities.

As Kerr surveyed the likely candidates for 1952, it seemed plausible that lightning might strike him.[30] The opposition was not formidable. Kefauver he dismissed as too liberal for the South and too much the reformer for the Democratic big-city bosses. Russell could not win northern support; Barkley was too old, Harriman too rich, and Stevenson too hesitant. In Kerr's mind, the only obstacle was his friend and leader, Harry Truman. Although Truman had said he favored the traditional two-term limit for presidents, there was no guarantee he would honor the tradition. The President was silent about his plans, but the Washington pundits fairly purred. The Alsop brothers reported that Truman was thinking of following the precedent of John Quincy Adams, who returned to the House after his defeat in 1828.[31] Washington rumors were always fanciful, but this one was fantastic. But Kerr was stymied until Truman publicly withdrew from the race.

Kerr's preparations for a possible campaign had been in the making for a long time. In late 1950 he subscribed to a national clipping service asking for stories on his candidacy and other potential Democratic nominees from representative regional papers.[32] He also began writing a newspaper column, "Senator Kerr Says," for Oklahoma consumption in December 1950.[33] In addition to reporting items of interest to his constituents, Kerr used the column to practice his campaign rhetoric and to attract coverage in major newspapers. He sniped at Taft, "He would rather be critical than informed," and demanded to know, "who does speak for the Republican party?"[34] The *New York Times* took the bait and reported that Kerr was "beginning to talk like a presidential candidate."[35] His campaign was launched.

Throughout 1951, Kerr continued to talk and act like a presidential candidate. His defense of Truman's dismissal of MacArthur put the President, as well as the national party, in his debt. Two seemingly unrelated events in the late spring were proof of his new stature in the Democratic party. In May, Kerr gave what was usually considered a routine luncheon at the Capitol for Oklahoma's new Democratic national committeeman, William Doenges. Vice-President Barkley and several Cabinet members, including Secretary of State Dean Acheson, attended and lingered to talk and be photographed. This was a gesture usually reserved for a prominent governor or a distinguished foreign parliamentarian, not for a political neophyte.[36]

The Democratic party also honored Kerr with an invitation to be the principal speaker at the Western States Conference in Denver in late May. CBS broadcast the speech, a colorful and imaginative attack on the Republicans as the war party.[37] But Truman, who did not even attend the meeting, stole the show. The President sent a letter regretting that he could not be present, but seemed to hint that "give 'em hell, Harry" would run in 1952.[38]

Carl Rice, Kansas national committeeman, reported the consensus at the meeting was that Truman could have the nomination if he wanted it. If not Truman, the Democrats considered Eisenhower, whose party preference was still unknown, a sure winner. Paul Douglas was the leading liberal candidate; and Barkley, Kefauver, McGrath, Rayburn, and Kerr were possible compromise choices.[39]

The Denver conference seemed to give party officials renewed hopes that the President would run and spare the party a divisive convention fight for at least another four years. There was also talk among the conferees about Kerr in the number two spot.[40] Truman's ability to campaign would probably be curtailed because of the Korean War, and Kerr was the ideal man to conduct a whistlestop tour denouncing Republicans and turning out the vote.

The Oklahoman probably never considered talk of a Truman-Kerr ticket as anything but a way to advance his own candidacy for the top job. He would not be a ceremonial subordinate to anyone, even President Truman, whom he admired and respected. He also knew the idea was politically unsound. Not only were he and Truman both from border states, but Oklahoma had only eight electoral votes. Kerr's appeal in the South was only moderate, and his reputation earned in the gas fight would be a handicap in northern and eastern cities. The two men also had the same highly partisan and purposely unsophisticated campaign style. If Truman ran, Senator Kerr would be the first to see the need for a vice-president to provide the pianissimo to Truman's fortissimo.

But Kerr did not discourage the rumors because he needed national publicity. And he suspected that while the President probably would not run, he still had not found a suitable successor. When—and if—Truman withdrew, Kerr wanted to be prominent enough to merit the President's endorsement.

Truman's off-again, on-again attitude toward renomination prevented him from promoting or training an heir. But as 1952 approached, he was primarily concerned with knocking down Estes Kefauver, "the self-invented presidential contender."[41] He considered Kefauver a "second-rate headline hunter" whose highly publicized crime investigations had damaged the Democratic party.[42] Truman, as well as party officials in Illinois, blamed the Tennessean's crime investigations and its spotlight on Chicago police scandals for party reversals in the 1950 elections. The President was particularly bitter about losing his majority leader, Scott Lucas.[43] And Truman was not alone in his concern about the Tennessean's unsuitability for the nomination. Few Democratic senators were sympathetic to Kefauver.

"It isn't that we don't like Estes, . . . but he isn't around for the infighting," one remarked. "He skims off the cream of the headlines and then he's off. He doesn't stick to the job and he doesn't cooperate."[44]

While there was widespread agreement that Kefauver had to

be stopped from playing the role of David to the Goliath of the professional politicians, the question was how. Representative Mike Kirwan, an influential member of the House Appropriations Committee, approached Truman to win his support for a Rayburn-led anti-Kefauver movement in early 1952.[45] If Truman did not run, Kirwan argued, Rayburn would be the best-known and most-experienced Democrat to lead the New Deal-Fair Deal coalition. Despite Rayburn's southern background, Kirwan felt he would be more acceptable to the northern party leaders than Russell.

But Truman had his own ideas about how to stall the Kefauver boom. His strategy, while complex, was to keep the various factions in the Democratic hierarchy off balance. Charles Murphy, the President's aide closest to labor, pushed Stevenson's candidacy, which pleased the ADA and some labor cadres. John R. Steelman, another White House assistant, supported Kefauver, which pleased the Teamsters Union and noneastern liberals. There was considerable antipathy among the Kefauver people toward the liberal, eastern wing of the party. They resented the Democratic hierarchy's apparent assumption that no candidate could lead the common man without a background of private preparatory school, eastern university education, and aristocratic associations.[46] Labor columnist Victor Riesel predicted that the White House gambit was to keep both Kefauver and Stevenson "strong enough to stay in the race and weak enough to prevent them from threatening control of the party machinery."[47] Then Truman could dictate the nomination.

Senator Kerr was undoubtedly aware of the President's stratagems, and early in 1952 he began to inch forward as a possible candidate. At the January Democratic party's midwestern conference in Kansas City, Kerr won the backing of several prominent state party leaders. Although the conference passed a resolution urging a Truman-Barkley ticket, several prominent national committeemen said they would favor Kerr if Truman did not run.[48] James Quigley, Nebraska's national committeeman, wanted to enter Kerr's name as a stand-in for Truman in the Cornhusker primary against Kefauver, but the Senator hesitated.[49] Kerr knew he would have to prove his ability as a vote-getter if the party was to take his candidacy seriously. In several sessions with Clark Clifford, he tried to evaluate which primary races would have the maximum impact.[50] But Truman's ambiguous position prevented Kerr from officially entering the race on his own.

Truman was still publicly undecided. Although he confided to his staff in November 1951 his intention not to seek reelection, he felt "it was both his right and duty to name a successor."[51] His first choice, Chief Justice Fred Vinson, refused because his health was precarious and he had no desire to leave the Supreme Court. There were other eager prospects, but none suited the Missourian.[52]

On January 6, 1952, Eisenhower allowed his name to be entered on the Republican ballot in the New Hampshire primary, and the quest for a suitable Democratic candidate intensified. Truman expected Eisenhower to win the Republican nomination,[53] so it was imperative that the Democrats begin grooming an attractive, well-known competitor. At the urging of several White House aides, the President became convinced, although reluctantly, that Adlai Stevenson, governor of Illinois, was the man. Truman was stunned when Stevenson refused to accept his help in securing the nomination, preferring to run for reelection in Illinois.[54] Within the week of Stevenson's refusal Estes Kefauver trounced Truman in the New Hampshire primary. Now not only was the President humiliated, he was also angry and vindictive. For a few days he even considered becoming a candidate after all.[55]

In late January, James Quigley consulted Frank McKinney, Democratic national chairman, about entering Kerr in the Nebraska primary as a stalking horse for the President. McKinney discussed the idea with Truman who "gave his tacit endorsement."[56] Although various polls indicated that the President was still leading Kefauver, the Tennessean's support was growing among rank and file Democratic voters.[57] Now the President switched to a new tactic. Not only did he publicly belittle the preferential primary as "mere eyewash," but he also "deliberately arranged to have primary holding states elect delegates committed to favorite sons who were stooges for him."[58]

But Senator Kerr remained cautious; he needed personal as-surances from Truman. Mrs. Kerr encouraged her husband to ask for Truman's help, convinced that he would gladly help Kerr get started in the primaries if for no other reason than his gratitude for the Senator's attack on MacArthur.[59]

Kerr met with the President in late January, and they agreed that the Oklahoman would enter the Nebraska primary as a stand-in for Truman against Kefauver. The President telephoned several prominent party officials in Kerr's presence and urged them to put their funds and organization at the Senator's disposal.[60] Most important of all, Truman promised to decide about his own can-didacy two or three weeks before the vote in Nebraska and to let the Senator know.[61] Assured of Truman's goodwill, Kerr an-nounced his entry in the Nebraska primary on February 6.[62] The Nebraska contest was crucial. "If Kerr whipped Kefauver in Ne-braska, President Truman could bow out in favor of Kerr, a man acceptable to him, who was proved a better vote getter than Kefauver."[63]

Kerr's campaign was a model of primary organization and finance. A hand-picked group of Oklahoma supporters with as-sistance from Ed Pauley, a Truman crony and California oil mil-lionaire who had played a key role in organizing and financing the drive that had assured Truman of the vice-presidential nomi-nation in 1944, raised the money.[64] Louis Johnson, Truman's for-mer secretary of defense and a major fund raiser in the 1948 campaign, returning from a trip to the West Coast, spread the word that Kerr was "the next choice after Truman for the nomina-tion."[65] He hinted that California, with the second largest delega-tion, would support Kerr; so Nebraskans should grab the lead. Bernard Boyle, a prominent Omaha attorney, directed activities in the state.[66] Ads appeared in Nebraska's 171 weekly newspapers, all of the dailies, and Kerr spoke almost daily over radio and television—this in addition to an exhaustive schedule of personal appearances. There was also special emphasis to reach labor and Negro voters in Omaha.[67]

Despite the money and organization, Kerr was the underdog in Nebraska.[68] Rex Hawks, the U.S. marshal in Oklahoma City and Kerr's long-time political associate, Aubrey, and B. B. went to Nebraska to appraise the situation. Hawks quickly became convinced that Kerr could not win. Anti-Truman sentiment was strong in the Cornhusker State, and Kefauver's popularity as a crime-buster grew steadily. Nebraskans, who had voted public ownership of all power plants, were hostile to the Kerr gas bill.[69] The Kerr-Kefauver contest also accentuated the split in the state party organization between the old-line Quigley faction and the so-called "New Lifers," an ADA-dominated group generally favoring Kefauver. The "New Lifers" charged that the state organization violated its neutrality pledge by opposing the Kefauver candidacy, but Quigley claimed he was acting as a private citizen, not in his capacity as Democratic national committeeman.[70] Hawks concluded, "Kerr was with the wrong crowd," and Kefauver would win.[71] He told the Senator the worst, but Kerr refused to believe it. He wanted so badly to win that he redoubled his efforts in what his most trusted aides told him was a futile endeavor.

The Oklahoman had never enjoyed the luxury of an easy campaign, so he worked exceptionally hard in Nebraska. One reporter observed that it was an Oklahoma tradition that regardless of the opponent Kerr always ran against Herbert Hoover, the Depression, four-cent cotton, and ten-cent hogs. "A lot of what he says is corn, and the Midwest thrives on it."[72] But Nebraska was unlike any campaign Kerr had ever fought or would wage again. He was going to lose and knew it. And he did what losers usually did, grasped at the one issue which would arouse the most people—communism. He implied that Kefauver was "soft on communism." He charged that Kefauver's Atlantic Union proposal would result "in surrendering our sovereignty to foreign countries without firing a shot."[73] Kerr had never pandered to these fears in his public career. Before 1952 he had always fought a campaign on the issues, had offered a definite program, and had rarely even mentioned an opponent, much less slandered him. But he was desperate to win and stooped lower than he ever would again.

Kefauver retaliated in an attempt to win the Catholic vote with false reports that Kerr, a prominent Baptist, had campaigned for Hoover in 1928 rather than endorse a papist, Al Smith.[74] In Omaha, the stronghold of Nebraska wets, he harped on Kerr's militant opposition to strong drink.[75] Neither candidate dignified the campaign with talk about substantive issues. But the bitterness in the Nebraska primary was not uncommon for a party searching frantically for a leader as the Democrats were doing in early 1952.

Three days before the voting, Truman withdrew from the race.[76] Senator Kerr was speaking at a Jefferson-Jackson Day dinner in Salt Lake City when he learned the news. He immediately announced that he was in the Nebraska race on his own merits, "win or lose."[77] But Truman's announcement came too late for Kerr to make an effective campaign in his own behalf. Kefauver defeated him 64,531 to 42,467.

Once again, as in the gas fight, Truman had reneged on his word to the Senator. Don McBride recalled, "Kerr was under the impression that he would have the blessing of Truman."[78] Kerr's staff felt that the President's failure to honor his promise to inform Kerr of his plans two or three weeks before the election would not have changed the outcome. But with more time, Kerr might have reduced the margin of defeat and certainly would have changed the nature of his campaign.[79]

Because of his qualified candidacy as a stand-in for Truman, many Nebraskans refused to take Kerr seriously. They were understandably reluctant to support anyone, Truman or Kerr, who might not really be a candidate. As a stand-in, Kerr inherited Truman's record and his enemies in Nebraska; and the President's belated withdrawal, with no hint of endorsement, left Kerr looking appropriately foolish on April 1, election day. It was astonishing that Kerr polled as many votes as he did given the bizzare circumstances. His loyalty to the President and the party doomed his campaign before it ever began. Kerr, and certainly Clark Clifford, probably suspected that Truman would not run, but their hopes for a possible presidential endorsement obscured their judgment. Regardless of their personal relationship, the Oklahoman should have realized that after the gas bill veto, Truman could never publicly sanction him. In the President's eyes Kerr was a political pariah—a special-interest, oil-and-gas senator.

Despite his self-confidence and arrogance, Robert Kerr, unlike Estes Kefauver, was not a maverick. He knew that the party would nominate the President's choice. With the likelihood of Eisenhower on the Republican ticket, Kerr knew that the Democratic nominee would have to be reasonably well known, but not offensive to any group or wing of the party; he should be from a populous, doubtful state with special appeal to urban and minority voters. Rationally, he knew there was no chance that he could capture the nomination. The Nebraska loss had destroyed any bargaining power he had hoped for in Chicago. But rationality seldom prevails against ambition. Lesser men than Robert Kerr had coveted the White House; deadlocked conventions had nominated some of them; and capricious voters had put a few in office while untimely death had elevated others to the top spot. So long as there was any possibility, Kerr was willing to try.

Kerr showed no despair about his chances for the nomination. After his loss to Kefauver he quipped, "If I run again, I'll have to learn to square dance, ride a bicycle and get a red headed wife."[80] The Cornhusker primary eliminated Kerr's strongest political selling point. Since he had considerable support from state party officials, he gambled that he could emerge from Nebraska as a vote-getter, a man popular with the rank and file. Despite the loss, he maintained that he still had pledges from seven of the twelve Nebraska delegates.[81]

When Kerr failed in Nebraska, many Oklahoma Democrats were not unhappy. Relations between the senior Senator and the state Democratic party organization were superficially cordial. But Kerr's wealth had enabled him to build a personal organization, and he was frequently at odds with prominent state politicians. Friends of his predecessor as governor, Leon C. Phillips, still opposed him. Roy Turner, who followed Kerr in the statehouse, had not forgotten that Kerr supported H. C. Jones in the 1946 governor's race. Since Turner planned to challenge Kerr for the Democratic nomination to the Senate in 1954, any setback was welcome. A. S. "Mike" Monroney, the junior Senator elected in 1950, endorsed Sam Rayburn's candidacy to avoid being embroiled in a possible Oklahoma Democratic party split over Kerr.

Elected to the House in 1939, Monroney served five terms under Rayburn's leadership. Publicly, Kerr remained neutral when Monroney moved to unseat veteran Elmer Thomas, but privately he endorsed the aging Thomas.[82] The Henryetta (Okla.) *Daily Free-Lance* noted that Monroney could document that he was on record as being for Rayburn before the first "Kerr for President" club was formed. "Of course, he wasn't on record for Rayburn before Kerr had White House aspirations. Monroney is not that old."[83]

The incumbent governor, Johnston Murray, was also cool toward Kerr's presidential aspirations. Kerr had sided with William O. Coe, Murray's primary opponent in the 1950 gubernatorial race.[84] Although Murray won 47 per cent of the primary vote, Coe, the nearest rival with 30 per cent, refused to retire as was customary. Before the runoff was completed, it was generally known that Kerr was contributing heavily to Coe. Some of the Senator's friends were critical of his involvement and warned him of possible difficulties when Murray won.[85]

Relations between the Senator and the Governor were understandably strained during the early months of the new administration. But by mid-1951 both saw the benefits of rapprochement. Despite a lingering rancor over the 1950 election, the Governor needed Kerr's help to arrange a truce among warring factions in the state party in an effort to stave off a rising Republican organization.[86] As frequently occurred in one-party states, the Democratic party in Oklahoma had developed ideologically into separate internal conservative and liberal wings. With the likelihood of another liberal candidate in the New Deal-Fair Deal tradition, Governor Murray feared the "Jefferson Democratic" wing of the party would desert to Taft or any other Republican candidate. He needed Kerr's prestige and organization to prevent any rupture in the party and to keep Oklahoma in the Democratic column, regardless of the national presidential candidate.

Kerr, not Murray, took the first step toward improved relations when he entertained the new national committeeman, William Doenges, in Washington that spring. Doenges was Murray's choice to replace Elmer Harber, a Shawnee banker who left the national committee to join the Reconstruction Finance Corporation in 1951. Oklahomans referred to Doenges as Murray's "political godfather" because he had bankrolled Murray's 1950 race.[87] Doenges had never held elective public office, but he had visions of being a senator. He eagerly supported Kerr's bid for the nomination with the hope that Murray would appoint him to Kerr's unexpired term.[88]

At Kerr's suggestion, the Oklahoma State Society in Washington hosted a lavish brunch to honor the visiting Governor in June 1951. Officially, Murray was in Washington to ask public road administrators for greater allocations of steel for Oklahoma; but he spent most of his time with Bill Boyle, Democratic National Committee chairman, and other party leaders. According to the *Tulsa World*'s Washington correspondent, Murray's acquiescence in Kerr's plan to be nominated as Oklahoma's favorite son had a price tag. Johnston Murray wanted Kerr's pledge to assist him in securing a diplomatic assignment in Central or South America when his term as governor ended in 1954.[89] As a boy, he had accompanied his father "Alfalfa Bill," who led a group of Oklahoma colonists to Bolivia. He was fluent in Spanish and knowledgeable about Latin American–United States relations.[90] Kerr probably agreed to do what he could, but first he had to be on the national ticket and the Democrats had to win the White House.

Despite the understanding with Kerr, Murray wanted to avoid offending any faction in the state party with a public endorsement of the Senator. Since he had warned party officials to "divest themselves of all affiliations with any candidates" early in 1952, he had to set the example.[91]

When the Democratic State Central Committee met in February, neither Murray, Doenges, nor Roy Turner was present and, therefore, could not be bound by any committee decision. Influenza had felled them as it often did politicians in February of an election year.[92] Seventy-five of the seventy-seven counties endorsed Kerr for the nomination, so the results were reported as unanimous.[93]

As enthusiasm for Kerr in Oklahoma was beginning to build, Kefauver defeated him in Nebraska. Governor Murray was not surprised at the outcome and called for "an Oklahoma delegation to the national convention which is uncommitted, either openly or under the table."[94] But E. K. Gaylord, Sr., publisher of Oklahoma City's two major newspapers and a persistent critic of Kerr, acknowledged that Truman's record and belated withdrawal had determined the outcome. In what many interpreted as a qualified endorsement, the influential editor said that Kerr, as an announced candidate with his own platform, would have been a formidable opponent for any contender, even the popular Kefauver.[95]

With this boost, Kerr decided to push for resolutions for instructed county delegates in areas where he was strong, but not in others, in the hope that there would be enough sentiment at the state convention to override Murray's wishes for an uninstructed delegation to Chicago. There was some opposition to Kerr at the April 12 county conventions, but most of the delegates to the state meeting were instructed to go along if the Senator showed enough strength to warrant an endorsement. The favorite son argument was persuasive enough to prevent the party schism from deepening further.

Prior to the state convention on April 28, the Governor maneuvered to gain control of the party. While it was customary for governors to work behind the scenes to see that their men were elected to state and national party offices, Murray announced his choices for state party chairman and national committeeman publicly. Jim Arrington, Kerr's long-time political ally who became state party chairman when Kerr was governor, wanted to stay in the job, but "no one was inviting him to continue."[96] Kerr was apparently willing to drop Arrington and to tolerate Murray's grandstanding, if these acts of political self-effacement would induce the Governor to accept an instructed delegation. Chicago was all that mattered.

Several days before the state meeting, Murray announced that Doenges was his personal choice for national committeeman and Smith Hester, a Purcell attorney, his candidate for party chairman. "Doenges and Hester see eye to eye with me on all important policy matters pertaining to the Democratic Party in Oklahoma."[97] Party politics in Oklahoma need not be democratic as long as Oklahoma politics remained Democratic.

There was some muttering from Kerr supporters about Murray's dictation, but it died down when the Governor denied any intention of blocking Kerr's candidacy. Murray was bartering tacit support of Kerr for domination of the state party. The Kerr people were in no position to challenge Murray, for, as the Senator readily admitted, "a fellow who is seeking delegates . . . wants most of all . . . those from his home state."[98]

Kerr's caution induced Murray to compromise. And the state convention enthusiastically endorsed the Senator as a favorite son. The thirty-six delegates were instructed to cast their twenty-four votes for him until he was nominated or until a majority decided to end the instruction.[99] Murray was selected to head the delegation, and the convention dutifully elected his designees to other party offices.[100] All the principals got what they wanted. Murray consolidated control of the state party, and Kerr received full support for the presidential nomination. With his rear flank secured, the Oklahoman began to build support elsewhere.

In April, Kerr opened his national headquarters in the Willard Hotel in downtown Washington, D.C. under the direction of Charles van Devander, a former public relations man for the Democratic National Committee. With an able staff to handle publicity and scheduling matters, Kerr concentrated on convention maneuvers. He believed that no candidate, not even Kefauver, would be victorious in the early balloting at Chicago. When the deadlock developed, Kerr wanted to be strong enough to emerge as the compromise choice. While most southerners preferred James F. Byrnes or Richard Russell, Kerr assumed that neither would be acceptable to the northern Democrats. Since he had co-operated with southerners on states rights' questions such as civil rights, tidelands oil, and statehood for Alaska and Hawaii, they would accept him. If necessary, Kerr's backers could switch to Russell without sacrifice of principle. The Georgian had a long record of support for public power and New Deal agricultural policy.[101] This was approximately the same strategy Kerr and Russell used to capture the Senate leadership for McFarland and Johnson in 1951—a coalition of South and West with Russell commander of the southern forces and Kerr organizing the West.

If circumstances favoring the "southern strategy" failed to develop, Kerr still had hope. He believed that northern liberals, anxious to avoid a repeat of the 1948 Dixiecrat rebellion, would not force either Kefauver or Stevenson on an unwilling South. In that event, he might emerge as the unity candidate—a middle-of-the-road, loyal party man.[102]

Although Kerr's only real hope lay in a deadlocked convention, he knew that Vice-President Alben Barkley would be the ideal unifying candidate. Barkley was seventy-four years old in 1952, but age was no barrier to political aspirations. Northern organization leaders, such as Frank McKinney and John McCormack, and southern moderates had talked of drafting Barkley when Stevenson continued to vacillate. Even before Barkley's July 6 official announcement that he was a candidate, Kerr regarded him as the greatest threat to his own nomination.[103]

Everything depended on Kerr's surviving the first ballot. Although he and Clifford had agreed in January that he should enter the primaries to establish a reputation as a vote-getter, Truman's delayed withdrawal prevented him from participating as a full-fledged candidate. In late February he had toyed with the idea of being a stand-in for the President in the California primary.[104] He believed that New York would reserve its ninety-four votes for Averell Harriman, whom he dismissed as the "party's professional bridesmaid," but California's sixty-eight votes were up for grabs. John B. Elliot, dean of the Golden State delegation, agreed to enter Kerr's name in the primary.[105] Clinton Anderson, one of the principals in the Senate coterie opposed to Kefauver, was urging Barkley to enter as a "stop-Kefauver" maneuver.[106] When Earle Clements, former Kentucky governor who resigned to take Barkley's Senate seat in 1949, approached Truman with the idea, he was told to check with Frank McKinney, Democratic National Committee chairman. McKinney said he was trying to clear the Truman delegates for Kerr but finally recommended that neither Barkley nor Kerr file in California. It would "be a bigger blow to Kefauver to have him win in California by default."[107] McKinney's advice prevailed when Kerr's attempt to get on the ballot failed. Six California assemblymen pledged to Truman refused to serve on a slate for the Oklahoman, saying that they had "never heard of Kerr."[108] Other Californians were uneasy about his role in the natural gas controversy, the tidelands bill, and the Central Arizona Project.[109] Finally, the growing anti-Truman sentiment convinced Kerr that California would be a pointless and costly battlefield. He canceled the effort on March 27.[110] Abandoning the California primary was a strategic retreat. Just before leaving for Chicago, Kerr wrote a Los Angeles delegate that he expected to "receive support from the California delegation after it becomes apparent that Kefauver will not get a majority."[111]

After the Nebraska debacle, Kerr decided that the party leaders were correct in their strategy of ignoring Kefauver. He certainly had no desire to risk another whipping. Quietly, he, along with Russell, Barkley, and Brien McMahon, withdrew from the District of Columbia primary leaving Averell Harriman to face Kefauver. Despite great talents, Harriman was destined to advise presidents, not to be one. Gael Sullivan, Kefauver's national campaign director, scoffed at Harriman's candidacy, calling him "the horsy set's Huckleberry Finn."[112] In a stunning upset, the New Yorker won almost 80 per cent of the vote largely because of his uncompromising advocacy of civil rights.[113]

The victory did not alter Harriman's image, but revealed a very important flaw in Kefauver's apparently booming candidacy. While a tireless and attractive campaigner, Kefauver was a superficial liberal, a southern Democrat, equivocal on civil rights. When the Chicago delegates searched the roster of possible nominees for a civil rights advocate they bypassed Kefauver without hesitation for Stevenson.

Harriman's victory over Kefauver led Arthur Schlesinger, Jr., to claim that the New Yorker was the immediate beneficiary of Kerr's collapsing candidacy in the Midwest.[114] It was conceivable that Harriman might develop some following in the Midwest where his family had extensive railroad holdings, but not enough to counterbalance the stigma of his New York City–Long Island–Washington, D.C. image. Kerr, who was reputedly almost as rich as Harriman, was quick to point out that he had made his money while Harriman inherited his. Kerr was the Everyman of the 1950's with enormous appeal in a society that still believed that, with hard work and a little good fortune, every man could succeed.

Kerr did not believe his candidacy was collapsing. At the National Press Club in early June he summarized the campaign. "Frankly, when I analyze my own chances and count the specific votes now pledged to me, I don't know how I can win. Yet when I analyze all the other candidates, and appraise their chances, and recognize the solid opposition against them, I don't see how I can lose. . . ."[115]

As the convention grew nearer, Kerr intensified his search for delegates. By the end of June he claimed to be the "only man seeking the Democratic nomination for President whose delegate strength is growing daily."[116] After the disappointing results in Nebraska, Kerr had resumed efforts to win delegates in the West. The western states, which included the territories of Alaska and Hawaii, enjoyed relative importance in the 1952 convention. With about one-eighth of the population of the United States, the region had more than one-sixth of the total voting strength at the convention. Nearly a quarter of its 210 votes were bonus votes, the party's reward to each state that had voted Democratic in the last election.[117]

Kerr visited every western state except New Mexico and the two territories before the end of June. Formidable allies in the Land of Enchantment, Senators Clinton Anderson and Dennis Chavez and Congressman Antonio M. Fernandez, looked after Kerr's interests there. Most of the party leaders in New Mexico wanted an uninstructed delegation, but the Albuquerque *Journal* predicted at the close of the state convention that Kerr would receive nine or ten of the state's twelve votes on the first ballot.[118]

The Oklahoman's alliance with the southern senators in opposition to statehood for Alaska and Hawaii in exchange for their support on oil and gas matters precluded any delegate votes from the territories. Clinton Anderson's warning that this swap would cost Kerr votes for the nomination in Chicago was correct.[119] When he appeared before the Alaska delegation at the convention, he told them, "I have been for statehood all along."[120] But even the glib Oklahoman was unable to explain away his vote to re-commit the statehood bill.

Despite the preliminary spadework of Kansas' National Committeeman Carl Rice and state Senator Bob George who traveled in the West as advance-men, there was little real enthusiasm for Kerr. In each state where there seemed no hope of breaking down resistance to instruction or where support was already pledged to a favorite son, Kerr asked for second ballot support, seemingly confident he would survive the first roll call. Although he ranked fourth in national polls conducted in the western states in mid-June, his supporters talked of growing delegate strength. They claimed enough votes in the western states having the unit rule to swing Idaho, Utah, Wyoming, Montana, New Mexico, Arizona, and Kansas, plus ten of twenty-two votes from Washington and one and one-half from Nevada for a total of 137½ votes on the first ballot.[121] This view of events differed considerably from reality. At best, Kerr could expect no more than 37½ votes from the western states.[122] With Oklahoma's twenty-four-vote bloc, he had a total of 61½ votes, a rather meager showing for a man who hoped to emerge as the unity candidate.

The Midwest was no more promising than the West. The internecine party struggle which hampered Kerr's campaign in Nebraska also hurt his efforts to win delegates in Kansas and North Dakota. His major supporter in the Sunflower State, Carl V. Rice, was retiring as national committeeman, a post he had held since 1932. In traditionally Republican Kansas, Rice had considerable influence as the chief dispenser of Democratic patronage, so the contest to replace him was a lively one. Rice's man, Kenneth T. Anderson, the Democratic gubernatorial candidate in 1950, won the race at the state convention in Hutchinson, but endorsement of Kerr did not follow as hoped. Kerr was the main convention speaker and, in fact, the only contender to appear personally in Kansas during the preconvention campaign. He made extensive efforts to secure the delegation's sixteen votes. Rice and George Burke, party chairman of the fifth congressional district, urged the delegation to go on record as pledged to Kerr, but John I.

Young, the state chairman, blocked the move. Anti-Rice delegates spread the story that Kerr had promised to make the Kansan national party chairman if he were nominated.[123] Although bound to the unit rule, the delegation went to Chicago unpledged and uninstructed.[124] Shortly after the state convention, Young and Anderson flew to Springfield to offer their support to Stevenson. A newspaper poll of the delegation taken just after the state convention indicated that few had decided to back any single candidate. Only three delegates publicly supported Kerr.[125]

The situation in North Dakota was similar to that in Kansas. As the traditional minority, the Democratic machinery existed primarily to allot federal patronage. Any struggle between the ins and outs was always bitter. David Kelly, the national committeeman, had dominated the party for over twenty years. In the early fifties an anti-Kelly faction developed among the Young Democrats, who were becoming a significant force nationally. Kelly managed to retain control of the state organization and won reelection to the national committee. But he did not move for a unit rule vote to be cast for Kerr on the first ballot as expected. He probably favored Kerr as a stalking horse for Truman but was unwilling to risk his own position in North Dakota by backing a loser. The four major contenders campaigned in North Dakota after the May 13 state convention, but "their efforts . . . had less influence on the North Dakota delegation than the desire of this group to be with the winner at the end of the convention."[126]

In Iowa, where the Senator campaigned only one day by air, an unofficial poll in the Cedar Rapids *Gazette* reported 2½ of the Hawkeye State's twenty-four votes for the Oklahoman.[127] In Minnesota, committed to Humphrey as a favorite son on the first ballot, Kerr asked for second ballot consideration.[128] He did not invest too much time in the Midwest, where he was widely remembered as the ogre behind the natural gas bill. Illinois was Stevenson territory and Kefauver had campaigned extensively and effectively, building on his win in Nebraska. Sixteen and one-half votes out of a possible 336 was all Kerr could realistically expect.

In the Northeast, the Oklahoman worked strictly through contacts in the national party hierarchy. A Pennsylvania delegate,

Clarence Brown, hosted a dinner in Kerr's honor, but few party leaders turned out.[129] Neither a brief trip to Maine nor an appearance before the New Jersey delegation at Princeton produced any results.[130] The only hint of support came from Massachusetts. Margaret O'Riordan, national committeewoman from Boston, promised Kerr at least six votes on the second ballot.[131] There was a rumor of some second ballot support from New York, but the Kerr staff in Washington wrote off the Northeast effort as wasted motion.[132]

The South belonged to Russell and Barkley, and Kerr was too careful a party man and too loyal a friend to transgress. He had all he was entitled to, Oklahoma's twenty-four votes, although Florida and Arkansas indicated they might move to him if he were still a serious candidate after the first roll call.[133]

In the six months before the Chicago convention Kerr exploited all his connections in the national Democratic party built over the years as a favorite banquet circuit speaker and successful fund raiser. The professionals knew and liked him. Men like Stevenson and Harriman seemed too fastidious for rough-and-tumble party politics; Kefauver had sought personal aggrandizement at the expense of the party; but Robert Kerr was one of them, a Democrat's Democrat. Unfortunately, these party officials did not make the nomination, contrary to myths about smoke-filled rooms. But even if they had, their ultimate concern for victory would not have altered the result arrived at in July in an open convention.

Kerr was the first Democratic candidate to arrive in Chicago, but his staff had been in town for over a month preparing a head-quarters at the Conrad Hilton Hotel. Joe Howell, a former *Tulsa Tribune* reporter, was in charge of local arrangements. A veteran of Democratic conventions, Howell believed in a campaign's appearing to gain momentum. "While ballyhoo did not necessarily win nominations, anytime a candidate's headquarters and bally-hoo began to fold you could bet his chances were disappearing too."[134] What they lacked in solid delegate support, Kerr backers made up in campaign paraphernalia and sheer bravura. They shipped fifty thousand pieces of campaign literature, thirty thousand small campaign buttons, and ten thousand large ones to hand out at the convention. A log cabin, symbolizing the Senator's birthplace and humble origins, appeared on the buttons. A cardboard replica was also set up in Kerr's $225-a-day Normandie Lounge headquarters in the hotel. Throughout the convention Kerr greeted delegates and posed for pictures in the cabin's doorway. Because of threatened trouble with the local musicians' union, plans to bring a thirty-two-piece Oklahoma all-girl band wearing kilts was scrapped. Instead, Howell hired a Chicago hillbilly band and a local square-dance team. "And as long as we paid them to keep performing the Kerr headquarters was crowded with people."[135]

To fill in lulls when the band was on break, Howell installed a jukebox which played a medley of favorites, such as "I Can't Say No," "I'm Yours," "All or Nothing at All," and "Was It a Dream?"[136] He also hired an organist to play tunes from the musical *Oklahoma!* on the large pipe organ just outside the entrance to the Normandie Lounge. There were photographs of projects and programs Kerr had supported and a brief film of the Senator's life which ran continuously. John O'Reilly of the New York *Herald Tribune* used considerable restraint when he described the Kerr headquarters as a "carnival."[137]

In spite of the ballyhoo and cacophony in the Normandie Lounge, Kerr was still seriously working for the nomination. He held a press conference shortly after arriving in Chicago on July 15 to boast of his delegate strength which he predicted would carry him through the perilous first ballot.[138] After six months of grueling travel, Kerr seemed fresh, rested, and confident. To a reporter who asked him how he responded to accusations "of making millions legitimately since the Democratic Party had been in power," Kerr quipped that "not even a Republican was able to make a million during the last GOP administration."[139] It was politics as usual. As one reporter summed up the candidates, "Senator Kerr is running against Hoover, Senator Kefauver, against sin, and the veep is running against time."[140]

Stevenson's June 30 statement at the Governors' Conference in Houston that he would not participate in a draft encouraged renewed talk of Truman. As the delegates gathered in Chicago, Democratic politicians and political writers were forecasting a ticket of Truman and Russell or Truman and Kerr.[141] This strong belief that Truman might yield to a draft was not based on any feeling that the President was being coy, but on the fear that the convention would be deadlocked and only Truman could lead the party to victory over Eisenhower. The Alsops predicted, "President Truman can swing at least 400 Democratic delegate votes to any candidate the convention likes; and can give at least 400 Democratic delegate votes to a candidate the convention does not like."[142] Kerr agreed. "The President will have more influence than any other delegate."[143] And with that observation, he announced he was flying to Washington to ask Truman for his support.

Senator Kerr was unable to see the President, who entered Walter Reed Hospital on July 16 with a virus infection and was incommunicado for several days. But it would have been a futile visit anyway. With Stevenson resisting the nomination and Harriman not a credible candidate, Truman had reluctantly agreed to support Barkley.[144]

Kerr's worst fears were now realized. If Barkley led the ticket his own candidacy was doomed. But the Barkley boom was brief. On the Sunday before the convention, labor leaders blocked him, ostensibly because he was too old "but also because they feared that the Kerr-Russell forces might unite behind his candidacy and exercise disproportionate control in the party."[145] Kerr was relieved when Barkley withdrew, sensing the renewal of his hopes of being the unity candidate. But this was merely self-deception. As long as there was any possibility that Barkley might actually head the ticket, Kerr at least had the opportunity for considerable influence during the campaign and in the administration if the Democrats won. But as the convention opened, no one but Kerr and a handful of faithful supporters kept up the pretense of victory.

Despite his reluctance to be a candidate, the Stevenson draft movement was steadily gaining momentum. As key party leaders from important states such as Pennsylvania, Indiana, and New Jersey began to swing toward the Illinoisan, Kerr showed the first sign of doubt. He considered the mild-mannered Stevenson who had backed away from the President's offer of full political support a contemptible ingénue. Kerr was so partisan and so ambitious that he could not conceive of any red-blooded Democratic governor spurning the presidency. On the day nominations began, Kerr issued a press release warning the party not to nominate Stevenson out of hysteria. "Governor Stevenson has made more serious accusations against himself than any of the other Democratic candidates have made against each other."[146] He cited the Governor's own comment that he was "mentally, physically and temperamentally unfit for the presidency." He also inferred something unsavory in Stevenson's psychological makeup because of his divorce and his character deposition for Alger Hiss.[147] This was not the kind of talk designed to conciliate and unify a fragmented party. It was the spleen of a bitter and disappointed man who had finally caught the scent of his own defeat in the rising wind of a Stevenson victory.

Nominations began at noon on Thursday, July 24. Alabama, first on the roll call, yielded to Georgia, whose senior senator, Walter George, nominated Richard Russell. Alaska yielded to Tennessee's governor, Gordon Browning, who invited the delegates to "climb aboard the Chattanooga Choo-Choo with Kefauver, a fearless man with a touch of nobility about him."[148] It was 2:35 P.M. before the Kefauver demonstration subsided and diminutive Congressman Carl Albert of Oklahoma, straining to be seen above the podium, nominated Robert Kerr—"a man physically, temperamentally and mentally fit for the office and ready and willing to lead the country at this time."[149]

Albert's allusion to Stevenson was bad taste, as well as bad politics. There was scattered applause from Kerr backers, but the general effect was a hushed embarrassment. After the seconding speeches and a brief demonstration, nominations continued—William Fulbright, Averell Harriman, Oscar Ewing, and Brien McMahon. At 5:00 P.M. Delaware's Governor Carvel and Indiana's Governor Schricker in an unorthodox, two-part nomination speech demanded that Stevenson not be permitted "to say no to the call of service."[150]

With Stevenson nominated, the roll call resumed. Idaho allowed Michigan to name Governor G. Mennen Williams; then the convention became embroiled in the debate over seating the Virginia delegation. Four hours elapsed before resumption of the nominating roll call. Keynote speaker Paul Dever, governor of Massachusetts, Senator Hubert Humphrey, and Vice-President Alben Barkley joined the lengthening roster of candidates. Finally, after several hours of confused maneuvering, interrupted with motions to adjourn, South Carolina and Louisiana were seated. The convention finally adjourned at two o'clock Friday morning after fourteen exhausting hours.

Balloting for the nomination began just after noon on Friday, July 25, but the inevitable polling of delegations delayed the results of the first ballot until 4:14 P.M. The tally was inconclusive: Kefauver—340; Stevenson—273; Russell—268; Harriman—123½; Kerr—65; Barkley—48½; and all others—111.[151] The Kerr boom collapsed with the first ballot. Arizona was the only state besides Oklahoma to give Kerr all its votes on the first ballot. The Apache State also had used its favored position in the roll call to yield to Oklahoma for Kerr's early nomination. And while there was some feeling that the Arizona delegation at Chicago over-represented the Kerr-Russell sentiment among Arizona Democrats, the first ballot support was probably a genuine expression of Arizona's gratitude for Kerr's vigorous support of the Central Arizona-Colorado River project.[152]

Kerr's preconvention claim of western strength did materialize, but hardly on the scale he had anticipated. His largest bloc of votes came from beyond the Rockies, twenty-six and one-half votes.[153] As expected, he gained no southern votes beyond Oklahoma's twenty-four. In the Midwest he received only fourteen votes, and one-half of one vote from Pennsylvania accounted for his northeastern support.[154]

True to his preconvention agreement, Kerr agreed to release the Sooner State's delegation on the second ballot. Governor Murray wanted to go with Russell, but a majority of the delegates decided to retain some freedom to maneuver in the interests of an ultimate revival of Kerr's candidacy if the deadlock persisted past the third ballot. They refused to join Russell's diehard support and were not yet convinced that Stevenson would be the winner. The delegation cast its twenty-four votes for Barkley, and Kerr's strategy prevailed.[155] The delegation stayed with Barkley until the end, voting for a candidate who, although officially nominated, had actually withdrawn two days earlier. They wasted their strength in pursuit of an illusion which, in retrospect, seemed more like a response of frustration than a plan for influence and possible victory.

Shortly after midnight, Orville Freeman of Minnesota moved to make the Stevenson nomination unanimous. Within a few hours Senator Kerr, bitter and disappointed, was on his way to his lakeside retreat. Just before departing he told Joe Howell to pack up the log cabin and send it to the Oklahoma headquarters. "It may have been the only thing Kerr remembered about the 1952 convention with pleasure."[156]

Kerr seldom spoke about his try for the nomination. Although he met with Stevenson early in August to plan for the campaign and performed his usual role giving rousing partisan speeches throughout the South and West, his heart, understandably, was not in it.[157] The loss in Chicago cut so deeply into his confidence and self-esteem that he could not discuss it with even close associates. Not until 1962, when he was the reputed "uncrowned King of the Senate," did he talk freely about what went wrong in 1952. But the ten years had not given him any objectivity. He blamed Truman's interference for his failure to be on the ticket. In a copyrighted interview, Kerr said he had been "assured Harry Truman would leave the convention alone." The Oklahoman admitted he was simply playing the odds; he figured he had "one chance in 50 of winning as the result of a deadlock. Had Truman stayed out of it, the ticket would have been Alben Barkley and Bob Kerr."[158]

Senator Kerr did not lose the nomination because of Truman's interference. His own reputation as a "special-interest, oil-and-gas Senator" determined the outcome. His leadership of the natural gas fight was a serious strategic error for a man with presidential aspirations. The complex controversy had been portrayed as a struggle between good and evil, and Kerr was doomed to the role of a perpetual villain.

Although he retained an executive outlook, Kerr had developed into an effective and influential legislator. By the 1960's the Senate would become the spawning ground for presidential candidates, but in the early 1950's both parties still looked to the statehouses and the battlefields for nominees. Robert Kerr had spent fifty-six years mastering the political craft only to learn that these skills were considered "black arts" and that the nation and party leaders professed to want something different from their presidents.

A great deal more than money was required to secure the presidential nomination. The futile campaign cost the Senator and his friends over a quarter of a million dollars, but he commented philosophically, "I've drilled dry holes that cost me a lot more . . . and had less fun."[159] A vast campaign treasury proved useless because the delegates at Chicago did not believe Kerr could win.

Senator Kerr's strategy of emerging as the compromise candidate of a deadlocked convention revealed an accurate and shrewd assessment of the state of the Democratic party in 1952. The Oklahoman realized the Democratic party was exhausted. At the end of a twenty-year winning streak, none of the established leaders seemed popular enough to win a presidential election. There was unspoken fear among the leadership that the party in 1952 was too fragile to survive a national free-for-all for the nomination. For the preceding generation the commanding figure of Franklin Delano Roosevelt and unifying events, like the response to the Depression and winning the war, had allowed the party to appear more cohesive that it actually was. The uncontested presidential nomination in 1948 had only seemed to test the strength of the coalition. Now there was no incumbent, no commanding figure, no great crisis. The Democratic party seemed ready to revert to its traditional collection of spokes in search of a wheel.

But Kerr erred when he tried to sell himself as a fresh face, a new figure, for he was unmistakably a political operator in the old tradition. All his support in the preconvention period came from the old guard in national and state party politics. He had been an exciting new personality in 1944 as he revitalized a war-weary party with his memorable keynote address, but in 1952 he was just another middle-aged senator.

Kerr's failure to achieve the nomination also revealed much about the changed nature of the presidency at the midpoint of the twentieth century. From the time of Theodore Roosevelt, the office had become progressively grand. Neither political party in 1952 would knowingly nominate the type of candidate who would remind them of a less sophisticated past. An uncouth, blunt man like Harry Truman probably would not have won the Democratic nomination had he not been an incumbent thrust into office by Roosevelt's death. Al Smith had been the exception for the Democrats, and his defeat reinforced this tendency. The Democratic party might cherish Jacksonian democracy, but in a presidential candidate it preferred Jeffersonian demeanor. Kerr was a kind of political fossil offering himself to a party unconsciously in search of a new kind of man.

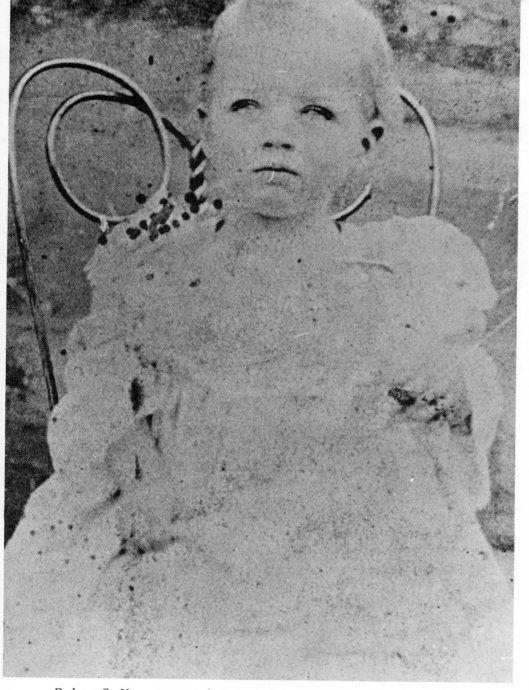

Robert S. Kerr as an infant in Indian Territory. Source: Kermac News.

William Samuel Kerr and Margaret Eloda Kerr, the Senator's parents. Source: Kermac News.

Robert S. Kerr,
Phi Delta.

Kerr as a collegeman with prophecy. From The Psagi, *1914*

The sophomore class at East Central Normal School in 1913. Kerr is fifth from the left, top row; "the giant of the class, liked by everyone," according to the yearbook. Source: Pontotoc County Historical and Genealogical Society, Ada, Oklahoma; used by permission.

Everybody knows Bob, but not everybody likes him. He knows this, but is not worried about it in the least. "Fair-minded men will differ on important questions," he says. He likes to fight, and this spirit is likely to lead him into politics. Once in, we venture that he will not stop before adding to his name M. C. or U. S. S.

ourtesy of East Central State University, Ada, Oklahoma.

*Kerr as an artilleryman in the U.S. Army in 1917. Source: Kermac
News.*

Kerr and his first wife, Reba Shelton, who died in childbirth in 1924. Source: Mrs. Estelle Dandridge, Ada, Oklahoma; used by permission.

M. O. Matthews, executive vice president of the Ideal Cement Company, with Kerr in the Ada law offices of Kerr, Lambert, Conn, and Roberts, about 1922. Source: Mrs. Warren B. Kice, Ada, Oklahoma; used by permission.

Kerr and his wife, Grayce Breene Kerr, whom he married in 1925.
Source: Kermac News.

Campaigning for Governor in 1942. Source: Kermac News.

Kerr as keynote speaker at the 1944 Democratic National Convention. Source: Robert S. Kerr Collection, University of Oklahoma.

Campaigning in 1948 with the Daughters of the Pioneers. Source: Robert S. Kerr Collection, University of Oklahoma.

Kerr compares colorful ties with Gene Autry, who helped in the 1948 senatorial campaign. Source: Robert S. Kerr Collection, University of Oklahoma.

Three members of the Class of '48: Lyndon B. Johnson (D., Tex.), Kerr, and Clinton P. Anderson (D., N.M.). Source: Robert S. Kerr Collection, University of Oklahoma.

Campaigning in the Nebraska presidential primary in 1952. Source: Robert S. Kerr Collection, University of Oklahoma.

Kerr congratulates Adlai Stevenson, the 1952 Democratic presidential nominee, as Lyndon Johnson looks on. Source: Robert S. Kerr Collection, University of Oklahoma.

Kerr, in a "feedsack blue" shirt and red galluses, campaigns in Tulsa for reelection in 1954. Source: Robert S. Kerr Collection, University of Oklahoma.

Senator Richard Russell (D., Ga.) and Kerr in one of their frequent discussions of legislative strategy. Source: Robert S. Kerr Collection, University of Oklahoma.

Kerr with his dog, Mr. Ling, in the Senator's Capitol Hill office.
Source: Robert S. Kerr Collection, University of Oklahoma.

The Kerr family: Breene, Kay, the Senator, Mrs. Kerr, Bill, Bob, Jr., and Robert S. Kerr, III with the family dog, Candy. Source: Robert S. Kerr Collection, University of Oklahoma.

Dean A. McGee presents Kerr with a lapel pen in 1956 commemorating the founding of Kerr-McGee Oil Industries, Inc. Source: Kermac News.

Lyndon Johnson and Speaker of the House Sam Rayburn (D. Tex.) join Kerr in celebrating the publication of his book, Land, Wood and Water *in 1960. Source: Kermac News.*

Oklahoma Democrats Carl Albert and A. S. "Mike" Monroney with Kerr. Source: Robert S. Kerr Collection, University of Oklahoma.

Kerr presides at a meeting of the Senate Aeronautical and Space Sciences Committee in 1961. Left to right: Clifford Case (R. N.J.), Margaret Chase Smith (R. Me.), Alexander Wiley (R. Wis.), Chairman Kerr, John Pastore (D. R.I.) and Stuart Symington (D. Mo.). Source: Robert S. Kerr Collection, University of Oklahoma.

Astronaut Gordon Cooper of Shawnee, Oklahoma with Kerr at Cape Canaveral in 1961. Source: Robert S. Kerr Collection, University of Oklahoma.

President Kennedy signing the legislation providing aid to dependent children in May, 1961. Kerr, HEW Secretary Abraham Ribicoff, Senator Harry Byrd (D. Va.) and Congressman Wilbur Mills (D. Ark.) look on. Source: Robert S. Kerr Collection, University of Oklahoma.

Kerr congratulates Senator Jennings Randolph (D. W. Va.) on his decisive vote against medicare in 1961. Source: Robert S. Kerr Collection, University of Oklahoma.

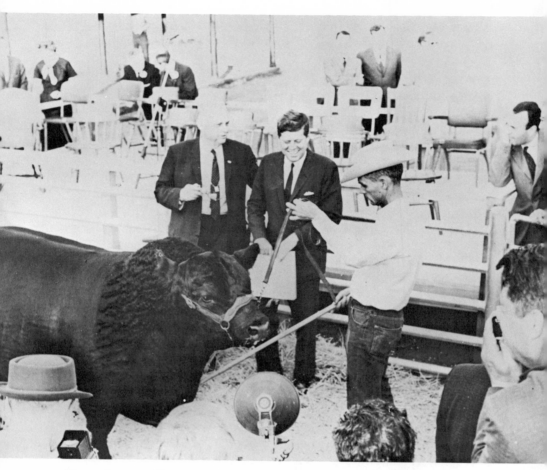

*Kerr shows off his prize bull to President Kennedy at the Kerr
ranch in Poteau in November, 1961. Source: Robert S. Kerr Collection, University of Oklahoma.*

CHAPTER VI
The Arkansas Project

Senator Kerr's defeat at Chicago in 1952 was, in Oklahoma parlance, "a trip to the party's woodshed." The whipping smarted but was not fatal. The effects, however, were significant and lasting. Clinton Anderson described Kerr after Chicago as a chastened individual. "He told me he would never again try for high public office because he knew where he stood with the people."[1] Kerr believed this humiliation was the price for "his courageous battle to protect the interests of Oklahoma and Oklahomans in the bitter fight over natural gas two years ago."[2] Unable to shed the stereotype of a parochial, special interest politician, Kerr now determined to exploit it.

When he returned to Washington for the opening of the Eighty-third Congress, he abandoned the flamboyant, headline-hunting tactics that had characterized his first four years in the Capitol. Within a year he faced a difficult reelection campaign. Roy Turner, his popular successor in the Oklahoma governor's office, planned to challenge him in the primary. To remain in national politics he must concentrate on Oklahoma problems.

At the first staff meeting of the new year, Kerr established new rules for everything from answering constituents' requests to accepting radio and television engagements. Matters of interest in Oklahoma were to have precedence. Oklahomans had to be reassured that "Big Bob Kerr" was on the job for them, twenty-four hours a day. When "Meet the Press" asked Kerr to appear in February to forecast the success of Eisenhower's legislative program, they were surprised to learn that the quotable Senator was not available. Other network radio and television shows received the same polite declination. Kerr was not sulking because of any real or imagined insults from the news media during the 1952 campaign. He had instructed Burl Hays to determine two crucial things before accepting any radio or television engagement: that the program would be broadcast in Oklahoma, and the subject should be of enough national importance or immediate interest to appeal to Sooners. Unless both conditions were satisfied, Kerr had no time to spare.[3]

This marked change in the Senator's political style was merely one part of a well-conceived new strategy. His goals were unchanged; his ambition for political power was unchecked; but his efforts were rechanneled. Denied the presidency, "he put more and more attention into becoming a power in the Senate—and in that field he succeeded mightily."[4]

This transformation from partisan heckler to elder statesman was a difficult and not altogether convincing one, but Kerr believed it was necessary. Eisenhower had carried Oklahoma in 1952 by over eighty-seven thousand votes, and Kerr's advisers cautioned him against endangering his tenuous, but crucial, support in Tulsa County by taking critical swipes at the popular President.[5] Besides helping his reelection, this conciliatory attitude was designed to produce a better working relationship with the Republicans who now controlled Congress. Even if the Democrats regained the majority in the next election, these new friendships would prove useful. Kerr was planning to fashion in Congress the kind of coalition he had in Oklahoma—a combination of rural and urban interests allied to promote industry and agriculture through mutual dependence on the development of natural resources, primarily water.

After two years on the Senate Public Works Committee, Kerr knew that every member of Congress wanted some favorite local public works project. These required federal money, and had to pass the gauntlet of the authorization-appropriations process. Kerr wanted to achieve enough seniority on the Public Works

Committee to pass on all requests for public improvements. With power to withhold or grant favors, he could influence any legislation he chose.

The Arkansas River Navigation Project was the key to this plan to acquire political power while bringing new prosperity to Oklahoma. Kerr's commitment to the Arkansas project was rooted in a genuine desire to reverse the trend of Oklahoma's declining population by attracting heavy industry and making the state's agricultural and mineral products more competitive through improved transportation facilities. As governor, Kerr had supported farm pond construction, and 66,700 ponds were built during his administration. He also became a national spokesman for conservation when he took the lead in mobilizing the effort to get legislation transferring World War II surplus machinery to soil conservation districts.[6] He had seen the tragedy of the dust bowl as a young man. In 1943, as governor, he witnessed a calamitous cycle of drought-flood-drought, which he later called "the flood of conviction."[7] For a week in early May torrential rains pelted eastern Oklahoma, washing out drought-withered crops, shearing off topsoil, digging deep ruts in the red earth, and sweeping away homes, bridges, livestock, and people. When the Arkansas River crested at Muskogee, its waters spilled out over a five hundred-mile area, destroying $31 million in property and taking twenty-six lives.[8]

At the height of the flooding, Don McBride worked late drafting a memo to Governor Kerr about the need for long-term planning to avert future disaster. He left the document at the mansion after midnight, and at eight the next morning Kerr was ready to act. McBride reminded the Governor that army engineers at Tulsa and Little Rock were studying the feasibility of a multi-purpose plan to develop the Arkansas basin to control floods and to provide navigation.[9] Kerr made an aerial tour of the area hardest hit by the flooding accompanied by Colonel Francis J. Wilson, the district engineer from the Tulsa office of the Corps of Engineers. While evacuation and disaster relief were being organized, Kerr moved to obtain the corps' commitment to develop the Arkansas basin. On May 22 he met with Major General Eugene Reybold, chief of the Army Corps of Engineers, at Muskogee. As they toured the flooded area, sloshing through the mud and talking to stunned and bewildered farmers, Kerr asked Reybold's help to implement the Arkansas plan. General Reybold was a natural ally. In 1938 as Southwest Division engineer, he had established a district office for the corps at Tulsa because of the intense local interest in water development.[10] The desolate scene alone was a persuasive argument, and Reybold, long committed to the multipurpose plan, agreed to act.[11]

When he returned to Oklahoma City, Kerr immediately summoned the state's two leading proponents of river development, Don McBride and Newton R. Graham. These men represented the dominant views in the complex "upstream versus downstream" debate over the nature of development. McBride, an engineer and head of the Oklahoma Planning and Resources Board, was sympathetic with the Department of Agriculture's approach of building small dams to improve the watershed and assist in soil conservation. Graham, a Tulsa newspaperman turned banker, also a member of the Planning and Resources Board, was a nationally known advocate of large downstream projects for flood control, power generation, and navigation. His dream of restoring water transportation on the Arkansas had earned him the title "Admiral of the Arkansas."[12]

Kerr consulted McBride and Graham in a deliberate effort to harmonize their divergent views and channel their expertise and enthusiasm into helping him secure federal funds for development. McBride, the technician, and Graham, the strategist, were a formidable combination. Both men knew the importance of a committed political advocate and quickly recognized this as an opportunity to achieve the goals of both groups. But Kerr saw much more. He remarked that he was amazed at the political potential in the project. "Here was a ready made issue which no one in politics was using."[13] He determined to make it his exclusively.

To the untrained eye the Arkansas River "looked like a vast sandbed . . . a scar on the face of our State. . . ,"[14] but the proposal to develop the Arkansas basin was not as fanciful as it seemed.

During most of the nineteenth century the Arkansas River had been the main highway of the Indian Territory. In the steamboat's heyday, $5 million worth of merchandise had been shipped into Oklahoma river towns. As late as 1870, steam packets from the Mississippi carried men and livestock to the flourishing cattle industry in Kansas.[15] During World II, Governor Kerr had seen tremendous industrial expansion follow the route of the inland waterways in the Midwest and the Northeast. He was eager for Oklahoma's coal, oil, zinc, and lead to share in the benefits of low-cost transportation. History and geography had penalized Oklahoma long enough. "We are willing to pay our part in Federal taxes, but we cannot forget that the Arkansas is the last of the great tributaries of the Mississippi to gain improvements for navigation."[16] Recognizing the need for co-operation with Arkansas, Kerr and Governor Ben Laney formed the Arkansas-Oklahoma Interstate Water Resources Committee late in 1943 with the dual function of building local support and lobbying in Congress.[17]

The war had suspended Corps of Engineers' civilian projects, and the new interstate committee used the delay to strengthen its case for the economic benefits from developing the Arkansas. When the corps's Board of Engineers for Rivers and Harbors called a public hearing in May 1945 to evaluate including the Arkansas plan in their postwar building program, the committee was ready. Their study showed that with only minor changes in the corps's original plan, the economic benefits would exceed construction costs. Graham testified that the public benefits would be $1.97 for each dollar invested.[18]

Despite the favorable hearings, the board failed to recommend any action. By late summer, Graham and McBride were alarmed that General Reybold, who favored the project, would retire before the board reported. If that happened, they would have to start all over in winning the new chief's endorsement. Kerr, Senator Elmer Thomas, Graham, and McBride asked Reybold to prod the board, but the General declined.[19] The group decided to appeal directly to the President. McBride argued that in the case of the Missouri basin, there had been disapprovals until President Truman took a personal interest. He urged Kerr to ask Truman to intervene with General Reybold with a request that the Arkansas plan be included in the corps's postwar program.[20]

The Governor, McBride, and Graham saw Truman on August 17, and the President agreed to write General Reybold requesting an early report.[21] On September 11 the board issued a report of partial approval. They recommended that the navigation features be deferred for several years.[22] In response to the President's letter General Reybold overruled the tenuous action and wrote an extremely favorable recommendation.[23] To assure the General of the wisdom of his action, Kerr predicted that the "Reybold Plan" to develop the Arkansas "forecasts prosperity and happiness for our people."[24]

The Governor now was impatient to begin. He met with Truman again on March 25, 1946, to discuss strategy for the upcoming rivers and harbors bill in Congress. Truman asked for a memo on what action was necessary, and Kerr promptly outlined the steps.[25] He asked the President's aid "in expediting the report with the Bureau of the Budget." He also suggested that Truman "request Congressman Mansfield, Chairman of the Rivers and Harbors Committee, to include the Arkansas River Report in a Rivers and Harbors bill this session of the Congress."[26]

The House committee set aside May 8–9 to hear the case for the Arkansas, but there was still no word from the Bureau of the Budget. So on May 10, Kerr was back in the Oval Office pleading his case.[27] Four days later, the hearings completed, he was still badgering the President. "The House members are awaiting an indication from you that you are going forward with this one."[28] He reiterated that the BOB's approval of the corps report would be "the greenlight for a rivers bill."[29] Finally, just a few days before the scheduled House debate, all the pieces fell into place.[30]

But there was a surprise in the House debate. Oklahoma City Congressman Mike Monroney proposed to strike the $55 million authorized for the Eufaula dam, an essential part of the Arkansas plan.[31] Kerr knew that Monroney was cool to the navigation aspects of the plan, but he never thought the Congressman would publicly defy the rest of the delegation. Monroney opposed the authorization on the ground that it committed Congress to a $435 million project to canalize the whole Arkansas River—a proposal he considered of dubious value and requiring more study. He suggested sarcastically that nine out of ten Oklahomans would be willing to appropriate money to pave the Arkansas River but not to canalize it.[32] The project's supporters denied that the Eufaula authorization committed the House to any more than the stated $55 million, and Monroney's motion failed 42–99.[33]

Under McClellan's (D., Ark.) skillful questioning, Governor Kerr easily won the Senate Commerce Committee's approval of his request to increase the House authorization to $150 million.[34] The Senate quickly approved the bill on July 5.[35] The large sum had been accepted in conference when, to the horror of the Arkansas-Oklahoma delegations, the House voted to recommit the conference report with specific instructions to delete the Senate increase for the Arkansas project and to hold the original House figure of $55 million. Although Congressman Monroney did not participate in the debate to recommit, he apparently convinced George A. Dondero, then the ranking Republican on the House Rivers and Harbors Committee, to move for recommittal. Dondero argued that the House conferees had agreed to the Senate figure by the margin of only one vote. He also claimed that the conference report violated the committee's informal decision to hold rivers and harbors authorizations to $500 million in the interest of economy.[36] The bill went back to conference, the Senate conferees acceded to the House figure, and the bill finally passed.[37] Although $55 million did not seem like an auspicious beginning, the Eufaula reservoir was the pivotal project in the navigation program. The 1946 Rivers and Harbors Act was the first step in constructing the nine-foot navigation channel from the Mississippi up the Arkansas and Verdigris rivers to the port of Catoosa, Oklahoma, fifteen miles east of Tulsa.

But there were still serious obstacles. Newton Graham considered Monroney "our greatest local problem." He won Kerr's approval "to conduct a quiet campaign in the Eufaula area and downstream organizing the people . . . to appear before the Congressional Committees in support of this request for funds."[38]

The long-term problem of securing continuous authorizations and appropriations for each part of the project convinced Kerr that Elmer Thomas needed help in the Senate. While he had been planning to run in 1948 when Republican Senator E. H. Moore's term expired, his increasing concern for the Arkansas project confirmed the timetable. Kerr was impressed with Thomas' influence over public works spending because of his position as chairman of the Appropriations Subcommittee for the Army, which funded rivers and harbors legislation on Appropriations. But he also saw the need for an Oklahoman on the Public Works Committee to shepherd the Arkansas plan through the authorizations process and to be in on the crucial conference stage. He planned to fight Monroney where it really mattered.

Kerr was also aware of the political problems facing the Arkansas project in Oklahoma. Most Sooners agreed that some kind of river basin development was desirable; but western Oklahomans were concerned with water scarcity, soil conservation, and irrigation, while eastern Oklahomans wanted flood protection and navigation facilities. Kerr had to unite these groups through their mutual interest in water. When he retired from the governor's office in 1947, he immediately plunged into an unofficial campaign for the Senate race in 1948. Since Congress traditionally considered rivers and harbors legislation only in election years, he was free to concentrate on Oklahoma matters. Oklahoma City was the immediate problem. E. K. Gaylord, Sr., influential publisher of the *Daily Oklahoman* and the *Oklahoma City Times*, was skeptical of the Tulsa planners' dreams. A persistent critic of valley authority development, Gaylord denounced the navigation project as bad fiscal policy.[39] Graham believed that Gaylord was the inspiration for Monroney's attempt to defeat the 1946 Eufaula authorization.[40] Kerr knew he must convince Oklahoma City civic leaders that they had as much to gain from supporting the project as did their Tulsa rivals. He persuaded the Chamber of Commerce to host a special meeting to interest city leaders in navigation. Graham spoke to the groups. "It took but little effort to show that they had stood largely by because they feared navigation to Tulsa and thereby let the development of possible water resources of central

and western Oklahoma fall far behind those of eastern Oklahoma."[41] The Oklahoma City group agreed to cooperate and
raised $20,000 to help with public education and lobbying
expenses.[42]

Although he concentrated on the election campaign in Oklahoma, Kerr did not neglect Washington. In the fall of 1946, Don
McBride resigned from the Planning and Resources Board to become the secretary-manager of the Washington-based National
Reclamation Association. Graham kept him advised of developments in the state.[43] In Washington, McBride arranged schedules
for Kerr's almost monthly visits and accompanied him to conferences with officials at the Interior Department, Bureau of Reclamation and Soil Conservation Service, and Corps of Engineers.[44]
Graham concentrated on strengthening his alliance with Fort
Smith editor, Clarence Byrns, who advised the Arkansas Senators
on water resource matters.[45]

Kerr won election to the Senate in 1948. He "talked nothing
but land and water and his opponents never had a chance."[46]
Graham and McBride urged the new Senator to seek a position on
the Public Works Committee, and, although Kerr preferred the
prestige of Appropriations or Finance, he followed their advice.[47]
Graham convinced the Senator that his chances of becoming a
chairman quickly were greater on Public Works, because "others
who are ahead in line indicate they desire other assignments."[48]
Senator Thomas was a power on Appropriations, but no part of
the Arkansas project could be funded until it was authorized, so
the Public Works Committee would be crucial to the project's
success.

A few days after he was sworn in, Kerr gave a luncheon for
the Oklahoma delegation where he presented a series of maps
and detailed plans concerning Arkansas navigation. He outlined a
strategy for securing the money and asked the delegation to join
the undertaking. As they walked back to the House after lunch,
Congressman Tom Steed (D., Okla.) commented to Carl Albert
that they had been in the presence of "a genius or a mad man."[49]

During his first term Kerr had difficulty obtaining funds for
the river project. The Korean War curtailed Corps of Engineers'

civilian projects, and later the Eisenhower Administration's emphasis on budget cutting starved the Arkansas plan. But Kerr accomplished two things which helped speed the project when his own seniority and relations with the Eisenhower Administration permitted.

The first achievement was to secure the establishment of a federal interagency study commission, the Arkansas-White-Red Basin Inter-Agency Committee (AWRBIAC) to prepare a comprehensive plan for multipurpose river development. The idea for this committee grew out of difficulties McBride and Graham had in trying to work with representatives of the Soil Conservation Service, Bureau of Reclamation, and Corps of Engineers. McBride actually drafted the essential part of the bill in October 1948, prior to Kerr's election. The original proposal included only the Arkansas and Red rivers, but Kerr added the White River because of its potential for extensive hydroelectric power development. The profits from these power projects would be useful in establishing a favorable cost/benefit ratio for more expensive watershed developments elsewhere in the three basins.[50]

The committee was designed to resolve conflicts among the various federal agencies responsible for water development, interstate disputes, federal-state disagreements, and clashes between advocates of "big dams" versus "little dams." "Kerr felt that by getting all the combatants involved and working together . . . his chances of getting Arkansas projects authorized and funded would be greater."[51]

The merit of this approach, which had been used successfully in the Missouri basin, was that the ratio of costs and benefits was computed basinwide, not for each individual project. Expensive irrigation works in western Kansas and Oklahoma could be justified because of the excess economic benefits from navigation in eastern Oklahoma, Arkansas, and Louisiana. Kerr also favored the basin concept because it broadened the political support in Congress.[52] The interagency committee affected eight states— one-sixth of the Senate and fifty-five members of the House.

Before introducing this proposal in the Senate, Kerr made certain he had Speaker Rayburn's backing in the House.[53] Rayburn also agreed to intercede with William M. Whittington (D., Miss.), the chairman of the House Public Works Committee.[54]

Despite the care to ensure support for the bill before the hearings and the Senator's insistence on broadening the study committee to encompass wider political support, the intended allies ambushed the proposal. The major opponents, Senators Long (D., La.) and McClellan and Chairman Whittington were united against any policy or administrative device which threatened the supremacy of the Corps of Engineers in water matters. Russell Long and other witnesses from the Red River basin feared that the "ace economists in the House Appropriations Committee" would use the study committee as an excuse to withhold further appropriations for flood projects in their area.[55] The army engineers had already constructed projects worth millions in the lower Arkansas, White, and Red river basins, and Congress had authorized an additional $2 billion in civil works there awaiting construction.[56] Lower basin pressure groups were satisfied with the corps's program and were unwilling to risk sharing their political influence and funds.

Senator McClellan's opposition to the Kerr plan was only a little less transparent. The Arkansan was concurrently the third-ranking Democrat on the Senate Public Works Committee, a member of the Appropriations Committee, and president of the powerful National Rivers and Harbors Congress.[57] A staunch ally of the Corps of Engineers, the Rivers and Harbors Congress saw Kerr's proposal as threatening the "efficient system that we have built up and . . . transferring . . . the functions to less competent, less experienced hands."[58] McClellan was adamant in his support of the Corps of Engineers. As a member of the Hoover Commission, he had made an impassioned defense against the recommendation to transfer the corps's public works functions to the Department of the Interior.[59] McClellan's main interest was in flood control in the lower Arkansas valley, projects which the corps was planning to build. He refused to back Kerr's proposal for a resource inventory unless the status of authorized projects was guaranteed and the army engineers retained the dominant agency position.[60]

Chairman Whittington was "a great admirer of the Corps of Engineers because of the work they had done in the lower Mississippi River and . . . perfectly willing to favor them . . . to keep them happy."[61] He was also vice-president of the National Rivers and Harbors Congress. On July 6, 1949, Whittington reported the rivers and harbors authorization bill with no hint that Kerr's study proposal had even been considered.[62] But the bill did contain authorizations of over $70 million dollars for corps projects along the Arkansas River.[63]

The Senate Public Works Committee included the Kerr plan, with several modifications, in its report on H.R. 5472. Elmer Staats, assistant director of the BOB, suggested most of the changes which he said would make the proposal acceptable to the President.[64] The Senate committee also added another $19 million for the Arkansas River projects, bringing the total that year to $89 million. The Senate approved the authorization section of the omnibus bill but withheld action on the rest until the following session.[65]

The following April, despite protests from Paul Douglas that "the potential sound of the steamboat whistle was taking away the sanity of men," the Senate passed H.R. 5472 with no further discussion of Kerr's study commission.[66] But the conferees, who included McClellan and Whittington, modified the proposal to ensure that the corps directed and dominated the interagency effort. They also added a provision to protect existing projects. The conference version scarcely resembled Kerr's original proposal, but he did not challenge the drastic changes. He voted for the bill, as did all the other senators from the affected region, except Schoeppel of Kansas.[67]

Although his basin study proposal had "practically been vetoed by the Corps,"[68] Kerr, as usual, had prepared an alternate strategy. The following day, Don McBride delivered a letter from Kerr to the President to Elmer Staats' office.[69] Kerr reminded Truman of his endorsement of a similar study commission for New England in a February 9, 1950, letter to Vice-President Alben Barkley. He asked the President to establish an interagency commission by executive order, along the lines of the Senate version in H.R. 5472, which had incorporated the executive branch's desired changes. Two weeks later the President instructed the department and agencies concerned to comply, and on June 12, 1950, the Federal Inter-Agency River Basin Committee created the Arkansas-White-Red Basin Inter-Agency Committee.[70] In a maneuver to appease the corps, the President suggested that the Department of the Army chair the study. In a little more than a month, Kerr had the study commission that Congress had for a year tried to deny him. The President's quick response to Kerr's request suggested that at the first hint of real trouble with the corps's supporters in Congress, Kerr and McBride had worked out an alternate route through the executive branch with Elmer Staats' help.[71] Kerr's appeal to the President was a clear signal to Congress and the Corps of Engineers that the Oklahoman was prepared to do whatever was necessary to further his scheme of developing the Arkansas.

Senator Kerr's success in obtaining the interagency study commission through executive order was not an intentional challenge to the traditional dominance of Congress and the Corps of Engineers in water resources programs, although it appeared that way to some. Since the early 1940's, Presidents Roosevelt and Truman had tried to break down that special Corps-Congress relationship which resulted in a patchwork of individual projects. The only semblance of planning was the striking coincidence of corps activity in the constituency of powerful members of the Appropriations and Public Works Committees. Executive branch attempts to impose a TVA-type of arrangement on the Arkansas valley repeatedly failed because Congress would not tolerate any interference in its direct relationship with the army engineers. President Truman probably embraced Kerr's proposal because it gave him more power over the executive agencies dealing with water. But Senator Kerr was interested in the policy-making arrangement only as a means to further the project.[72]

Kerr was ready to defend the corps position if it accelerated the Arkansas project. The Flood Control Act of 1948 had authorized the construction of three dams in northeastern Oklahoma, primarily designed for silt and flood control. The corps wanted to substitute one large dam near Keystone, Oklahoma, but had been unsuccessful against the combined efforts of the Soil Conservation Service, the private utilities, and the railroads. McBride and Graham were convinced that the corps's approach would accelerate the Arkansas project and improve the crucial cost/benefit ratio for the entire project. The potential for hydroelectric power production and city and industrial water storage in the Keystone reservoir made the larger dam economically attractive.[73] Kerr's testimony, prepared in consultation with the corps, was largely instrumental in the decision to build a single dam.[74] This decision to back the corps helped smooth ruffled feelings among the corps' supporters in Congress and probably saved millions of dollars and several years of construction time on the Arkansas River project.

The outbreak of the Korean War virtually suspended all work on the river project as the corps shifted to military construction. In Oklahoma, the project received another blow when veteran Senator Elmer Thomas lost the Democratic nomination to Congressman Mike Monroney. Thomas' defeat was a double misfortune because of his seniority on the Senate Appropriations Committee. Although Monroney stressed his opposition to the river project during his campaign against Thomas, Newton Graham hoped he would modify his position after he saw how Thomas gained in the primary runoff in eastern Oklahoma.[75] But the Oklahoma City Congressman had a well-established reputation for independence stemming from his efforts in the House to defeat a measure to increase the price of oil, which many of his own constituents favored.[76]

The reasons for Monroney's opposition were complex. The rivalry between Oklahoma City and Tulsa probably influenced him, as did the editorial stance of the Oklahoma City newspapers.[77] Some Arkansas enthusiasts believed he wanted to cut the Corps of Engineers' spending in eastern Oklahoma to obtain more funds for the Soil Conservation Service in western Oklahoma.[78] Graham, who was often unreasonably distraught over Monroney's failure to co-operate, even hinted darkly that Monroney was in league with congressmen from the "older sections of the North and East to oppose the plan for the Arkansas and thus refuse to help build an area which will compete for [their] industries and people."[79] There were also rumors that Monroney had received large contributions in 1950 from stripper oil well owners who feared that Oologah dam waters would inundate their wells before all the oil was recovered.[80]

If Kerr doubted Monroney's sincerity in opposing navigation on the grounds that it was too costly, he never said so publicly. His strategy was to obtain Monroney's public support and vote for certain aspects of the river project, such as bank stabilization to protect farmland, without compromising his opposition to navigation.[81] Working through Graham, Kerr also obtained an agreement with Sinclair Oil Company for a depletion schedule to allow full recovery of the oil the Oologah's waters threatened.[82]

By 1952 when Monroney still had not relented, Kerr decided on stronger measures. Don McBride complained to Graham, "We do not think it appropriate for the junior Senator to oppose the development of Oklahoma's water resources." He implied that the senior Senator would appreciate help from his friends in eastern Oklahoma, "to bring Monroney around."[83] This was the signal Graham had been waiting for. He quickly outlined a strategy. "Arrange key men who, when a flood comes to the Verdigris, will get all the folks aroused and demand that Mike come down and get his feet wet too."[84]

Unfortunately, the weather did not co-operate. The prolonged drought in the Southwest paralleled the drought in appropriations for the Arkansas. Without a flood, the river advocates had to try a different kind of persuasion. Graham wanted to put political pressure on the junior Senator. "Monroney does not care for economics. He looks to votes and is only impressed by organized votes."[85] With financial backing from the ABDA, Graham organized a letter-writing campaign of prominent citizens urging Monroney to join the rest of the delegation in working for the Arkansas project.[86]

But Kerr grew tired of coddling Monroney. In 1955, as the new chairman of the Public Works Committee's Subcommittee on

Rivers and Harbors and Flood Control and with a Democratic majority restored to the Congress, Kerr was impatient to move ahead. Don McBride wrote to Newton Graham that Kerr was convinced that "if the right person would sit down and talk to Senator Monroney, without having a crowd . . . Mike would still come around."[87] He suggested two names. Graham chose Joe Jarboe, a prominent businessman and rancher, who supported river development. Jarboe had managed Monroney's 1950 campaign in eastern Oklahoma. At the suggestion of the Tulsa banker, Verser Hicks, Jarboe agreed to fly to Washington to discuss the political realities with Monroney.[88] Jarboe told the junior Senator that his continued opposition to the Arkansas would lead to a gigantic and well-financed effort to unseat him in 1956. Up to this point the Kerr people and the Arkansas supporters had carefully chosen tactics that did not imply force. But even the stubborn and independent-minded Monroney understood that with growing state and national prestige, Kerr would not hesitate to crush him.

On May 10 Monroney capitulated. He sent a telegram to Jarboe, who was attending a Tulsa Chamber of Commerce meeting with representatives of area towns to plan their appearance at the May 16 House Appropriations Subcommittee hearings. Monroney agreed to testify in favor of funds for the Oologah project.[89] In his statement to the subcommittee, Monroney admitted he had changed his mind. He claimed that the inclusion of water-storage facilities to complement flood-control features was decisive. He did not mention the word "navigation," although everyone present knew the Oologah dam was crucial to the plan to bring barges from the Arkansas up the Verdigris River to Catoosa, Oklahoma. But Kerr was satisfied. While Monroney was not ready to work for navigation, at least he had stopped talking against it.[90]

Monroney's nonconformity was worrisome to Kerr, but he was not essential to the project's success, as was Arkansas' John McClellan. A senior member of the Senate Appropriations Committee, his importance was magnified when Elmer Thomas failed to win renomination.[91] McClellan had been cool to Kerr's interagency study commission; but, once assured that the corps' position would not be challenged, he co-operated fully.[92] With the reduction in federal funds available for river development during the Korean War, stiff opposition to the Arkansas plan developed among congressmen who lived on other rivers which had been under development for a longer time. There was a 50 per cent reduction in appropriations for river development on the Arkansas in 1950–51 as against a 25 per cent reduction nationally. Newton Graham warned the members of the ABDA, "It is not a matter of economy nor is it a matter of partisanship."[93] The need for concerted action within the Arkansas basin congressional delegations was now imperative. Briefly in late 1950, Kerr had feared that McClellan and Arkansas' Governor Sidney McMath would abandon the basinwide program in an effort to get whatever funds they could for projects within their state. Kerr learned that the Bear State delegation planned to ask Truman for appropriations to begin construction on the Dardanelle dam on the main stream of the Arkansas. McClellan believed the construction would be justified as necessary for the war effort because of the dam's potential to produce hydroelectric power.[94] Kerr had agreed the previous year to do all he could to help with the Dardanelle project, an integral part of the navigation plan. But he knew the Corps of Engineers would not agree to close a dam at Dardanelle until Keystone and Eufaula were completed as there was no silt-storage space in Dardanelle and the reservoir would quickly choke up.[95] Now Kerr feared that the war atmosphere would result in a desperate "every man for himself" grab for funds that would destroy years of work on the basin plan. He also sensed that the slightest hint of disunity within the Arkansas basin forces in Congress would shatter their fragile but growing bargaining strength. McBride appealed to Graham for help. The Tulsan called Clarence Byrns, who agreed "to tell McClellan that Dardanelle is out until Keystone and Eufaula are completed and to get him to work toward that goal."[96] In April, Graham and Byrns traveled to Washington, where they convinced the Arkansas delegation to follow Kerr's lead.[97] It would have been unwise, if not impossible, for Kerr to conduct these negotiations. The Arkansas Senators were senior to him, and he knew that every member of both delegations was more likely to respond to local pleas, which they felt was their proper representative role. Such a request from a junior member might arouse fears that he was exploiting them to further his own reputation.

Although the Oklahoma, Arkansas, and Kansas congressional delegations were solidly behind the river plan by 1952, the project stalled. McBride despaired of any progress until the Democrats returned to power. "With these lousy Republicans in office there is no chance of getting any appropriations for construction . . . in the Arkansas River."[98] A new approach to water policy in the Eisenhower Administration, the President's concern with budget cutting, and a Republican Congress combined to smother the Arkansas project. Eisenhower's emphasis on reducing federal activity in water development and hydroelectric power generation in favor of a "partnership" arrangement with state and local communities and private concerns sharing the cost meant that projects which emphasized expensive flood-control and navigation features would have to attract massive local funding to survive.[99] In the Arkansas basin, which had been losing population since the thirties and needed water development to stimulate diversified industrial growth, that kind of local money was simply not available. And the lack of emphasis on the production of hydroelectric power in the Arkansas plan also discouraged potential private investment.

The administration's "no new starts" policy, an attempt at balancing the federal budget, also penalized the project.[100] Then another economically inspired move threatened to undermine the whole basis of the project. In early 1954 the administration announced that all executive agencies involved in water matters would adhere strictly to uniform criteria for making cost allocations and evaluations of proposed multipurpose projects. The criteria, the so-called Bureau of the Budget Circular A-47, were formulated in the last days of the Truman Administration.[101] The standards were so restrictive that many in Congress and the executive agencies believed that large numbers of worthwhile projects would be eliminated. This action was, of course, another presidential attempt to weaken the special relationship between the Appropriations and Public Works committees in Congress and the agencies concerned with water. Eisenhower was using a budgetary weapon where Roosevelt and Truman had tried to alter administrative arrangements, but the effect was the same. Inevitably, Congress would have to confront the President to resolve the issue.

In 1955 Kerr began preparing for that confrontation. His reelection in 1954 elevated him to ranking Democrat on the Public Works Committee and chairman of the Subcommittee on Rivers, Harbors and Flood Control, where he had final say over what projects were authorized. The subcommittee chairmanship also entitled him to an *ex-officio* seat on the Appropriations Subcommittee on Public Works, which funded Army Corps of Engineers civil projects.[102] The Senate rules permitted an *ex-officio* member the same right to speak and vote as any full member. Traditionally, *ex-officio* members were not as influential as regular members of Appropriations, but Kerr quickly became an exception.[103] Although some regular members of Appropriations "resented his forays and his acid tongue," few tangled with Kerr.[104] *Ex-officio* status also entitled the Oklahoman to participate in the all-important conference committee sessions where final critical decisions were made. Kerr announced to his constituents that he would use the new positions on Public Works and Appropriations "to obtain roads, soil, water, and other public works projects needed in Oklahoma."[105]

This was precisely the route to power Kerr had envisioned in 1949. When the Democratic leadership refused his original request for a seat on Appropriations, Kerr settled down on Public Works to serve a patient and productive apprenticeship.[106] After an initial losing bout with the army engineers over the interagency study committee, the Oklahoman changed tactics. He began to cultivate the Corps of Engineers. As low-ranking member of the Subcommittee on Rivers and Harbors, Kerr adopted the full committee's traditional protective attitude toward the corps. As subcommittee chairman, Kerr made friends at every level of the army engineers. He secured invitations for them to speak at local functions, held appreciation dinners in their honor, and repeated public praise of their accomplishments. He used his position with the

Public Works Committee to favor the corps over other agencies and to shield it from a certain amount of executive control.[107]

In his efforts to win the corps's support, Kerr did not neglect other people whose allegiance could facilitate his plan. In 1954 he invited Kenneth Bousquet, professional staff assistant to Senator Allen Ellender (D., La.) on the Appropriations Subcommittee on Public Works, to tour eastern Oklahoma. During that trip Bousquet met local river advocates such as Graham and members of the Arkansas Basin Development Association. He was impressed with the breadth of local support and convinced that development in the Arkansas, White, and Red river basins would benefit the whole country through dispersing industrial growth and helping to reverse the downward population trend in Oklahoma and Arkansas.[108]

In 1955 Graham urged Kerr to use his new position "to exercise great power for good," which meant to push the corps to implement the Arkansas plan. "They [the corps] know their master's voice and heed it."[109] He suspected that the Chief of Engineer's decision in 1954 to reclassify the Arkansas plan as "deferred for further study" was politically motivated.[110] Within a few months of Kerr's becoming the subcommittee chairman, the Arkansas project was restored to active status.[111] Kerr credited the interagency committee's report, which was completed in 1955, with convincing the corps to reactivate the Arkansas plan.[112] While it was useful in providing data to justify the economic benefits of river development, Kerr's prominence on the Public Works Committee was primarily responsible "for restoring the Arkansas to the living."[113]

The most significant harbinger of success for the Arkansas project was the return of a Democratic majority to the Congress in 1955.[114] The swing back to the Democrats did not forecast a major change in national mood or policies. But the southern conservatives who dominated the Democratic party in Congress were in power again—good news for Kerr and the plan to navigate the Arkansas.

In his January 17 budget, Eisenhower requested funds for thirty-nine new starts for water development.[115] Most of these were relatively small projects without hydroelectric features. They all emphasized the administration's goal of establishing partnerships in which local interests assumed a large part of the cost. The new budget included funds for ongoing flood-control projects by the Corps of Engineers in the Tulsa Conservation District. Despite this decision to reactivate the Arkansas plan, there was no money in the budget for dams at Oologah, Keystone, or Eufaula. These projects were vital to the multipurpose development scheme, and Kerr decided to use them to test the government's commitment to the navigation project.

His strategy was to have the money included as an amendment to the Public Works Appropriation bill, H.R. 6766, during Senate hearings and then fight to keep the money in conference. An experience in 1951 illustrated the merits of this approach. Because of serious floods in the Mississippi-Missouri river system earlier that year, President Truman asked Congress for additional money for flood control. The House had already acted, so the request was added in the Senate.[116] In floor debate, Senator Monroney tried to have the supplemental funds for the Oologah dam deleted, but Kerr defeated him, only to see the provision eliminated in conference.[117] The House conferees were in an economy mood,[118] and Representative Clarence Cannon, chairman of House Appropriations and the conference committee, permitted no item originating in the Senate to stay in the bill unless it was in the state or district of one of the conferees. "When Kerr learned what happened, he knew he had to get on that committee."[119] In 1955 he was in position.

Events on the House side were somewhat more dramatic than in the Senate. The House Appropriations Committee report on H.R. 6766 followed the President's requests and included no funds for construction on any of the key Arkansas River dams. At Chairman Cannon's insistence, the committee had made so many cuts in river projects in all parts of the country that a minor revolt was brewing for the floor debate.[120] Muskogee Democrat Ed Edmondson sensed an opportunity to act but hesitated to ask for funds for the Arkansas, fearing an adverse floor vote which would prevent the House conferees from accepting the same item as a Senate

amendment. Kerr saw the situation as an opportunity to trade
Oklahoma's House votes to help other dissident delegations restore
funds for their public works projects. He suggested a co-operative
alliance between the Oklahoma and Arkansas House members.
Edmondson's amendment "restoring" $450,000 each for construc-
tion of the Eufaula reservoir and the Dardanelle dam passed after
a bitter debate.[121] Other delegations imitated the Oklahoma-
Arkansas strategy, and, as a result, the House-passed version of
the bill contained $86,376,558 more than the committee had
authorized.[122] The Senate was no problem. "Competing against
time and many other projects, we persuaded the Senate Appropriations Public Works Subcommittee to concur with the House on
Eufaula [and the Dardanelle dam] and to add to the House list,
Markham Ferry, Keystone and Oologah dams."[123] There was one
minor, but significant, incident during the Senate debate which
revealed the Senate power structure's rapid and complete acceptance of Kerr's preeminence in river, harbor, and flood control
matters. Senator Fulbright proposed a floor amendment to increase
the appropriation for the Dardanelle dam to $1 million.[124] But Al-
len Ellender, the peppery chairman of the Appropriations Subcommittee on Public Works, slapped it down.[125] Ellender was not
reprimanding Fulbright for being greedy, but reminding him that
any bargaining on these matters would take place properly between the chairman of the Appropriations Subcommittee and the
chairman of the authorizing subcommittee, not on the Senate
floor.

With Kerr on the conference committee, the money for construction starts on the Arkansas was safe. He did agree to a reduction in planning funds for the Keystone to give the appearance of
accommodation and compromise. Ellender remarked that Kerr
was at his very best in the informal give and take of a conference
committee.[126] Kerr had never been modest about his accomplishments, but he was particularly anxious that Oklahomans clearly
understand his role in the 1955 appropriations. In his newsletter,
"Senator Kerr Says," and in a letter to Colonel Francis J. Wilson of
the Arkansas Basin Development Association, he denied that he
was the *sole* reason for the appropriations, but "of course, it was

fortunate that I was a member of the Committee of Congress which considered the appropriations, and also that I was a member of the conference committee, where I could keep the money in the bill."[127]

President Eisenhower reluctantly signed the bill although it contained $1.5 billion for 107 projects not in his original budget. He specifically objected to new construction funds for the Arkansas, which he felt committed the government to millions more to finish the project.[128] A long-range commitment was exactly what Kerr had in mind. Although the Senator seemed jubilant as he hailed 1955 as "the finest year of progress in the long struggle to develop Oklahoma's soil and water resources," he was less sanguine in private.[129] He cautioned Graham that local supporters might drift away since "the fight to start the dams is finished." Kerr realized that the administration was sincere in its attempts to curtail federal spending on public works as a way to balance the budget. He anticipated that the President would use administrative strictures to retard new construction starts and predicted "the fight to finish the dams just started."[130] His worst suspicions soon became reality. Although there was no actual impoundment of funds, budgetary regulations, cumbersome administrative procedures in the Corps of Engineers, and technical aspects of awarding federal contracts delayed the release of appropriated funds.[131]

In the late summer of 1955 there was widespread flooding in several northeastern states. The *New York Times*, which often viewed western flood-control projects as "pork barrel," declared that flood protection in the northeastern and middle Atlantic states was "grossly inadequate."[132] On January 12, 1956, the Eisenhower Administration responded with a request for supplemental money to start five new flood-control projects and to complete the planning for seventeen more. Four days later in the annual budget message, the President requested construction money for the seventeen projects. He did not request funds to continue work on Eufaula and Dardanelle.[133]

The President's announcement that Oklahoma's development would be delayed in favor of the northeastern states stung Kerr. He saw the supplemental appropriation outside the regular budget as a Republican ruse to favor the Northeast.[134] Eisenhower was pushing Oklahoma aside "to help political favorites in 1956, after they had been opposed to any water program anywhere, until the recent floods . . . put them on the hook. . . ."[135] The Oklahoman vowed "to fight every inch of the way" to see that the Arkansas was funded equitably with projects in other regions.[136] This was no idle threat. If Kerr failed to get appropriations for the Arkansas, he would use his Public Works Subcommittee to bottle up authorizations for other public works projects.[137]

Despite the blast at Eisenhower, Kerr feared that the major problem with getting funds for the Arkansas might be the attitude of the Corps of Engineers. High officials in the corps had been cool toward the navigation project in the Truman Administration, and Kerr feared that their failure to request funds in the 1957 budget indicated a continued lack of interest.[138] He decided to find out why.

He asked Allen Ellender for help in the spring appropriation hearings.[139] At the hearings in April, Kerr and Ellender probed the executive branch's decision-making process attempting to locate responsibility for the "unfair" treatment of the Arkansas project. An exchange between Kerr and General Itschner, chief of Army Engineers, revealed that the Bureau of the Budget was the culprit. Itschner explained that BOB placed a "limitation of $275 million . . . as being the *total cost when completed*, of all the new starts that they would permit us to incorporate within our fiscal year 1957 budget." The corps needed a minimum of $1.5 million to begin on the Keystone dam, so in view of the budget limitations, they shelved costly plans for the Arkansas.[140]

For Kerr, the conflict with the BOB was no different from any other political problem. All he need do was find a common interest with policy makers there and trade his influence in Congress for their co-operation at budget drafting time. The common denominator was readily apparent — the fortunes of the Republican party in the Sooner State. The GOP had one member in the Oklahoma congressional delegation, Representative Page Belcher. As Congressman from the Tulsa area, Belcher favored river development. He and other leading Republicans from the Arkansas basin met with Republican National Chairman Leonard Hall and BOB Director Rowland Hughes late in December 1955 in a futile effort to convince the administration to include adequate funds for continuing the Arkansas plan in the new budget.[141]

As the 1956 elections approached, the Republican hierarchy was anxious to help its congressional candidates who faced strong opposition. Sherman Adams invited Belcher to a strategy luncheon at the White House. When asked how the administration could help in his campaign, Belcher replied, "I face the loss of my seat to a Democrat over this river thing. If Ike doesn't help me, he's putting a knife in my back."[142] Adams immediately instructed Fred Seaton, presidential adviser on water and conservation and later secretary of the interior, to "take care of Page on this Arkansas thing for me."[143] At Seaton's suggestion, Belcher wrote the President alerting him to the political repercussions for the GOP in Oklahoma and the President's entire water program if Senator Kerr's pet project were delayed further. Seaton also arranged a meeting at the White House between BOB officials and the Oklahoma delegation on March 12, where Kerr gave a detailed explanation and justification of the program to the President's representatives. Shortly after the appropriations hearings where General Itschner, under Kerr's and Ellender's questioning, revealed that budgetary limitations and not corps personnel were stalling the Arkansas project, the administration relented. Although Eisenhower refused to reverse the BOB decision against the Arkansas, fearing he would be criticized for doing so for strictly political reasons, he agreed to "yield to the wishes of Congress." Seaton informed Belcher that the President had promised "if the Congress appropriates the money . . . , I will not stand in its way."[144]

The Congressman immediately telephoned Kerr. Although the Senator was jubilant—pounding his desk with his fist and shouting, "We're in business, my God, we're in business,"—he was concerned that the President might "forget" the agreement. Kerr's skepticism was no reflection on Eisenhower's integrity. The Oklahoman had had two disappointing experiences with a president of his own party who had been unable, if not unwilling, to honor a confidential agreement for political reasons. He did not want to be frustrated a third time.

Eisenhower's refusal to reverse the BOB meant that the initiative for increased appropriations had to come from the Corps of Engineers. But when Don McBride told them of Belcher's understanding with the administration, they were reluctant to request the funds needed for construction, fearing they would be turned down again. Recognizing that the corps was unwilling to endanger millions of dollars committed to its other civil works projects, McBride asked Belcher for written assurances that BOB would honor the corps' requests for the Arkansas. BOB officials struggled to avoid a written commitment, but Kerr insisted, knowing that nothing less would convince the corps. Belcher finally dictated the essence of a letter in which the BOB agreed "we will be guided by the will of Congress in scheduling of funds for construction of appropriate features [of the Arkansas River] development."[145]

Kerr predicted that the President would sign the spending bill that was $38 million more than he requested. "The simple reason [was] that there are a number of able Republican Senators from the western states who are up for re-election this year and I know what they are going to whisper in his ear."[146] Faithful to his promise to Page Belcher, Eisenhower initialed the 1957 Public Works Appropriations Act which contained funds for three projects on the Arkansas River and four dozen more not included in the original budget message.[147]

Every dollar appropriated for the Arkansas project in 1956 was testimony to the remarkable co-operation within the Oklahoma and Arkansas congressional delegations and to the formidable legislative skills of Senator Kerr. Senators and representatives from the twenty-seven states throughout the Mississippi valley mobilized to support the project.[148] At Kerr's request, Speaker Rayburn smoothed the way with the House conferees to make sure that funds added in the Senate for the Keystone dam would be retained.[149] After eight months of exhaustive negotiations and bargaining, Kerr triumphantly reported "navigation is no longer a dream."[150]

Kerr labeled 1956 "the Gold Star year for the Arkansas," but recognized that the major work had just begun. Each new flood-control bill had to contain authorizations for new projects that were a part of the comprehensive basin plan. Then he had to secure appropriations for these new projects, as well as ongoing funds to keep construction progressing. To accomplish all this, Kerr needed maximum support in Congress. His technique to disarm potential opposition was to support every major river development, water conservation, and flood-control project that came before his Rivers and Harbors Subcommittee. He worked tirelessly to secure authorization and later funds for the Niagara Project, the St. Lawrence Seaway, the Central Arizona Project, the Columbia River Storage Reservoir, the Hells Canyon Reservoir, and the Glen Elder Dam. In most instances where there was apparently insoluble conflict between private and public interests, such as happened in the Niagara Project and in the TVA refinancing scheme, Kerr devised an acceptable compromise.[151] He aided Texas members on the Trinity River Project and helped them secure the location of the NASA headquarters in Houston in return for their consistent support of the Arkansas.[152] With these alliances, he cut through party loyalties, geographical boundaries, sectional prejudices, and philosophical differences to accommodate fellow members. And he let it be known to those coming before his subcommittee "that authorization of their projects required that they take their place in a line headed by his Arkansas project."[153]

Kerr also co-ordinated a successful team effort to keep pressure on key committees and party leaders in both houses. Senate Democratic Majority Leader Lyndon Johnson was a powerful ally.[154] As a member of the Democratic Policy Committee, the Oklahoman joined Johnson and Richard Russell in planning the daily calendar. No detail of the Arkansas plan—from the complex engineering studies on bank stabilization to fixing the hours of floor debate—was too trivial for Senator Kerr.

On the Senate Appropriations Committee, where John McClellan was a senior member, Kerr relied chiefly on his friendship with Allen Ellender, chairman of the Subcommittee on Public Works, to protect and increase the Arkansas appropriations. In the late 1950's he followed the Louisianan's pattern of attacking foreign aid as waste and extravagance, while supporting public works on the grounds that they paid for themselves.[155] At Kerr's urging, Monroney relinquished his position on the Banking and Currency Committee in 1959 for an opening on Appropriations. There he joined McClellan and Ellender on the Subcommittee on Public Works. This proved to be a vital move because most of the money required for the Arkansas River project was actually voted after Kerr's death in 1963.

Within his own subcommittee of the Public Works Committee, Kerr created a close sense of cameraderie among Republicans and Democrats that produced unanimous bipartisan support for virtually every bill that emerged. A newsman who covered the Rivers and Harbors Subcommittee hearings on controversial TVA financing in 1957 marveled at the casual conduct of the members who were forever diverting the testimony with amiable jibes and lengthy anecdotes.[156]

In the House of Representatives, Speaker Rayburn lent his prestige and persuasive powers when Kerr needed them.[157] Carl Albert, who became democratic whip in the Eighty-fourth Congress, Edmondson on Public Works, Steed, Stigler, and Norrell (D., Ark.) on Appropriations were all in strategic positions to guide Arkansas River bills. Page Belcher was not only helpful in dealing with the administration, but his sincere endorsement of the navigation plan also persuaded many House Republicans not to oppose the measure.

The key men who decided the fate of the Arkansas in the House were Clarence Cannon, chairman of the Appropriations Committee, and Michael Kirwan, chairman of the Appropriations Subcommittee on Public Works. Kerr courted their favor carefully. The aging Cannon "was a regular Scrooge when it came to appropriations."[158] He frequently reduced funds for Missouri River projects in his own district in the interests of economy. The Eisenhower Administration's emphasis on budget-cutting and skepticism about committing the Congress to $1.2 billion for the Arkansas River was compatible with Cannon's natural frugality.[159] Without Kirwan, this combination would have been disastrous.

Kerr and Kirwan were very much alike. They shared similar backgrounds, and both were hard-driving, competitive personalities. Like Kerr, Kirwan believed that water development was the catalyst of prosperity. To him barges in the port of Catoosa, Oklahoma, meant jobs everywhere. "Prosperity means people will buy cars. And every car . . . has some steel in it made in my hometown of Youngstown, Ohio."[160]

Congressman Kirwan favored a project for diverting water from Lake Michigan into the Illinois Waterway, a 325-mile system of canals and rivers from Chicago to the Mississippi River. "Senator Kerr made a pitch with Mike Kirwan that he would do everything he possibly could through the Senate Public Works Committee to get the diversion bill authorized . . . if . . . Kirwan would help him as Chairman of the House Public Works Appropriations Subcommittee to keep the Arkansas project on schedule." Both men kept the bargain. "He [Kirwan] saw to it that we got our appropriations as we needed them."[161]

Senator Kerr understood that Kirwan "like most men . . . appreciated being recognized by people in authority." He entertained the Ohioan frequently as his guest in Oklahoma, flying him back and forth on the Kerr-McGee plane, hosting dinners in his honor at the Arkansas Basin Development Association, and touring the river project to cement his association with it.[162] The Oklahoman also found other ways to thank Kirwan for his help. In 1960 Kirwan, as chairman of the House Democratic Campaign Committee, was low on funds for the fall congressional races. At an unpublicized breakfast meeting in Washington, Kerr asked the Oklahoma delegation to raise $13,000 for crucial House contests outside Oklahoma. Kerr's pep talk emphasized Kirwan's importance in the House committee structure for appropriations to the Department of Interior and the Bureau of Indian Affairs. He never mentioned Kirwan's assistance on the Arkansas project because there was no need to. Oklahoma quickly paid her assessment.[163]

There were no major conflicts in Congress over funding the Arkansas navigation project after 1956, but the struggle between Kerr and the executive branch continued uninterrupted until the Democrats took office in 1961. Eisenhower's promise not to withhold funds appropriated for the Arkansas was neither an endorsement of the project nor a commitment that substantial budget requests would be automatic in the future. Just a few days after McBride wrote Colonel Wilson that Kerr was "batting 1000%," Eisenhower vetoed the 1956 rivers and harbors authorization bill containing $1.6 billion in new projects. The legislation authorized eight new reservoirs out of a total of ninety-nine projects in four-teen river basin programs.[164] Although not part of the Arkansas system, the projects located on tributary streams of the Red River were certainly important to the overall development of Oklahoma's water resources. The President said that at least thirty-two projects, representing a total of $530 million, had not been properly studied or reviewed according to law.[165] This veto, the first rejection of public works legislation since 1940 and just prior to a national election, emphasized the President's seriousness about balancing the budget.[166] Kerr was furious. He characterized the veto as "un-justified, ill-advised and arbitrary" and was already planning his next move.[167] The House and Senate Democrats on Public Works would introduce identical bills the following session. "If the President repeats his veto, we will pass it anyway."[168]

In 1957 the administration requested funds to continue the work started with the 1956 appropriations.[169] Kerr managed to obtain an additional $500,000 above the BOB request from the Senate Appropriations Committee and to hold on to that increase in conference.[170] Despite the appropriations, no new starts on the Arkansas were authorized, as Kerr had predicted.

Although the administration had promised not to withhold construction funds, they delayed advertising bids on the Oologah project late in 1957. BOB director, Percival Brundage, ordered a "re-appraisal" of all new river and harbor contracts because of concern about economic recession in the midst of rising living costs.[171] Kerr was touchy about news stories that discussed the review of "pork barrel projects," and the old sectional animosity kindled in the gas fight flared.[172] He believed that blocking the construction of public works projects would result in deepening the recession. He criticized Brundage, "Ike's appointed Czar," and the President for ignoring the will of Congress in holding appro-priated money in reserve.[173]

As the economic situation worsened, the administration

reluctantly began to release soil and water project funds previously withheld.[174] To signify a more liberal spending policy, Maurice Stans replaced Brundage as BOB director.[175] Senator Kerr predicted that Stans would work hard to harmonize the differences between Congress and the BOB. He took the first step by inviting Stans to tour the entire navigation project as his guest. "Partly as a result of the Director's 'look-see' trip, the Budget Bureau now accepts and supports the Arkansas navigation program. . . ."[176]

While Kerr was sparring with the BOB, an authorization bill finally passed in the second session of the Eighty-fifth Congress. The President called it a "stupid" bill and vetoed it as he had done a similar one in 1956.[177] An angry exchange between congressional Democrats and administration supporters followed, reflecting the widening gulf on water and power project policy.[178] But 1958 was an election year, and, in the midst of a sharp recession, both parties really wanted some sort of public works legislation. Senator Kerr and the ranking Republican on Public Works, South Dakota's Francis Case, concentrated on working out a compromise the President could accept.[179]

Kerr was so anxious for new starts to keep the Arkansas on schedule that he bridled both tongue and well-known temper. In the hearings before his subcommittee, he was so gentle with Robert Merriam, deputy director of the BOB who outlined the administration's objections to S. 497, that the press commented on this obvious switch in tactics.[180]

In the debate on the Kerr-Case compromise bill, the Oklahoman said that the new bill contained only projects the BOB had "approved or accepted and acquiesced in. . . ."[181] To no one's surprise, BOB had acquiesced in thirty-seven new starts for the Arkansas. The new law also contained Kerr's twice-vetoed provision allowing the corps and the Bureau of Reclamation to include storage space for future municipal and industrial water in all their projects.[182] This provision not only recognized the need to plan water supply projects in anticipation of population needs, but it also was a step in liberalizing the cost/benefit criteria used to determine a water proposal's economic feasibility.[183]

Paul Douglas credited a little-noticed innovation that Kerr

initiated in 1956 in the public works bill as effectively neutralizing potential opposition. Beginning in 1955, the Senate Appropriations Committee considered all funding for Corps of Engineers water projects, Reclamation Bureau, and the Southwestern, Southeastern and Bonneville Power Administrations in a single bill.[184] As a new subcommittee chairman on Public Works, Kerr delayed hearings on individual bills for single projects to make up an omnibus bill. In response to a plea from Hubert Humphrey "for some action on S. 3231," Kerr replied that the Minnesota bill would fare better in an omnibus approach than being reported out to committee by itself.[185] In their crusade against pork barrel spending, Douglas and other economizers had used "the supporters of irrigation legislation against the supporters of rivers and harbors legislation." In 1958 Kerr combined all these measures into a single bill. "The two sets of sponsors were now tied together as allies, instead of competing as rivals. Bob Kerr became the champion of both kinds of projects."[186]

The President and congressional Democrats under Kerr's leadership clashed again over federal spending for public works in 1959. The President recommended "no new starts" in his budget, but he did ask for over $43 million to continue work underway on the Arkansas. The House Appropriations Committee objected to "this unrealistic policy [no new starts] which . . . would ultimately dry up the water resources program for the nation."[187] Congress approved a bill calling for sixty-seven new starts in defiance of the administration's ban.[188] The President promptly vetoed the measure and asked Congress for a new bill "to finance only projects under construction." A House move to override the veto failed, lacking one vote.[189]

The Democrats, with their large congressional majorities, were determined to shatter the administration's ban.[190] In April, the Senate had created a Select Committee on National Water Resources with Kerr as chairman. The committee was to survey national water needs and recommend changes in federal policy.[191] The Democrats intended to make the proper development of the nation's waterways and other natural resources an issue in 1960.

Secretary of the Interior Fred Seaton, who had been instrumental in settling the 1956 conflict over the Arkansas, suggested that the administration might be willing to compromise and accept a few new starts. Kerr, Ellender, and Kirwan met and agreed on a plan to retain all the sixty-seven projects, with a 2½ per cent cut in appropriations. Both houses readily agreed, only to have the President veto the second version also. As the House prepared to vote to sustain the veto, the reasons for Kerr's insistence on retaining all sixty-seven projects became clear. The bill provided money to start new flood-control and water development projects in the home districts and states of many Republicans. All the publicity over budget-cutting and the Democrats' harangue that Republican penny-pinching was retarding the economy and strangling natural resources development prompted a spontaneous grass roots opposition to the President's policy.[192] House Minority Leader Charles Halleck was unable to keep Republicans in line. The only way he managed to hold down the margin against the President was to persuade some Republican members not to vote.[193]

In the Senate, eleven of thirty-four GOP senators voted to overturn the veto. Virginia's Byrd and Ohio's Lausche were the only Democrats who supported the President.[194] This was the first of Eisenhower's 146 vetoes in seven years to be overturned. The *Wall Street Journal* attributed the outcome to "basic practical politics rather than broad philosophical considerations."[195]

Congress' victory over the administration in 1959 ended the disputes over new starts and appropriations for all practical purposes. Kerr's preeminence in water policy was so complete that the House rarely quarreled with any increases he slipped in for the Arkansas in Senate hearings or debate. Appropriations for the Arkansas began to grow as if by geometric progression.[196] One observer recalled seeing "Senators with tears in their eyes because of Kerr's refusal to let their projects move ahead until they voted the way Kerr wanted."[197]

The ease with which Kerr obtained appropriations after 1959 was not enough for him. He began to move up the completion date from the scheduled 1973 target. At an ABDA dinner in January 1961 in his honor, Major General Robert J. Fleming, Jr., the new Southwest Division army engineer, told an excited audience that the Arkansas basin was merely a problem of economics. "To be completed in 1972–73—nuts—if you give us the money we will expedite the program and could finish it in 1967."[198] General Fleming's announcement that he would lop six years off the construction schedule was probably the result of too much preprandial hospitality and his eagerness to make a good impression. Kerr was not present but learned of the remark immediately. The next morning he telephoned the corps headquarters in Washington asking for a specific schedule of appropriations required to meet Fleming's new deadline. The army engineers must have been horrified at such a gaffe, but they produced the figures. To complete the Arkansas project in 1967, the annual average appropriation would have to be in excess of $187 million dollars, a staggering sum even for Robert S. Kerr.

The Oklahoman knew there were limits to how large a chunk he could expect from each year's appropriations. Any major increase for Oklahoma reduced the amount left over for all other projects and, in effect, reduced his power to trade for the votes he needed. Ken Bousquet, of Ellender's Appropriations subcommittee staff, urged him not to appear too greedy. He also pointed out the dangers of appearing to favor the corps in one area of the country.[199] After careful and thoughtful analysis, Kerr settled on a more cautious approach. At a meeting of the entire Oklahoma delegation with the top army engineers, Kerr announced that Oklahoma would compromise on 1970 as the completion date, a schedule which required $141 million in annual appropriations.[200]

The return of the Democrats to the White House forecast halcyon days for the Arkansas. The Kennedy Administration's extravagant approach to water policy was a direct contrast to the penury of the Eisenhower years. The new President promised a high level of federal activity in water and power projects and a generous program of appropriations for new starts.[201]

Senator Kerr, of course, had approached Kennedy about support for the Arkansas long before inauguration day. The Southern Baptist Kerr campaigned extensively for Kennedy in 1960, although it endangered his own reelection to the Senate.[202] Before the election, Kerr gave the President-elect a special aerial tour of the

Arkansas navigation system to see the developments since Kennedy's last visit in 1958, while stumping for Oklahoma congressional candidates.[203] Kerr described how the projects had been more than twenty-five years in the making. Kennedy replied cryptically, "They didn't gain a thing by waiting, did they?"[204] Kerr interpreted this as an indication that Kennedy would support larger appropriations for the Arkansas if elected. Although Nixon had carried Oklahoma, Kerr reassured fearful Sooner congressmen that the "Kennedy Administration will go along with the figures [Kerr's new schedule for appropriations for the early completion of the Arkansas] and by so doing will help see that Oklahoma goes along with it four years from now."[205]

The first Kennedy budget demonstrated the President's good faith. By 1962 more than one-third of the $1.2 billion cost had been appropriated.[206] Despite the cornucopia of appropriations under Kennedy, Kerr never relaxed the grip on public works legislation, the secret of his ability to produce votes for floundering administration bills. In the debate on the $2.3 billion water projects bill in 1962, the largest since World War II, Kerr demonstrated his control over the Senate. Caleb Boggs (R., Del.) tried to delete two projects in the Columbia River basin on the grounds that feasible alternative private projects were available. Majority Leader Mansfield (D., Mont.), Lee Metcalf (D., Mont.), and Congressman Arnold Olsen (D., Mont.) supported the projects. Kerr warned Boggs, and anyone who dared support him, "if the Montana project is stricken from the bill, the Senator from Oklahoma will make a motion to strike the Delaware River Projects. . . ."[207] If Kerr had followed through on his threat, $194.4 million for projects in Delaware, New York, New Jersey, and Pennsylvania would have been lost. Predictably, Boggs' amendment failed.[208] Kerr would tolerate no challenge to the beloved Arkansas project or his own authority.

In September 1962, at the ground-breaking ceremony at the Port of Muskogee, Senator Kerr appeared driving a gold-colored bulldozer—an appropriate symbol of his political power. Within a few months he was dead. Although he did not travel in the first river boat to Tulsa as planned, the project was completed on time.

Senator McClellan and Congressman Edmondson took the lead
in obtaining appropriations. Don McBride, after a brief stint on
the Public Works Committee, joined Senator Monroney's staff
where he concentrated on the Arkansas project. He was as committed to the project as Kerr had been, and when President Johnson asked him to become a director of the TVA in 1967, he refused
until Johnson pledged to do everything in his power to see that the
Arkansas project was completed on schedule.[209]

By the time of the official opening of the Arkansas River
Navigation System (renamed the McClellan-Kerr Arkansas River
Navigation System) in June 1971, most of the project's early critics
were convinced of its merits. Within two years the commercial and
industrial development in the Arkansas basin directly related to
the project totaled over $3 billion, while flood control projects
in the Tulsa District in 1973 alone prevented over $83 million in
damage. The best previous record was $16.5 million in damages
averted in 1970. Although the Arkansas project was still short of
its goal of three billion kilowatt-hours of electricity a year in
March 1974, power plants along the waterway generated 2.3 billion kilowatt-hours in 1973, more than double the previous record
set in 1969. Freight tonnage moved within the system declined
slightly in 1973, but traffic in and out of the waterway system
gained substantially. And in 1973 corps officials predicted that the
attractiveness of low-cost water transportation would be reflected
in the 1974 figures as more wheat, coal, and fertilizer were shipped
on the Arkansas because of rising fuel prices.

The most startling impact of the Arkansas River Navigation
System was the creation of the single largest recreation attraction
in the Southwest. With the completion of the waterway's recreational facilities, the Tulsa District ranked first nationwide in
attendance for recreational purposes. Although it was difficult to
compute the monetary value of this activity, retail sales in Oklahoma's water-rich eastern counties rose dramatically, and local
merchants credited the money spent for recreation with priming
their sluggish economy.[210]

CHAPTER VII
The Eisenhower Years

By the time Senator Kerr returned to Washington in 1953, he had banked the fires of presidential ambition. They flickered briefly in 1956, then finally cooled and went out.[1] Kerr cauterized the wounds with hard work. Intent on a new plan to secure as much federal money as possible for the growth and development of Oklahoma, his first job was to win reelection. The humiliation of the Chicago convention had diminished his popularity in the Democratic party in Oklahoma, and he anticipated a difficult primary race against Roy J. Turner, his successor as governor.

Eisenhower's easy victory in Oklahoma in 1952 also compounded Kerr's political problems. Although the GOP had never been exceptionally strong in the Sooner State, Kerr's election strategy was to "pretend you're running against Herbert Hoover's sinister host of reactionary Republicans, the greatest living experts in sin."[2] Knowing Kerr's instinct for the jugular, Clark Clifford and Don McBride cautioned against partisan attacks on the popular new President.[3] For a few years Kerr managed to create the general impression of co-operation with the Eisenhower Administration, but his advisers were constantly warning him to curb his zest for partisan wisecracks. "You are about a year ahead of Mr. John Q. Public," a supporter wrote in 1953. "Wait 'til [Ike] blunders and those who are hurt complain. . . ."[4]

But as the 1956 election approached, Kerr allowed a lifelong disdain for the Republican party to obscure his judgment. In a newsletter comment on the ailing President's health, he quoted a story in the *Army-Navy-Air Force Journal* of December 24, 1955, that the Army was preparing a suite at Letterman General Hospital in San Francisco for the President's use during the 1956 convention.[5] The *New York Times* carried the story on page one the following day.[6] Within a few weeks, David Lawrence's syndicated column appearing in numerous Oklahoma papers reported Kerr saying, "The Republicans would try to keep Eisenhower alive by the use of drugs." What began as a partisan jab verged on becoming malicious slander.

Kerr hastily attempted to explain that his original statement had been garbled. An editor of the Muskogee *Times-Democrat*, who reprinted the Lawrence column, apparently attributed the statement to the Senator, while he maintained that the slur was actually Richard Neuberger's (D., Ore.). Unfortunately, despite Lawrence's insistence that his original story had been altered and that he did not quote Kerr; the Oklahoman was never able to erase the impression that he had kicked Eisenhower when he was down.[7]

In spite of this unfortunate incident, Kerr lived up to his pledge to work with the President "to achieve national security and peace and *any goal that will serve the welfare of our country and the best interests of Oklahoma*" during the early Eisenhower years.[8] But he had carefully qualified the terms of his support, and they did not include the administration's agricultural policy. As early as 1952, demand for farm products had started to decline as the extraordinary needs of the Korean War subsided. Despite the subsequent drop in farm prices, as well as in farm income in 1953, agricultural production remained high. The federal government, in an attempt to buoy farm income, began to acquire huge surpluses of some items under price support policies.

In Oklahoma and other southwestern states, bad weather and shortages of credit aggravated declining beef prices and rising production costs, creating a crisis in the beef industry. As soon as the Eighty-third Congress convened, Kerr introduced legislation to require price supports to beef producers at 100 per cent of parity.[9] The Oklahoma legislature petitioned the President and Secretary of Agriculture Ezra Taft Benson for similar relief in

February.[10] Benson responded that price supports should be used to provide insurance against disaster, but not to encourage uneconomic production which resulted in heavy surpluses.[11] Kerr denounced Benson's failure to stand behind the Republican party's campaign promise to back 90 per cent of parity price supports and demanded his resignation.[12]

The conflict between Benson and Kerr intensified. In July, during Senate debate on a drought aid bill to provide credit to stockmen, Kerr failed to obtain cattle supports at 90 per cent of parity. By the end of 1953, he had an issue and a Republican opponent to blast in his 1954 reelection campaign.

As expected, Roy J. Turner, known to Oklahomans as the "champion of the turnpikes," announced he would oppose Kerr for the Democratic Senate nomination.[13] The Kerr-Turner rivalry stemmed from the development of the Oklahoma City oil field in the 1930's.[14] Both men were oil millionaires, and both were prominent in national Democratic circles—Kerr, as national committeeman and keynoter in 1944 and Turner as head of the Truman-Barkley clubs in 1948. Turner had declined an opportunity to join Truman's second administration as secretary of agriculture in order to finish his term as governor.[15] At the 1952 Democratic National Convention, Turner served as chairman of the National Committee's Agricultural Division. But he had been cool to Kerr's presidential aspirations, preferring Kefauver instead.[16] Senator Kerr's loss of prestige after the 1952 debacle probably convinced Turner to challenge him in 1954.

A majority of Oklahoma political writers polled early in that election year picked Turner to defeat Kerr. They believed that Turner, the more conservative candidate, would draw substantial strength from Oklahoma City and Tulsa, where many of Republican philosophy masqueraded as registered Democrats. Turner would benefit from Kerr's New Dealer-Fair Dealer image.[17]

Kerr, however, enjoyed the advantage of incumbency and the gratitude resulting from his lengthy participation in federal patronage. He also had wider voter appeal throughout the state than Roy Turner did. Kerr was the leading Baptist layman in Oklahoma and a prominent dry, while Turner, a Methodist, had

earned both groups' enmity in the struggle to repeal state pro-
hibition in 1949.[18] Teachers groups, old-age pensioners, and blacks
remained as loyal to Kerr as senator as they had been to him as
governor.[19] And despite his meager support of organized labor,
the Oklahoma CIO favored his reelection on the strength of a
promise that he would support labor legislation in the future.[20]

The 1954 primary was a difficult reelection campaign for
Robert Kerr. The enormous popularity he had enjoyed shortly
after his term as governor had begun to subside. During his first
term in the Senate, he had acquired a reputation for political
maneuvering that caused even some traditionally free-wheeling
Oklahoma politicians to blanch. And his abortive try for the
Democratic presidential nomination in 1952 was an embarrassing
memory that had dimmed and slowed his rising political star.

Facing a rich and powerful opponent, Kerr decided to abandon the sentimental practice of announcing in his hometown,
Ada. Instead, he opened on April 13 with a statewide radio and
television broadcast, outlining a "square deal" for Oklahoma and
calling for a halt to the trend toward recession.[21] As always, Kerr
concentrated on his strengths. The campaign theme was the need
for seniority to be an effective senator for Oklahoma. In every
appearance, he stressed his experience in Congress.[22]

Kerr skillfully used the seniority argument to woo oil men
who had previously opposed him because of his identification
with the New Deal. He circulated a letter from Russell B. Brown,
general counsel of the Independent Petroleum Association of
America, lauding Kerr's vigilance on the Senate Finance Committee to withstand attacks on "the present provisions in the
Internal Revenue Act relating to intangible drilling and development costs of oil and gas wells."[23]

Prominent civic leaders in traditionally Republican Tulsa
backed Kerr in 1954 because of his demonstrated commitment
to river development. "He is the only one with any seniority and
has always worked to reverse the trend of shrinking population
in Oklahoma."[24] And the benefits of seniority were not lost on
the cunning rural voter who had always asked, "what's in it for
me?"[25]

At the outset of the primary campaign Kerr declared, "I am not running against Mr. Turner. I am running . . . on the basis of my record and my program. Any mention of my opponent will be by him, not me."[26] Then, in characteristic fashion, Kerr began to blast the Republicans, but in 1954 Benson and the farm problem had replaced Hoover and the Depression. Kerr vowed "to hang [Benson's] hide on every barn door in Oklahoma."[27] He portrayed the Secretary of Agriculture as a callous and incompetent bureaucrat determined to pulverize the small farmer. "I would just as soon be in hell with my back broke—as to be a farmer standing before Benson . . . expecting to get either sympathy, charity or assistance."[28]

Kerr's solution to the farm problem was to restore price supports on grain sorghum and to provide subsidies at 90 to 100 per cent of parity to relieve the drought-plagued cattle producers. Despite the emphasis on farm prosperity, Kerr did not neglect the interests of the cities. He sent thousands of letters over the signatures of leading farmers in each county to the nearby townspeople depicting the need for price supports as another measure to help restore business prosperity.[29]

Turner, a successful cattle rancher, also favored government subsidies to bolster the livestock market, but he wanted a floor under beef prices to guarantee a minimum of twelve cents a pound for lower-grade meat.[30] This was essentially the position of the Oklahoma Cattlemen's Association, an organization of large cattle ranchers. Without mentioning Turner's name, Kerr skillfully characterized his opponent's proposal as another Benson-style attempt to eliminate the small cattleman and farmer.[31]

Although well financed and adequately staffed, Turner's campaign failed to develop into a significant threat to Kerr's reelection. Turner's personal jealousy and bitterness toward Kerr gave his statements a pettiness that was out of place in the frontier-style politics that still prevailed in Oklahoma. His selection of Gomer Smith, a perennial Kerr opponent, as his campaign director probably influenced the waspish tone of the campaign.[32] Turner tried to dismiss Kerr's seniority saying that he did not want a seat on "any high finance committee or public works committee to build

big dams and get elected president."[33] Alluding to the Senator
as "the man who wasn't there," Turner charged Kerr with excessive
absenteeism during the Eighty-third Congress. Although he maintained this was a habit Kerr acquired as governor, he seemed
unable to decide if Kerr were away running for the presidency
or away busy expanding his business ventures, or both. "From
the first day he entered politics, Kerr has used the power of his
office to pile up personal reward."[34] In a special campaign edition
of the Sulphur *Times-Democrat*, Turner repeated all the canards
about Kerr's conflicts of interest.[35] When the Senator failed to
take the bait, Turner became shrill and frenzied. He campaigned
with evangelical fervor denouncing Kerr like a tent revivalist condemning Satan. Kerr was the "great pretender" who "craves wealth
and . . . craves power."[36] Despite the personal attacks and the
increasing viciousness of the accusations, Kerr refused to respond
or even mention Turner's name.

Kerr's relentless battering of Benson and his insinuations
about big cattle ranchers foiled Turner's strategy to defeat him
in rural areas. Since Roy Turner was a poor public speaker, his
advisers planned to counter Kerr's oratorical talents by "selling
their man as a friendly, easy to meet fellow who can do the job in
Washington without having to make high flown speeches."[37] While
Turner was probably wise in not trying to match Kerr's forensic
abilities, he misjudged Kerr's campaign style "back home." No
Oklahoman since Will Rogers was more accessible or folksy than
"Big Bob Kerr." Hatless, in rolled-up shirtsleeves and red galluses,
he stood for hours in the blistering Oklahoma sun listening intently
to weatherbeaten farmers' hard luck stories about the ravages of
wind and drought. The Turner campaign utterly failed to perceive
the secret of Kerr's success in a rural campaign. Always when he
campaigned, but especially in farming and ranching communities,
Kerr listened more than he talked. Born into Oklahoma's rural
poverty and raised with a passionate and intense identification
with the land, Robert Kerr understood and cared about the problems of the little farmer. When he hunched up his big frame and
stuck his face close to a man so he could catch every word, the
concern in his eyes was genuine. No amount of artifice could

equal the patriarchal compassion Robert Kerr came to feel for his native state. He had offered his talents to the nation, and she had refused; now he intended to devote himself to Oklahoma, and she would flourish. Kerr was a mystifying combination of oil tycoon, calculating politician, and country-store raconteur. Rural Oklahomans traveled miles to see him in a campaign. And more than once they braved flash floods, washed-out roads, and tornadic winds to vote for him.

There were fifteen candidates in the spring primaries—nine Democrats, four Republicans, and two independents. Campaign activities ran the gamut from elegant cocktail receptions among high Republican circles in Tulsa to Democrat Raymond Haywood Field's "hot corn bread and cold buttermilk open house" in Ardmore.[38] Several local races were so savagely contested that Governor Murray called up the National Guard and declared martial law to maintain surveillance at the polls in five counties.[39] The two major Democratic contenders probably spent in excess of $1 million each, but Oklahoma's campaign spending laws made it impossible to estimate accurately. Kerr's traditional opponents— the liquor lobby, Texas-backed oilmen, and Republicans—supposedly contributed heavily to Turner's campaign.[40] Kerr once estimated that "the winner spends about 50 cents per vote received,"[41] but that the votes not received were the costly ones. Extravagant spending was as much a part of campaigning in Oklahoma as barbecues and cowboy bands. The standing joke in Oklahoma was that a Democratic primary put more money into circulation that a "good cotton or calf crop."[42]

Although Kerr led the Democratic ticket in sixty-four counties and polled 238,543 votes to Turner's 205,241, the combined tallies of his eight opponents kept him from receiving a majority.[43] Turner carried only thirteen counties, including the urban centers in Tulsa, Oklahoma, Cleveland, and Canadian counties. A week after the primary, as Oklahomans were beginning to anticipate an expensive and colorful runoff, Roy Turner suddenly withdrew. Saying that he was out of money and out of the race, Turner claimed that a deluge of cash on Kerr's side had altered the results.[44] While Turner had some financial problems, his decision to quit came after sounding out the other Democratic candidates and finding himself short of the votes, not money, needed to defeat Kerr. Commenting on Turner's decision, the Pawhuska *Journal-Capital* quipped, "And to think that Kerr might have been president if all the other candidates had given up in the last presidential election."[45]

In the general election, Kerr defeated Republican Fred M. Mock, an Oklahoma City attorney, with a margin of 73,114 votes.[46] Although the Republican gubernatorial nominee, Ruben Sparks, had predicted that Democrats would cross party lines, as in 1952, "to clean up that *other* mess in Washington," Kerr's victory followed a big sweep through the southern half of the state and the collapse of Republican strength in Tulsa and Oklahoma counties.[47] Fears about a deepening recession, especially in agriculture, and dwindling public confidence in Benson's willingness to help Oklahoma farmers and cattlemen strengthened Kerr's campaign. Although the plan to develop the resources of the Arkansas River was a secondary issue, Tulsa's Republican civic and business community was sold on the argument that if the eastern part of the state wanted industrial growth they would get it only through supporting the Democratic state ticket—and Robert S. Kerr.

The 1954 elections returned Congress to the Democrats. Kerr became chairman of the Subcommittee on Rivers and Harbors and Flood Control and assumed a coveted seat on Senate Appropriations as an *ex-officio* member. He was in a unique position to influence both the authorization and appropriations for public works projects.[48] He immediately announced to his constituents that he was planning "to build up enough pressure from Democrats and Republicans alike who are interested in water all over the country" to push through legislation on the Arkansas.[49]

In an unexpected maneuver, Kerr also became the third-ranking Democrat on the Senate Finance Committee. This happened when Senator Walter George relinquished the chairmanship to Virginia's Harry Byrd to assume the top spot on the prestigious Foreign Relations Committee.[50] With the Virginian ailing and nearing seventy, Kerr confidently assumed he would be chairman of Finance before his second term was over.[51]

When the Democratic Congress convened in 1955, many senators considered Robert Kerr the logical choice for majority leader, but the Oklahoman showed no eagerness for the assignment.[52] Kerr had been Lyndon Johnson's champion in 1951 for the Whip's job, and he had supported the Texan as McFarland's successor for minority leader in 1953.[53] Johnson's successful policy of constructive but muted opposition during the first two years of the Eisenhower Administration and his deft handling of the McCarthy censure were ample testimony to his suitability to lead the Democratic majority.

Kerr, unlike Johnson, was not interested in the day-to-day maneuvering and the tedium of parliamentary details that were the heart of the leader's job. Johnson was fascinated with intrigues and manipulations, while Kerr was more interested in results. The Oklahoman eschewed the aura of official position for the substance of power. As majority leader, Johnson reveled in the trappings of legislative authority—hideaway offices in the Capitol, an ever-growing retinue of staff assistants, intimate sessions with selected members of the press at the end of a long legislative struggle, and easy access to the popular Republican President. Both men hungered for power, but Johnson needed public acclaim, praise, constant reassurance, and applause.[54] Kerr was satisfied with the private word, the respectful—sometimes fearful—glance, the unspoken acknowledgment.

"Why be the mule when you can hold the reins?" Kerr always replied when asked why he never sought the leader's job.[55] By 1955 Kerr had accepted the harsh political verdict that "an oil man from the Southwest can't be elected president."[56] No longer interested in higher office, "Senator Kerr did not want to be tied down to the horrible job of leadership . . . because he had too many other things he felt had to be done."[57]

The Oklahoman also suspected that Johnson intended to use the leadership position to build a national reputation as a responsible legislative leader with the hope of capturing the Democratic nomination in 1960. Kerr knew the folly of such thinking. Active in Democratic presidential politics since 1940, he never succumbed to the myth that senators were major political forces in their own states or that getting a senator's vote in Congress was tantamount

to getting his delegation's support at a national convention. In
his abortive campaign in 1952, Kerr had worked strictly through
established party professionals and activists within each state,
not through Democratic national officeholders. Despite misgivings
about the wisdom of Johnson's long-range plans, Kerr was interested more in the present. He believed he could accomplish
what he wanted for Oklahoma through a close, influential personal relationship with the leadership. With Russell's co-operation,
he helped Johnson fend off a weak challenge from Democratic
liberal James E. Murray (D., Mont.).

The Kerr-Johnson relationship that developed after the mid-
1950's was very complex. They shared a special kinship that grew
out of their disputed elections in 1948 and mutual admiration
for Sam Rayburn.[58] Kerr, a shrewd judge of political as well as
business talent, had advised Johnson on profitable financial investments in land, cattle, and bank stock.[59]

In addition to financial counsel, the Senator often advised
Johnson on complicated legislation. "Once when White House
officials traveled secretly to Capitol Hill to give Johnson a confidential peek at a new Eisenhower farm bill, they were taken back
to find Kerr waiting for them with Johnson."[60] But in public,
Kerr always deferred to Johnson's position as majority leader.
With the Oklahoman's wholehearted co-operation, Johnson often
assumed the role as the liberals' shield against Kerr's unpredictable
temper and tongue. Johnson would warn a liberal senator that he
was "courting danger if he continued to bait vicious-tongued Bob
Kerr. . . ." At other times, he begged Kerr to stop teasing liberal
senators on the floor about their wanting just a "teeny weeny
dam."[61] Kerr was often in the cloakroom ready to emerge if Johnson needed a vote or to remain at gin rummy if the Majority
Leader wanted absences. Helping Lyndon Johnson was a sure way
to help Oklahoma.

Johnson's style of leadership created the perfect atmosphere
for Kerr's growing power within the Senate after 1955. When he
inherited the Democratic leadership in 1953, Johnson realized that
the Senate was "a decentralized institution where power resided
in committee chairmen and ideological bloc leaders, in addition

to central party leaders."[62] That arrangement was a threat to his own ascendency. Always at his best in a one-to-one relationship, the Texan worked to create an atmosphere in which virtually every Democrat and certain Republicans had an opportunity to distinguish themselves. With Russell's blessing, Johnson tinkered with the hallowed seniority system to permit new senators one good committee assignment instead of making them cool their heels for years on the Post Office and Civil Service or District of Columbia committees. With the appearance of fairness, Johnson was actually able to dispense favors with greater flexibility than the rigid seniority system of the past permitted. He rewarded "good" liberals, such as Humphrey and Kennedy, with early assignment to the Foreign Relations Committee, while forcing "bad" liberals, such as Kefauver and Douglas, to wait until seniority and political expediency brought them important committee positions.[63] After the 1956 elections, Johnson persuaded Clinton Anderson to request a seat on Foreign Affairs in order to thwart a similar request from Estes Kefauver. Since both men had been elected in 1948, Johnson declared a standoff. He then awarded the seat to John F. Kennedy, the popular young Massachusetts senator whom Johnson wanted to draw into his political orbit.[64] "Johnson's blatant favoritism to Kennedy was analyzed in Washington as an attempt to build political alliance with Kennedy and lay the groundwork for a Johnson-Kennedy ticket in 1960."[65] The Majority Leader's dexterity in making an individual senator's personal success synonymous with party success gave Kerr the impetus he needed to push for even larger public works expenditures as the Democratic party's response to a Republican-induced recession.

The Democratic landslide in the 1958 elections triggered twenty months of frenzied activity prior to the 1960 nominating conventions. As one presidential aspirant after another surfaced, Johnson discouraged the friends and supporters who urged him to enter the race.[66] While Johnson agonized over his political future, he also faced a reelection campaign for the Senate in 1960. Sam Rayburn, who feared the repeat of the 1928 disaster if the Democratic party nominated another Roman Catholic from an

eastern seaboard state, was determined that Johnson "must run
. . . for the sake of the nation and the party, even if he did not
want to."[67] The only outcome "Mr. Sam" dreaded more than the
possible dissolution of his beloved party was the prospect of
Richard M. Nixon in the White House.[68]

While Kerr shared Rayburn's fears for the future of the Democratic party, his reasons for supporting Johnson stemmed from
more immediate and practical concerns. In 1960 Kerr, too, faced
reelection; his name and campaign would be linked with the
national Democratic ticket. Only once before, when Harry Truman
carried Oklahoma in 1948, had Kerr been on the ballot during a
presidential year. Eisenhower carried the Sooner State in 1952
and 1956, and the Republicans were sure to contest the Senate
race. Although the practice of separate ballots for presidential,
congressional, and state races tended to reduce coattail effects
in Oklahoma elections,[69] Kerr anticipated a well-financed and
carefully organized Republican challenge. If he were encumbered
with a Catholic candidate as the presidential nominee, his Senate
seat might actually be endangered.

A poll of Oklahoma editors taken in June 1959, which showed
that a majority favored Johnson, probably influenced Kerr's cal-
culations about 1960.[70] Most observers concluded that the religious issue, not party affiliation, would determine the outcome in
Protestant Oklahoma. Kerr, a leading Baptist layman, was well
aware of the blurred line between theology and politics in Oklahoma. With his own political future uppermost in his mind, he
decided early to support Johnson. Never mentioning the inflam-
matory subject of religion, Kerr stated, "Oklahoma's interests
would be better cared for if Johnson were president and not a
fellow from back east."[71]

Though ready to work for Johnson, Kerr disagreed sharply
with the Texan's strategy to secure the nomination. Primarily
the work of Johnson's congressional intimates Earle Clements and
Bobby Baker, the plan was predicated on the Texan's reputation
as a legislative genius with vast influence on congressmen and
senators throughout the nation. Kerr and Clinton Anderson disagreed with the campaign's critical assumption that members of

Congress influenced and directed Democratic party politics within their own states.[72] Both men had learned the truth of the political axiom that "power rises ultimately from beyond the Potomac."[73] And Kerr's 1952 experience had taught him that the nomination seeks no man. If Johnson relied on his political allies in the Senate to round up delegates with the hope of emerging from a Kennedy-Humphrey or Kennedy-Kefauver deadlock as a unity candidate, Kerr believed he was bound to fail.[74]

The Oklahoman suggested an alternative approach which recognized Johnson's stature as a legislative leader but also relied on building a base of delegate support in the South and West. The plan was first aired at a hearing of Kerr's Select Committee on Water Resources in Idaho in October 1959. Commenting on California Governor Pat Brown's proposal that the western states form a bloc in support of a presidential candidate, Kerr said he agreed — and Johnson was the man. He also hinted that the Texan had considerable support in the border states.[75]

Kerr's plan had possible merit as a strategy, but its implementation in the hands of Johnson's campaign people revealed their gross misconception of the political realities of 1960. Despite Kerr's and Anderson's warning that there was no ready mechanism for transferring power from Capitol Hill to the nation and then back to the national convention, the Johnson campaign relied on Carl Hayden in Arizona, Edwin Johnson in Colorado, Mike Mansfield in Montana, and Tom Dodd in Connecticut.[76] In almost every case, each state delegation was already committed to Kennedy — to the complete surprise of its own senator.

When the Democratic National Convention recessed late Wednesday night after nominating Kennedy on the first ballot, a majority of delegates and members of the press predicted that the vice-presidential nominee would be Stuart Symington or Henry Jackson (D., Wash.). Kerr was still in his hotel suite the following morning when Johnson summoned him to discuss Kennedy's offer of the second spot on the ticket. He told Rex Hawks and W. A. "Moon" Underhill, his attorney, he was afraid Johnson would say yes. Speaker Rayburn was already there and arguing bitterly against the offer when the Oklahoman arrived. Kerr sided with

Rayburn, telling Johnson he would be ruined in Texas if he ran on the same ticket with a Catholic—a ticket certain to lose.[77] Although he did not say so, Kerr was loathe to see Johnson leave the Senate for anything less than the presidency, lest his own influence within the Senate be drastically curtailed. With Johnson as majority leader, Kerr had pushed through Congress the most ambitious water development-public works program in the twentieth century. Oklahoma and Robert Kerr had received enormous dividends from this twelve-year-old political partnership. In Kerr's thinking it seemed a waste for Johnson-the-coalition-builder to become Johnson-the-ribbon-cutter.[78]

Kerr and Rayburn were not alone in opposing the idea,[79] but Bobby Baker and Congressman Hale Boggs (D., La.) stiffened Johnson's inclination to run with shrewd appeals to his political vanity. They argued that he must accept because without his presence on the ticket, Kennedy would lose and Richard Nixon would be elected President.[80] It was evident that Johnson wanted to say yes. One by one, his friends grudgingly assented. The Speaker reluctantly admitted that with Johnson as the vice-presidential candidate, there was a possibility of salvaging the ticket and saving the nation. While Rayburn's "cerebral horror of a Nixon presidency" outweighed his "instinctive fear of a Catholic candidate,"[81] Kerr found Nixon more humorous than sinister. He had frequently taunted the humorless Republican, mocking him as "Moby Dick Nixon and his whale of a pet Checkers." And Kerr knew that Johnson's political ambitions could be satisfied only with the presidency. Since he had argued that Johnson's reliance on his reputation as majority leader was a mistake in 1960, he could see that the Texan might have a better chance eight years hence. As vice-president he would have an opportunity to emerge as a national figure as Nixon had done.[82] Sensing that further opposition was futile, Kerr relented. By the next day in an interview with the correspondent from the *Daily Oklahoman*, Kerr was taking credit for convincing Johnson to accept the number two spot and booming the benefits for Oklahoma. "With Johnson as Vice President our part of the country will have a voice in determining policy and making decisions."[83]

Kerr supported the Kennedy-Johnson ticket despite fears that the anti-Catholic bias in Oklahoma might impair his own reelection. But he balked at Johnson's attempt to ram Kennedy's "medicare" plan through the postconvention session of the Eighty-sixth Congress. By late June when Johnson and Rayburn settled on their strategy of a rump session to increase the Majority Leader's leverage at the Democratic National Convention and build up the party record for the election, Kerr had already decided to introduce his own health care bill.[84]

Although opposed to the compulsory nature of various health insurance proposals in Congress in the late forties and fifties, Senator Kerr had long acknowledged the federal government's responsibility to "enable low income groups to secure the necessary health services. . . ."[85] He was also a strong and consistent supporter of the income replacement concept of Social Security. In the 1950's Kerr was instrumental in efforts which extended the system's protection to an additional 7.5 million persons.[86] In 1956 he led a move within the Senate Finance Committee to convince Walter George to support a plan for cash payments to permanently disabled persons over fifty. The same year he also won passage of an amendment to permit women to receive Social Security benefits at sixty-two rather than at the age of sixty-five. The disability amendment, a new departure in the types of protection afforded the individual through the social insurance programs of the Social Security Act, was the opening wedge for the ultimate passage of Medicare in 1965. George consented when Kerr suggested that the proceeds from a small increase in the payroll tax be reserved for disability payments in a separate trust fund.[87] This scheme functioned so well that in 1960, Kerr easily won approval of a provision to drop the fifty-year minimum age requirement.[88]

Throughout the 1950's public concern over the federal government's proper role in providing health care for the aged intensified. The major proposals in Congress reflected the conflicting approaches which crystallized prior to the 1960 presidential elections. Organized labor, some Republicans, and Democratic party liberals—the Democratic Advisory Council, northern urban con-

gressmen and senators, and the ADA—favored a compulsory
health insurance system for people over sixty-five financed through
the Social Security payroll tax.[89] The opponents of compulsory
health insurance consisted of a majority of Republicans and southern Democrats in Congress, business and insurance groups, and
the American Medical Association (AMA). They sought a nar-
rower federal role in a voluntary system. Their proposals centered
on various reinsurance schemes to help private insurance companies offer voluntary coverage at a moderate cost for high-risk
groups such as the elderly and the chronically ill.[90] Despite their
abhorrence of direct federal health care, the advocates of a voluntary system recognized the problem of the medically indigent and
included provisions for their care under public welfare programs.

Most of the 1960 campaign rhetoric and press coverage focused on such glamorous issues as the missile gap, Eisenhower's
record, Castro, and the fate of the Cuban people. But the leading
contenders in the presidential race gradually began to realize that
the American voter was vitally concerned with the mundane problems of paying his rising medical bills. In March, Kennedy's praise
of the Forand bill sent Nixon and Secretary of Health, Education
and Welfare Arthur Flemming first to the President and then to
Republicans on the House Ways and Means Committee pleading
for some kind of bill to take the pressure off GOP candidates
in the fall campaign.[91] Kennedy's aides, who had been working
with Wilbur Cohen on a medicare bill since 1958, recognized the
election potential of the issue.[92]

A cataract of mail deluged a Congress which was unwilling
to act, but fearful of the election consequences of inaction. After
considerable internal debate, the administration unveiled its own
medicare plan—a combination of federal and state subsidies to
private health insurance companies covering indigent persons over
sixty-five.[93] While offering broader coverage than the Forand bill,
the administration proposal was more expensive. And no one
liked it. The AMA branded it socialistic, while the AFL-CIO said
it was an insurance boondoggle. West Virginia Democrat Burr
Harrison of the House Ways and Means Committee depicted it
as a "Townsend-Rube Goldberg scheme . . . [which] calls for every-

thing except prenatal care for persons over 65."[94] Richard Nixon, the Republican heir apparent, said nothing.

No one on Capitol Hill was surprised when the Ways and Means Committee rejected both the administration's so-called Flemming plan and the Forand bill. But the administration's bill meant that both political parties now accepted the federal government's obligation to help the elderly with medical expenses. Some kind of health care legislation seemed destined to pass before the November election.

In late spring, Walter Reuther persuaded Democratic congressional leaders that the Republicans' failure to push for medicare legislation would be a major issue in the fall campaign. Lyndon Johnson, who ached to have labor's endorsement when he arrived in Los Angeles, decided to modify his position. He and Rayburn saw this as the perfect issue to demonstrate the Majority Leader's legendary talents. Rayburn persuaded Ways and Means Chairman Wilbur Mills (D., Ark.) to work for a modest substitute proposal, while Johnson went to see his ally on Senate Finance, Robert Kerr.[95]

By the time the Majority Leader appealed for help, the Oklahoman's bill was ready. Faced with the possibility of an unpopular national ticket and the certainty of health care financing as a major issue in the 1960 campaign, Kerr had begun seeking a position somewhere between the extremes of Flemming and Forand as early as 1959. In June 1959 members of his Washington staff, along with several Oklahoma congressmen, met with representatives of the Oklahoma State Medical Association to exchange ideas. The doctors unanimously opposed any legislation to finance health care payments at taxpayers' expense. They voiced the medical profession's traditional concerns about government interference in doctor-patient relationships, regulation of fees, and hospital choice. But the Oklahoma physicians genuinely feared that the Forand-type program would weaken community incentive to build and support local hospitals and clinics. This was particularly crucial in the rural areas of Oklahoma.[96]

While the House Ways and Means Committee conducted hearings on the Forand Bill in March 1960, a group of influential

Oklahoma doctors called on their senior Senator. They said they were now opposed to any federal program to finance health care payments. Kerr, impatient with this unrealistic attitude, refused to support their extreme position. He suggested that they spend a couple of days on Capitol Hill talking to people and then come back to see him. He warned them, "In my judgment you're going to get the whole kit and kaboodle. They're going to tack the Forand Bill on some measure coming out of the Finance Committee if you don't come up with an alternative."[97] In less than a week the doctors were back. Shaken by what they had heard and chastened in their judgments, they asked Kerr's help in drafting a substitute bill.[98] Now Kerr had what he wanted. The Oklahoma medical leaders had come to him, and he would be sure to remind them of their indebtedness if his reelection were threatened. His role in working for a compromise on health care financing would be useful in demonstrating to conservative Oklahomans his independence if the Democratic national ticket and platform proved as unsatisfactory as he anticipated.

Although extremely knowledgeable about social insurance and welfare matters, the Oklahoma Senator probably agreed with Paul Douglas that a Social Security expert was "a man with Wilbur Cohen's telephone number."[99] Kerr had known the University of Michigan professor of public welfare administration from his days with the Social Security Administration under Truman. Cohen was also a close friend of Lloyd E. Rader, the long-time director of Oklahoma's Department of Public Welfare and Kerr's chief adviser on Social Security and public welfare legislation.[100] Senator Kerr also knew that Cohen had helped draft the Forand proposal, and he "thought Wilbur Cohen had as fine a mind and was as dedicated to his profession as any man he had ever seen."[101] Kerr needed Cohen's professional expertise; he would supply the political artistry.

In mid-May 1960, in response to Rayburn's plea, Wilbur Mills presented a compromise health care plan to an executive session of Ways and Means.[102] Patterned on the administration's federal-state matching program, the Mills plan provided less-generous benefits to the aged but gave the states more discretion over the scope of their programs.[103]

As soon as he learned the details of the Mills plan, Kerr asked Cohen's opinion. Although Mills had consulted him, Cohen did not draft the legislation. When he told Kerr he had reservations about the plan,[104] the Senator invited him to Washington to help prepare alternate legislation. Committed to any incremental step that might lead to a comprehensive health insurance program, Cohen quickly accepted the invitation.[105]

Kerr assigned Bill Reynolds of his personal staff to work with Cohen and Lloyd Rader in drafting a suitable alternative to the Forand bill. But first he asked them to work out a proposal based on how much money the Forand payroll tax would raise and then determine how many benefits that amount of money would buy. He did this because he knew most legislation was written in reverse—the author first decided on the benefits desired and then devised a system to fund them.[106] When the analysis was completed, Kerr was convinced that "a medicare program financed through the Social Security payroll tax might bankrupt the old age and survivors insurance and disability program." As he shook his head in disagreement, he kept repeating, "To many people, that [Social Security] is the only retirement they have."[107] He knew that as the cost of living rose, medical benefits would have to keep pace, and that meant raising the payroll tax. Always the realistic politician, he said, "I'm afraid that in the future . . . the Congress in an election year will put on some added benefits and won't have the guts to increase the payroll tax. . . . Once they do that, they will have destroyed the solvency of the Social Security fund and the federal government will have to step in and make a general appropriation."[108] He opposed the means, not the goal.

When Congress reconvened after the July conventions, "Kennedy, with more of an eye to the voters than to Senate arithmetic, declared that 'this Congress should not adjourn before it enacts a comprehensive, adequate plan to meet . . . medical needs.'"[109] The Kennedy people persuaded the sponsors of various medicare bills to unite in support of a plan Senator Anderson had offered as an amendment to the recently passed House Social Security amendments.[110] With Johnson's help, they intended to force a test vote to dramatize the magnitude of the health care issue. The likelihood of defeat was not an unpalatable prospect since medical care for the aged could become the clarion call of the Democratic campaign.

While Senator Kerr believed that the Social Security payroll tax was not the appropriate method to finance health care, his overwhelming concern was to secure legislation that would help him win the votes of physicians and conservatives in Oklahoma in 1960 when he ran for reelection. "He felt that he would lose a lot of votes among Baptists and Methodists if Jack Kennedy—a Catholic—ran for president, and he wanted to show Oklahoma that he was not 100 percent for Kennedy in order to retain some anti-Kennedy votes for himself."[111] He asked Cohen and Rader to draft a bill incorporating the federal-state grant features of the administration program to guard against the possibility of presidential veto. Using that format, Kerr cautioned them to keep an eye on the Oklahoma welfare statutes to insure that the Sooner State was treated as well as any other.[112]

Election year politics, as well as a keen sense of what Congress would accept, governed Kerr's strategy in the Senate Finance Committee and later in floor debate. He had warned Oklahoma doctors that mere opposition would not forestall a Forand-type program, and he was not convinced that most Finance Committee members who earlier opposed anything in the health field realized they could not vote down the Social Security approach without producing a substitute. The conservative Democrats and Republicans on Finance generally followed Chairman Byrd's lead, and the Virginian was openly hostile to any tampering with the Social Security payroll tax. Despite their public insistence on an "all or nothing" fight for a Forand-type bill, Kerr believed that the Finance Committee liberals—Anderson, Gore, and Douglas—could be placated with any program that would establish the principle of federal responsibility for health care. He also planned to introduce legislation to drop the fifty-year age requirement for disability benefits under Social Security, one of Anderson's pet proposals.[113] With an eye toward the House, Kerr knew that any health plan with Social Security financing ran the risk of becoming hopelessly entangled in the Rules Committee. If it should pass the Congress, President Eisenhower would surely veto it.[114] Kerr believed that the Democrats should work for a plan that could become law. With these contingencies in mind, he presented his own health care proposal when Senate Finance met in August.[115]

Kerr's plan incorporated much of the Mills proposal, but offered potentially greater federal assistance than the House measure. Financed from general revenues, the plan increased federal "vendor" payments to states under the existing Old-Age Assistance (OAA) program. It also created a new federal-state matching program for the medically indigent—persons not covered under the OAA but judged too poor to meet their medical bills. The Kerr-Mills proposal, as the plan was known, contained the standard language characteristic of existing public assistance legislation. The federal share was tied to the recipient state's per capita income, the low-income states receiving the greatest assistance.[116]

On August 13, 1960, the Senate Finance Committee rejected Senator Anderson's proposal to tie medicare into the Social Security system but approved the Kerr-Mills plan of direct federal grants to the states.[117] Kerr's assurance to the committee that his plan had administration backing probably accounted for the swift acceptance. Since Kerr and Secretary of the Treasury Robert Anderson were close personal friends, such co-operation was not unlikely.[118] The *Wall Street Journal* hinted that Eisenhower was adroitly using Kerr as "a secret weapon in the Senate to hold spenders on a leash. . . ."[119] In predicting Kerr-Mills chances of passing, the Oklahoman admitted the odds were only 50–50. But he cautioned, "The alternative is no bill at all."[120]

Liberal opposition ebbed as bipartisan support crystallized. In a news conference, President Eisenhower endorsed the Kerr-Mills approach.[121] To avert a severe rift threatening the Democratic party already burdened with the task of electing a Catholic president, Wilbur Cohen returned to Washington in August to persuade Kennedy's aides, Theodore Sorensen and Myer Feldman, that the Forand approach was dead. Cohen argued that if Kennedy made the adoption of a Social Security-financed program an either/or situation—Forand or Kerr-Mills—the Senate's conservative coalition would choose the milder Kerr bill. Such action would pit Democrat against Democrat just before a national elec-

tion and probably obliterate any hope of enacting health legislation for years to come. Cohen also tried to persuade them that
the Kerr-Mills plan should be regarded as a foot in the door.
For him "it was not a situation of alternatives, but of supple-
ments."[122] Kerr's role in the Cohen mission was unclear, but the
professor's argument to the Kennedy staff mirrored the Senator's
views with absolute fidelity.

When Senator Kerr appeared in the Senate chamber on Monday to discuss the legislation, it was clear that Cohen had been
successful. Kerr briefly outlined his plan. Almost in passing he
remarked that one of the merits of the Kerr-Mills approach was
that it could be implemented as early as October 1, 1960.[123] He
only mentioned this attractive feature once, but every member
up for reelection heard it and understood the implications. Despite
the Democratic nominee's announcement the previous weekend
that Kerr-Mills "did not go far enough" and his promise to fight
for the Anderson amendment on the floor, Kennedy, who was
present throughout the speech, failed to respond to the Oklahoman.[124]

At this point, Walter Reuther was urging Kennedy, Johnson
and Rayburn to "crack the whip of party discipline" over Democrats to vote a unified front for the Social Security approach.
But because of growing support for Kerr-Mills, the Kennedy people decided to forego a confrontation with Kerr. Instead, their
plan was to attempt to "pile a Social Security financed program
on top of the federal-state cost sharing principle already passed
by the House and approved by Senate Finance."[125] They believed
this combination would broaden the coverage of each plan and
spare fellow Senators the political pain of having to choose one
plan over the other. Hitching the Anderson amendment to the
Kerr-Mills plan would risk a veto, but vetos were ideal campaign
fodder.[126] The politics of health care legislation had become more
important than the contents of the proposals.

The Senate debate in mid-August was a foretaste of the colorful and bitterly contested election campaign that would follow.
No new arguments were heard and no new coalitions appeared,
but the presence of both presidential candidates throughout the

three-day debate heightened public interests in the Senate's traditionally muffled proceedings. Vice-President Nixon was on hand for the straight party vote defeat of the administration-backed Javits amendment, a program patterned on Kerr-Mills.[127] The *New York Times* reported that Nixon moved freely about the floor like a party whip, rounding up votes to defeat his rival's proposal.[128] Knowing that he would inherit the Democrats' opprobrium if Eisenhower vetoed the bill, Nixon had to defeat the bill in Congress. When the vote came, nineteen Democrats joined thirty-two Republicans in rejecting the Social Security approach.[129] The Democratic vote for the Anderson amendment was large because most senators did not think it had any real chance to pass. Several who voted yes later admitted that they wanted to be in position to claim loyalty to their liberal backers while assuring their conservative supporters that they would not have voted that way "if it had counted."[130] A great many of those votes probably came from senators who understandably did not want to offend the young man who might be their president within a few months. Kennedy, who was standing near Douglas when the vote was announced "remarked bitterly that the Southerners would not support the national needs and declarations of our Party, but would demand their full share of the perquisites and patronage . . . in the coming Presidential election."[131] With the Kennedy-Anderson proposal defeated, there was no contest on the Kerr amendment. It passed with only two dissenting votes.[132]

In retrospect it seemed clear that parliamentary procedure, as well as election politics, doomed the liberals' plan for the Kennedy-Anderson amendment to ride piggyback on Kerr-Mills. Senate rules stipulated that floor amendments, such as Kennedy-Anderson, were decided before voting on amendments, such as Kerr-Mills, which were a part of the Finance Committee's reported version of the omnibus Social Security bill. The piggyback scheme would have worked only if the vote on Kennedy-Anderson had followed, not preceded, the Kerr-Mills proposal. Johnson and Rayburn, who were obliged to work closely with the Kennedy campaign because of the Majority Leader's place on the national ticket, probably acquiesced in the charade for campaign purposes, but it was unlikely that such shrewd parliamentarians either planned the maneuver or anticipated its success.

Senator Kerr did not gloat over the triumph, although he had created a legislative milieu so flexible that every Democrat could interpret the events to fit his particular political situation. His own reactions were mixed. He confided to Wilbur Cohen that he regretted having to go against the party nominee, but the religious bias of his constituents and the political prominence of Oklahoma doctors left him no choice.[133] "I don't get any votes in Boston and New York. Mine all happen to come from Ada and Oklahoma City, Tulsa, Stigler and areas like that."[134] To Oklahomans who saw Kerr as disloyal to the national ticket or who thought the bill too narrow, he defended his action on the grounds of sheer practicality. "I felt that in fairness to the people over 65 I should work for the passage of a bill that could become a law, and not for the passage of one that had no chance of ever being of benefit to anybody."[135]

The conferees cleared the bill within hours of final passage and retained the major provisions of the Kerr-Mills plan as it had emerged from Senate Finance.[136] But rumors began circulating on Capitol Hill that the President was threatening to veto the bill because of its very liberal matching formulas. Eisenhower thought the bill was unusually favorable to the lower-income states, particularly Oklahoma and Arkansas.[137] Senator Kerr quickly intervened with the White House through Charles Schottland, commissioner of Social Security. Schottland explained to the President that through the complex formula for matching funds rural-agricultural states with low per capita incomes inevitably received a greater percentage of federal matching funds than richer, industrialized states.[138] Schottland was technically correct that Oklahoma and Arkansas were not favored over other states, for Mississippi occupied the bottom rung on the income scale below them. But it was no coincidence that southern Democrats who controlled the decisive votes received the most favorable federal matching formulas for their states in the Kerr-Mills plan.[139] Hardly anyone, save the men who wrote the bill "with an eye to Oklahoma welfare statutes," noticed the fine print which provided a total of $16 million for the Sooner State with no corresponding increase in state spending.[140]

The Kerr-Mills bill of 1960 reflected the prevailing sentiment concerning the appropriate role of the federal government in providing health care services to the elderly more accurately than it mirrored the social philosophy of its chief proponent. Senator Kerr's attempts to find an approach that was acceptable to the medical community in Oklahoma was as much a response to the political realities within his own state as recognition that the federal government could not institute any more extensive medical care program than the nation's physicians were willing to support. Always wary of hampering his freedom to maneuver and negotiate in state and national politics, Kerr refused to become snared in ideological traps. Shortly after the passage of the Kerr-Mills bill, Bill Reynolds was back in Oklahoma working on the re-election campaign. A local medical organization he approached said they would support Kerr if he would write a letter saying he would always oppose the Social Security approach to health insurance. The Senator declined. "There may come a time when in my judgment it becomes the procedure to do it. Right now I don't think it is, but I don't know what's going to come in the future."[141] Kerr was elected to a third term that fall, but his margin of victory was the smallest of his entire career. He complained to a friend that despite his efforts on Kerr-Mills, the medical profession had proved a fickle ally. "After all I did to save the doctors from themselves, I got only 22% of their votes. . . ."[142]

CHAPTER VIII
Kerr and Kennedy

When the post convention session of Congress adjourned in September 1960, Senator Kerr seemed to be the only Democrat for whom the three weeks had not been a hot, tedious, and miserable ordeal. Tailored for the anticipated Johnson campaign, the special session had soiled the Texan's image as the crisp and masterful leader and trapped the Democratic presidential nominee in the Senate chamber when he longed to be on the road. It seemed that every proposal the Kennedy-Johnson team tried to push through was either mangled in committee or choked in the House.

But Kerr was satisfied. Just before returning to Oklahoma for his third senatorial campaign, he told a friend, "I have a health care bill my doctors and my welfare people agree to."[1] Although he had only nominal primary opposition in 1960, Kerr faced a formidable Republican challenger in the general election.[2] And internal rifts within the state Democratic party compounded the problem that few Oklahoma Democrats were enthusiastic about the national ticket. Kerr had never enjoyed the luxury of a safe seat, but—except for the race against Roy Turner—1960 was shaping up as the most difficult campaign of his career.

The schism in the Oklahoma Democratic party was rooted in the 1958 election of the youthful Tulsa County attorney, J. Howard Edmondson, as governor. Brother of Muskogee Congressman Ed Edmondson, the thirty-three-year-old lawyer emerged in first place from a primary slate of eleven candidates.[3] Edmondson's courtroom performances had stirred statewide attention, and he had attracted a vigorous, intelligent, and sometimes ruthless following of young men known as the "crew cuts." Intent on reforming the Sooner State, they conducted a "prairie fire" runoff campaign in which they capitalized on the fresh candidate's youth, speaking talents, and photogenic face. Television was a natural medium for the attractive and personable attorney. One rating authority testified to his appeal when it reported, "Edmondson held his audience one night against the Lone Ranger."[4] Edmondson overwhelmed his primary opponent and defeated the Republican challenger in the fall with the largest majority on record.[5]

Despite his substantial victory, the Edmondson Administration encountered serious problems from its first day in office. As the spokesman of the urban wing of the Oklahoma Democratic party, the young Governor confronted a staid, rural-oriented, "Old Guard"-dominated legislature, and a bitter feud was inevitable. Edmondson also alienated many supporters through his early and enthusiastic promotion of John Kennedy's campaign for the Democratic nomination.

As early as 1958, Kerr's Oklahoma advisers began warning of a possible challenge from one of the ambitious Edmondson brothers.[6] Drew Pearson nourished the most persistent rumor that both brothers would try for the U.S. Senate—Ed for Kerr's seat in 1960 and J. Howard for Monroney's in 1962.[7] Despite the Edmondsons' immediate denial, Kerr and Monroney began closing ranks against the Muskogee pair.[8] Both Senators knew that at the first sign of age or slowing down, a youthful opponent would pounce. What had begun as a nonaggression pact in the mid-fifties became a political mutual assistance agreement for the approaching sixties.

Monroney and Kerr differed frequently on state and national party politics. Monroney supporters usually opposed Kerr's candidate in gubernatorial primaries, and the Senators backed different aspirants for the Democratic presidential nomination in 1952, 1956, and 1960. Their co-operation in Congress did not begin until

1955 when Monroney ceased to oppose Kerr's plan to navigate the Arkansas River.[9] Aware of their dissimilar legislative interests, Kerr deferred to Monroney on matters concerning aviation, a growing industry in Oklahoma in the fifties, while keeping control of water matters.[10] After an initial rift over the appointment of a director for the Tulsa Federal Housing Administration, their staffs worked closely to avoid future public disagreements. When the Democrats returned to power in 1961, Thomas Finney, Monroney's administrative assistant, worked out an agreement with Burl Hays to divide the patronage equally so that there could be no conflict.[11]

Most observers considered the junior Senator more liberal, an impression that reflected style and emphasis more than actual voting records. A former Scripps-Howard political writer, Monroney was comfortable among news pundits and the diplomatic corps on the Washington social circuit. Elected to the House in 1936, the natty Representative received the 1945 Collier's award for "Distinguished Congressional Service" for his role in modernizing Congress through the Legislative Reorganization Act.[12] As Oklahoma voters grew more conservative in the fifties, Monroney turned his attention to the problems of the state's burgeoning number of civil servants and defense workers. He traveled abroad extensively as a delegate to the International Parliamentary Union and wrote the legislation which resulted in the International Development Association.[13] While Kerr publicly scoffed at Monroney's notion that Europe's scenic wonders could compare with the mountains of Leflore County, both men recognized the effectiveness of their "decent fellow-tough guy" partnership.[14] "Bob roughs them up and I smooth them down," was Monroney's description of their teamwork.[15]

As Monroney's hold on the electorate weakened in his second term, his Senate colleagues urged him to spend more time in Oklahoma. But he countered that time in Oklahoma was time away from Oklahoma's business in Washington. Kerr disagreed. He knew that the voters sensed Monroney's faltering interest in issues vital to the state. He remarked that he could stay in Washington every weekend and the newspapers would still report "Kerr speaks at Pawhuska," "Kerr Attacks Republicans in Guymon," but Monroney could go home three times a week and never get credit for it.[16]

Despite his long career on Capitol Hill, Monroney was never part of the Senate power structure. In 1958, when he wanted a seat on Appropriations, Kerr spent two days buttonholing the right members, especially Johnson and Russell. When the appointment was announced, Monroney gratefully acknowledged Kerr's assistance in his press release.[17] One reporter, who had characterized the relationship as "bordering on Alphonse-Gastone [sic]" in 1958, said it was clearly "Damon and Pythias" by 1960.[18]

As presidential nominating politics gathered momentum early in 1960, Governor Edmondson attempted to gain control of the Democratic party's machinery with the hope of casting Oklahoma's twenty-nine votes for John F. Kennedy.[19] Democratic State Chairman Lloyd Benefield had resigned late in 1959, and the Governor announced his choice was Pat Malloy, a Tulsa attorney. Kerr—along with former-Governor Raymond Gary, Carl Albert, and other Sam Rayburn loyalists among Sooner congressmen— wanted to bind the delegation to Lyndon Johnson. Monroney, while praising Johnson, remained unaligned. He wished for a deadlock between Kennedy and Johnson so that Stevenson might have a third try for the White House.[20]

Edmondson, intent on dominating the delegation, decided to fight Kerr's candidate, Gene McGill, in the precinct and county conventions. Although the Edmondson-Malloy forces triumphed in the urban centers, McGill was elected and the delegation pledged to Johnson.[21] Edmondson and Kerr reached an understanding that the Governor would not promote a candidate against the Senator if Kerr would use his influence to dampen growing opposition to Ed Edmondson in the second district.[22] At Kerr's insistence, the Governor was named as a delegate to the July convention in Los Angeles, although his one-half vote went to Johnson under the unit rule.[23] Relishing the role of maverick, Edmondson made one of the seconding speeches for Kennedy. The Sooner delegation booed him, and Johnson never forgave this public insult.[24] Kerr, too, was visibly angry, but he probably sensed that Edmondson's

action in defying his own delegation was more than mere petu-
lance. The Edmondsons of Muskogee, like the Kennedys of Boston's Back Bay, represented a challenge to the existing political
order in their states. Impatient with the old leaders and the old
ways, supremely confident of their ability to solve any problem
and eager to govern, both men signified the changing of the guard
in the Democratic party. As the generation of Franklin Roosevelt
and Harry Truman gave way, it was inevitable that Edmondson
should cast his lot with Kennedy and shun Kerr.

With a Catholic leading the national ticket on a platform
demanding the end of the oil depletion allowance, Kerr's reelection
campaign seemed doubly cursed.[25] He faced the delicate task of
appearing close enough to the nominee to reassure Oklahoma's
petroleum industry of Kennedy's true intentions while maintaining
a respectful distance so he could conduct an independent campaign, free from the passions he expected the religious issue to
generate. At first he ignored Kennedy and stressed his friendship
with Johnson.[26] In August, Dean McGee gave a party at the Skirvin
Hotel in Oklahoma City to celebrate the publication of Kerr's
book, *Land, Wood and Water*.[27] With Lyndon Johnson and Sam
Rayburn heading a guest list of the Sooner State's leading businessmen, publishers, and officeholders, politics soon predominated
over literary events. That afternoon at a picnic on the Kerr-Mac
Ranch, Johnson predicted that Kerr would play an even greater
role in the Senate after the election. For Kerr, this seemed the
appropriate opening to portray the vice-presidential candidate
as Oklahoma's special emissary on the Democratic national ticket.
The Senator assured his guests that Johnson would "go further in
making a great man out of our nominee for president than any
other man could."[28]

When troubled representatives of the state's petroleum industry seemed ready to fly to Kerr's Republican challenger because of
fears that the Democratic presidential nominee really meant to
halt the depletion allowance, the Senator patiently reminded them,
"Congress, not the President, controls depletion."[29] Implying that
Kennedy's hard line on depletion was merely sop to the liberals,
Kerr recalled that a large portion of the Kennedy family fortune

was invested in Texas oil.[30] Drumming the theme that his seniority on the Finance Committee, where tax legislation was written, was the "key to his ability to serve Oklahoma better," Kerr convinced the oil interests to stay with him for another term.[31]

The religious issue was more difficult. According to a national census of church memberships in 1957, three Protestant groups predominated in Oklahoma—Baptists, Methodists, and the Disciples of Christ.[32] With a congregation of almost four hundred thousand, the Baptists enjoyed wide influence in Oklahoma politics. Historically, Baptists in Oklahoma had voted Democratic while Methodists usually voted Republican.[33] Senator Kerr was Oklahoma's most prominent Baptist layman and a conspicuous contributor to Baptist charities and educational institutions. In previous elections, he relied on Baptist support as a considerable portion of his predictable electoral strength. But in 1960 his adherence to the Baptist faith conflicted sharply with his allegiance to the Democratic party. It was a painful and saddening experience for him.

Four days after the Democratic convention adjourned, Kerr was busy trying to placate Oklahoma's fears about Catholicism. In a letter to Sam Scantlan, an official of the Oklahoma Southern Baptist General Convention, he described Lyndon Johnson as the guarantor that Kennedy "would at all times place his duty to his country first and not in response to or directly from any religious hierarchy."[34] Despite repeated public and private assurances that he accepted Kennedy's statement expressing belief in "an America where the separation of church and state is absolute . . ." Kerr was unable to calm the anti-papist hysteria.[35] Baptist ministers across the state found the election rich in sermon material to boost slumping summer attendance. Kerr's own pastor, Herschel Hobbs of the First Baptist Church in Oklahoma City, delivered a sermon, "Who are the Bigots?" attacking Kennedy's appeal for the Catholic vote.[36]

Disregarding Kerr's plea that the presidential campaign bypass Oklahoma, Kennedy's managers decided early in October to add a stopover in the Sooner State.[37] It seemed futile to waste precious final hours in pursuit of eight electoral votes when the state's large Republican majorities in 1952 and 1956 indicated that Nixon would probably carry Oklahoma again. And there was always the possibility that Johnson's presence on the ticket might be sufficient to persuade doubtful Democrats to vote for the ticket out of neighborliness. Kennedy had little to gain from the appearance, but Kerr seemed certain to suffer.

The Democratic nominee arrived in Oklahoma City on Thursday before the election, and Senator Kerr introduced him to an overflow crowd at the Municipal Auditorium as "a patriotic Catholic Democrat for President."[38] The late summer campaign had clearly been a strain on the sixty-four-year-old Kerr. He liked to campaign in the expansive, passionate style of Bryan or with the hammering staccato of ridicule that characterized Truman. But the tenseness of the 1960 campaign had forced him to weigh every response. Watchful caution had replaced his usual charisma. But sensing something different in the atmosphere as he prepared to introduce the young presidential candidate, Kerr suddenly abandoned the wariness of August and September. He pleaded with the crowd, "Why my Baptist father and my Baptist mother would turn over in their Democratic grave if they thought I would not speak up for my nominee for President."[39]

The next day it was clear that Kerr had miscalculated the response to his introduction of Kennedy. The Oklahoma Baptist Convention assembled hurriedly to debate a resolution to censor him for supporting a Catholic. Some of the more militant individuals favored the extreme action of "churching" him.[40] But Kerr would not be intimidated. He responded stiffly that he had signed an oath to support the Democratic nominee and he would not be pressured into breaking his word.[41]

Election day 1960 was a serious disappointment for Oklahoma's leading Democrat. Nixon won 59 per cent of the vote; and, although Kerr retained his Senate seat by 89,000 votes, he lost counties he had never failed to carry with large margins in both primaries and general elections. His Republican opponent, B. Hayden Crawford, had campaigned almost exclusively on the issue that Kerr was using his position in Washington to promote legislation designed to favor Kerr-McGee in the sale of helium and uranium to the federal government.[42] Despite some evidence that Crawford's accusations were based on fact, most voters seemed unconcerned. Even the *Tulsa Tribune*, traditionally the severest critic of Kerr's politics as well as his ethics, dismissed Crawford's charges as "silly."[43] The issue of Kennedy's religion, not Kerr's ethics, drained away at least one hundred thousand votes from the Senator's expected margin of victory.[44]

The morning after the election was the lowest point of Robert Kerr's public career. The towering and vigorous Oklahoman seemed suddenly shrunken and spent. Secluded in his Oklahoma City office in the Kerr-McGee headquarters, he confided to Bill Reynolds that he did not think he would run again. "After what my Baptist friends did to me in this campaign, I just don't think I can take it anymore."[45] That same evening Kerr was scheduled to speak at the First Baptist Church in Shawnee. Oklahoma Baptist University, the school Kerr had supported so generously, was located there. When the arrangements were made months earlier, the intention was to celebrate the leading Baptist's certain re-election to the United States Senate. Ironically, the topic Kerr had announced was "loyalty." Reynolds, who accompanied him to Shawnee, said he never heard a worse speech. The Senator felt betrayed. "It hurt him tremendously and it made him mad, but it hurt . . . more than it angered him."[46]

When Kerr returned to Oklahoma City late that night, he learned there had been a call from Hyannisport, Massachusetts. Early the next morning the call went through. John Kennedy joked about running behind Stevenson in Oklahoma and assured Kerr that he had never expected to carry the state. He said he knew that Kerr's endorsement had cost him dearly. "But I want you to know one thing," the President-elect promised, "I'll never forget it." Senator Kerr would see to it that he kept his word.[47]

In mid-December, Kennedy and Johnson met with Majority Leader Mansfield and Speaker Rayburn in Palm Beach, Florida, to discuss legislative strategy for the Eighty-seventh Congress. After a great deal of talk about how to dilute the power of the House Rules Committee and the likelihood of alienating vital southern support through attempts to curb filibusters in the Senate, they settled on a plan. They would delay civil rights to keep down emotional issues and push the President's domestic program—aid to depressed areas, aid to education, increasing the minimum wage to $1.25, and medicare.[48]

Another topic that dominated these planning sessions was the space program. Kennedy had emphasized space and the missile gap in the campaign.[49] But Johnson still considered the space program his personal domain. His Senate Preparedness Subcommittee's hearings in the wake of Sputnik II were the catalyst for national interest in space and the missile gap issue had been his unique contribution to the 1960 presidential campaign.[50] Johnson wanted to be named chairman of the Space Council and intended to use his ties to the Senate Aeronautical and Space Sciences Committee to create an interesting and visible role as vice-president.[51] Since Kerr was the new chairman of the Senate Space Committee, Johnson suggested that he be invited to Palm Beach to confer on plans for expanding American efforts in outer space.[52]

Kerr arrived at the Kennedy retreat in Florida the day after Christmas. Immediately, there were conflicting reports about the purpose of the visit. Douglas Dillon, slated to be secretary of the treasury in the new administration, was also present. Some reporters speculated that Kennedy wanted Kerr's help on Senate Finance to halt the drain on U.S. gold reserves that had accelerated in the last years of the Eisenhower Administration.[53] Others said that Kennedy was after Kerr's endorsement of future legislation to cut tariffs, while hinting at exemptions and possible subsidies for Oklahoma's suffering lead and zinc industries.[54] Hugh Sidey, *Time*'s Washington correspondent who was present, said Kerr's visit to Florida to discuss space matters was a ruse. Brooklyn Congressman John J. Rooney (D., N.Y.), chairman of the House Appropriations Subcommittee for State, Justice and the Judiciary, was also there to be softened up to permit increases in the skimpy booze allowances" for ambassadors so Kennedy could appoint such nonmillionaires as John Kenneth Galbraith and Charles "Chip" Bohlen.[55] One Kennedy aide remarked to a wire service reporter afterwards, "When you get into outer space there's just no end to the range of subjects you might chance on."[56] Whatever Kennedy's stated reason for including Kerr, he probably wanted an opportunity to size up the Oklahoman at close range.

Kennedy had already decided he needed a skilled and respected lieutenant to guide his program through Congress. Johnson, as vice-president, was now an outsider to the Senate he had once dominated. There had been rumors of a growing revolt against the Texan during the final days of the Eighty-sixth Congress. Even Richard Russell had predicted that "Lyndon was living on borrowed time as a strong Majority Leader."[57] Kennedy suspected that Johnson's old enemies in Congress might turn on him if he tried to use the former Majority Leader's talents on Capitol Hill. And some of Kennedy's closest advisers, particularly his brother Robert, feared Johnson would try to dominate the new administration's legislative politics "by emerging as the vital intermediary between White House liberals and Senate conservatives."[58] The President-elect, as a former senator, knew instinctively that Johnson's guidance would not be tolerated in the absence of his previous power.

Since Kennedy clearly intended to assume the initiative of government which he believed his predecessor had let slip to Congress, Mike Mansfield seemed the ideal majority leader. Where Johnson's pushing, goading style made him masterful in opposition, Mansfield's inclination was toward housekeeping, not empire building. An introspective, accommodating, gentle person, Mansfield seemed willing "as Johnson was not, to accept the consequences of other men's bad judgments."[59] As early as December 1960, it was predictable that under Mansfield's loose rein, the Senate would return to what it had been throughout most of its history, "a hundred disparate adults."[60] The Montana Senator was an acceptable manager, but Kennedy needed more.

The President-elect faced the prospect of serious problems with the Eighty-seventh Congress. The 49.7 per cent of the voters who had elected Kennedy on a promise "to get this country moving again" also had elected what appeared to be an immovable Congress. Although the Democrats retained substantial majorities in Congress, the Republicans gained twenty-two seats in the House of

Representatives.[61] Events in the House appeared due in part to the
return of normally GOP seats swept away in the Democratic
victories in 1958. But this meant trouble for the Democratic
President because most of those twenty-two vanished Democrats
had been staunch liberals who would have supported the Kennedy
Administration.[62] A revitalized coalition of Republicans and
conservative Democrats could destroy the new administration's
agenda of social and economic legislation.

Almost every major item in Kennedy's proposed legislative
program had been rejected or emasculated in the last Eisenhower
Congress. In electing a more conservative Congress in 1960 than
in 1958, the voters "showed something less than public outrage
at the record."[63] Kennedy confronted the prospect of political
frustration and impotence unless he ensured that his performance
in Congress matched his promise in campaigning.

Senator Kerr was in the unique position to be either the
administration's best friend or most effective enemy. As the
ranking Democrat on Senate Finance, he favored monetary and
fiscal policies to stimulate economic growth.[64] Trade legislation,
tax revision, and medicare—all destined for the Finance Committee—would have to pass his scrutiny. From his vantage point
on the Public Works Committee, he could assist in the administration's aggressive approach to natural resource development and
conservation. And as chairman of the Aeronautical and Space
Sciences Committee, Kerr could be indispensable for Kennedy's
costly moon program. But most important for Kennedy, whose
friends in Congress Johnson described as "the minnows," Kerr's
intimates—Russell, Rayburn, Hayden, Ellender, Eastland, Kirwan,
and Bridges—were "the whales."[65]

Although Kerr and Kennedy had served together in the Senate
eight years, their paths had seldom crossed. As a senator, Kennedy
sponged up ideas and experimented with a range of issues from
labor legislation to foreign policy, while Kerr stuck to the familiar.
Both men understood the play of traditional political forces—
organized labor, farmers, business, and ethnic groups—and both
were modern in their use of research, expert opinion, and public
relations techniques. But unlike Kennedy, Kerr viewed every

problem through the prism of his home state. He decided national issues of trade and tax policy after determining their effect on Oklahoma wheat, oil, and gas; state, rather than national, concerns guided him on health care. Something in Kerr's personality and background made it virtually impossible for him to embrace causes or ideas beyond his own experience. While this concentration on the familiar explained a great part of his success as a legislator, it also explained his failure to reach the presidency.

Other members of Kerr's generation in the Senate dismissed Kennedy as a playboy, a dilettante. But Kerr, who was in the habit of probing beneath the surface, probably saw beyond Kennedy's casual and rather elusive exterior the calculating toughness of an ambitious and self-confident politician. Kerr's philosophy, which a reluctant admirer once described as "what works is fine; if it doesn't work, the hell with it,"[66] was more akin to Kennedy's than the young President's admirers cared to admit. The Oklahoman respected winners, and when John Kennedy was elected Kerr told Bill Reynolds the only thing the President lacked was a little experience. "He knows where he's going and he's going to get there."[67]

When the President-elect and the Oklahoma Senator faced one another in Palm Beach, the contrast was striking. One reporter remembered "two men whose styles [were] as dissimilar as a derringer and a shotgun."[68] Basically unemotional and impersonal, calculating rather than fervent, Kennedy seemed the antithesis of Kerr. But the "good ole boy" recognized the Boston-Irish scrapper under the veneer of glamour and urbane charm. The major difference between them was that, as Kerr had grown older and his hopes of the presidency faded, he had begun to find inherent pleasure in political manipulations. For Kennedy, the great sport of politics was of passing interest, he cared only for the result—power. The Oklahoman had intimidated many lesser men, but Kennedy was not threatened because he remained essentially detached.

For Robert Kerr other men were either equals or subordinates. He saw everyone in terms of political power and responded to them after determining how they could help him. But even the arrogant Oklahoman knew that the President of the United States was very different from a Senate colleague. President Kennedy was far more important to Oklahoma's interests than Senator Kennedy of Massachusetts had ever been. For Kerr the invitation to Palm Beach was "an opportunity to do a little courtin'."[69]

During the December visit, Kennedy asked for the Senator's help in getting his legislative program through Congress, and Kerr agreed. The young President-elect had handled the situation deftly in appealing to Kerr's own sense of pride and place. Kennedy's private and respectful recognition of his dependence on Kerr's unofficial leadership was the Senator's personal triumph. He promised to work for those parts of the Kennedy program he agreed with and to continue opposing others—namely medicare. The deal was struck.[70]

There was later a great deal of speculation about the tribute Kerr had extracted from the administration in exchange for his help.[71] While there was no doubt that he wanted "to get as many Blue Chips from the President . . . as he could in his pocket," it would have been out of character for the Oklahoman to set a fixed price.[72] In politics, as in business, Kerr preferred a flexible arrangement where he would trade up or down as the circumstances warranted. President Kennedy was well aware that Kerr saw the completion of the Arkansas River Navigation Project as his personal monument. Should the President's memory falter, Kerr would be there to remind him. Years later at the dedication of the Robert S. Kerr Dam near Sallisaw, Lyndon Johnson told of an incident he had witnessed which helped illuminate the Kerr-Kennedy understanding. Johnson was with the President one afternoon when Senator Kerr called to report that a key administration bill had finally cleared Congress. The conversation continued for a few minutes, then cradling the receiver, Kennedy remarked to the Vice-President, "Senator Kerr always expects something in return . . . but you find it is always a bargain."[73]

After Kennedy's "high C" at the inauguration in January 1961, Congress settled into the pedestrian routine of appropriating funds to keep the government functioning. Except for Kennedy family antics, the most exciting topic in Washington was the proposed expansion of the space program. The President's appointment of James E. Webb as director of the National Aeronautics and Space Administration (NASA) revealed much about the program's future direction and the less-than-subtle influence Senator Kerr enjoyed. Webb had little background in science but "was familiar with every important backstair entrance in Washington."[74] An official in the Truman Administration, first at the Bureau of the Budget and later as an undersecretary of state, Webb joined Kerr-McGee industries in the 1950's. Johnson suggested Webb's name to Kennedy when his personal choice, Donald Cook, declined the job, and Kerr was understandably pleased.[75] Jerome B. Wiesner, who Kennedy named special assistant for science and technology had also been associated with Kerr-McGee Industries as a consultant.[76] Senator Monroney, as chairman of the Senate Commerce Committee's Aviation Subcommittee, also had a lively interest in the future of space flight. The *Tulsa Tribune* correctly predicted that Oklahoma's monopoly on crucial appointments affecting space would be very beneficial to the state.[77]

Senator Kerr had assumed the chairmanship of the Senate Aeronautics and Space Committee somewhat reluctantly in 1961. He had been so preoccupied with the Public Works Committee, where he was frequently acting chairman because of Dennis Chavez' poor health and prolonged absences, that he seldom attended hearings on space matters. When Chavez died in November 1962, most observers thought Kerr would give up the chairmanship of Space to preside over Public Works. Instead, he relinquished the position to Patrick McNamara, a gravel-voiced, chain-smoking liberal Democrat from Michigan, who had been a plumber and union leader before his election. But Kerr had sacrificed nothing. During the fifties he had used his position as chairman of the Rivers and Harbors and Flood Control Subcommittee to construct a vast network of favors and rewards which were the basis of his unprecedented ability to produce a majority in support of a wide range of issues in the sixties. So long as he retained the subcommittee position, his power base was secure. And it was also true that he had obtained almost all the "land, wood and water" projects Oklahoma could absorb.

But before he publicly renounced a claim on Chavez' legacy, he conferred privately with McNamara. Kerr told the Michigander that he would remain as chairman of the Senate Space Committee provided that McNamara promised priority consideration for all authorizations that Kerr specified—namely those for the Arkansas River Navigation Project and all other projects affecting the Sooner State. McNamara, a comparative neophyte in terms of seniority, probably saw this as an unprecedented opportunity and quickly assented to the procedure. But as a security measure, Kerr quietly transferred Don McBride to the Public Works Committee payroll "to ride herd in the absence of Senator Kerr from the meetings."[78] It was not a sudden infatuation with conquering a new world that prompted Kerr's decision in favor of the Space Committee, but the realization that the benefits for Oklahoma were virtually unlimited.

When he returned from Palm Beach, Senator Kerr promised the greatest boom in Oklahoma since the land run. "With my new committee chairmanship, I shall make every effort to help Oklahoma get a full measure of both private and public facilities in this field."[79] He immediately reshaped the committee's professional staff for this purpose. Abolishing the title of staff director, he hired Carter Bradley, former manager of United Press International in Oklahoma, as chief clerk. Bradley's job was to serve as liaison man with NASA and to work with Kerr's press assistant, Malvina Stephenson, to publicize the space program in Oklahoma.[80] Bill Reynolds, who usually worked on Finance Committee matters, was also transferred to the Space Committee. Kerr's staff regularly sent all space hearings and documents to Oklahoma Chamber of Commerce personnel and interested business firms.[81]

For the first few months, Kerr underplayed his new position. He insisted, "My ignorance is colossal," and rebuffed all interviews until he amassed an armor of information.[82] But there was another reason for his caution. Kerr could do little until the President made a decision on manned flight. After the January 16 meeting in Johnson's Capitol hideaway office where Kennedy revealed the Wiesner Committee's critical report of NASA indicating that the investment of resources for manned flight were not justified, Kerr feared the space bonanza might fizzle.[83] A few days later he announced a special inquiry into U.S. achievements in space as compared with the Soviet Union. He clearly intended to resort to "national security" pleas to support the space program.[84]

The Oklahoman was also anxious not to offend Lyndon Johnson by seeming to invade his domain. Johnson continued to use the Space Committee staff after becoming vice-president and even considered sitting with the committee during hearings. But after the stiff opposition to Mansfield's suggestion that the vice-president be allowed to preside at the Senate Democratic Caucus, Kerr made it clear to the Vice-President that he was welcome in hearings as a guest, but not with senatorial privileges.[85] As Kerr worked more closely with Kennedy throughout 1961 and 1962, his Senate colleagues believed he slowly pulled away from Johnson.[86]

Just as renewed Soviet pressure against the western powers in Berlin, plus political turmoil in the Congo and Southeast Asia, triggered demands for accelerated defense spending, Russian Astronaut Yuri Gagarin's successful earth orbit on April 12, 1961, prompted calls for increased funds for NASA. Responding to Kennedy's request for specific recommendations about the space program, Johnson went to the Hill to get congressional backing for increased spending.[87] Kerr and Styles Bridges, the ranking Republican on the Space Committee, assured the Vice-President of bipartisan support for a program to promote American superiority in space. As chairman of the influential Republican Policy Committee, ranking GOP member on Space and Appropriations, and second to Saltonstall on Armed Services, Bridges was a formidable institutional power as well as a long-time Kerr ally. A hardline anticommunist, the New Englander supported space programs primarily because of their potential military significance. The Bridges-Kerr teamwork on the Space Committee ensured that virtually every spending request received unanimous backing during Kerr's tenure as chairman.[88]

Alan Shepard's successful suborbital flight on May 5 probably erased any lingering doubts Kennedy had about the Johnson-Kerr recommendation that manned flight should take precedence over other NASA programs. At a convention of national radio and television broadcasters meeting in Washington on May 10, Kerr revealed that Kennedy had accepted the views of civilian space agency personnel and congressional space experts over his White House science advisers.[89] Kennedy's May 25 message to Congress on "Urgent National Goals" echoed Kerr's argument that the people of the free world needed to do something spectacular in space to counter the belief that the Russians were ahead.[90]

Senator Kerr moved rapidly to respond to the President's revised budget request for an additional $549 million for NASA in 1962.[91] The day before Kennedy's message, the House had authorized $1.4 billion for NASA, which the Senate Space Committee increased by another $384 million.[92] The Senate debate was perfunctory—only five members spoke and policy questions hardly intruded. As one observer noted, "The resemblance was one akin to war, a time when every Senator knew that to ask too many questions is tantamount to treason."[93] By early August, the appropriations process was complete. The country was firmly committed to spend billions to land an American on the moon in a race that "had little to do with the requirements of science" but a great deal to do with prestige and politics.[94]

Senator Kerr had been busy with efforts to ensure that Oklahomans shared in the space program. In the midst of news about the Gagarin flight and a state visit from West German Chancellor Konrad Adenauer, Kerr, James Webb, and Harold Stuart of Tulsa invited the President to address the "First National Conference on the Peaceful Uses of Space" to be held in Tulsa, May 26–27.[95] The meeting was designed to give representatives of Oklahoma's Chambers of Commerce and industries an opportunity to meet officials and technicians from NASA, the Department of Defense, and other space-related agencies. As the featured speaker at the Tulsa conference, Kerr hinted that Sooners could count on landing their share of contracts flowing from the $5.7 billion, five-year program Kennedy had requested the day prior to the conference. Max Genet, director of the Oklahoma Department of Commerce, reported that while twenty-nine companies were already engaged in research and production activities related to space, he expected a five-fold increase in space-related activity within the year. When asked to spell out the effects of the President's space push in dollars, Kerr replied coyly, "You wouldn't want me to show my hole card, would you?"[96]

After the initial press release, there had been a deliberate attempt to underplay the Tulsa conference, probably to avoid charges of conflict of interest. And since the President was unable to attend, the meeting lacked celebrity status.[97] But anyone seeing the original announcement—which noted that the head of NASA, prominent Defense Department officials, Edward R. Murrow, the director of USIA, and senior executives from RCA, ITT, McDonnell Aircraft, and Convair Astronautics would attend—could not have mistaken it for a routine public information exercise. Despite the questionable circumstances, there was only one note of criticism. Congressman John Rhodes (R., Ariz.), a member of the House Appropriations Subcommittee on Independent Offices, which had jurisdiction over NASA funding requests, wrote James Webb that he had a nagging feeling that politics had intruded into NASA affairs. "Any similarity between the name Kerr-McGee and the name of the member of the other body who also happens to be chairman of the Senate Committee on Aeronautics and Space Science is not coincidental."[98] To avoid any further possible criticism, NASA decided to hold several similar conferences in other major cities.[99] By the end of 1962, it was clear that Senator Kerr's pork barrel instincts were not limited to land, wood, and water. Douglas Aircraft and North American Aviation, two giants in the space industry, opened plants in Tulsa, with North American planning a substantial expansion when the Arkansas navigation project was completed in 1970.[100] By the time of his death, Kerr was steadily attaining his dream of overtaking California as the leading state in space construction.[101]

Senator Kerr's support of the President's ambitious and expensive manned-flight venture generated numerous dividends for Oklahoma in areas other than space. In return for Kerr's promise to lend his influence to selected aspects of the New Frontier legislative program, the administration gave him a virtually blank check for water resources. Early in 1961, the Oklahoma Senators hosted a breakfast in Tulsa where Kerr introduced Secretary of the

Interior Stewart Udall saying how wonderful it was "to have a man in the Cabinet who is deeply interested in land and water development." Udall responded, "It is just as wonderful to have a Senator like Oklahoma's Kerr . . . who [has] such a deep interest in these matters."[102] Oklahoma water projects were financed to the hilt in the first Kennedy budget and then increased again in Congress with no resistance from the traditionally frugal Bureau of the Budget.[103] When the U.S. Public Health Service selected sites for seven regional water pollution and demonstration research laboratories, Ada, Oklahoma, Kerr's birthplace, headed the list. In announcing the $2.5 million facility, Kerr admitted that "we had to have some help from the White House, and I am grateful for that."[104]

Despite the appearance of harmony between Kerr and the Kennedy Administration, a rift over patronage in 1961 revealed just how fragile the alliance was. Under the arrangements to share patronage equally with Senator Monroney, Kerr had nominated Rex Hawks for the job of federal marshal and, at Aubrey Kerr's urging, Luther Bohanon as the federal judge for the northern, eastern and western districts of Oklahoma. This so-called roving judgeship was vacant because of the death of William R. Wallace in 1960.[105] With an impressive "due bill" for handling six major parts of Kennedy's 1961 legislative program—the highway bill, revision of aid to dependent children under Social Security, the temporary increase in the federal debt limit, water antipollution legislation, expansion of unemployment compensation, and funds for the space program—Kerr was astonished when the Justice Department refused to act on either appointment.[106]

According to a 1953 agreement, the Justice Department submitted nominations for the federal bench to the American Bar Association's Standing Committee on the Federal Judiciary for evaluation.[107] The Oklahoma ABA president, a Republican attorney from Tulsa, reported unfavorably on Bohanon's qualifications to the standing committee.[108] Attorney General Robert Kennedy apparently miscalculated his brother's dependence on the Senator's good humor, as well as his goodwill and refused to go against the ABA's verdict that Bohanon was "not qualified."

In July, a Justice Department investigator, John Siegenthaler, arrived in Oklahoma City to make inquiries about the judicial nominee. Kerr denied that he had instigated the visit but admitted telling Robert Kennedy that the Attorney General's position was untenable without personal knowledge that Kerr's recommendation was not a good one.[109] Then on August 4, Assistant Attorney General Byron F. "Whizzer" White visited Oklahoma City and Tulsa to confer with attorneys of the ABA. But still nothing happened. Kerr, though impatient and irritable, calmly announced that if the President attempted to nominate someone other than Luther Bohanon, he would block Senate confirmation.[110] The *Daily Oklahoman*'s Washington correspondent noted, "Kerr's political plum was slowly becoming a prune."[111] Clearly the judgeship was no longer the issue; Robert Kerr's prestige was.

In an effort to loosen the logjam at Justice, Rex Hawks went to see Assistant Attorney General White ostensibly about the unexplained delay on his appointment. Hawks had served as U.S. marshal during the Truman Administration; and, as a member of the Oklahoma Bureau of Investigation in Kerr's gubernatorial administration, he was well known at Justice. White assured him that no one opposed his appointment but that the Attorney General was unwilling to act until the conflict over the judgeship was resolved. He also made it clear to Hawks that Robert Kennedy was reluctant to renege on the agreement with the ABA for fear of alienating the legal profession. If Kerr would simply make another recommendation for the judgeship, Hawks' appointment would go right through. Hawks was noncommittal but reported directly to Kerr's Senate office. The Senator listened impassively, then telephoned the President's office requesting an appointment for 5:30 that afternoon.[112] The following day, August 17, the White House issued a press release announcing the President's intention to appoint Luther Bohanon.[113]

In recounting the interview to Burl Hays and Rex Hawks, Kerr said he told Kennedy that his three choices for the judgeship were, "Bohanon, Bohanon, and Bohanon." If the President were unwilling to allow the Senator this courtesy, "Kennedy had better get himself another boy."[114] The implication was that Senator Kerr would not lift a finger to help with the important tax and trade legislation planned for the coming session.

It was unlikely that President Kennedy was aware of the serious nature of the quarrel between his brother and the Senator. Preoccupied with the Vienna summit and the increasing Soviet pressure which resulted in the Russians sealing the borders of East Germany, patronage matters were of minor concern. But he quickly recognized the repercussions if Kerr were not appeased. In terms of political power, the Oklahoman was infinitely more important to the President than the American Bar Association. Kennedy also probably sensed, if he did not yet know for certain, that while Kerr was infinitely flexible in politics—as long as he could explain a shift in his vote rationally—he would never go back on the promise to his own brother.

The day Bohanon's nomination reached Capitol Hill, the Senate passed the controversial Foreign Assistance Act of 1961. The new law replaced the ten-year-old Mutual Security Act by separating military from nonmilitary aid. Although the Senate accepted the provision for a five-year authorization for development loan funds, the members insisted on annual appropriations, not the direct Treasury financing that the President had requested.[115] Before the final voting, there were rumors that the administration was sitting on federal judgeships until the bill passed Congress, hoping that the lure of patronage would convince wavering Democrats to support the bill.[116] Senator Kerr denied that his vote for the foreign aid bill was a matter of patronage. A consistent opponent of foreign aid spending in the Eisenhower Administration, he had voted against "expenditures of billions in other countries when I couldn't get millions for Oklahoma." But he added, circumstances had changed. The Kennedy Administration "has endorsed every proposal I favor for Oklahoma."[117] Kerr had actually decided to support the administration's revised foreign aid program, which gave special attention to the problem of U.S. gold reserves, as early as April.[118] But if Kennedy had refused him the Bohanon appointment, he probably would have retaliated, and the foreign aid vote was the most immediate weapon. There was no reason to doubt Kerr's statement that no one in the administration had talked to him about the foreign aid bill in connection with the judicial appointment. When you did business with Senator Kerr, a great deal was merely understood.

The thunderheads which had threatened the sunny relationship between Kerr and Kennedy quickly dispersed, although the Attorney General never forgave Kerr.[119] Any lingering doubts about restored good relations vanished when the White House announced that the President would visit Senator Kerr overnight at his ranch outside Poteau, Oklahoma.[120] The news came as a complete surprise to Governor J. Howard Edmondson, a Kennedy clan intimate who had asked the President to come to Oklahoma on several occasions. The Governor immediately called Kenneth O'Donnell, the White House appointments secretary, demanding to know the reason for the visit. O'Donnell disclaimed any special knowledge saying that the President had described the trip as "personal." Edmondson, who was reputed to be a possible replacement for Lyndon Johnson in 1964, was frantic to know Kennedy's true purpose. Unable to reach Kennedy by telephone, he flew to Hyannisport and tracked the President to the golf course. In response to Edmondson's almost hysterical questioning, the bemused Kennedy wryly replied, "Why Howard, I'm going to Oklahoma to kiss Bob Kerr's ass."[121]

Kerr's office announced that the President would dedicate a new scenic highway in eastern Oklahoma.[122] This "scenic highway" was a nine-mile stretch of road from the town of Big Cedar (population: 2) through the Ouachita National Forest. One editorial writer described it as "a mountain road that starts nowhere in particular and goes to a suburb of the same place."[123] But anyone familiar with the administration's legislative package for 1962— trade expansion, tax revision, and medicare—knew those bills would have to travel a road that ran directly through the Senate Finance Committee. It was easy to understand why the President would "travel so far to dedicate so little."[124]

The presidential helicopter touched down at Big Cedar, Oklahoma, on October 30, a crisp fall afternoon. Sixty thousand friendly Oklahomans waited to see the young President whose name had been an anathema in the Sooner State just a year earlier.

Kennedy made a brief speech, snipped the tape opening the highway after a flurry over the misplaced shears, and was whisked away for a private evening at Kerr's ranch.[125] The Senator's home was as big and boastful as its owner. Located on a bluff overlooking a picturesque river valley, the 321-foot-long native stone-and-glass house consisted of fourteen thousand square feet, three kitchens, nine bedrooms, eleven baths, and a playroom outfitted as a ship for the grandchildren. Kerr had wanted a modest retreat similar to his cabin on Lake Pelican in Minnesota, but a mere husband in private life, he had yielded to Mrs. Kerr's grander plans. The house was elegantly furnished in the Chinese manner and reflected her interest in antiques. Kerr had begun buying the fifty-two thousand acres of land in 1954 after determining the Oklahoma county with the greatest annual rainfall. He revitalized the land with rich grasses, which also provided grazing pasture for the magnificent herd of two thousand Black Angus cattle. Although he spent fewer than two dozen nights in the house, Kerr, whose father had been a tenant farmer, was enormously proud of the ranch. He often talked of using it to teach small ranchers and farmers how to replenish the exhausted land in this economically depressed part of the state.[126]

With the President a captive audience, Senator Kerr had invited the district and division chiefs of the Corps of Engineers, replete with models and charts, to explain progress on the Arkansas River Navigation Project.[127] After the detailed briefing an experienced White House correspondent concluded that if there were any immediate political fallout from the visit, it would show up in appropriations for Oklahoma water projects.[128] The following year Kennedy recommended $66.1 million for Oklahoma water development. The administration also approved $9.5 million in government loans and grants under the new Area Redevelopment Act for building twin lodges at Lake Eufaula—twelve times larger than any other grant.[129]

President Kennedy paid Kerr a distinct compliment in traveling to Big Cedar, but he also put the Senator under enormous obligation. While predictions that Kerr might be on the ticket in 1964 or that he had agreed to soften his opposition to medicare seemed unjustified, one forecast was accurate. When the second session of the Eighty-seventh Congress convened, Robert Kerr was clearly "the new wagon master of the rocky road to the new frontier."[130]

Kerr's emergence in 1962 as the only man in Congress who was a powerful force in his own right occurred because of a peculiar combination of weakened congressional leadership, a politically unattractive legislative program, and the Oklahoman's own institutional power and dominating personality. Without Lyndon Johnson, the upper chamber had lapsed into feudalism as power drifted from the majority leader to the several "lords" of the Senate. The fifties had been an aberration: in the sixties the Senate was back to its old self—disorganized, often unmanageable, and fiercely independent. The sixteen standing committee chairmen—ranging from staunchly conservative southerners like Russell, Byrd, Ellender, and Eastland to mildly liberal westerners like Chavez, Anderson, and Magnuson—set the tone. Political analysts writing of the "barons of the Senate," described Kerr as the greatest of the sixteen.[131]

Senator Mansfield was simply too mild-mannered to be an effective leader. His failure to prod Harry Byrd to hasten consideration of key Kennedy proposals in the Finance Committee, particularly tax and trade legislation, created a tangle of legislation at the end of summer when most senators were anxious to be at home campaigning for the November elections. And his inept handling of the southern filibuster on the literacy test bill had given Senate liberals license to filibuster the administration's communications satellite bill.[132] Although Hubert Humphrey assumed greater prominence as Mansfield's Whip than he had as Johnson's, his status was fuzzy because he held no chairmanships. While he was never to eastern and midwestern liberals what Russell was to southern and most western Democrats, Humphrey's technical mastery of the institution at fifty-one earned him the reputation "as the man to see if you want to get something done."[133] This was probably a greater tribute to his zest for Senate chores than an estimate of his influence.

On the House side, the leadership situation was no better.

Rayburn's death in November 1961 elevated Kennedy's old Massachusetts political enemy, John McCormack, to the speakership, and Carl Albert became majority leader. Albert was an old friend, having placed Kerr's name in nomination at the 1952 convention. Presidential intimates believed Kennedy favored Richard Bolling for Rayburn's job, but the Missouri Congressman was unable to muster a challenge.[134] Although Kennedy had refused to endorse the northeast-southwest package of McCormack and Albert which Kerr favored, his courtesy and kind words to the McAlester Congressman during his visit to Oklahoma in 1961 implied his acceptance of the inevitable. Unlike Bolling, Albert had not been a reliable administration supporter, but he was an important link to the eleven southern House committee chairmen and to Robert Kerr.[135]

President Kennedy had little taste for the wearying and mundane task of courting Congress, but he wanted a bountiful legislative harvest for the fall elections, so White House contacts with the Hill intensified. Early in 1962 Larry O'Brien, special assistant for congressional relations, held a four-hour bipartisan briefing session for six hundred aides to senators and congressmen to explain the President's legislative program.[136] O'Brien's Chautauqua," as Interior Secretary Udall dubbed the event, was an isolated success, but it did not compensate for direct and frequent contact between the man in the White House and the voting legislator on Capitol Hill.

Some efforts at intensified liaison backfired. New York Democrat Otis Pike publicly requested that the White House stop trying "to twist his arm," while a southern Democrat complained of being harassed with ten White House calls in one week asking him to support raising the debt ceiling after he had announced his intention to do so.[137] Other congressmen smirked at veiled threats because the men who made them were either politically impotent or uninformed. During the 1961 fight to enlarge the House Rules Committee, Secretary Udall told Alton Lennon (D., N.C.) that a saline water conversion plant might not be built in his district if he did not vote to expand the committee. Lennon voted no and got the plant anyway.[138] When tempers flared over the 1962 farm bill, the White House told another congressman there would be no new post office in his district if he continued to oppose the administration. The member voted as he pleased because the new post office was already being constructed.[139]

The President's reluctance to deal personally with Congress often stemmed from a wish to husband his legislative credits for measures like the trade bill and tax revision. To bypass a legislative struggle, as well as to avoid embarrasing southern Democrats, he resorted to an executive order to end discrimination in federal housing.[140] But this action raised cries that he was usurping Congress as the policy making branch of government. Such criticism was only natural from influential Democratic lawmakers who believed they had exercised some power in policy determination during the Republican years and now felt ignored.[141]

The program Kennedy outlined in the 1962 State of the Union Address—discretionary power to cut income taxes to combat recession, broad tariff-cutting powers, a system of medical care for people over sixty-five financed through Social Security, and tax revision—was not abhorrent because it was liberal, but because it had little political appeal.[142] Nineteen sixty-two was an election year in which only the medicare proposal possessed much vote-getting power, but even its sparkle seemed limited to the northern cities. As spring faded into summer, the President summoned Mansfield, Humphrey, Russell, and Kerr to discuss ways to speed consideration of key proposals.[143] Although the Ways and Means Committee had stalled on medicare, the House had passed the President's tax revision proposals at the end of March, and Wilbur Mills was promising a report on the trade bill within a few days. Since Senate Finance Chairman Harry Byrd was out of sympathy with both tax and trade legislation and an avowed opponent of medicare, the problem was how to get the administration's program through the Finance Committee unscathed and onto the Senate floor.[144] White House strategists proposed postponing the tax bill and jumping to trade which they feared might die if left to the last days of what promised to be a very lengthy session. But Kerr disagreed. Since Finance had started hearings on the House-proposed tax bill on April 2, he felt Byrd would resent the administration's interference with the committee's scheduled business. The administration and the Senate leadership were dependent on Kerr to get both trade and tax to the floor, so they accepted his counsel. But before he delivered on either, he demonstrated his independence as well as his enormous influence in defeating the administration's medicare bill a second time.

In his State of the Union Message, Kennedy challenged the heavily Democratic Congress to pass the health care legislation scuttled just before the 1960 election. Senator Anderson, who was seated next to Kerr, led the applause. "Kerr, grinning . . . reached across and playfully attempted to quiet Anderson's clapping hands."[145] The New Mexican probably sensed that despite his smile, Kerr was not playing.

When the second session of the Eighty-seventh Congress began, the administration's medicare plan, known as the King-Anderson bill, was stuck in the House Ways and Means Committee. With Chairman Mills opposed "until I have reason to believe that it is going to get enough support to pass," the committee moved on to other business.[146] Despite administration attempts to win committee support for a cannibalized version of an earlier Javits-Rockefeller proposal, still nothing happened.

Unable to generate any great enthusiasm for medicare in Congress, Kennedy, at the urging of organized labor and the National Council of Senior Ctizens for Health Care, decided to appeal to the American public. On May 20, with the mercury registering ninety degrees, Kennedy appeared before 17,500 people at Madison Square Garden. Bert Parks was master of ceremonies for a program that included a full symphony orchestra, medleys from *Porgy and Bess*, tenor Robert Merrill of the Metropolitan Opera, and a sing-along session with Mitch Miller.[147] For some reason, the President discarded his carefully prepared text and spoke extemporaneously, but "he delivered his message without his customary clarity and grace . . . it was a shambles." Kennedy seemed to have forgotten the lessons of the 1960 campaign "that arousing a partisan crowd in a vast arena and convincing the skeptical TV viewer at home required wholly different kinds of presentation."[148] The following night Dr. Leonard Larson, president of the American Medical Association, in a television appearance at an empty Madison Square Garden warned older Americans not to confuse Kennedy's popularity with infallibility.[149]

Although most administration supporters agreed that Kennedy's performance was a disaster,[150] Senator Kerr seemed to waver in his belief that he could defeat medicare. Abraham Ribicoff, secretary of HEW, had been saying since early February that Kerr-Mills was "a most laudable piece of legislation, but needs to be supplemented by a version of King-Anderson."[151] Kerr was realistic enough to see that "sooner or later there was going to be a Social Security financed mechanism," and when that happened, he wanted to be in a position to have some degree of control over its form.[152] A few days after the New York rallies, he met privately with Wilbur Cohen and Larry O'Brien to discuss a possible compromise, but nothing came of the meeting.[153]

Stymied by the delphic Mills in the House, Senate medicare proponents decided to try a procedural end-run. Earlier in the year in an interview on Kenneth Keating's (R., N.Y.) television program, "Let's Look at Congress," Majority Leader Mansfield hinted that the Senate might force consideration of medicare as a rider to a bill from Ways and Means.[154] With debate scheduled on the administration's public welfare amendments for July 2, the appropriate vehicle was at hand. H.R. 10606, the welfare bill, offered both an immediate increase in public aid to the needy and the possibility of reducing the cost of such aid in the future through rehabilitation and vocational programs for welfare recipients. Such legislation had substantial political appeal for both spenders and economizers in an otherwise barren election year.[155]

On June 29, Senators Anderson and Javits introduced a compromise medical insurance plan as an amendment to the administration's welfare bill.[156] This new version incorporated several features designed to appeal to enough liberal Republican votes to get it adopted.[157] Despite the cosmetics and the five Republican cosponsors, the controversial Social Security financing mechanism of the original King-Anderson Bill was intact.

During the eleven days of desultory and ill-attended debate on H.R. 10606, Kerr was busy making sure that the Anderson-

Javits amendment would be rejected. Although most senators doubted that the House would accept the amendment since it was essentially a revenue measure which had skirted normal legislative channels, Kerr believed his prestige depended on the ability to defeat the measure in his own bailiwick. Judging that the vote would be extremely close, he concentrated on a handful of pivotal Democrats and Republicans.

To escape the distractions of his Capitol Hill office, Kerr rented a suite in the Statler Hilton hotel in downtown Washington. At five A.M. on July 5, returning from an Independence Day speaking engagement in Oklahoma, he met with Bill Reynolds and two analysts from the Legislative Reference Service to scrutinize the amendment section by section probing for a weakness. When the day was over, he had found it. The provisions relating to nursing home facilities were flawed. For the next week, Reynolds called every state department of welfare to determine if their nursing homes would meet the amendment's proposed standards. For several senators "this was the real clincher . . . when they found their nursing homes would not qualify."[158] Kerr believed that this issue was especially crucial in securing the votes of two influential New England Republicans, George Aiken of Vermont and Margaret Chase Smith of Maine.[159]

Kerr approached Mrs. Smith directly because of their congenial relationship as colleagues on the Senate Space Committee, but winning Aiken's vote was a more difficult problem.[160] Though often intensely partisan, Aiken took pride in his independence. Direct lobbying was a sure way to lose his vote, so Kerr chose an indirect approach. During the Senate debate, Kerr, as floor manager for the welfare bill, happened to linger near Aiken's desk one day. He was deep in conversation with a Republican who opposed the medicare amendment. "The fellow kept asking questions that he had asked before, but Kerr patiently explained the amendment to him." The Vermonter remained motionless at his desk throughout the discussion, watching and listening intently. After the vote, Bill Reynolds, who had witnessed the event, marveled at Kerr's patience with the persistent questioner. Kerr laughed heartily and admitted to a charade. "Why I was talking to Senator Aiken and that fellow just gave me the opportunity."[161]

There was no standing room in the Senate galleries and staff members packed the rear of the chamber near the cloakroom as the Clerk began to call the roll on July 17. The question was on Senator Kerr's motion to table the Anderson-Javits medicare amendment. The Oklahoman was slumped at his desk apparently unconcerned. The tally sheet in front of him, which he and Bobby Baker had been over many times, indicated the vote would be 50–50.[162] With Carl Hayden reluctantly supporting the amendment, Kerr needed only one defector from the administration ranks. Then Hayden would switch, and the amendment would be lost 52–48.[163]

As the roll call proceeded, Senator Kerr seemed pleased. Hayden, though present when his name was called, remained silent. It was not yet clear if the leadership would need him. When the Clerk reached the last of the M's, there was a ripple from the galleries as conservative South Dakota Republican Karl Mundt voted no—in favor of the administration. Kerr was furious. The plodding Mundt, arriving late, was obviously confused. He thought a negative response was a vote against medicare. But when the roll call reached the R's, there was an audible gasp from senators and spectators as Jennings Randolph (D., W. Va.), a stalwart Kennedy supporter, rose and voted yes—against the administration. After hurried explanations from his aides, Mundt corrected his vote, and the tally was 51–48. The measure was shelved. Hayden, free of his obligation to the leadership raised the final count to 52 to table and 48 against.[164]

Despite Mundt's slip, Jennings Randolph cast the decisive vote.[165] In an interview just off the Senate floor following the vote, he told reporters he "was not interested in making a gesture to our senior citizens when I feel so convinced that there will be no action in the other body this year on the subject that is not generated by the House Ways and Means Committee."[166] Randolph neglected to say that West Virginia had overspent her federal welfare funds by about $11 million and faced the prospect of unmanageable state debt. He had probably discussed his state's predicament with Kerr in June when the Oklahoman received an honorary degree from West Virginia's Salem College, which Randolph's father had founded. Personal as well as political friends, they shared an interest in Baptist philanthropies, and Kerr had campaigned for the West Virginian in 1960 when he was elected to Democrat Matthew M. Neely's vacant seat.[167] Kerr promised to help the Panhandle State with an amendment to the welfare bill covering the deficit.[168] HEW Secretary Ribicoff and Undersecretary Wilbur Cohen conferred with Kerr on the amendment, and both men personally assured Randolph they would go along with whatever Senator Kerr promised him.[169] On July 3, Kerr unobtrusively secured a voice vote to pass an innocuous looking provision which made certain federal payments retroactive to July 1, 1961, to states which had trained unemployed parents for useful jobs.[170]

Kennedy learned of the amendment and feared what Randolph had promised Kerr in return. He called the West Virginian several times during the debate urging him not to desert the administration's cause. The President also arranged for Democratic party leaders throughout West Virginia, along with labor and welfare groups, to talk to him.[171] Randolph later admitted that he had been "under the heaviest pressure not to vote to table," but his alliance with Kerr held.[172] Within hours of a television statement characterizing the Senate vote as a "serious defeat for every American family," Kennedy retaliated. He instructed the budget director, David Bell, to notify the West Virginian that a costly and controversial project he wanted was being dropped. Sorenson tried to excuse the harsh action, saying he had "no doubt that Senator Kerr could channel more funds into West Virginia than we could reroute."[173]

The 1962 medicare debacle was humiliating for the Kennedy Administration, but their own handling of the amendment probably hurt them as much as Senator Kerr's opposition. The strategy, designed to circumvent both House Ways and Means and House Rules, was certain to fail. The best the administration could hope for was to give urban Democrats an opportunity to make a record that would be useful in the fall elections. Although the administration knew that Congress frequently voted on bills strictly for political window dressing, they learned the painful lesson that the legislative branch reserved the right to choose what battles it would lose. This was particularly true of the Senate. Several Democrats, including influential southerners like Russell, Sparkman, and Hill probably would have voted against tabling if the bill had gone through normal legislative channels. But they resented not only being put on the spot on a politically uncertain issue but also squandering their votes on a strategy doomed to failure in the House. Other southern Democrats, who feared civil rights legislation more than they disliked medicare, saw the possible implications of this strategy and voted with Kerr.[174] Still others, like Randolph, feared that the entire welfare bill might be lost in conference if the medicare provision were attached.[175]

Despite the Press Gallery gossip that "what Kerr wants, Kennedy gets,"[176] the Oklahoman's victory on medicare was neither surprising nor unwarranted. Kerr had been working quietly for over six months lining up votes against the day he would need them. The day before the vote the *Oklahoma City Times'* Washington correspondent wrote that Kerr was "cashing in all his due bills on this one."[177] Reynolds said that Kerr was certain of Randolph's vote and hoped for Hayden's at least ten days before the July 17 roll call. But he kept still because the White House effort, relying on Johnson's vote to break a probable tie, had peaked. On the day of the vote the White House suddenly realized that they were in danger, and by that time it was too late.[178]

Although some pundits thought Kerr's opposition on medicare might dampen the "spirit of Big Cedar," the relationship between the Senator and the President was actually strengthened.[179] When a reporter on NBC's "Meet the Press" asked Kerr how he justified his opposition to medicare when he had supported and led the floor fights on most other Kennedy proposals, he replied, "No man in the Senate respects or loves the President of the United States more than I do, but I love the people of Oklahoma more than I do the President of the United States."[180] Later, when Kerr was at the White House, he noticed the President examining the transcript. Apparently embarrassed at his own effulgence, he sheepishly explained, "Mr. President, I had to say what I said there about you and the people of Oklahoma . . . for my sake—and for your sake."[181] Despite mutterings about Kerr's villainy in some quarters at the White House, President Kennedy never wavered in his confidence that the Oklahoman would honor the bargain struck at Palm Beach.

At nine A.M. the morning following the medicare vote, Senator Kerr and Treasury Secretary Douglas Dillon were busily reviewing the administration's tax revision bill pending in the Senate Finance Committee.[182] Before the Eighty-seventh Congress adjourned in October, Senator Kerr played the leading role in securing adoption of the first omnibus tax revision since 1954 and enactment of significant innovations in American trade policy designed to match the architecture of world trade patterns in the 1960's.[183] Kerr's emergence after mid-1962 as the administration's most-valued ally on Capitol Hill probably explained why he no longer rattled off, "What's in it for Oklahoma?" at every opportunity. Contrary to *Saturday Evening Post* columnist Joseph Kraft's assessment that the provincial Oklahoman "showed signs of beginning to understand the New Frontier view of national politics," it seemed more accurate that the administration had become the legislative captive of the man whose fundamental political philosophy of "what's good for Oklahoma is good for the nation," remained unchanged.[184]

The Kennedy Administration's concessions to the domestic oil industry and acceptance of larger budget requests to speed the Arkansas River Navigation Project were the price for Kerr's leadership on both tax and trade. According to a Treasury official, Kennedy's omission of revisions in the petroleum depletion allowance in the 1962 tax bill was deliberate. "There was no point in starting off with that. We [didn't] want to lose the support of Senator Kerr."[185] In July, when the unlikely coalition of conservatives Byrd and Williams (R., Del.) and liberals Gore, Douglas, and McCarthy seemed ready to smother the administration's investment incentive feature in the Finance Committee, the President summoned Kerr. While Kennedy argued that this proposal was the key to bringing the economy out of recession, Kerr seemed detached. In response, he asked Kennedy why the Budget Bureau opposed the Arkansas project. "So it went, tax bill versus Oklahoma pork." Finally Kerr said he could not move against the logjam on the tax bill until the administration moved on the Arkansas. Smiling, Kennedy replied, "You know, Bob, I never really understood that Arkansas River bill before today."[186]

In exchange for abandoning an earlier protectionist stance on trade, Kerr extracted the President's commitment to retain a system of import quotas to protect the domestic oil industry.[187] Once he had Kennedy's word, he publicly opposed the independent oil producers' efforts to write specific limits on oil imports into the trade bill, offering his own prestige as a guarantee that the administration would not injure the domestic producers. "If I do a job on this bill," he told a group of skeptical oil men, "then don't you think I'll have more bargaining power with the President for the oil industry?"[188]

Kerr's remarkable performance on both tax and trade matters, as well as his role in stopping a liberal filibuster that threatened the administration's communications satellite bill in July, proved "that there was a lot more to Bob Kerr than homilies and billingsgate."[189] The man whom so many had dismissed in 1952 as a church basement orator, long on platitudes and Biblical quotations, in 1962 earned the laureate "the uncrowned King of the Senate." Kerr's lifelong habit of thorough, painstaking preparation explained much of his success in handling the administration's legislative program. His absorbent mind was so quick and his mastery of complicated tax law and trade practices so complete that many senators of both parties followed him on these complex issues without hesitation.[190] Senator Gore, who opposed Kerr in the 1962 tax debate, conceded that he was "undoubtedly the most influential Senator on tax matters in our history."[191]

Kerr's strong ties to the southern Democrats and his rapport with the westerners facilitated his task as floor manager for a northern Democratic President. Because of his adroit handling of the tax bill and the chairman of Senate Finance, Harry Byrd, at first bitterly opposed to the investment credit feature of the bill,

ultimately voted for final passage.[192] As the symbol of fiscal con-
servatism in the country, Byrd's acquiescence on both tax and trade
became the administration's stamp of respectability within the
business community.

And Kerr's reputation for generosity with his own money, as
well as the government's, also helped. A Republican on the Finance
Committee admitted that it was difficult for him to vote against
Kerr because the Senator had helped raise money for his last
election.[193] In the same vein, a Democrat's commenting on Kerr's
handling of Public Works remarked, "Two birds in the hand from
Bob Kerr are worth one in the bush from Jack Kennedy."[194]

Despite his impressive record in the Eighty-seventh Congress,
Kerr was no shadow leader. If a bill did not interest him or was
not within the jurisdiction of one of his committees, he left it alone.
And even if he did take an interest, there were limits to his ability
to persuade. Without the official position as majority leader, he
lacked the "baubles of Johnson's power"—coveted committee assignments and scarce office space.[195] But his vitriolic tongue and
his often unpredictable temper were the real reins on his power.
Robert Kerr was more feared than loved, and there was no anti-
dote for the sting of his ridicule. His old friend Clinton Anderson,
more frequently an antagonist than an ally in the 1960's, noticed
"a growing number of complaints from . . . Senate colleagues
about Bob's high pressure tactics." As the Eighty-seventh Congress
ended, he predicted that a major resistance movement was forming
to "cut Bob's power back significantly."[196]

Congress did not adjourn until October 13, perilously tardy
for an election year. Although exhausted from the hectic late
sessions and the Washington heat, Kerr had no time for a vacation.
His only recreation, besides endless games of gin rummy, was
fishing, but it was already too cool for angling at his Minnesota
retreat. Elections were less than a month away, and his colleague
Monroney needed help. The Democratic party's prominence in
Oklahoma was seriously threatened. The Republicans, whose
organization had been perfected in the Eisenhower years, were
concentrating their efforts on electing a governor and a senator,
and Kerr confided to close friends he feared they might win both.[197]

At a meeting of prominent Democrats three weeks before the election, Senator Kerr announced that he planned to campaign extensively for Monroney, although he continued his strong support of W. P. Atkinson, the Democratic gubernatorial candidate. Kerr was anxious for another bout with B. Hayden Crawford, who had challenged him in 1960, and was now the candidate against Monroney.[198]

Monroney disliked the earthy aspects of politics and did little electioneering on his own behalf, while Kerr toured the state reiterating the theme "Let's keep the team together."[199] Monroney, who had said his greatest ambition was to be the "oldest junior Senator,"[200] was reelected, and the Republicans won the governor's race. Kerr's strategy and his personal campaign accounted for Monroney's return to Washington, but the weeks of traveling had tired him even more.

The election over, Kerr, though haggard and beginning to show his sixty-six years, seemed unable to rest. He had assumed so much personal responsibility for the administration's legislation program that he hurried back to Washington to consult on the top-priority tax reduction and reform bill planned for the 1963 opening of Congress. He was also busy with a plan to recoup a $25 million authorization for a dam at Waurika, Oklahoma, which he had dropped during the conference on the 1962 Public Works bill as a concession to Representative Howard W. Smith (D., Va.). Despite the ritual of sacrifice, Oklahoma still had received $200 million or 10 per cent of the money appropriated in the bill. Lest anyone think Kerr was slipping he told reporters, "Judge Smith got his pound of flesh. The people got a bill. But we'll be back next year."[201]

In addition to his obligations in Washington, Kerr was anxious to examine a new drilling rig Kerr-McGee had perfected and was using off the Louisiana coast. He decided to fly to the Gulf Coast for a quick inspection and a brief visit with Dean McGee. Rex Hawks drove him to the airport in Oklahoma City where a company plane was waiting. Usually gregarious, Kerr seemed subdued during the brief ride. He slumped exhausted, his deeply lined face showing the strain of the last few months. At the airport the two men said good-bye, shook hands, and the Senator boarded the plane. As Hawks waited for the takeoff, Kerr suddenly reappeared in the doorway and walked back down the ramp. He seemed concerned that he had been aloof on the trip out and gripped Hawks hand to thank him for driving him to the plane. He also mentioned his great affection for this friend of twenty years. Then, as he turned to reboard, he said in a low voice, "Rex, if anything happens to me, do what you can for Bob Jr."[202]

On Sunday, December 16, Kerr entered Bethesda Naval Hospital with a "mild virus infection." He had no history of heart trouble, but the exertions of climbing all over the twenty-story drilling rig, coming on top of a grueling year in the Senate and a statewide campaign, had taken their toll. The next day doctors confirmed that the Oklahoman had suffered a mild heart attack and would have to tone down his frenetic life. The Senator told his son Breene that he planned to spend more time in Poteau relaxing because "now I have a reason to say no."[203] Mrs. Kerr flew up from Poteau but assured that the Senator merely needed rest, she returned to Oklahoma to finish preparations for the family Christmas celebration. On December 27, Bobby Baker informed Senator Mansfield that "the Doctor assured me that Senator Kerr will be ready to carry a full load by June 1st.[204]

By New Year's Day, the Senator seemed restored to his old vigor. He was sitting on his bed that morning regaling his doctor with stories about his first trip to New York City, a visit to Coney Island, and his original encounter with a New York cabbie. Kerr always loved a funny story on himself. Laughing heartily, he stopped in midsentence; his arm jerked; and he fell back on the pillows, dead.[205]

Kerr's sudden death meant further schism for Oklahoma's turbulent Democratic party and exposed Governor Edmondson's raw ambition. Under Oklahoma statute, the governor filled any Senate vacancy with the appointee holding office until the next general election. It was no secret that Edmondson had been eying Kerr's Senate seat since the late 1950's; now it was suddenly within his grasp. Most "old guard" Democrats favored naming Robert S. Kerr, Jr. It would have been an appropriate gesture of respect to the Senator's memory, and since the young Kerr had no aspirations for a political career, it would have allowed the party time to find a suitable successor for the general election in 1964. Lyndon Johnson, who knew of Kerr's wishes through Rex Hawks, endorsed the junior Kerr; but the Kennedy Administration, particularly Robert Kennedy, favored Edmondson—a reliable and eager vote for the New Frontier.[206]

Political realities as well as opportunism determined Edmondson's decision. Kerr had been the only Sooner governor ever elected to higher office. Edmondson probably concluded that his best hope for the Senate was to resign and have the new governor appoint him. Not only did he lack Kerr's financial resources and political organization to keep his candidacy alive for twenty-three months, but Edmondson was no longer popular. Elected with a record margin in 1958, he was about to leave office as the most controversial chief executive since "Alfalfa Bill" Murray.[207] Nine days before his term ended, Edmondson resigned. George Nigh, his successor, immediately appointed him to the United States Senate.

Edmondson's maneuver further enraged opponents in his own party. Although the Democrats managed to retain Kerr's seat for another term, it was probably due more to the GOP's strategy of concentrating on a few major offices at a time than to superior Democratic electoral strength.[208] By 1968, when former Republican Governor Henry Bellmon defeated Mike Monroney with considerable ease, it was clear that one-party politics was over in Oklahoma. Although Robert Kerr had not dominated Oklahoma politics the way Harry Byrd did in Virginia, he was certainly the Democratic party's titular leader. And in crucial moments, such as the struggle for party leadership in 1960, he was influential enough to arrange an acceptable compromise. Without settled leadership at the top, the Democratic party returned to the factionalism that had characterized so much of its early history nationally as well as in the Sooner State.

Kerr's untimely death also had profound and immediate effects in Washington. It altered the prospects for the President's 1963 legislative program and accelerated a change in the long-range balance of power within the Senate. Without the Oklahoman as an effective counterweight to Finance Committee Chairman Harry Byrd's almost total opposition to New Frontier economic policy, it seemed unlikely that Kennedy's proposed tax cut would survive Byrd's antipathy for increased federal budgets.

With Kerr absent from the Senate's cloakrooms and corridors, the administration had to depend on individual members of varying prestige and influence, where for two years the Oklahoman had managed the major legislative proposals singlehandedly. *Newsweek*'s Kenneth Crawford, in describing the magnitude of Kerr's influence within the Senate, said he had achieved the ultimate in equality. "Like the other 99 Senators, [Kerr] cast only one vote when the roll was called. Unlike most of them, he influenced the votes of a considerable number of his colleagues on a wide range of issues. . . ."[209]

President Kennedy joined Kerr's Senate colleagues, his family, and hundreds of admirers for the final tribute at the First Baptist Church in Oklahoma City. Among the eloquent eulogies and remembrances that filled the national and state press, a simple editorial in the Duncan *Daily Banner* seemed to express best what his death meant to thousands of Oklahomans who thought of him as a close friend as well as a masterful legislator: "We never again can rest on our oars and say, 'Bob Kerr will take care of it.'"[210]

Epilogue

Kerr's sudden death on January 1, 1963, stunned both his family and his colleagues in Washington. Since they remembered the brawny Oklahoman only as a vigorous and tireless politician, they seemed unable to comprehend the loss. Thousands throughout the Sooner State grieved as if one of their own family had died. As his children matured and established families and Mrs. Kerr devoted more time to her antique business and building the house in Poteau, Senator Kerr substituted his work in Washington for family pleasure. After 1952 he never wavered from the vow to devote all his efforts to furthering the interests of Oklahoma. Through his work to fund the Arkansas River Navigation Project and a concern that the entire state benefit from his tenure in the Senate, Kerr became a twentieth-century patriarch. Yet despite his prominence in Washington, he never lost touch with constituents because he was genuinely concerned for their welfare. More than a decade after his death, Oklahomans remembered him with affection. Almost every recollection began with a personal anecdote about how the individual recalled frequently seeing Kerr in shirtsleeves on a town's square of a city's busy corner, head cocked, listening to whomever stopped to talk. Kerr was always a familiar figure, never a remote politician away in Washington.

A worldly and sophisticated politician, Kerr embodied the cunning shrewdness of the frontier of his boyhood. But he deliberately shunned the patina of life on the Potomac which often separated the successful politician from his humble origins—and frequently from his seat in Congress. Senator Kerr was never graceful or cosmopolitan or smooth, but neither was Oklahoma.

Except for Oklahomans, few people outside Washington had ever heard of Robert Samuel Kerr. His power within the Senate developed in the late fifties and matured only in the two years before his death. It was too recent and too complex to earn him a national reputation. The domineering figure of Majority Leader Lyndon Johnson overshadowed most of his Senate career, but as an intimate of the Senate power structure, Kerr cared little for appearances. Yet in the sixties, when a member of the Capitol press corps wrote that, "Mr. Kennedy asked; Mr. Kerr decided," the Oklahoman was pleased.[1]

Kerr's death contributed to the gradual restoration of the regular Democratic leadership's authority in the Senate, but it did not presage a return to the Senate of the 1950's. When Lyndon Johnson became Vice-President, he left a void that Mike Mansfield had neither the inclination nor the ability to fill as majority leader. But the Senate was still accustomed to strong leadership, and the President needed a co-operative and influential ally. So it seemed only natural that a politician of Kerr's intelligence, vigor, and skill should simply take over once he negotiated the terms to his advantage.

In the Senate, Robert Kerr was an individual rather than an institutional power. His greatest asset was a wholly undoctrinaire approach to politics. Faced with a legislative problem, he was remarkably free of preconceived ideas, a quality that enhanced his role as the legislative broker for the Kennedy Administration. Depending on the circumstances, he was a protectionist or a free trader, a free spender or an economy advocate, an enthusiastic champion of the large corporation or a compassionate solicitor for the aged pensioner or the abandoned child.

Kerr's flexibility did not mean that he was devoid of a defined political philosophy. His was a materialistic view of politics equal to "promoting the general welfare." He saw the federal government's proper role as funding and expanding the economy through political action to widen and stabilize the general social system in which individuals made their way. Kerr assumed the characteristic American political position of talking Jeffersonian rhetoric while practicing Hamiltonian principles. The link between these two was a conception of individualism and freedom based on each person working out his talents in a stable and expanding social system.

Senator Kerr was neither a unique figure nor an aberration in American politics. His attitude toward internal improvements was the same as Carl Hayden's toward the Central Arizona Project, George Norris' toward TVA, and that of politicians who secured federal funds to subsidize highways, railroads, airlines and inner-city reconstruction. There was no difference in funding the Arkansas River Navigation Project, a traditional effort to develop a rural area, and securing federal monies to fight urban crime or improve urban housing. Only the problems varied from place to place, not the political means.

In a less abrasive and aggressive man, this flexibility might have been lauded as the high art of pragmatic politics. But in Robert Kerr, it was condemned as opportunism. His unwavering support of the oil and gas industry, the origin of his personal fortune, killed whatever chance he had of winning the Democratic nomination in 1952. And his personal code admitted no conflict in using his legislative prowess to benefit the second largest industry in his home state. He dismissed criticism from the liberals of his own party with the remark, "If Oklahomans didn't like it, they wouldn't elect me."[2]

Robert Kerr saw national politics as a forum to accommodate local interests. For him the representative system of government was literal. "Every Senator and member of the House represents one or more of our basic elements . . . and the sum total of those pressures working through Congress is the catalyst that produces our laws," he told his constituents.[3] If southwestern oil and gas producers' interests conflicted with eastern coal miners' or northern consumers', Kerr believed Congress should resolve the dispute through the democratic process of majority rule. And he devoted more than fourteen years to making certain that when it mattered for Oklahoma, he would have the votes.

Kerr did not hit his stride politically until after 1952. In his mature years, his single-minded purpose was to regenerate the state he loved so well, to restore the vigor and confidence of territorial days that the relentless winds and lingering hard times of the Depression had beaten down. In doing so, he added to his own wealth, but that was not his basic motive. Business was a diversion and riches the pleasing result, but politics was his passion. His deepest hunger was for political power. Had Kerr chosen his own epitaph, it probably would have been the assessment of his career that appeared in the Cushing (Okla.) *Daily Citizen* on the day of his burial: "If Will Rogers was Oklahoma's most loved citizen, then Kerr was its most powerful."[4]

NOTES

NOTES
Chapter I

1. The sources on Kerr's family and early life are scarce and often contradictory. This account was based on the Ada (Okla.) *Evening News*, September 6, 1936; Ray Parr, *The Daily Oklahoman*, July 26, 1942; Laura M. Messenbaugh, "William Samuel Kerr," *The Chronicles of Oklahoma*, v. 20 (September, 1941): 250–51; "Biographical Sketch of Robert S. Kerr," no date, Robert S. Kerr Papers, Western History Collection, Bizzell Memorial Library, University of Oklahoma, Norman, Oklahoma. Cited hereafter as Kerr Papers.

2. J. Hugh Biles, *The Early History of Ada* (Ada: The Oklahoma State Bank, 1954), p. 146.

3. Joseph Kraft, "King of the U.S. Senate," *Saturday Evening Post*, v. 236 (January 5–12, 1963): 27. Cited hereafter as Kraft, "King of the U.S. Senate."

4. Ada (Okla.) *Evening News*, September 6, 1936.

5. *Daily Oklahoman*, September 23, 1962.

6. Edwin C. McReynolds, *Oklahoma: A History of the Sooner State* (Norman: University of Oklahoma Press, 1954), p. 391. Also see John Huddleston Nabors, "Robert S. Kerr, Baptist Layman: A Study of the Impact of Religion and Politics on the Life of an Oklahoma Leader," M.A. thesis, University of Oklahoma, 1964. Cited hereafter as Nabors, "Robert S. Kerr, Baptist Layman."

7. J. David Cox, "Senator Robert S. Kerr and the Arkansas River Navigation Project: A Study in Legislative Leadership," Ph.D. dissertation, University of Oklahoma, 1972, p. 14. Cited hereafter as Cox, "Senator Robert S. Kerr and the Arkansas River Navigation Project." Also see Parr, *Daily Oklahoman*, July 26, 1942. McFarland was a senator from Arizona, 1941–1953.

8. Parr, *Daily Oklahoman*, July 26, 1942.

9. Marquis Childs, "The Big Boom From Oklahoma," *Saturday Evening Post*, v. 221 (April 9, 1949): 23. Cited hereafter as Childs, "The Big Boom From Oklahoma."

10. Parr, *Daily Oklahoman*, July 26, 1942.

11. Joe Stocker, *Oklahoma City Times*, June 11, 1940; Nabors, "Robert S. Kerr, Baptist Layman," p. 12.

12. On Kerr's military career see Stocker, *op. cit.;* and T. P. Tripps, *Harlow's Weekly,* December 9, 1933. For copies of official induction and discharge papers see Scrapbook I, 1917–1941 in Kerr Papers.

13. Kraft, "King of the U.S. Senate," 27.

14. Otis Sullivant, "Robert S. Kerr: Realist in Politics," in J. T. Salter, ed., *Public Men In and Out of Office* (Chapel Hill: University of North Carolina Press, 1946), p. 426. L. E. Rader, director of Institutions, Social and Rehabilitative Services of the Oklahoma Public Welfare Commission, was a friend and adviser to Senator Kerr throughout his career. "I became acquainted with Senator Kerr during the early 1930's when he was a candidate for commander of the American Legion. At times, I also attended the Sunday School class taught by Senator Kerr in the Old Criterion Theater in Oklahoma City." L. E. Rader letter to the author, May 1, 1974. On Kerr's election as state American Legion Commander, see the *Daily Oklahoman,* July 26, 1925. As state commander, Kerr became acquainted with Baird Markham, adjutant general of the Oklahoma National Guard, who was later assistant to E. W. Marland at Marland Oil. The Marland Oil Company later was sold to Continental Oil, and Marland became governor. On the Kerr-Markham relationship see "Aubrey Kerr Interview" and "Travis Kerr Interview," Tapes and Transcripts, Public Relations Department Files, Kerr-McGee Oil Industries, Oklahoma City, Oklahoma, courtesy of John Ezell.

15. Tripps, *Harlow's Weekly,* December 9, 1933.

16. Parr, *Daily Oklahoman,* July 26, 1942. Parr is the only source that mentions Kerr's first marriage to Reba Shelton. According to close associates, Senator Kerr never spoke of his first wife, although he maintained contact with Reba's mother. See Kerr letters to Mrs. Shelton, Kerr Papers.

17. Daniel Seligman, "Senator Bob Kerr, the Oklahoma Gusher," *Fortune,* v. 59 (March, 1959): 182. Cited hereafter as Seligman, "Senator Bob Kerr."

18. See "Mrs. Robert S. Kerr," biographical sketch prepared for the 1952 campaign, June 26, 1952, Kerr Papers. Also Rex Hawks, interview with the author, April 3, 1974. Cited hereafter as Hawks Interview.

19. Childs, "The Big Boom From Oklahoma," 23. See Elizabeth Carpenter, *Washington Post,* February 11, 1952.

20. Seligman, "Senator Bob Kerr," 182; Dean A. McGee, *Evolution Into Total Energy, The Story of Kerr-McGee Corporation* (Princeton: Princeton University Press for the Newcomen Society in North America, 1971), p. 8. Kerr's association with Dixon Brothers probably began earlier than 1926, but the Senator always used the 1926 date as the formal beginning of the relationship. John Ezell interview with the author.

21. Seligman, "Senator Bob Kerr," 182.

22. *Ibid.,* 184. Dean McGee said that drilling in the early 1930's in Oklahoma City was not as dangerous as it has been portrayed because the oil pressure was significantly reduced. See "Interview with Dean McGee," Tapes and Transcripts, Public Relations Department Files, Kerr-McGee Oil Industries, courtesy of John Ezell.

23. Kerr had led numerous membership drives and fund-raising activities for the YMCA and the Red Cross in Oklahoma City. He served twice as the state chairman of the Infantile Paralysis Fund Drive and was a newly elected director of the Chamber of Commerce. See "Biographical Sketch of Senator Robert S.

Kerr for the 1952 Presidential Campaign," Kerr Papers. Scrapbook I, 1917–1941 in the Kerr Papers also contains hundreds of news clippings giving the details of these various activities. See also Stanley C. Draper to Kerr, January 25, 1935, Kerr Papers.

24. Seligman, "Senator Bob Kerr," 184; Cox, "Senator Robert S. Kerr and the Arkansas River Navigation Project," p. 18.

25. Anderson-Kerr Petroleum Company made its first public offering of 125,000 $5-per-capital-share stock in 1936. See the *Chicago Herald and Examiner Finance*, October 20, 1936; also the *Daily Oklahoman*, October 26, 1938.

26. On Lynn, see "Travis Kerr Interview" and "Dean Terrill Interview," Tapes and Transcripts, Kerr-McGee Public Relations Department Files, Kerr-McGee Oil Industries, courtesy of John Ezell. Quote is from "Terrill Interview." On the formation of Kerlyn Oil see *Chicago Herald and Examiner Finance*, April 14, 1937; and the *Daily Oklahoman*, April 14, 1937. See also the *Annual Report of the Anderson-Kerr Petroleum Company*, June 28, 1937, Public Relations Department Files, Kerr-McGee Oil Industries.

27. For the specific terms of the agreement, see auditor's statement in *Annual Report of Kerr-McGee Oil Industries*, June 30, 1949, Public Relations Files, Kerr-McGee Oil Industries. For Kerr's version of the arrangement see Seligman, "Senator Bob Kerr," 184; and McGee, *Evolution Into Total Energy*, pp. 14–17. The Anderson-Kerr Company had been associated with Phillips Petroleum as early as 1935, in drilling on gas leases in a field in Moore County, Texas. Phillips had gas leases in Texas which they farmed out to Anderson-Kerr and agreed to supply money to drill the first ten wells. In return for Anderson-Kerr's repayment of the cost of the original wells, Phillips agreed to give up their interest in the rest of the field and to purchase all the gas produced. The Moore County gas field was the only stable production the company had for years. For details see *Second Annual Report of Anderson-Kerr Oil Company, 1936*, Public Relations Department Files, Kerr-McGee Oil Industries. John Ezell Interview. Also see Anderson-Kerr S.E.C. Registration under the Securities Act, 1933, dated September 22, 1936. Copy at Kerr-McGee Archives, courtesy John Ezell.

28. On the acquisition of uranium properties and milling facilities, see *Annual Report of Kerr-McGee Oil Industries*, June 30, 1952 and June 30, 1955 respectively, Public Relations Department Files, Kerr-McGee Oil Industries.

29. Seligman, "Senator Bob Kerr," 184; McGee, *Evolution Into Total Energy*, pp. 18–19. On potash see *Annual Report of Kerr-McGee Oil Industries*, June 30, 1955; and on helium see *Annual Report of Kerr-McGee Oil Industries*, June 30, 1961, Public Relations Department Files, Kerr-McGee Oil Industries.

30. Robert Novak, *Wall Street Journal*, January 2, 1963. Also see Allan Cromley, *Daily Oklahoman*, February 2, 1963.

31. *Daily Oklahoman*, October 19, 1935.

32. Statement quoted in clipping from *The Oil and Gas Journal* (January 23, 1936), copy in Scrapbook I, 1917–1941, Kerr Papers.

33. Seligman, "Senator Bob Kerr," 184, 188. For information on Kerr as president of the Mid-Continent Oil and Gas Association, see *Tulsa World*, November 21, 1936; *Daily Oklahoman*, November 20, 1937; Chicago *Daily News*, November 30, 1937; *Tulsa Tribune*, November 3, 1939. Also see clippings in Scrapbook I, 1917–1941, Kerr Papers.

34. Sallisaw (Okla.) *Times*, October 24, 1941.

35. U.S. Congress, Joint Committee on Printing, *Biographical Directory of the American Congress, 1774–1961* (Washington: Government Printing Office, 1961), p. 1160. Cited hereafter as *Biographical Directory*.

36. *Daily Oklahoman*, October 29, 1935.

37. Stephen Jones, *Oklahoma Politics in State and Nation, 1907 to 1962*, I (Enid: The Haymaker Press, Inc., 1974), p. 46. Cited hereafter as Jones, *Oklahoma Politics*.

38. For an account of Marland's life see John Joseph Mathews, *Life and Death of an Oil Man: The Career of E. W. Marland* (Norman: University of Oklahoma Press, 1951) and Arrell M. Gibson, *Oklahoma: A History of Five Centuries* (Norman: Harlow Publishing Corp., 1965), pp. 378–83. Cited hereafter as Gibson, *Oklahoma*. Also see James Ralph Scales, "The Political History of Oklahoma, 1907–1949," Ph.D. dissertation, University of Oklahoma, 1949, pp. 373–93. Cited hereafter as Scales, "Political History of Oklahoma."

39. *Daily Oklahoman*, October 26, 1938. Cox, "Senator Robert S. Kerr and the Arkansas River Navigation Project," p. 20. Also see Scales, "Political History of Oklahoma," p. 400.

40. Kerr's "fishing" party consisted of W. J. Holloway, former governor and chief political agent for the oil industry, A. L. Crable, state superintendent of public instruction, and Henry G. Bennett, president of Oklahoma A & M College and a leading Baptist layman. See El Reno (Okla.) *American*, August 25, 1938; R. M. M'Clintock, *Oklahoma City Times*, August 18, 1938; and Joseph Howell, *Tulsa Tribune*, January 20, 1939.

41. *Harlow's Weekly* (December 2, 1939): 9.

42. *Tulsa World*, January 1, 1940.

43. *Daily Oklahoman*, April 19, 25, 1940. One Oklahoma writer praised Kerr's frank ambition. "It is to the everlasting credit of gruff, hearty Bob Kerr that he managed to acknowledge his election as Democratic National Committeeman Monday without saying this was a great and wholly unexpected honor." See Stocker, *Oklahoma City Times*, June 11, 1940.

44. Parr, *Daily Oklahoman*, July 27, 1942.

45. M. H. Shepard to Ben Dwight, June 19, 1950, Kerr Papers. There is extensive material on the Phillips-Kerr split in Scrapbook I, 1917–1941, Kerr Papers. For the best articles analyzing the breach as it developed, see R. M. M'Clintock, *Oklahoma City Times*, August 18, 1938; Ernest M. Hill, Holdenville (Okla.) *Daily News*, August 30, 1940; *Tulsa World*, January 10, 1940; and Ernest M. Hill, Alva (Okla.) *Review-Courier*, July 25, 1941. Kerr wrote a series of articles in 1940 supporting Roosevelt which were widely reprinted. See *Tulsa Tribune*, October 6, 13, 20, 27, and November 3, 1940. On Phillips' opposition to the New Deal, see Scales, "Political History of Oklahoma," p. 430.

46. "I called Kerr . . . and told him to get his lobbyists out of the Capital." Phillips quoted in the Norman (Okla.) *Transcript*, May 15, 1942. Also see Howell, *Tulsa Tribune*, July 9, 1941. The quote in the text appeared in the Frederick (Okla.) *Daily-Leader*, July 22, 1941.

47. On the possibility of Bennett's candidacy, see the Vinita (Okla.) *Daily Journal*, September 29, 1941; the *Daily Oklahoman*, October 19, 1941; and Ernest M. Hill, Hobart (Okla.) *Chief-Democrat*, October 28, 1941.

48. *Tulsa Tribune,* December 15, 1941.

49. On the firing of three Kerr supporters from the Tax Commission, see the Norman (Okla.) *Transcript,* July 14, 1941. For additional dismissals, see *Daily Oklahoman,* October 16, 1941; Stillwater (Okla.) *Gazette,* November 7, 1941; Blaine (Okla.) *Democrat,* November 6, 1941; Lawton (Okla.) *News Review* and Newkirk (Okla.) *Reporter* November 5, 1941.

50. Scales, "Political History of Oklahoma," p. 436.

51. Smith ran for governor in 1934 and for the U.S. Senate in 1936 and 1938. In 1937 he was elected as a Democrat to the 75th Congress to fill a vacancy in the fifth congressional district. See Duncan (Okla.) *Banner,* February 12, 1942, and *Biographical Directory,* p. 1616.

52. Childs, "The Big Boom From Oklahoma," 118.

53. On settlement of Oklahoma and the development of economic, religious, and political patterns, see Solon J. Buck, "The Settlement of Oklahoma," *Transactions of the Wisconsin Academy of Science, Arts and Letters,* v. 15, pt. 2 (1907): 385–400; Jones, *Oklahoma Politics,* pp. 131–33. Also see V. O. Key, *American State Politics* [1st edition] (New York: Alfred A. Knopf, 1956), pp. 220–22.

54. "Oklahoma Politics," *Life,* v. 13, no. 2 (July 13, 1942): 21–27.

55. *Daily Oklahoman,* Lawton (Okla.) *Constitution-Morning Press,* and the *Tulsa World,* March 15, 1942. For Kerr's attack on isolationists nationally and in the Senate, see the Poteau (Okla.) *Sun,* May 8, 1941. For Kerr's urging of more aid for Britain and the use of convoys, see the Wewoka (Okla.) *Democrat,* May 14, 1941.

56. Kerr received 196,656 votes to Otjen's 180,454. See Samuel A. Kirkpatrick and David R. Morgan, *Oklahoma Voting Patterns: Presidential, Senatorial and Gubernatorial Elections* (Norman: University of Oklahoma, 1970), p. 32. Cited hereafter as *Oklahoma Voting Patterns.*

57. Sullivant, *Daily Oklahoman,* January 12, 1947.

58. For county breakdowns of voting, see Kirpatrick, *Oklahoma Voting Patterns,* p. 32.

59. Cox, "Senator Robert S. Kerr and the Arkansas River Navigation Project," p. 20.

60. Jones, *Oklahoma Politics,* p. 50; Scales, "Political History of Oklahoma," p. 434.

61. Gibson, *Oklahoma,* p. 385.

62. Childs, "The Big Boom From Oklahoma," 119.

63. Gibson, *Oklahoma,* p. 386.

64. Claude R. Thorpe, "Robert S. Kerr's 1948 Senatorial Campaign," M.A. thesis, University of Oklahoma, 1967, p. 2. Cited hereafter as Thorpe, "Robert Kerr's 1948 Senatorial Campaign."

65. The following summary of Kerr's governorship is based on Gibson, *Oklahoma,* pp. 385–95; Scales, "Political History of Oklahoma," pp. 428–66 Cox, "Senator Robert S. Kerr and the Arkansas River Navigation Project," pp. 21–22; Sullivant, *Daily Oklahoman,* January 12, 1947; and clipping files of the *Daily Oklahoman* and the *Oklahoma City Times,* 1943–1947.

66. Scales, "Political History of Oklahoma," pp. 447–48.

67. Sullivant, *Oklahoma City Times,* January 12, 1947, Kerr Papers.

68. Don McBride Interview, June 15, 1974. Cited hereafter as McBride Interview.

69. Thorpe, "Robert Kerr's 1948 Senatorial Campaign," p. 2.

70. Sullivant, *Oklahoma City Times*, January 12, 1947, Kerr Papers.

71. Scales, "Political History of Oklahoma," p. 465.

72. Seligman, "Senator Bob Kerr," 188; also see *New York Times*, July 2, 1944.

73. McBride Interview. For text of speech see *New York Times*, July 20, 1944; for editorial comment on the speech see *Daily Oklahoman*, July 21, 1944; *New York Times*, July 20, 1944.

74. Childs, "The Big Boom From Oklahoma," 119.

75. Margaret Truman, *Harry S Truman* (New York: Morrow & Co., Inc., 1973), p. 181. Cited hereafter as Truman, *Harry S Truman*. She says that Kerr acted on direct orders from Democratic party treasurer, Ed Pauley. "Ed Pauley later recalled that Bob Kerr paled when he pointed his finger at him. . . . He would have made an ideal compromise candidate. But he was a good Democrat, and he sacrificed his personal ambitions without a moment's hesitation, when he got the signal." Also see Cromley, *Daily Oklahoman*, June 20, 1962.

76. Perry (Okla.) *Daily-Journal*, November 1, 1948.

77. Owen Townsend to Kerr, December 10, 1946, Kerr Papers. Townsend, a former state senator, wrote to urge Kerr to enter the Senate race upon Moore's death, for "it appears to me that the old rascal has only about two more years to live." Moore died in 1950.

78. Thorpe, "Robert Kerr's 1948 Senatorial Campaign," pp. 4–5.

79. *Ibid.*, p. 16.

80. *Ibid.*, p. 17.

81. Scales, "Political History of Oklahoma," pp. 343, 361.

82. Eugene Lorton, Republican editor and publisher of the *Tulsa World*, financed the Smith campaign with $10,000 because he believed no other candidate had the necessary glamor to defeat Kerr. Senator Moore's administrative assistant in Washington was also assigned to help run the Smith campaign in Oklahoma. See Thorpe, "Robert Kerr's 1948 Senatorial Campaign," p. 19.

83. Thorpe, "Robert Kerr's 1948 Senatorial Campaign," p. 3.

84. *Ibid.*

85. *Ibid.*, p. 5. William Kerr Interview, April 27, 1976.

86. Thorpe, "Robert Kerr's 1948 Senatorial Campaign," p. 6; Hawks Interview. (For organizational details, correspondence, list of workers, and contributors to the 1948 campaign see Kerr Papers, Boxes 107–111.)

87. McBride to Kerr, May 13, 1948; Ben Dwight to Harrington Wimberly, April 26, 1948, Kerr Papers; *Tulsa Tribune*, October 13, 1948.

88. Thorpe, "Robert Kerr's 1948 Senatorial Campaign," p. 5; Kerr to Matthew J. Connelly, February 28, 1948; and Matthew J. Connelly to Harry S Truman, June 25, 1947, Harry S Truman Library, Independence, Missouri. Cited hereafter as Truman Papers. Kerr's staff also conducted periodic opinion surveys in 1947–1948. Senator Kerr used these to keep the President informed of Oklahoma sentiment on national issues and to guide his own campaign efforts. For details of the surveys see Box 117, Kerr Papers.

89. John Morton Blum, ed., *The Price of Vision: The Diary of Henry A.*

Wallace, 1942–1946 (Boston: Houghton Mifflin Company, 1973), p. 546; *Oklahoma City Times,* February 13, 1946. In 1941 there was a rumor that Kerr would succeed Ickes as National Petroleum Coordinator. See Joseph Howell, *Tulsa Tribune,* October 7, 1941 and Shawnee (Okla.) *Daily Star,* November 13, 1941.

90. *Daily Oklahoman,* March 14, 1946; *Rocky Mountain News,* November 17, 1946; Kerr to Julius L. Kabotsky, December 13, 1946; Kerr to E. P. Ivory, December 19, 1946, Kerr Papers; *Washington Post,* February 20, 1947.

91. Thorpe, "Robert Kerr's 1948 Senatorial Campaign," p. 5.

92. The *Tulsa Tribune's* poll of late spring showed Kerr leading in Oklahoma County and third in Tulsa County. In eastern Oklahoma counties such as Okmulgee and McIntosh, where voter interest was very low, Kerr was leading. Overall, Kerr led in sixty-seven counties, was tied with Smith in four, and Smith led in six. See Howell, *Tulsa Tribune,* June 4, 1948.

93. Thorpe, "Robert Kerr's 1948 Senatorial Campaign," p. 13. C. B. Akers to Horace Clark, June 17, 1948, Kerr Papers.

94. Kerr to Lincoln Battenfield, March 8, 1948, Kerr Papers.

95. After the 1948 Truman landslide, Kerr wrote the President praising his strategy for recognizing the farm vote as a key to the Democratic victory. Kerr to Truman, November 4, 1948, Truman Papers.

96. Altus (Okla.) *Times-Democrat,* June 4, 1948.

97. Kerr saw the musical a dozen times and never tired of hearing the soundtrack.

98. Robert S. Kerr, "Radio Broadcast from Collinsville, Oklahoma," June 11, 1948, Kerr Papers.

99. W. C. Alston to Kerr, June 18, 1948, Kerr Papers.

100. Seminole (Okla.) *Producer,* June 8, 1948, Kerr Papers.

101. Guymon (Okla.) *News Herald,* June 3, 1948, Kerr Papers.

102. Gomer Smith received 73,511; Mac Q. Williamson, 48,670; Ora J. Fox, 35,817; and Glen D. Johnson, 24,513. The remaining candidates finished in the following order: Wilburn Cartwright, James E. Berry, Fletcher Foley, G. A. Gentry, and L. G. Burt. See State of Oklahoma, Oklahoma State Election Board, *Directory of the State of Oklahoma, 1953* (Guthrie: no publisher, 1954). J. William Cordell, secretary of the Election Board compiled the figures. Cited hereafter as *Directory of the State of Oklahoma, 1953.*

103. Political advertisements appearing in Tishomingo (Okla.) *Johnston County Capitol-Democrat,* July 22, 1948, and in the Ada (Okla.) *Evening News,* July 15, 1948, Kerr Papers.

104. Burl Hays Interview, June 26, 1974. Cited hereafter as Hays Interview.

105. Cushing (Okla.) *Daily Citizen,* July 22, 1948; Howard Wilson, Durant (Okla.) *Daily Democrat,* June 3, 1948.

106. N. S. Allen to Kerr, July 26, 1948; G. S. Ramsay to Kerr, July 19, 1948, Kerr Papers.

107. Kerr to J. Howard McGrath, July 9, 1948, Truman Papers; Kerr to Richard R. Nacy, August 13, 1948, Kerr Papers.

108. Kerr: 168,861; Smith: 124,519. See *Directory of the State of Oklahoma, 1953,* p. 30.

109. *Daily Oklahoman,* April 26, 27, 1948.

110. *Directory of the State of Oklahoma, 1953,* p. 31.

111. Bill Henthorne, *Tulsa World,* October 17, 1948.

112. *Daily Oklahoman,* October 17, 1948.

113. Thorpe, "Robert Kerr's 1948 Senatorial Campaign," p. 54.

114. The Oklahoma Progressives and the States Rights Democratic (Dixie-crat) party failed to win the legal right to appear on the November ballot. The Democratic party, through control of the courts, prevented both groups from scattering its vote in 1948. See *Ibid.; Cooper* v. *Cartwright,* 195P2d 290 (1948); Gerald L. K. Smith to Wilburn Cartwright, April 8, 1948, Wilburn Cartwright Collection, Western History Collection, Bizzell Memorial Library, University of Oklahoma, Norman, Oklahoma. Cited hereafter as Cartwright Papers.

115. *Daily Oklahoman,* September 29, 1948.

116. Okemah (Okla.) *Daily Leader,* September 29, 1948, Kerr Papers.

117. Childs, "Washington Calling," copy sheet of column written about the 1948 election, Kerr Papers.

118. Enid (Okla.) *Enid Events,* October 28, 1948, Kerr Papers.

119. Quoted in address by Robert S. Kerr, September 17, 1948, Kerr Papers.

120. Thorpe, "Robert Kerr's 1948 Senatorial Campaign," p. 56.

121. *Tulsa Tribune,* October 7, 1948. An editorial quoted a prominent Baptist layman, Garland Keeling, who was "sick and tired of having Bob Kerr using my denomination to further his political fortunes."

122. *Daily Oklahoman,* September 30, 1948.

123. *Daily Oklahoman,* September 30, October 12, 15, 1948; Howell, *Tulsa Tribune,* October 15, 1948.

124. Childs, "The Big Boom From Oklahoma," 119.

125. "Address of Ross Rizely," September 11, 1948, Kerr Papers.

126. J. W. Sanford to Stanley Synar, June 21, 1948; form letter from Sanford to Negro voters, no date, Kerr Papers.

127. "Address by Robert S. Kerr," September 17, 1948, Kerr Papers.

128. Cecil Brown, *Tulsa World,* October 12, 1948; Leon Hatfield, *Oklahoma City Advertizer,* October 14, 1948; *Daily Oklahoman,* October 13, 1948.

129. L. G. Burt to Kerr, October 25, 1948, Kerr Papers; *Tulsa Tribune,* October 9, 1948.

130. "Report of the Subcommittee on Privileges and Elections to the Committee on Rules and Administration of the United States Senate on Oklahoma First and Second Primaries Held in 1948," mimeographed copy in Kerr Papers.

131. The clubs served primarily to circumvent Oklahoma's election law which limited primary campaign expenditures to the unrealistic sum of $3,000. Clubs permitted candidates to spend freely since they are not mentioned in the law. All experienced candidates used this device to spend more rather than risk defeat because of niggardly expenditures. See Oklahoma, State Election Board, *Primary and General Election Laws of the State of Oklahoma, Annotated (1947),* p. 55.

132. October 7, 1948, Kerr Papers.

133. Oliver Benson and others, *Oklahoma Votes, 1907–1962* (Norman: University of Oklahoma Press, 1964), p. 39. Also see Kirkpatrick, *Oklahoma Voting Patterns,* p. 6.

134. Charles N. Haskell, Oklahoma's first governor, ran for the Senate

against incumbent Robert L. Owen in 1912 and was defeated. This trend was not broken until Kerr's election.

Chapter II

1. The skylight was removed during renovations in the 1950's. Senator Henry Cabot Lodge (R., Mass.) declared that the modern ceiling with its indirect lighting system made the Chamber look "like a glorified cocktail bar." See Paul McBride, Washington, *Sunday Star*, September 3, 1956.

2. William A. Robinson, *Thomas B. Reed, Parliamentarian* (New York: Dodd, Mead & Company, 1930), p. 77.

3. Membership did not reach one hundred until the 87th Congress.

4. William S. White, *Citadel: The Story of the U.S. Senate* (New York: Harper & Brothers, 1956), pp. 93, 94, and Chapter VII, "The Senate and the Club." Cited hereafter as White, *Citadel*. Some scholars disagree with White's definition of the Inner Club. See Richard F. Fenno, Jr., *The Power of the Purse: Appropriations Politics in Congress* (Boston: Little, Brown and Company, 1966), p. 509. Cited hereafter as Fenno, *The Power of the Purse*.

5. White, *Citadel*, p. 84.

6. Kraft, "King of the U.S. Senate," 26.

7. Lyndon Johnson served as Vice-President and President.

8. *Biographical Directory*, p. 478; Clinton P. Anderson with Milton Viorst, *Outsider in the Senate: Senator Clinton Anderson's Memoirs* (New York: The World Publishing Company, 1970), pp. 10–13, 85, 86, 110–14, 295–96, 316. Cited hereafter as Anderson, *Outsider in the Senate*.

9. In the 1950's, when Anderson supported the Republicans' plan for flexible price supports, many Democrats from states without wheat, corn, or other basic crops followed his lead. See Harry McPherson, *A Political Education* (Boston: Little, Brown and Company, 1972), p. 27. Cited hereafter as McPherson, *A Political Education*.

10. Rowland Evans and Robert Novak, *Lyndon B. Johnson: The Exercise of Power* (New York: The New American Library, 1968), pp. 6, 30. Cited hereafter as Evans and Novak, *Lyndon B. Johnson*. Johnson was elected to the 75th Congress to fill a vacancy at the death of James P. Buchanan. He served in the House from April 10, 1937, to January 3, 1949. He had been an unsuccessful candidate for the Senate in 1941. See *Biographical Directory*, p. 1128.

11. Evans and Novak, *Lyndon B. Johnson*, p. 6.

12. *Ibid.*, p. 28.

13. *Ibid.*, p. 32.

14. See Anderson in U.S. Congress, Joint Committee on Printing, *Memorial Address in Behalf of Senator Robert S. Kerr* (Washington: Government Printing Office, 1963), p. 49. Cited hereafter as *Memorial Addresses*. Kerr also campaigned for John Sparkman's reelection in Alabama in 1948. See Sparkman to Kerr, May 21, 1948, Kerr Papers.

15. Kerr and Anderson shared joint ownership of a bank in Grants, New Mexico, and participated in uranium milling in Arizona and potash development in New Mexico. Kerr financed Johnson's early ventures into expanding his radio-television interests in Austin, Texas. Hawks Interview.

16. McPherson, *A Political Education*, p. 28.

17. Kerr made periodic trips to the Kellogg Health Sanatorium in Battle Creek, Michigan, where he subsisted on Special K cereal and exercise. He called the place the poor man's Maine Chance. Hawks Interview. Also see Cromley, *Oklahoma City Times*, March 20, 1959, and *Daily Oklahoman*, January 1, 1961, on Kerr's weight problem.

18. "The 88th Congress; What will JFK Get?" *Newsweek*, v. 61 (January 14, 1963): 13–14.

19. McPherson, *A Political Education*, p. 42.

20. Childs, "The Big Boom From Oklahoma," 119.

21. Kerr and his Washington staff maintained excellent working relationships with scores of people throughout the Washington bureaucracy. Once a year Senator Kerr hosted a party honoring people in the executive agencies who had been especially helpful on some problem important to Oklahoma. This generated a great deal of goodwill as well as useful information. Hawks Interview.

22. Cromley, *Oklahoma City Times*, June 26, 1958.

23. Kraft, "King of the U.S. Senate," 27.

24. Theodore Schad Interview, March 13, 1973.

25. Kraft, "King of the U.S. Senate," 27.

26. William A. Reynolds, "Social Security Administration Project," Oral History Research Office, Columbia University, 1967, p. 1. Cited hereafter as Reynolds, "Social Security Transcript."

27. Cromley, *Daily Oklahoman*, February 2, 1963. After Kerr's death, Burl Hays, found a folder several inches thick of notes and IOU's from people Kerr had loaned money. The notes were primarily records, as Kerr was a very orderly man, especially about money. He never really expected these debts to be repaid. Hays Interview. See Kerr to Robert Rone, January 24, 1944, Kerr Papers.

28. Cromley, *Daily Oklahoman*, February 2, 1963.

29. "Senator Kerr Says," July 31, 1959, Kerr Papers.

30. William Baker English, "Senator Robert S. Kerr: A Study in Ethos," Ph.D. dissertation, University of Oklahoma, 1966, pp. 94–95.

31. The youngest child, Bill, left for college in the fall of 1955. The Kerrs sold their home on Wyoming Avenue and moved to an apartment in the Sheraton Park Hotel. In October, Mrs. Kerr opened an antique shop, Kerr and Company, in Georgetown. She did interior decorating for many prominent government officials including the Greenwich, Connecticut, home of Robert B. Anderson, former deputy secretary of defense. Mrs. Kerr became disenchanted with politics after the Senator's defeat for the presidential nomination in 1952. She did not like Washington society, which operated on seniority, and since they did not drink, the Kerrs rarely enjoyed Washington social life. Mrs. Kerr sold Kerr and Company in the late 1950's and returned to Oklahoma. She divided her time between her home and the Black Angus Restaurant which they owned in Poteau. Mrs. Kerr described her interest in decorating and the restaurant "as absorbing

to me as angus cattle are to the Senator." See Alice DeWeese, Pine Bluff (Ark.) *Commercial*, February 6, 1962, Kerr Papers; Cromley, *Daily Oklahoman*, September 18, 1955; *Oklahoma City Times*, January 25, 1957; Hawks Interview.

32. Hays Interview.

33. Seligman, "Senator Bob Kerr," 137.

34. Nabors, "Robert S. Kerr, Baptist Layman," p. 63.

35. Senator Kerr preferred the southwestern tradition of doing business verbally. He had three telephones, two on the desk and one underneath. He frequently used all three at once acting as moderator in a telephone conference. See Cromley and John Dexter, *Daily Oklahoman*, October 31, 1954.

36. Senator Gale McGee (D., Wyo.) lauded Kerr for saving the original Peace Corps appropriation with a funny story. "The rest of us spend days preparing speeches. You come in, give a one minute off the cuff statement and make the rest of us look like we're wasting our time." See *Tulsa Tribune*, August 25, 1961.

37. English, "Senator Robert S. Kerr," pp. 168–72.

38. Cox, "Senator Robert S. Kerr and the Arkansas River Navigation Project," p. 81.

39. Albert Gore, *Let the Glory Out: My South and Its Politics* (New York: Viking Press, 1972), p. 124. Cited hereafter as Gore, *Let the Glory Out*.

40. Kraft, "King of the U.S. Senate," 27.

41. Paul H. Douglas, *In the Fullness of Time: The Memoirs of Paul H. Douglas* (New York: Harcourt, Brace Jovanovich, Inc., 1971), pp. 231, 235–36, 465. Cited hereafter as Douglas, *In the Fullness of Time*.

42. Kraft, "King of the U.S. Senate," 27.

43. *New York Times*, January 11, 1963.

44. Cox, "Senator Robert S. Kerr and the Arkansas River Navigation Project," p. 81.

45. Confidential source.

46. Seligman, "Senator Bob Kerr," 137. In the 1954 debate on atomic energy legislation, Gore suggested that the proponents needed a speech explaining the basic details of the patent questions involved. Kerr agreed to give the speech if Gore provided the information. Gore recalled, "I had prepared about one page, and he spoke for three hours and a half, authoritatively." See Gore to Kerr, September 7, 1954, Kerr Papers.

47. Neil MacNeil, *Dirksen: Portrait of a Public Man* (New York: The World Publishing Company, 1970), p. 212.

48. Evans and Novak, *Lyndon B. Johnson*, p. 38.

49. McPherson, *A Political Education*, p. 42.

50. Carter Bradley quoted in Cox, "Senator Robert S. Kerr and the Arkansas River Navigation Project," p. 86.

51. Douglas, *In the Fullness of Time*, p. 235.

52. Childs, "The Big Boom From Oklahoma," 22–23, 118–20.

53. *Tulsa Tribune*, January 2, 1963.

54. Clipping from a Tulsa paper, December 23, 1948, Kerr Papers.

55. McPherson, *A Political Education*, p. 44.

56. Cromley, *Daily Oklahoman*, January 7, 1960.

57. Hays Interview. Kerr consistently refused invitations from his close friend Albert Gore to attend Senate round-table foreign policy discussions with

such notables as Dean Acheson, Gardner Means, Henry Kissinger, and George Kennan. See Columbia (S.C.) *Record*, May 26, 1952, Kerr Papers.

58. Kraft, "King of the U.S. Senate," 26.

59. *Oklahoma City Times*, June 12, 1962.

60. Spessard Holland (D., Fla.) recalled Kerr's unbending efforts for Oklahoma in a crucial conference on public works appropriations. "I shall never forget the delightful way that he wangled some particularly desirable things from his standpoint and those of his constituency in Oklahoma, from the conference of the other body." See Holland, *Memorial Addresses*, pp. 40–41.

61. Kerr to Mrs. Robert B. Grant, August 3, 1961, Kerr Papers.

62. Ed Edmondson, *Memorial Addresses*, p. 25.

63. *Daily Oklahoman*, August 20, 1962.

64. Fenno, *The Power of the Purse*, p. 527.

65. Kerr quoted in Reynolds, "Social Security Transcript," pp. 9–10.

66. Kerr to Allen J. Ellender, March 22, 1956, Kerr Papers.

67. Michael Kirwan was chairman of the Subcommittee on Public Works of House Appropriations. This subcommittee approved appropriations for the Arkansas project in the House. The Kerr-Kirwan relationship is discussed in detail in Chapter VI. Clarence Cannon, the tough octogenarian chairman of the House Appropriations Committee was unsympathetic to the Arkansas project but rarely overrode Kirwan's recommendations in full committee. Bridges, the most influential Republican in the Senate after Robert Taft's death, was a close friend of Kerr's. As ranking Republican on Senate Appropriations and Armed Services, Bridges had considerable influence and institutional power. Fellow senators viewed Aiken as a composite of early American virtues. Although he could be as intensely partisan as Strom Thurmond (D., S.C.), he was fair minded and often voted with the Democrats on foreign policy and on progressive rural legislation. Kerr often went to extreme lengths to win Aiken's vote because his endorsement could swing significant numbers of Republican votes.

68. Eugene McCarthy, *Memorial Addresses*, p. 55.

69. *Ibid.*, p. 56.

70. Lawton (Okla.) *Constitution-Morning Press*, January 3, 1963.

71. Donald R. Matthews, *U.S. Senators and Their World* (Chapel Hill: The University of North Carolina Press, 1960), pp. 93–102. Cited hereafter as Matthews, *U.S. Senators and Their World*. Anderson, *Outsider in the Senate*, p. 98.

72. White, *Citadel*, p. 82.

73. "There are 13 of us here who served together as wartime governors, which makes the work most pleasant from the very beginning. Needless to say we shall be hoping to have you join us as the 14th." See Holland to Kerr, March 8, 1947, Kerr Papers.

74. Matthews, *U.S. Senators and Their World*, p. 103.

75. Hays Interview.

76. Kerr liked to see his staff informally. He had impromptu lunches in the Senate cafeteria to discuss political matters several times weekly. In the early years, he and Mrs. Kerr entertained the staff and their spouses at monthly dinners in their home. Later, the Senator entertained in the private dining room reserved for senators in the Capitol. See Reynolds, "Social Security Transcript," p. 2.

77. McPherson, *A Political Education*, p. 25.

78. Reynolds, "Social Security Transcript," p. 2.

79. Hays Interview.

80. Stephenson, *Tulsa Tribune*, May 12, 1950.

81. Hays Interview. McBride Interview.

82. Trask was Kerr's personal secretary and began his service while the Senator was still in private business. Ben Dwight, chief of the Choctaws from 1930 to 1937, was Kerr's administrative assistant in Washington. He was responsible for office management, patronage matters, and legal problems. Burl Hays, designated "chief clerk," took the Senator's dictation for speeches and public statements, did editorial tasks, and kept a watch on political developments in the state. Hays succeeded Dwight as administrative assistant in 1953. See Stephenson, *Tulsa Tribune*, May 15, 1950; Frosty Troy, *Tulsa Tribune*, February 22, 1962.

83. Stephenson, *Tulsa Tribune*, May 12, 1950. *Oklahomans in Washington*, a directory prepared for the 1952 campaign for the presidential nomination, lists Don McBride as Manager, Oklahoma Water Development Association, with his office in Room 362 of the Senate Office Building, Kerr's suite. See Kerr Papers.

84. McBride also brought his own secretary, Florine McNabb, who had been with him since he was chairman of the Oklahoma Planning and Resources Board. Unlike her boss, she was on the Senate payroll. See Stephenson, *Tulsa Tribune*, May 12, 1950.

85. Hays Interview.

86. *Ibid.* Clifford also represented Kerr-McGee Oil Industries during this period. See *Wall Street Journal*, October 18, 1954. Senator Kerr paid some personnel costs in Washington through the Kerr-McGee corporation, and also used his personal funds for staff assistance. See Kerr to Ernest Black, June 15, 1955, Kerr Papers. Also see Robert Allen Reports, Charleston (W. Va.) *Charleston Daily Mail*, no date, Kerr Papers. An Oklahoma colleague, Tom Steed (D.), estimated that Kerr spent "$100,000 a year of his own money to supplement his government allowance for staff." Steed quoted in Cox, "Senator Robert S. Kerr and the Arkansas River Navigation Project," p. 87. Whatever the cost, the investment freed Kerr to concentrate on activities that would give him access to the Democratic power structure and a voice in its councils.

87. Matthews, *U.S. Senators and Their World*, pp. 148–58.

88. "Appropriations stands at the apex. . . . It is truly a committee sought by those who are and want to be influential." See Stephen Horn, *Unused Power: The Work of the Senate Committee on Appropriations* (Washington, D.C.: The Brookings Institution, 1970), p. 33. Cited hereafter as Horn, *Unused Power*.

89. Alben Barkley to Kerr, November 20, 1948; Kerr to Barkley, November 23, 1948, Kerr Papers.

90. Fenno, *The Power of the Purse*, p. 526; Horn, *Unused Power*, p. 10.

91. Five southerners were appointed to the Senate Appropriations Committee: Allen Ellender (La.), in his third term; Lister Hill (Ala.); Harley Kilgore (W. Va.); John McClellan (Ark.); and Willis Robertson (Va.), all in their second term. Clyde R. Hoey (N.C.) and J. Howard McGrath (R.I.) filled the vacancies on Finance. See *U.S. Congressional Directory, 1949*, p. 189.

92. The six choices were Appropriations, Finance, Public Works, Interstate

and Foreign Commerce, Interior and Insular Affairs, and Armed Services. These preferences reflected Kerr's assessment of their importance within the Senate structure for what he wished to accomplish in Oklahoma. See Kerr to Barkley, November 23, 1948, Kerr Papers.

93. Hawks Interview.

94. Speech to the National Reclamation Association, Phoenix, Arizona, October 31, 1947, Kerr Papers.

95. *Congress and the Nation, 1945–1964* (Washington, D.C.: Congressional Quarterly Service, 1965), p. 772. Cited hereafter as *Congress and the Nation.*

96. See "Senator Kerr Says," 1950–1962, Newsletter Files, Kerr Papers.

97. Anderson, *Outsider in the Senate*, p. 273.

98. Bill reported from House Appropriations Committee, March 28, 1949, passed House on a voice vote March 30, 1949. See *Congressional Quarterly Almanac—1949* (Washington, D.C.: Congressional Quarterly Service, 1949), pp. 210–11. Cited hereafter as *Congressional Quarterly Almanac—*Date.

99. *Ibid.*, p. 213.

100. Senator Thomas introduced a bill, S. 2459, August 19, 1949, to establish a national fuels policy. See *Congressional Record*, 81st Congress, 1st Session, p. 11743.

101. *Ibid.*, pp. 11367, 11436–37.

102. *Ibid.*, p. 11453.

103. The roll-call vote was 47–35, August 23, 1949. *Congressional Quarterly Almanac—1949*, p. 213.

104. Don McBride to M. H. Shepard, August 16, 1949, Kerr Papers.

105. *Congressional Record*, 81st Congress, 1st Session, p. 11454.

106. *Tulsa Tribune*, August 31, 1949.

107. The Senate adopted the original Rule XXII following the furor over President Wilson's proposal for arming American merchant ships before the nation's entry in World War I. In its original form, the rule required two-thirds of those present and voting to stop debate. Over the years interpretations and precedents which held that cloture could not be applied to procedural questions rendered the rule impotent. Cloture was further weakened in 1948 during a filibuster over President Truman's anti-poll tax bill. The president *pro tempore*, Arthur Vandenberg (R., Mich.), ruled that cloture could not be applied to a motion to proceed to consideration of a bill. Vandenberg conceded that his ruling meant that "the Senate has no effective cloture rule at all." See *Congress and the Nation*, p. 1426, and Anderson, *Outsider in the Senate*, p. 94.

108. McPherson, *A Political Education*, p. 19.

109. *Congressional Quarterly Almanac—1949*, p. 586.

110. Cromley, *Daily Oklahoman*, May 20, 1962. This explanation of Kerr's relationship with the southern leaders did not appear until late in his career when Allan Cromley included it in an article explaining his role as Kennedy's "shadow leader."

111. Anderson, *Outsider in the Senate*, p. 133.

112. Cromley, *Daily Oklahoman*, May 20, 1962.

113. The vote was 63–23. See *Congressional Quarterly Almanac—1949*, p. 671.

114. *Ibid.*, p. 586.
115. *Congressional Record*, 81st Congress, 1st Session, p. 2667.
116. McPherson, *A Political Education*, p. 50.
117. Douglas, *In the Fullness of Time*, p. 207.

Chapter III

1. Section 1(b) reads as follows: "The provisions of this Act shall apply to the transportation of natural gas in interstate commerce, to the sale in interstate commerce of natural gas for resale for ultimate public consumption for domestic, commercial, industrial, or any other use, and to natural-gas companies engaged in such transportation or sale, but shall not apply to any other transportation or sale of natural gas or to the local distribution of natural gas or to the facilities used for such distribution or the production or gathering of natural gas." 52 Stat. 821 (1938).

2. See Columbian Fuel Corporation Case, 2 F.P.C. 200 (1940). Similar cases in which the FPC commissioners openly declared that they had no jurisdiction over the independent producers and gatherers of gas are discussed in Charles B. Crenshaw, "The Regulation of Natural Gas," *Law and Contemporary Problems*, v. 19 (1954): 336, n. 62. For a full discussion of the question of regulation of the natural gas industry see Burton N. Behling, "Federal Regulation of the Natural Gas Industry," a paper for presentation at a session of the American Economic Association, December 29, 1949, in Kerr Papers; Frederick F. Blachly and Miriam E. Oatman, *Natural Gas and the Public Interest* (Washington: Granite Press, 1947); William Cary, *Politics and the Regulatory Agencies* (New York: McGraw-Hill Book Co., 1967); Louis M. Kohlmeier, Jr., *The Regulators: Watchdog Agencies and the Public Interest* (New York: Harper & Row, 1969); Eugene O. Kuntz, *A Treatise on the Law of Oil and Gas* (Cincinnati: W. H. Anderson Co., 1962); James McKie, *The Regulation of Natural Gas* (Washington, D.C.: American Enterprise Association, Inc., 1957); Edward J. Neuner, *The Natural Gas Industry: Monopoly and Competition in Field Markets* (Norman: University of Oklahoma Press, 1960).

For a discussion of the thesis that wellhead regulation of price was a mistake and resulted in a regulation induced shortage of natural gas, see Paul W. MacAvoy, *Price Formation in Natural Gas Fields: A Study of Competition, Monopoly, and Regulation* (New Haven: Yale University Press, 1962). See also MacAvoy, "The Rationale for Regulation of Gas Field Prices," and E. W. Kitch, "Regulation of the Field Market for Natural Gas by the Federal Power Commission," in MacAvoy, ed., *The Crisis of the Regulatory Commissions: An Introduction to a Current Issue of Public Policy* (New York: W. W. Norton & Company, Inc., 1970), pp. 152–68 and 169–86.

3. 3 F.P.C. 416 (1943).

4. The commission initiated the study September 22, 1944, under the statutory authority of the Natural Gas Act of 1938, Section 14(a), 52 Stat. 821; 15

USC 717. For the complete findings see FPC, *Natural Gas Investigation* (Docket No. G-580), 12 parts (Washington: April 1948). Copy in Harrington Wimberly Papers, Western History Collection, Bizzell Memorial Library, University of Oklahoma, Norman, Oklahoma. Cited hereafter as Wimberly Papers.

5. Burton N. Behling, "Federal Regulation of the Natural Gas Industry." A paper presented to the American Economic Association, New York, December 29, 1949, p. 6. Copy in Kerr Papers. Cited hereafter as Behling, "Federal Regulation."

6. For testimony from industry representatives and producer-state officials, see FPC, *Natural Gas Investigation* (1947), *Transcript*, pp. 20–21, in Wimberly Papers.

7. H.R. 2185 was introduced February 24, 1947, and S. 734 was introduced on February 28, 1947. See *Congressional Record*, 80th Congress, 1st Session, pp. 1410, 1526.

8. U.S. Congress, House, Committee on Interstate and Foreign Commerce. *Hearings to Amend the Natural Gas Act Approved June 21, 1938, as Amended*, April 14–18 and May 28–29, 1947, 80th Congress, 1st Session (Washington: Government Printing Office, 1947), pp. 10–12. Cited hereafter as House, *Hearings to Amend the Natural Gas Act, 1947*.

9. Harry S Truman to Nelson Lee Smith, April 9, 1947, Truman Papers. Also cited in House, *Hearings to Amend the Natural Gas Act, 1947*, p. 38.

10. *Hearings to Amend the Natural Gas Act, 1947*, p. 10.

11. *Congressional Record*, 80th Congress, 1st Session, p. 8055.

12. U.S. Congress, House, Committee on Interstate and Foreign Commerce. *Amending the Natural Gas Act Approved June 21, 1938, as Amended*, Report No. 800 to accompany H.R. 4051, 80th Congress, 1st Session (Washington: Government Printing Office, 1947), p. 2. Cited hereafter as House, *Report No. 800*.

13. *Interstate Natural Gas Co. v. Federal Power Commission*, affirmed, 331 U.S. 682 (1947), pp. 690–91; *New York Times*, June 17, 1947. Among the best law journal articles on the case are Robert E. Hardwicke, "Some Consequences of Fears by Independent Producers of Gas of Federal Regulation," *Law and Contemporary Problems*, v. 19 (1954): 342–60; and Raoul Berger and Abe Krash, "The Status of Independent Producers Under the Natural Gas Act," *Texas Law Review*, v. 30 (1951): 29–61.

14. See Nelson Lee Smith to Charles A. Wolverton, July 10, 1947, Kerr Papers. Also reprinted in U.S. Congress, House Interstate and Foreign Commerce Committee, Subcommittee on Petroleum and Federal Power. *Hearings on H.R. 79 and H.R. 1758 and H.R. 982, Natural Gas Amendment (Production and Gathering)*, April 5, 6, 7, 25, and 26, 1949, 81st Congress, 1st Session (Washington: Government Printing Office, 1949), pp. 271–72. Cited hereafter as House, *Hearings on H.R. 79*. For Priest bill see *Congressional Record*, 80th Congress, 1st Session, p. 8394.

15. For the House adoption of the Rizley bill, see *Congressional Record*, 80th Congress, 1st Session, pp. 8750–51; for Senate Committee vote, see *Congressional Quarterly Almanac—1947*, p. 355.

16. F.P.C. Docket No. R-106, August 7, 1948, Kerr Papers.

17. F.P.C. Docket No. R-106, August 11, 1947, p. 3, Kerr Papers.

18. See Leland Olds and Claude Draper to Tom Stewart, February 18, 1948, in U.S. Congress, Senate Interstate and Foreign Commerce Committee, Subcommittee on H.R. 4051. *Hearings on Amendments to the Natural Gas Act, H.R. 4051*, 80th Congress, 2nd Session, February 4, 5, 6, 9, 10, 11, 12, and 18, 1948 (Washington: Government Printing Office, 1948), pp. 544–58. Cited hereafter as Senate, *Hearings on H.R. 4051*. Tom Stewart (D., Tenn.) was chairman of the Senate Committee.

19. *Ibid.*, p. 220. For the complete text of the Olds-Draper report see, FPC, *Natural Gas Investigation* (Docket No. G-580), *Report of Commissioner Leland Olds and Commissioner Claude L. Draper* (Washington, 1948). Copy in Wimberly Papers.

20. See FPC, *Natural Gas Investigation* (Docket No. G-580), *Report of Commissioner Nelson Lee Smith and Commissioner Harrington Wimberly* (Washington, 1948). Copy in Wimberly Papers. They opposed the Rizley bill but favored the Priest bill, H.R. 4099. See Smith and Wimberly to Tom Stewart, March 1, 1948, in Senate, *Hearings on H.R. 4051*, p. 539.

21. For other amendments, see *Ibid.*, p. 358, 360, 377. On April 13, the Senate committee voted 9–4 not to report H.R. 4051, see *Congressional Quarterly Almanac—1949*, p. 355.

22. See Chapter I.

23. McPherson, *A Political Education*, p. 64.

24. *Ibid.*

25. John Osborne, "Natural Gas and the Authoritarian 'Liberals,'" *Fortune* (May 1952): 126.

26. *Ibid.* Wimberly's appointment was presumably a favor to Kerr for his support of Truman's candidacy for the vice-presidential nomination in 1944. An Altus, Oklahoma, publisher in the 1940's, Wimberly was Democratic state chairman during Kerr's gubernatorial administration. See Scales, "Political History of Oklahoma," p. 456. Harrington Wimberly Interview, January 24, 1975.

27. Joseph Alsop, *The Seattle Times*, October 9, 1951, Kerr Papers.

28. *Congressional Quarterly Almanac—1948*, p. 456.

29. See U.S. Congress, Senate, Subcommittee of Interstate and Foreign Commerce Committee. *Hearings on the Nomination of Thomas Chalmers Buchanan . . . to the Federal Power Commission*, 80th Congress, 2nd Session, April 29, May 6, 13, 25, 26, and June 1, 1948 (Washington: Government Printing Office, 1948) and *Congressional Record*, 81st Congress, 1st Session, pp. 7250–54.

30. Don Emery to Kerr, November 10, 1948, Kerr Papers. Alvin Richard, an attorney for the Pure Oil Company, was also of considerable help to Kerr in drafting S. 1498. See Kerr to Richards, April 7, 1950, Kerr to Luther Bohanon, April 3, 1950 in Kerr Papers.

31. *Congressional Record*, 81st Congress, 1st Session, p. 3776.

32. H.R. 79 by John E. Lyle (D., Tex.) and H.R. 1758 by Oren Harris (D., Ark.).

33. Copy of S. 1498, Kerr Papers.

34. See House, *Hearings on H.R. 79*.

35. *Ibid.*, p. 219.

36. *Ibid.*, p. 193.

37. U.S. Congress, House, Interstate and Foreign Commerce Committee.

Report to Accompany H.R. 1758. Report No. 1140, 81st Congress, 1st Session, July 28, 1949 (Washington: Government Printing Office, 1949). Cited hereafter as House, *Report No. 1140.*

38. *Ibid.*, p. 9.

39. *Ibid.*, pp. 17–19.

40. *Ibid.*, pp. 20–23; 24–28.

41. See *Congressional Record*, 81st Congress, 1st Session, p. 10777.

42. *Ibid.*, pp. 10784, 10845, 10871.

43. E. C. Johnson to Kerr, May 3, 1949, Kerr Papers.

44. Evans and Novak, *Lyndon B. Johnson*, p. 8.

45. *Ibid.*, p. 9.

46. The Brown brothers purchased the pipelines from the government after World War II for $143,127,000 for their Texas Eastern Transmission Corporation. See Alfred Steinberg, *Sam Johnson's Boy: A Close-up of the President from Texas* (New York: The Macmillan Company, 1968), p. 243. Cited hereafter as Steinberg, *Sam Johnson's Boy.* Also see Evans and Novak, *Lyndon B. Johnson,* p. 18.

47. Thomas L. Stokes quoted in Evans and Novak, *Lyndon B. Johnson*, p. 35. Leland Olds was born in Rochester, New York, in 1891, the son of George D. Olds, who became president of Amherst College. Olds had considered a career in the ministry, but after graduating from Amherst in 1912, he studied economics and sociology at Harvard. Before entering the army in 1918, he worked for the Shipbuilding Labor Adjustment Board and the National War Labor Board. After the war he was a researcher for the American Federation of Labor and then a writer for the *Federated Press,* a left-wing labor news service. See Olds obituary in *New York Times*, August 5, 1960.

48. U.S. Congress, Senate, Subcommittee of Interstate and Foreign Commerce Committee. *Hearings on S. 1498, A Bill to Amend the Natural Gas Act, Approved June 21, 1938, as Amended,* 81st Congress, 1st Session, May 17, 18, 24, 26, and 31 and June 7, 8, 1949 (Washington: Government Printing Office, 1949), p. 30. Cited hereafter as Senate, *Hearings on S. 1498.*

49. *Ibid.*, pp. 92–93.

50. *Ibid.*, p. 47.

51. F.P.C. Docket No. R-106, August 11, 1947, p. 1.

52. For Olds' early comments see Federal Power Commission, *The First Five Years Under the National Gas Act* (Washington, 1944), 3ff, copy in Wimberly Papers. Also see 3 F.P.C. 32; 2 F.P.C. 704 and 127F. 2nd 153 (1942); *New York Times*, January 6, 30, 1944.

53. See F.P.C. *Olds-Draper Report*, pp. 1–13, Wimberly Papers.

54. The quote is from House, *Hearings on H.R. 79*, p. 276. Olds made similar statements in the Senate hearings. See Senate, *Hearings on S. 1498*, p. 213.

55. Senate, *Hearings on S. 1498*, p. 93.

56. Gerald D. Nash, *United States Oil Policy, 1890–1964: Business and Government in Twentieth Century America* (Pittsburgh: University of Pittsburgh Press, 1968), p. 219. Cited hereafter as Nash, *United States Oil Policy.*

57. Senate, *Hearings on S. 1498*, p. 201.

58. *Ibid.*, p. 284.

59. *Ibid.*, p. 248.

60. *Ibid.*, p. 93.

61. *Ibid.*, p. 4.

62. *Ibid.*, pp. 229, 231, 233, 235–36, 237, 246, 350–51, 358, and 399.

63. See brief for the FPC before the U.S. Supreme Court, Case No. 733, October Term, 1946, pp. 43–44, Kerr Papers.

64. Senate, *Hearings on S. 1498*, p. 220.

65. Charles H. Rhyne quoted in Peter Edson, *Washington Daily News*, February 24, 1950, Kerr Papers, Rhyne, the Washington representative of the National Institute of Municipal Law Officers, did not testify at the hearing. Anne X. Alpern, solicitor for the City of Pittsburgh testified for the organization. See Senate, *Hearings on S. 1498*, pp. 456–60.

66. U.S. Congress, Senate, Interstate and Foreign Commerce Committee. *Amendments to the Natural Gas Act, Report to Accompany S. 1498*, Report No. 567, 81st Congress, 1st Session, June 24, 1949 (Washington: Government Printing Office, 1949). Cited hereafter as Senate, *Report No. 567*.

67. "Subcommittee Substitute for S. 1498," typed memorandum dated June 19, 1949, and "Report of the Committtee on Natural Gas, Section of Mineral Law," American Bar Association, St. Louis, Missouri, Don Emery, chairman, September 7, 1949, Kerr Papers.

68. Senate, *Report No. 567*, p. 1.

69. Frank Pace, Jr., to Truman, Memorandum on S. 1498, July 22, 1949, Truman Papers.

70. See Nelson Lee Smith to Charles A. Wolverton, July 10, 1947, Kerr Papers.

71. Pace to Truman, July 22, 1949, p. 2, Truman Papers.

72. See Truman notation on Charles S. Murphy to Truman, July 25, 1949, Truman Papers.

73. Elmer B. Staats to Edwin C. Johnson, August 1, 1949, Truman Papers.

74. Murphy to Truman, July 25, 1949. At the bottom of the memo, Truman wrote, "I approve of Mr. Murphy's suggestion," dated July 26, 1949, Truman Papers.

75. Kerr to Truman, August 11, 1949, Kerr Papers.

76. Kerr to Truman, August 12, 1949, Truman Papers.

77. *Ibid.*

78. Douglas, *In the Fullness of Time*, p. 464.

79. Ralph K. Huitt, "National Regulation of the Natural-Gas Industry," in Emmette S. Redford, ed., *Public Administration and Policy Formation* (Austin: University of Texas Press, 1956), pp. 92–93; Steinberg, *Sam Johnson's Boy*, p. 294.

80. Evans and Novak, *Lyndon B. Johnson*, p. 31.

81. *Tulsa Tribune*, September 28, 1949.

82. Lowell Mellett, *Washington Post*, no date, clipping in Kerr Papers.

83. *Tulsa World*, October 6, 1949.

84. Joseph P. Harris, "The Senatorial Rejection of Leland Olds: A Case Study," *American Political Science Review*, v. 45, No. 3 (September, 1951): 674–92. Cited hereafter as Harris, "The Senatorial Rejection of Leland Olds." For Bridges' statement see *Congressional Record*, 78th Congress, 1st Session, p. 5044.

85. See *Congressional Record*, 78th Congress, 2nd Session, p. 7692; U.S.

Congress, Senate, Subcommittee of the Interstate and Foreign Commerce Committee. *Leland Olds Appointment to the Federal Power Commission*, 78th Congress, 2nd Session (Washington: Government Printing Office, 1944).

86. Harris, "The Senatorial Rejection of Leland Olds," 686; Nash, *United States Oil Policy*, pp. 224–25.

87. *Tulsa World*, October 4, 1949.

88. John Lyle was born September 4, 1910, and elected to the Texas House of Representatives in 1941. He resigned in 1942 to enlist in the U.S. Army and was elected to the U.S. House of Representatives in 1944 while still serving overseas. *Biographical Directory*, p. 1244.

89. U.S. Congress, Senate, Subcommittee on the Nomination of Leland Olds, Interstate and Foreign Commerce Committee. *Hearings on the Reappointment of Leland Olds to the Federal Power Commission*, 81st Congress, 1st Session (Washington: Government Printing Office, 1949), p. 100. Cited hereafter as Senate, *Reappointment of Leland Olds, 1949*.

90. Truman to E. C. Johnson, October, 1949, Truman Papers.

91. *Congressional Record*, 81st Congress, 1st Session, p. 13759.

92. Willard Edwards, Washington *Times Herald*, October 5, 1949, copy in Kerr Papers.

93. *Congressional Quarterly Almanac—1949*, pp. 774–75. See also *Congressional Record*, 81st Congress, 1st Session, p. 13858.

94. *Washington Post*, October 6, 1949.

95. Arthur Krock, *New York Times*, October 6, 1949.

96. For Ives' remarks see, *Congressional Record*, 81st Congress, 1st Session, pp. 14365–66; Dulles' remarks, p. 14370.

97. Byrd quote in Evans and Novak, *Lyndon B. Johnson*, p. 36. Senator Forrest Donnell (R., Mo.) said in the Senate debate that "no official, not even the President of the United States, has the right to direct or instruct the Senate." *Congressional Record*, 81st Congress, 1st Session, p. 14236.

98. Evans and Novak, *Lyndon B. Johnson*, p. 36.

99. Editorial in the Washington *Evening Star*, October 8, 1949, copy in Kerr Papers.

100. See *Congressional Record*, 81st Congress, 1st Session, pp. 14021, 14212, 14235, 14336, 14357.

101. *Congressional Record*, 81st Congress, 2nd Session, pp. 14386–87.

102. For various views of Kerr's role see Evans and Novak, *Lyndon B. Johnson*, p. 36; Mellett, *Washington Post* clippings, no dates, in Kerr Papers; Douglas, *In the Fullness of Time*, pp. 463–64; and Harris, "The Senatorial Rejection of Leland Olds," 677.

103. Douglas, *In the Fullness of Time*, pp. 463–64.

104. *Ibid.*, p. 464.

105. *Tulsa Tribune*, September 28, 1949.

106. See Senate, *Reappointment of Leland Olds*, p. 103.

107. *Congressional Record*, 81st Congress, 1st Session, pp. 14215–17.

108. Evans and Novak, *Lyndon B. Johnson*, p. 39.

109. Steinberg, *Sam Johnson's Boy*, p. 244.

110. Evans and Novak, *Lyndon B. Johnson*, p. 36. See also Harold L. Ickes, *The Secret Diary of Harold L. Ickes: The Lowering Clouds, 1939–1941*, v. III

(New York: Simon and Schuster, 1954), pp. 578, 580, 585, 619.

111. Evans and Novak, *Lyndon B. Johnson*, p. 36.

112. Mellett, Washington *Evening Star*, October 1, 1949.

113. "Questions to Senator Kerr from Marquis Childs," handwritten response from Kerr, no date, Kerr Papers.

114. Senators Wayne Morse (R., Ore.) and William Langer (R., N.D.) were the only Members to defend Olds against the communist charges. See *Congressional Record*, 81st Congress, 1st Session, pp. 14360–64; 14366–70.

115. William Cary, chairman of the SEC from March 1961 to August 1964 criticized Olds' political ineptness. "Whether he likes it or not, as the head of an agency he is in politics." Cary, *Politics and the Regulatory Agencies*, p. 139.

116. Osborne, "Natural Gas and the Authoritarian 'Liberals,'" 124.

Chapter IV

1. Debate on S. 1498 began March 16, 1950. See *Congressional Record*, 81st Congress, 2nd Session, p. 3439.

2. Osborne, "Natural Gas and the Authoritarian Liberals," 126.

3. See *Philadelphia Inquirer*, February 16, 1950; *Labor*, January 7, 1950; Donald Woods, *CIO News*, February 13, 1950; *Oil Reporter*, August 11, 1949; Mellett, Washington *Evening Star*, March 14, 1950.

4. Representative Sidney Yates (D., Ill.) quoted by Gerry Robichaud, Chicago *Sun Times*, February 26, 1950.

5. Mellett, Washington *Evening Star*, March 23, 1950.

6. See Kerr handwritten notes on the gas bill, 1950, Kerr Papers.

7. *Ibid.*

8. Muskogee (Okla.) *Phoenix*, March 27, 1950. Also see Robert A. Taft, "Washington Report," no. 42, April 5, 1950. Copy in Kerr Papers.

9. Muskogee (Okla.) *Phoenix*, March 27, 1950.

10. On March 24, 1950, five days before the vote, Kerr's tally showed forty sure "yes" votes. Tally sheet in replica of Kerr's Senate Office at Kerr Museum, Poteau, Oklahoma.

11. McBride Interview.

12. *Congressional Record*, 81st Congress, 2nd Session, p. 3440.

13. *New York Times*, February 25, 1965.

14. See Paul I. Wellman, *Stuart Symington: Portrait of a Man with a Mission* (Garden City, N.Y.: Doubleday & Company, Inc., 1960), p. 41. Cited hereafter as Wellman, *Stuart Symington*.

15. *Congressional Record*, 81st Congress, 2nd Session, p. 3571.

16. *Ibid.*

17. Copy of news clipping, no date, no paper, in Kerr Papers.

18. *Congressional Quarterly Almanac—1950*, p. 600.

19. Robert S. Allen and William V. Shannon, *The Truman Merry-Go-*

Around (New York: Vanguard Press, Inc., 1950), pp. 282–83. Cited hereafter as Allen and Shannon, *Truman Merry-Go-Around.*

20. Quoted in *Tulsa Tribune,* March 17, 1950.

21. *Congressional Record,* 81st Congress, 2nd Session, p. 3450.

22. *Ibid.*

23. *Ibid.,* p. 3452.

24. *Ibid.*

25. *Ibid.,* p. 4194.

26. Johnson quoted in *Tulsa World,* March 29, 1950. Also see George Bryan, WCBS, March 28, 1950, radio copy in Kerr Papers.

27. *Congressional Record,* 81st Congress, 2nd Session, p. 3466.

28. *Ibid.,* p. 3474.

29. "Election Issues Grow Hot," *USNWR,* v. 29 (October 23, 1950): 20.

30. *New York Times,* March 17, 1950.

31. McPherson, *A Political Education,* p. 76.

32. *Congressional Record,* 81st Congress, 2nd Session, pp. 3452–53.

33. *Ibid.*

34. See clipping files on gas bill, 1949–1950, in Kerr Papers. These clippings are not identified regarding source or date.

35. See *Congressional Record,* 81st Congress, 2nd Session, pp. 3614, 3788–89.

36. *Ibid.,* p. 4020.

37. *Ibid.,* p. 4012.

38. McPherson, *A Political Education,* p. 30.

39. See Childs, *Washington Post,* March 28, 1950.

40. Douglas wrote "I felt inadequately matched against Kerr, who had a detailed knowledge of the industry. . . ." Douglas, *In the Fullness of Time,* p. 465.

41. Douglas, *In the Fullness of Time,* p. 465.

42. *Ibid.* Also see Douglas to Edmund G. Brown, May 31, 1957. Paul H. Douglas Papers, Chicago Historical Society, Chicago, Illinois. Cited hereafter as Douglas Papers.

43. Allen and Shannon, *Truman Merry-Go-Around,* p. 276.

44. *Congressional Record,* 81st Congress, 2nd Session, p. 3615.

45. All New England Republicans, with the exception of Bridges, voted against the Kerr bill. Rumor was that Bridges received campaign contributions from Phillips Petroleum in exchange for his vote. See Tyler Abell, ed., *Drew Pearson Diaries, 1949–1959* (New York: Holt, Rinehart and Winston, 1974), p. 326. Cited hereafter as Abell, *Drew Pearson Diaries.*

46. *Congressional Record,* 81st Congress, 2nd Session, p. 3625.

47. Huitt, "National Regulation of the Natural Gas Industry," p. 95.

48. *Congressional Record,* 81st Congress, 2nd Session, p. 3627.

49. *Ibid.,* p. 3724.

50. *Ibid.,* pp. 3626, 3724.

51. *Congressional Quarterly Almanac—1950,* p. 600.

52. *Congressional Record,* 81st Congress, 2nd Session, p. 3630.

53. *Congressional Quarterly Almanac—1950,* p. 600; *Congressional Record,* 81st Congress, 2nd Session, pp. 3778–79.

54. Mellett, Washington *Evening Star,* March 23, 1950.

55. Evans and Novak, *Lyndon B. Johnson,* p. 48.

56. *Ibid.*

57. *Congressional Record*, 81st Congress, 2nd Session, pp. 3760–61. Copy of letter in Truman Papers.

58. *Ibid.* The article appeared in the *St. Louis Post-Dispatch*, March 18, 1950.

59. Pearson, *Washington Post*, March 29, 1950.

60. *Congressional Record*, 81st Congress, 2nd Session, p. 3458.

61. *Ibid.*, p. 4019.

62. *Ibid.*

63. *Ibid.*, p. 4022; *Tulsa Tribune*, March 25, 1950.

64. *Tulsa Tribune*, March 25, 1950; Paul McBride to Kerr, memo, no date, Kerr Papers.

65. Pearson, *Washington Post*, March 29, 1950.

66. *Congressional Record*, 81st Congress, 2nd Session, pp. 4297–98.

67. J. Tracey Reynolds, *Tulsa World*, March 25, 1950; Murphy draft of letter for Truman, April 13, 1950, letter not sent, Truman Papers.

68. *Congressional Record*, 81st Congress, 2nd Session, p. 4299.

69. Reynolds, *Tulsa World*, March 25, 1950.

70. *Congressional Record*, 81st Congress, 2nd Session, p. 4299.

71. *Tulsa World*, March 31, 1950.

72. McPherson, *A Political Education*, p. 49.

73. *Washington Post*, April 2, 1950.

74. Robert Bendiner, "The Raid on the Gas Fields," *The Nation*, v. 170 (March 11, 1950): 218–19.

75. *Congressional Record*, 81st Congress, 1st Session, p. 10779; *Congressional Quarterly Almanac—1949*, p. 719.

76. Edson, Washington *Daily News*, February 24, 1950.

77. *Ibid.*

78. Stephenson, *Tulsa Tribune*, March 2, 1950.

79. Edson, Washington *Daily News*, n. d., Kerr Papers.

80. *Tulsa Tribune*, March 17, 1950.

81. See Blackwell (Okla.) *Journal-Tribune*, March 2, 1950; Clinton (Okla.) *Times-Tribune*, March 2, 1950, Kerr Papers.

82. Robert Allen, St. Louis *Post-Dispatch*, February 23, 1950, Kerr Papers.

83. McBride quoted from Kerr's 1949 speech before the National Reclamation Association in Phoenix and from his 1950 speeches before the Mississippi Valley Association in St. Louis and the Water Conservation Conference in Chicago. McBride to Noble, March 11, 1950, Kerr Papers.

84. For Millikin on Kerr bill see *Congressional Record*, 81st Congress, 2nd Session, pp. 3564–70.

85. Charles M. La Follette, national director of ADA, to Scott Lucas, February 16, 1950; Nathan E. Cowan, CIO legislative director to Scott Lucas, February 20, 1950. Lucas forwarded copies of both telegrams to Senator Kerr, Kerr Papers.

86. See Douglas to Palmer Hoyt, *Denver Post*; Douglas to Jonathan Daniels, *The Raliegh News and Observer*; Douglas to Barry Bingham, *The Courier-Journal*, *The Louisville Times*; Douglas to Martin S. Ochs, *Chattanooga Times*; Douglas to Ralph McGill, *The Atlanta Constitution*; Douglas to Paul M. Warner, *The Philadelphia Enquirer* and Douglas to Harry Wade, *The Detroit News*, varying dates in March 1950, Douglas Papers.

87. Robert Wallace, "New Gouge for Consumers," *New Republic*, v. 122 (March 13, 1950): 11–13.

88. *Washington Post*, March 18, 1950.

89. *New York Times*, March 18, 1950.

90. Edson, Washington *Daily News*, February 24, 1950; see Mellett, Washington *Evening Star*, March 14, 1950; Pearson, *Washington Post*, March 23, 1950, and March 24, 1950.

91. See J. M. Cordell, secretary, Oklahoma State Senate to Kerr, March 28, 1949. Transmits a copy of S. Con. Res. No. 12 passed the Senate on March 17, 1949, and House on March 22, 1949, Kerr Papers. Copy of resolution in Kerr Papers.

92. *Daily Oklahoman*, March 1, 1950; Durant (Okla.) *Daily Democrat*, March 3, 1950.

93. *Washington Post*, February 24, 1950.

94. Frank Edwards, WOR, March 27, 1950, radio copy in Kerr Papers.

95. Kenneth Banghart, WNBC, April 15, 1950, radio copy in Kerr Papers.

96. "High Ride for Gas," *Time*, v. 55 (April 10, 1950): 20.

97. *Ibid.*

98. Edwards, WOR, April 15, 1950, radio copy in Kerr Papers.

99. Muskogee (Okla.) *Phoenix*, March 25, 1950.

100. Carmen (Okla.) *Headlight*, March 11, 1950, Kerr Papers.

101. Edwards, WOR, March 30, 1952, radio copy in Kerr Papers.

102. Allen and Shannon, *Truman Merry-Go-Around*, p. 185.

103. Robert Albright, *Washington Post*, April 1, 1950.

104. Allen and Shannon, *Truman Merry-Go-Around*, p. 183.

105. *Ibid.*, p. 191.

106. *Congressional Record*, 81st Congress, 2nd Session, p. 4566.

107. Allen and Shannon, *Truman Merry-Go-Around*, p. 184.

108. See Rayburn to Truman, April 3, 1950, Sam Rayburn Library, Bonham, Texas. Cited hereafter as Rayburn Papers. Kerr to Al Reese, July 14, 1950, Kerr Papers.

109. *Congressional Record*, 81st Congress, 2nd Session, p. 4567.

110. *New York Times*, April 1, 1950; *Daily Oklahoman*, April 1, 1950; Allen and Shannon, *Truman Merry-Go-Around*, pp. 191–92; *Congressional Quarterly Almanac—1950*, p. 714. Ninety-seven Democrats and 79 Republicans voted for the bill; 115 Democrats and 58 Republicans and one American Laborite voted no.

111. Kerr to Bohanon, April 3, 1950, Kerr Papers.

112. Draft of Press Release on Passage of the Natural Gas Act, Kerr Papers.

113. *Ibid.*

114. See Alonzo L. Hamby, *Beyond the New Deal: Harry S Truman and American Liberalism* (New York: Columbia University Press, 1973), p. 348. Cited hereafter as Hamby, *Beyond the New Deal.*

115. *Philadelphia Enquirer*, March 30, 1950, Kerr Papers.

116. Thomas L. Stokes, March 31, 1950, no paper, Kerr Papers.

117. Allen and Shannon, *Truman Merry-Go-Around*, p. 73.

118. *New York Times*, April 7, 1950.

119. Rayburn to Truman, April 3, 1950, Rayburn Papers.

120. Truman to Rayburn, April 6, 1950, Rayburn Papers.

121. La Follette to Truman, April 6, 1950, Truman Papers.

122. Hamby, *Beyond the New Deal*, p. 346.

123. "Natural-Gas Blowoff," *Newsweek*, v. 35 (April 3, 1950): 18.

124. *Tulsa Tribune*, April 7, 1950.

125. *New York Times*, April 6, 1950; Mellett, Washington *Evening Star*, April 12, 1950.

126. *New York Times*, April 6, 1950.

127. Douglas, *In the Fullness of Time*, p. 466.

128. *New York Times*, April 6, 1950.

129. McBride Interview; Breene Kerr Interview, April 27, 1976. Breene Kerr confirmed that Truman had promised Senator Kerr that he would accept the gas bill.

130. Clip Boutell to Kerr, April 13, 1950; Ben Dwight to Boutell, April 14, 1950, Kerr Papers.

131. Quoted in Pearson, *Washington Post*, April 10, 1950.

132. La Follette to Truman, April 6, 1950, Truman Papers; Edward Jamieson, *Tulsa World*, April 10, 1950; McBride Interview.

133. The FPC reported 5 1/2 million residential users, while the Bureau of Mines counted 13 1/2 million homes in 35 states for a total of 43 million individuals. Edwards, WOR, April 5, 1950, radio copy in Kerr Papers.

134. Chapman to Frank Pace, Jr., Director, BOB, April 6, 1950, Truman Papers.

135. Hamby, *Beyond the New Deal*, p. 347; Allen and Shannon, *Truman Merry-Go-Around*, pp. 97–98.

136. Elmer Staats to William J. Hopkins, April 14, 1950, Truman Papers.

137. Fort Worth (Texas) *Star-Telegram*, April 12, 1950.

138. *Ibid.*

139. Murphy to Truman, April 13, 1950, Truman Papers.

140. Truman to Kerr, April 13, 1950, Murphy draft of memo with notation "not sent," Truman Papers.

141. U.S. Congress, House of Representatives, *Message from the President of the United States Returning Without Approval the Bill (H.R. 1758) to amend the Natural Gas Act Approved June 21, 1938, as Amended.* Doc. No. 555, 81st Congress, 2nd Session, April 18, 1950 (Washington: Government Printing Office, 1950), pp. 1, 2.

142. Cecil Holland, Washington *Sunday Star*, April 16, 1950; Kerr to Reese, July 14, 1950, Kerr Papers.

143. Holland, Washington *Sunday Star*, April 16, 1950, Kerr Papers.

144. *Ibid.*

145. *New York Times*, April 19, 1950.

146. Hamby, *Beyond the New Deal*, p. 348.

147. *New York Post*, April 17, 1950, Kerr Papers.

148. Davis quoted in Hamby, *Beyond the New Deal*, p. 348.

149. Chicago *Daily News*, April 18, 1950.

150. McBride Interview.

151. *New York Times*, April 17, 1950.

152. Eisenhower favored the legislation, but vetoed the bill because Senator Case alleged that a representative of the gas industry had offered him a bribe to vote for the bill.

153. Kerr to Foster, April 19, 1950, Kerr Papers.

Chapter V

1. Anderson, *Outsider in the Senate*, p. 96. Kerr and Russell had similar careers. Both were popular governors; both tried for the presidency in 1952 and failed; and both returned to the Senate where they continued to have impressive careers. Although Kerr died before his supremacy was threatened, Russell lived to see age and ill health diminish his influence.

2. Richard Russell, *Memorial Addresses*, pp. 64–65.

3. "Oklahoma's Kerr—The Man Who Really Runs the U.S. Senate," *Newsweek*, v. 60 (August 6, 1962): 15.

4. Representative Everett McKinley Dirksen (R., Ill.) upset Lucas; and James Henderson Duff, former governor of Pennsylvania, defeated Myers. Five senators were defeated, leaving the Democrats with a majority of 49 to 47 Republicans. The Democrats lost 28 seats in the House, retaining a majority of 235 to 199 Republicans. Seven Democratic governors lost, giving the GOP 25 statehouses compared to 23 for the Democrats. See *Congress and the Nation*, p. 10.

In Lucas' case leadership duties had kept him in Washington when he should have been home campaigning. Clinton Anderson saw other causes for his defeat—his opposition to McCarthy that alienated Illinois Catholics, his failure to push a welfare bill supported by Illinois miners, and Kefauver's crime hearings in Chicago one week before the election. See Anderson, *Outsider in the Senate*, p. 107.

5. For quote see McPherson, *A Political Education*, p. 15. Lucas opposed two major items in Truman's legislative program. In 1947 he voted to override the President's veto of the Taft-Hartley Act, and he opposed the tough civil rights plank in the 1948 platform. See Evans and Novak, *Lyndon B. Johnson*, p. 40. Scott Lucas was not constituted to impress his own or the President's views on the heterogenous Democratic membership of the Senate.

6. Anderson believed that "Russell . . . would be under an obligation and would, by the force of his leadership, bring the rest of the southern contingent along with him." See Anderson, *Outsider in the Senate*, p. 108.

7. *Ibid.* Evans and Novak, *Lyndon B. Johnson*, p. 42.

8. *Ibid.*

9. Randall B. Ripley, *Power in the Senate* (New York: St. Martin's Press, 1969), p. 65. Cited hereafter as Ripley, *Power in the Senate*. Also see Ray Tucker, *Tulsa World*, July 12, 1951.

10. McBride Interview; Hays Interview; *Colliers* (January 5, 1952): 52, Kerr Papers; and Evans and Novak, *Lyndon B. Johnson*, pp. 41–42.

11. *Ibid.*, p. 42; Anderson, *Outsider in the Senate*, p. 109.

12. McPherson, *A Political Education*, p. 14.

13. *Tulsa World, Tulsa Tribune*, and *Oklahoma City Times*, November 14, 1950.

14. *Tulsa World*, November 15, 1950.

15. McBride Interview.

16. Evans and Novak, *Lyndon B. Johnson*, p. 33.

17. McPherson, *A Political Education*, pp. 13–14.

18. *Ibid.*, p. 51.

19. *Daily Oklahoman*, April 12, 1951.

20. See Kerr's speech to the Midwest Conference of Democratic Party Leaders at Denver, *New York Times*, May 24, 1951. Copy of speech in Kerr Papers.

21. *Daily Oklahoman*, April 9, 1951.

22. Hays Interview.

23. The *Tulsa Tribune* criticized Kerr for daring to ridicule the General. While willing "to excuse the President's action," the paper deemed "Kerr in a class with Drew Pearson for calling the great soldier, MacArthur the Magnificent." See *Tulsa Tribune*, April 17, 1951.

24. See Jack Cleland, *Tulsa World*, August 12, 1962.

25. *Ibid.*

26. The professed shock over Chairman Wallgren's vote to exempt the Phillips Company showed how completely the proregulatory forces had deluded themselves. Wallgren was under considerable pressure from Oscar Chapman when he reluctantly joined in supporting the President's decision to veto the Kerr gas bill. But nothing in his record as a legislator or as a governor justified the liberals' belief that Wallgren would continue Olds' crusade for regulation. Yet the President had fought so stubbornly to save Olds that it seemed impossible that he would name a commissioner of divergent views. The very swiftness of Wallgren's confirmation was a sign that the gas forces considered him manageable, despite Paul Douglas' warning that the appointment was like "hiring a nurse to murder a baby." For the Douglas quote see Joseph Alsop, *Seattle Times*, October 9, 1951, Kerr Papers. On Wallgren's decision to support a veto see Allen and Shannon, *Truman Merry-Go-Around*, p. 98. On Wallgren's record see Hamby, *Beyond the New Deal*, pp. 335–36.

The truly unexpected vote in the Phillips case came from Claude Draper, the seventy-six-year-old Wyoming Republican, who had dissented from the commission's self-denying Rule No. 139 and had supported the veto. His vote to exempt the Phillips Company caused rumors that he had "come around" in response to pressures from the oil and gas lobby. There were also reports that Draper's request to be renamed to the FPC, when his term expired in 1951, was delayed until he agreed to reverse himself on the Kerr bill. For Draper's decision to exempt Phillips, see FPC Docket No. G-217, 90, P.U.R. (NS) 325 (1951), pp. 355–56 and Osborne, *Fortune*: 126. On rumors that Draper had been pressured in the Phillips case, see Pearson, *Washington Post*, July 19, 1951, and Alsop, *Tulsa Tribune*, October 11, 1951.

For a detailed discussion of the Phillips case see Huitt, "National Regulation of the Natural Gas Industry," pp. 97–101; Hawkins, *The Field Price Regulation of Natural Gas*, pp. 20–24; Neuner, *The Natural Gas Industry*, pp. 80–111; and

McKie, *The Regulation of Natural Gas,* pp. 23–26.

27. Douglas, *In the Fullness of Time,* p. 466.

28. See Alsop, *Tulsa Tribune,* October 11, 1951. For Kerr's offer to correct "the gross inaccuracies and the erroneous conclusions your column contained," see Kerr to Alsop, October 12, 1951, Kerr Papers. Alsop failed to respond either by letter or in his column.

29. Walter Lippman, New York *Herald Tribune,* July 17, 1952.

30. McBride Interview.

31. Joseph and Stewart Alsop, *Washington Post,* February 5, 1952. Adams served in the Senate from 1803 until his resignation in 1808. After his term as President, he was elected to the House and served from 1831–1848. See *Biographical Directory,* pp. 459–60.

32. Kerr to Press Intelligence, Inc., December 1950, Kerr Papers.

33. Kerr to various editors, December 18, 1950, Kerr Papers.

34. "Senator Kerr Says," January 4, 1951, Kerr Papers.

35. *New York Times,* January 5, 1951.

36. James Free, *Tulsa World,* May 17, 1951.

37. *Tulsa World,* May 24, 1951; *Oklahoma City Times,* May 25, 1951.

38. Truman to William Boyle, Jr., May 23, 1951, Truman Papers; *Rocky Mountain News,* no date, Kerr Papers.

39. Albright, *Washington Post,* May 27, 1951.

40. *Oklahoma City Times,* May 25, 1951.

41. Doris Fleeson, Washington *Evening Star,* no date, 1952, Kerr Papers.

42. Quotation from Hamby, *Beyond the New Deal,* p. 483. Also see Joseph Bruce Gorman, *Kefauver: A Political Biography* (New York: Oxford University Press, 1971), pp. 117–30; William Howard Moore, *The Kefauver Committee and the Politics of Crime, 1950–1952* (Columbia: University of Missouri Press, 1974), 235–36.

43. Albright, *Washington Post,* January 24, 1952; Fleeson, Washington *Evening Star,* no date, 1952, Kerr Papers.

44. Quotation in Fleeson, Washington *Evening Star,* no date, 1952, Kerr Papers.

45. Pearson, *Washington Post,* January 20, 1952.

46. Louisville *Courier-Journal,* May 18, 1952, Kerr Papers.

47. Victor Riesel, *Daily Oklahoman,* February 19, 1952.

48. *Daily Oklahoman,* January 27, 1952.

49. Sullivant, *Daily Oklahoman,* March 9, 1952; Josephine Ripley, *Christian Science Monitor,* February 7, 1952.

50. Clark Clifford to Kerr, January 4, 1952, Kerr Papers. Clifford sent Kerr a set of memos on presidential primaries.

51. Truman, *Harry S Truman,* p. 527; Hamby, *Beyond the New Deal,* p. 481.

52. Truman, *Harry S Truman,* p. 528.

53. Hamby, *Beyond the New Deal,* p. 402.

54. Truman, *Harry S Truman,* p. 482.

55. Hamby, *Beyond the New Deal,* p. 483.

56. *Oklahoma City Times,* February 7, 1952.

57. George Gallup, *Washington Post,* February 14, 1952; Marin Relman, Washington *Evening Star,* February 10, 1952, Kerr Papers.

58. Fleeson, Washington *Evening Star*, no date, 1952, Kerr Papers; *New York Times*, January 31, 1952.

59. Hawks Interview.

60. *Ibid.*

61. Hays Interview.

62. *Daily Oklahoman*, February 6, 1952.

63. Leslie Carpenter, *Tulsa Tribune*, February 12, 1952.

64. Robert S. Allen, Miami (Fla.) *Daily News*, February 22, 1952, Kerr Papers; Hamby, *Beyond the New Deal*, p. 57.

65. Allen, "Senator Kerr is Hot Presidential Dark Horse," no date, no paper, Kerr Papers.

66. Woodward (Okla.) *Daily Press*, March 4, 1952, Kerr Papers.

67. Sullivant, *Daily Oklahoman*, March 9, 1952. Dean Baugh, executive secretary of the Nebraska AFL, said labor was "just waiting for word from labor in Oklahoma before going all out for Kerr." See Norman (Okla.) *Transcript*, February 24, 1952, Kerr Papers.

68. Stokes, Washington *Evening Star*, March 24, 1952.

69. Allen, "Nebraska, Now or Never for Kerr," no paper, no date, Kerr Papers.

70. Paul T. David, Malcolm Moos, and Ralph M. Goldman, eds., *Presidential Nominating Politics in 1952*, V (Baltimore: The Johns Hopkins Press, 1954) pp. 295–96. Cited hereafter as David, *Presidential Nominating Politics*.

71. Hawks Interview.

72. Inez Robb, *Tulsa World*, no date, 1952, Kerr Papers.

73. *Daily Oklahoman*, March 28, 1952.

74. Longview (Tex.) *Daily News*, March 20, 1952, Kerr Papers.

75. *Daily Oklahoman*, March 29, 1952.

76. Truman, *Harry S Truman*, pp. 532–33.

77. *Daily Oklahoman*, March 30, 1952.

78. McBride Interview.

79. Hays Interview.

80. "Kefauver Knocks Out Kerr," *Life*, v. 32 (April 14, 1952): 41.

81. Muskogee (Okla.) *Times-Democrat*, April 7, 1952, Kerr Papers.

82. Leland Gourley, Henryetta (Okla.) *Daily Free-Lance*, February 20, 1952, Kerr Papers.

83. *Ibid.*, Editorial, February 19, 1952, Kerr Papers.

84. *Daily Oklahoman*, April 6, 1952.

85. See W. R. Wallace, Judge, U.S. District Court, to Kerr, January 3, 1951, Kerr Papers; David, *Presidential Nominating Politics*, III, p. 303.

86. Beckell Eubanks, *Christian Science Monitor*, February 19, 1952, Kerr Papers.

87. John M'Williams, *Tulsa Tribune*, January 12, 1952.

88. Carpenter, *Tulsa Tribune*, June 25, 1951; Henthorne, *Tulsa World*, July 22, 1951.

89. Henthorne, *Tulsa World*, July 22, 1951.

90. Gibson, *Oklahoma*, pp. 372, 406. On the Bolivian colony see Keith L. Bryant, Jr., *Alfalfa Bill Murray* (Norman: University of Oklahoma Press, 1968), pp. 151–72.

91. "Statement Regarding Democratic Party Politics," Johnston Murray Collection, Western History Collection, Bizzell Memorial Library, University of Oklahoma, Norman, Oklahoma. Cited hereafter as Murray Papers.

92. M'Williams, *Tulsa Tribune*, February 25, 1952.

93. M'Williams, *Tulsa Tribune*, February 27, 1952. Coal and Washita counties were present, but did not vote.

94. "Press Release on Nebraska Primary," Murray Papers; *Oklahoma City Times*, April 2, 1952.

95. *Daily Oklahoman*, Editorial, April 3, 1952.

96. See Checotah (Okla.) *Democrat*, July 5, 1951, Kerr Papers.

97. "Statement from Governor Regarding National Committeeman and Democratic State Chairman," no date, Murray Papers.

98. *Daily Oklahoman*, April 8, 1952.

99. David, *Presidential Nominating Politics*, III, pp. 306–307; *Daily Oklahoman*, April 28, 1952.

100. David, *Presidential Nominating Politics*, III, pp. 306–307.

101. Fleeson, Washington *Evening Star*, March 12, 1952.

102. Robert L. Riggs, Louisville *Courier-Journal*, February 10, 1952, Kerr Papers.

103. Kerr quoted in Bristol (Conn.) *Press*, June 27, 1952, Kerr Papers.

104. See Samuel W. Yorty to Kerr, February 5, 1952, Kerr Papers.

105. Leslie Claypool, Los Angeles *Daily News*, March 24, 1952, Kerr Papers.

106. Abell, *Drew Pearson's Diary*, p. 206.

107. *Ibid.*

108. Robert Engler, *The Politics of Oil: A Study of Private Power and Democratic Direction* (New York: The Macmillan Company, 1961), pp. 402, 373.

109. *Ibid.* Kerr was absent when the tidelands bill, S.J. Res. 20, passed the Senate, April 2, 1952, but he had refused to take part in the debate "to avoid the charge that he was an interested party." Kerr-McGee had major investments in offshore drilling and high expectations for new finds in the Gulf of Mexico.

110. James Bassett, *The* (Los Angeles) *Mirror*, March 26, 1952, and *Examiner*, March 27, 1952, Kerr Papers.

111. Kerr to Albert T. Otis, June 26, 1952, Kerr Papers.

112. See Riggs, Louisville *Courier-Journal*, May 18, 1952, Kerr Papers.

113. Hamby, *Beyond the New Deal*, p. 485; Jay Walz, *New York Times*, June 18, 1952.

114. *New York Post*, June 22, 1952, Kerr Papers.

115. Carpenter, *Tulsa Tribune*, June 6, 1952.

116. Salt Lake City *Deseret News*, June 30, 1952, Kerr Papers.

117. The Democrats gave four votes at large to each state carried in the last presidential election. Oregon was the only western state to vote Republican in 1948. See David, *Presidential Nominating Politics*, V, p. 21.

118. Albuquerque *Journal*, June 28, 1952, Kerr Papers. "Kerr's candidacy was being sold to the delegates with the argument that it would benefit New Mexico Democrats more in the coming general election campaign to have backed Kerr than to have climbed on the bandwagon of the winner." Quoted in Albuquerque *Journal*, June 22, 1952, Kerr Papers.

119. Pearson, Perry (Okla.) *Daily Journal*, May 23, 1952, Kerr Papers.

120. See David, *Presidential Nominating Politics*, V, p. 265.

121. George Mack, *Topeka Capitol*, June 22, 1952, Kerr Papers.

122. Three from Idaho, 3 from Wyoming, 1 from Nevada, 10 from New Mexico, 6 1/2 from Washington, 4 from Utah, 6 from Arizona and 4 from Kansas. An AP poll of July 23 showed Kerr's delegate strength in Wyoming was 1, although his fanatical supporters claimed 3 votes. The claim of 10 votes in Washington was groundless. Senator Kerr was present at the Washington state convention when a last-minute appeal from a Stevenson supporter resulted in a vote for an uninstructed delegation. While a clear defeat for the Kefauver supporters, there was no groundswell for Kerr. An AP poll at the close of the Washington state convention showed 12½ votes for Kefauver, 2 for Stevenson, ½ for Harriman, ½ for William O. Douglas and 6½ unknown. See David, *Presidential Nominating Politics*, V, pp. 53, 178.

Utah's delegation decided to give some support to each of the three senators running, "to avoid antagonizing members of a body that would remain powerful on matters affecting Utah." See David, V, p. 95.

Montana was casting its twelve votes for its senior Senator, James E. Murray, who was ineligible for the presidency because he was not a native-born American. See David, V, 21.

The Colorado delegation had shown marked enthusiasm for Harriman during the state convention. Observers predicted that more than half of the 16 votes would go to any Truman-backed candidate, and they did not consider Kerr strong enough to merit the President's endorsement. See David, V, p. 76.

123. Mack, *Topeka Capital*, June 22, 1952, Kerr Papers.

124. David, *Presidential Nominating Politics*, V, pp. 320–26.

125. *Ibid.*

126. *Ibid.*, IV, p. 254.

127. *Ibid.*, pp. 211–12.

128. *Ibid.*, p. 185.

129. *Ibid.*, II, p. 282.

130. *Ibid.*, pp. 21, 208.

131. O'Riordan to Kerr, June 22, 1952, Kerr Papers; *Tulsa Tribune*, June 23, 1952.

132. R. Donald Slee to Kerr, May 1, 1952, Kerr Papers. Slee was a member of the New York state Democratic Committee.

133. J. Irwin Walden to Kerr, June 21, 1952, Kerr Papers. Walden was the secretary-treasurer of the Democratic Executive Committee. W. C. Mahan, *Arkansas Gazette*, July 1, 1952, Kerr Papers.

134. Howell, *Tulsa Tribune*, March 27, 1974.

135. *Ibid.*

136. Edward C. Burks, *Baltimore Sun*, July 21, 1952, in Kerr Papers.

137. Howell, *Tulsa Tribune*, March 27, 1974.

138. *Chicago Tribune*, July 16, 1952.

139. Ashville (N.C.) *Times*, July 15, 1952, Kerr Papers.

140. *Phoenix Gazette*, July 18, 1952, Kerr Papers.

141. Paul Martin, Rochester (N.Y.) *Times-Union*, July 18, 1952, Kerr Papers; Phillip Geyelin, *Wall Street Journal*, July 22, 1952.

142. Quoted in David, *Presidential Nominating Politics*, I, pp. 107–108.

143. Carpenter, *Tulsa Tribune*, July 18, 1952.

144. Joseph H. Miller, *Philadelphia Inquirer*, July 18, 1952, Kerr Papers; Truman, *Harry S Truman*, pp. 541–42.

145. Geyelin, *Wall Street Journal*, July 22, 1952.

146. *Chicago Tribune*, July 24, 1952.

147. *Ibid*.

148. *Chicago Tribune*, July 25, 1952. For Senator George's speech see Democratic National Committee, *Official Report of the Proceedings of the Democratic National Convention, 1952* (Washington: Democratic National Committee, 1952), pp. 280–83; Browning's speech, pp. 287–89. Cited hereafter as *Proceedings, 1952*.

149. *Chicago Tribune*, July 25, 1952. For the text, see *Proceedings, 1952*, pp. 292–95.

150. *Chicago Tribune*, July 25, 1952. For details on the Carvel-Schricker agreement, see David, *Presidential Nominating Politics*, I, pp. 137–38. For Schricker's speech, see *Proceedings, 1952*, pp. 317–20; for Carvel's, pp. 320–25.

151. *Proceedings, 1952*, p. 456. Also see David, *Presidential Nominating Politics*, I, pp. 152–53.

152. David, *Presidential Nominating Politics*, V, p. 159. Arizona's votes went to Russell on the second and third ballots. See *Proceedings, 1952*, pp. 484, 488.

153. Idaho 3; Wyoming 1 1/2; Utah 2 1/2; Nevada 1/2; New Mexico 4 1/2; Arizona 12; Oregon 2 1/2. See David, *Presidential Nominating Politics*, I, p. 153, and *Proceedings, 1952*, p. 456.

154. Kansas actually cast 4 votes for Kerr but before the end of the roll call asked permission for its total vote to be recorded in favor of Stevenson. See *Proceedings, 1952*, p. 454.

155. "Oklahoma, although bound under the unit rule, votes unanimously from their hearts and not from a piece of paper for our friend and neighbor, Barkley." *Proceedings, 1952*, p. 481.

156. Howell, *Tulsa Tribune*, March 27, 1974.

157. *Washington Post*, July 31, 1952; Waco (Tex.) *News Tribune*, October 15, 1952, Kerr Papers.

158. Saul Pett, Lawton (Okla.) *Constitution-Morning Press*, September 23, 1962. Kerr Papers.

159. *Ibid*.

Chapter VI

1. Anderson, *Outsider in the Senate*, p. 275.

2. Joe N. Groom, "The Night Watch," no paper, no date, clipping in Kerr Papers.

3. Hays Interview.

4. Anderson, *Outsider in the Senate*, p. 275.

5. Eisenhower: 518, 045–Stevenson: 430, 939. See Luman H. Long, ed., *World Almanac, 1968* (New York: Doubleday and Co., Inc., 1968), p. 234. Clark Clif-

ford approved a draft of Kerr's January 1953 newsletter: "I believe you strike exactly the right note and that there will be a general commendation for your pledge of support to Ike in the foreign policy field. I feel strongly that this is the line to follow until the time for the break comes." See Clifford to Kerr, December 29, 1952, Kerr Papers.

6. See John Robert Ferrell, "Water Resource Development in the Arkansas Valley: A History of Public Policy to 1950," Ph.D. dissertation, University of Oklahoma, 1968, p. 148; Cited hereafter as Ferrell, "Water Resource Development in the Arkansas Valley." *Daily Oklahoman*, December 9, 1945; *New York Times*, January 17, 1946; McBride to Kerr, October 17, 1956, Kerr Papers.

7. Robert S. Kerr, *Land, Wood and Water* (New York: Fleet Publishing Corporation, 1960), p. 159. Cited hereafter as Kerr, *Land, Wood and Water.*

8. See U.S. Congress, House of Representatives. *Arkansas River and Tributaries, Arkansas and Oklahoma*, House Document 758, 79th Congress, 2nd Session, July 30, 1946 (Washington: Government Printing Office, 1947), pp. 5–6, 7–39. Cited hereafter as *House Document 758.*

9. This study was authorized in the Flood Control Act of 1938. See G. B. Pillsbury, brigadier general, acting chief of Engineers to Elmer Thomas, October 14, 1937, Thomas Papers, Western History Collection, Bizzell Memorial Library, University of Oklahoma, Norman, Oklahoma.

10. Newton Graham, "History of the Arkansas," a typed report to the membership of the Arkansas Basin Development Association, p. 2, Arkansas Basin Development Association Papers. Cited hereafter as ABDA Papers.

11. This account is based on information in Professor William Settle's unpublished manuscript on the history of the Tulsa District of the Corps of Engineers, cited hereafter as Settle, Ms. See also Jim Henderson, "The Men Who Built the Waterways," *Tulsa*, v. 48 (May 27, 1971): 33; McBride Interview; Kerr, *Land, Wood and Water*, pp. 157–59; Cox, "Senator Robert S. Kerr and the Arkansas River Navigation Project," p. 105; and Ferrell, "Water Resource Development in the Arkansas Valley," pp. 130–31.

12. *Tulsa World*, August 7, 1960. For a discussion of the upstream-downstream controversy see Robert J. Morgan, *Governing Soil Conservation: Thirty Years of the New Decentralization* (Baltimore: Johns Hopkins Press, 1965); Irving K. Fox and Isabel Picken, *The Upstream-Downstream Controversy in the Arkansas-White-Red Basins Survey* (University, Alabama: University of Alabama Press, 1960); John V. Krutilla and Otto Eckstein, *Multiple Purpose River Development* (Baltimore: Johns Hopkins University Press, 1958); Arthur A. Maass, *Muddy Waters: The Army Engineers and the Nation's Rivers* (Cambridge: Harvard University Press, 1951); Elmer T. Peterson, *Big Dam Foolishness: The Problem of Modern Flood Control and Water Shortage* (New York: Devin-Adair Co., 1954); Ferrell, "Water Resource Development in the Arkansas Valley," pp. 137–47.

13. Howell, *Tulsa Tribune*, January 3, 1963; Kerr, *Land, Wood and Water*, p. 159.

14. J. Howard Edmondson, *Memorial Addresses*, p. 187.

15. Kerr, *Land, Wood and Water*, pp. 148–50; Grant Foreman, *A History of Oklahoma* (Norman: University of Oklahoma Press, 1945), p. 7; Muriel H.

Wright, "Early Navigation and Commerce Along the Arkansas and Red Rivers in Oklahoma," *Chronicles of Oklahoma*, v. 8, no. 1 (March 1930): 69.

16. Kerr, *Land, Wood and Water*, p. 157.

17. The committee was composed of Newton Graham as chairman, Don McBride, and Elmer T. Harber, the director of the Arkansas Association. Clarence F. Byrns, Reece Caudle, and David Terry represented Arkansas. See Kerr, *Land, Wood and Water*, p. 180; Cox, "Senator Robert S. Kerr and the Arkansas River Navigation Project," p. 109; Arkansas-Oklahoma Interstate Water Resources Committee, *Additional Benefits in the Proposed Plan for Comprehensive Improvement of the Arkansas River Basin* (Tulsa: States of Arkansas and Oklahoma, May 1945), Kerr Papers. Cited hereafter as Arkansas-Oklahoma, *Additional Benefits*.

18. Arkansas-Oklahoma, *Additional Benefits*, pp. 6–7, Kerr Papers; Newton Graham, "History of the Development of Water Resources of the Arkansas Basin" (August 2, 1947), p. 3, ABDA Papers; Kerr, *Land, Wood and Water*, p. 181.

19. Graham, "History of the Development of Water Resources of the Arkansas Basin," p. 3, ABDA Papers.

20. McBride to Kerr, August 1, 1945, Kerr Papers.

21. See Settle, Ms.; Kerr to Truman, August 25, 1945, Truman Papers.

22. See *House Document 758*, p. 18.

23. See Reybold letter, September 20, 1945 in *House Document 758*, p. 3; Graham, "History of the Arkansas," p. 3, ABDA Papers.

24. Kerr to Reybold, September 25, 1945, Kerr Papers.

25. Graham to Col. F. J. Wilson, January 9, 1946, ABDA Papers. Graham quoted a letter from Truman to Kerr which he had seen.

26. Kerr to Truman, April 2, 1949, Truman Papers.

27. The meeting is mentioned in Kerr to Truman, May 14, 1946, Truman Papers.

28. *Ibid.*

29. *Ibid.*

30. U.S. Congress House of Representatives, Committee on Rivers and Harbors, *The Improvement of the Arkansas River and Tributaries, Arkansas and Oklahoma*, 79th Congress, 2nd Session, May 8–9, 1946 (Washington: Government Printing Office, 1946), pp. 2–34.

31. *Congressional Record*, 79th Congress, 2nd Session, p. 6280.

32. *Ibid.*

33. Senator Thomas told Graham that, despite the relatively small authorization, the House committee had approved the entire project "and that any part of the project could be appropriated for." See Graham, "History of the Development of Water Resources of the Arkansas Basin," p. 4, ABDA Papers.

34. U.S. Congress, Senate, Commerce Committee, *Hearings on H.R. 6407*, June 10, 11, 12, 13, 14, 1946, 79th Congress, 2nd Session (Washington: Government Printing Office, 1946), p. 468.

35. *Congressional Record*, 79th Congress, 2nd Session, p. 8323.

36. This was agreed upon before the Arkansas-Oklahoma delegations testified. See *Congressional Record*, 79th Congress, 2nd Session, pp. 8476–77; Gra-

ham, "History of the Development of Water Resources of the Arkansas Basin," p. 4, ABDA Papers.

37. U.S. Congress, House of Representatives, Conference Committee, *Report No. 2472*, 79th Congress, 2nd Session (Washington: Government Printing Office, 1946). Also see *Congressional Record*, 79th Congress, 2nd Session, p. 8523. Public Law 79–525.

38. Graham, *ABDA Minutes*, May 19, 1947, ABDA Papers.

39. *Oklahoma City Times*, Editorial, "Oklahoma Doesn't Want Arkansas Valley Authority," January 22, 1942; also see *Oklahoma City Times*, October 11, 1945.

40. Graham to John H. Dunkin, August 9, 1949. ABDA Papers.

41. Graham, *ABDA Minutes*, May 19, 1947, ABDA Papers.

42. *Ibid.* Colonel Wilson told Dr. William Settle that later on, to escape Gaylord's wrath, the Oklahoma City Chamber of Commerce had to quit acting directly and that leading members worked through organizations such as the Water Foundation. Settle to author.

43. See ABDA Papers, 1947–48, for extensive correspondence between Graham and McBride.

44. See Settle, Ms.; McBride Interview.

45. See ABDA Papers for Graham-Byrns correspondence.

46. Graham to N. R. Patterson, August 16, 1949, ABDA Papers.

47. See Chapter II.

48. Graham to ABDA members, "Program of Work for 1949," December 8, 1948, ABDA Papers.

49. Quoted in Cox, "Senator Robert S. Kerr and the Arkansas River Navigation Project," p. 202.

50. Graham to Byrns, February 4, 1943; Graham, *ABDA Minutes*, May 19, 1947, ABDA Papers; *Tulsa Tribune*, October 15, 1948; Ferrell, "Water Resource Development in the Arkansas Valley," p. 158; Settle, Ms.

51. Cox, "Senator Robert S. Kerr and the Arkansas River Navigation Project," p. 116.

52. Ferrell, "Water Resource Development in the Arkansas Valley," p. 159.

53. Kerr to Rayburn, February 3, 1949, Rayburn to Kerr, February 12, 1949, Rayburn Papers. Kerr introduced S. 1576 in the Senate on April 13, 1949. See *Congressional Record*, 81st Congress, 1st Session, p. 4447.

54. See Kerr to Graham, March 2, 1949, ABDA Papers.

55. U.S. Congress, Senate, Committee on Public Works, Subcommittee on Flood Control-Rivers and Harbors, *Hearings . . . H.R. 5472*, Pt. 1, 81st Congress, 1st Session, 1949 (Washington: Government Printing Office, 1949), pp. 644, 687–707; U.S. Congress, House of Representatives, Committee on Public Works, *Flood Control Act of 1949*, Hearings on H.R. 5472, 81st Congress, 1st Session, 1949 (Washington: Government Printing Office, 1949), pp. 993–1004.

56. Fox and Picken, *The Upstream-Downstream Controversy in the Arkansas-White-Red Basins Survey*, p. 7.

57. See Robert DeRoose and Arthur A. Maass, "The Lobby That Can't Be Licked," *Harper's Magazine*, v. 199 (August 1949): 25. See also Benton J. Strong, "The Rivers and Harbors Lobby," *New Republic*, v. 121 (October 10, 1949): 13–15.

58. Quoted in Ferrell, "Water Resource Development in the Arkansas Valley," p. 174.

59. For proposal see the U.S. Commission on Organization of the Executive Branch of the Government, *Reorganization of the Department of the Interior,* March 15, 1949 (Washington: Government Printing Office, 1949), pp. 81–89; U.S. Congress, Senate, Committee on Expenditures in the Executive Departments, *Reorganization Act of 1949: Hearings . . . on S. 516,* February 2, 3, 7, 9, 10, and 15, 1949, 81st Congress, 1st Session (Washington: Government Printing Office, 1949). McClellan was chairman of the committee. Kerr favored the Hoover Commission recommendation concerning the Corps of Engineers and told the House Public Works Committee that if they adopted the proposals, his bill would not be needed. See Senator Kerr's speech to the Third National Water Conservation Conference, September 22, 1949, Kerr Papers. Also see, U.S. House of Representatives, Committee on Public Works, *Flood Control Act of 1949, Hearings . . . on H.R. 5472,* pp. 989–990.

60. See Ferrell, "Water Resource Development in the Arkansas Valley," p. 175.

61. McBride quoted in *Ibid.,* pp. 176–77.

62. U.S. Congress, House of Representatives, Public Works Committee, *Report to Accompany H.R. 5472 . . . ,* House Report No. 696, 81st Congress, 1st Session, July 16, 1949 (Washington: Government Printing Office, 1949), p. 139.

63. H.R. 5472 passed the House August 22, 1949. See *Congressional Record,* 81st Congress, 1st Session, p. 11999.

64. For Staats' testimony see U.S. Congress, Senate, Committee on Public Works, Subcommittee on Flood Control—Rivers and Harbors, *Hearings . . . on H.R. 5472,* Pt. 2, pp. 886–96. Also see U.S. Congress, Senate, Committee on Public Works, *Report to Accompany H.R. 5472 . . . ,* Senate Report No. 1143, 81st Congress, 1st Session, October 7, 1949 (Washington: Government Printing Office, 1949), p. 74.

65. *Congressional Record,* 81st Congress, 1st Session, pp. 14761–62.

66. *Congressional Record,* 81st Congress, 2nd Session, p. 5283.

67. *Ibid.,* p. 6565.

68. McBride quoted in Cox, "Senator Robert S. Kerr and the Arkansas River Navigation Project," p. 118.

69. Kerr to Truman, May 5, 1950, Truman Papers.

70. Truman to Kerr, May 18, 1950 includes a copy of Truman to Agency Head, no date, Truman Papers.

71. Kerr suspected trouble with Senator Long and others on behalf of the corps as early as March 1949. See Kerr to Graham, March 2, 1949, ABDA Papers.

72. See Ferrell, "Water Resource Development in the Arkansas Valley," p. 214.

73. Graham testimony in Senate, *Hearings . . . on H.R. 5472,* Pt. 1, pp. 728–31.

74. *Ibid.,* pp. 725–27; *Tulsa World,* June 4, 1971.

75. Graham, "Confidential memo to ABDA Membership," August 25, 1950, ABDA Papers.

76. Settle, Ms.

77. *Ibid.*

78. "It's as simple as that, and his reason has the wholehearted support of *The Daily Oklahoman.*" See Graham to Col. F. J. Wilson, November 23, 1954, ABDA Papers.

79. Graham, "Memo to ABDA Membership," March 23, 1950, ABDA Papers.

80. Graham to McBride, September 7, 1951, ABDA Papers.

81. Graham reports of a meeting with the Arkansas delegation in early 1951. "Senator Kerr asked him [Monroney] directly if he would support the reservoir program including Keystone and Eufaula and the bank stabilization program and Monroney said, 'yes.'" See Graham to ABDA members, April 5, 1951, ABDA Papers.

82. Graham to McBride, September 7, 1951, Philip J. Kramer to Graham, December 21, 1951, ABDA Papers.

83. McBride to Graham, June 18, 1952, ABDA Papers.

84. See Graham to Verser Hicks, June 18, 1952, Graham to McBride, June 24, 1952, ABDA Papers. This was the plan Graham had used to win Thomas over in 1943.

85. Graham to John Dunkin, November 19, 1954, ABDA Papers.

86. For representative letters see Verser Hicks to Monroney, October 15, 1954, Gordon Watts to Monroney, January 3, 1955, ABDA Papers. Also see Russell Rhodes to Monroney, May 9, 1955, Kerr Papers.

87. McBride to Graham, March 29, 1955, ABDA Papers.

88. When Graham reported this progress to McBride, he carefully noted, "I did not 'show' in the effort." See Graham to McBride, April 12, 1955, ABDA Papers.

89. Settle, Ms.

90. For Monroney's statement see U.S. Congress, House, Committee on Appropriations, Subcommittee on Public Works. *Public Works Appropriations for 1956*, Pt. 3, 84th Congress, 1st Session, May 1955 (Washington: Government Printing Office, 1955), pp. 425–28.

91. Graham to ABDA members, August 25, 1960, ABDA Papers.

92. *Daily Oklahoman*, September 21, 1950.

93. Graham to ABDA members, March 23, 1950, ABDA Papers.

94. Graham, "Confidential Report to ABDA Members," August 25, 1950; Graham to John Mayo, November 9, 1950, ABDA Papers.

95. McBride to Graham, August 15, 1949, Kerr Papers.

96. Graham to McBride, March 19, 1951, ABDA Papers.

97. Graham to John Mayo, April 8, 1951, ABDA Papers.

98. McBride to Graham, February 1, 1954, ABDA Papers.

99. See Dwight David Eisenhower, "Annual Message to the Congress on the State of the Union," February 2, 1953, *Public Papers of the Presidents of the United States, 1953* (Washington: Government Printing Office, 1954), pp. 26–27 and "Statement by the President Approving a Statement of Policy on Electric Power by the Secretary of the Interior," August 18, 1953, pp. 573–74. Cited hereafter as Eisenhower, *Public Papers*.

100. *Congress and the Nation*, p. 835.

101. Up to March 12, 1954, the criteria were not binding, but merely guidelines.

102. The Appropriations Subcommittee on Public Works was composed of four units; Kerr was an *ex-officio* member of the unit on civil functions.

103. ". . . [Kerr's] aggressiveness and his power within the Senate establishment enabled him to transcend the restrictions to rivers and harbor items. . . ." Horn, *Unused Power*, p. 52.

104. *Ibid.*

105. "Senator Kerr Says," January 20, 1955, Kerr Papers. Also see Horn, *Unused Power*, p. 50; Fenno, *The Power of the Purse*, p. 556.

106. See Chapter II for Kerr's brief service on Interior.

107. "At the height of his power, Kerr became the spokesman for the corps. He had the power to reject or push corps proposals. They had to come to him with hat in hand." McBride quoted in Cox, "Senator Robert S. Kerr and the Arkansas River Navigation Project," p. 205.

108. Kenneth Bousquet Interview. March 13, 1974.

109. Graham to Kerr, April 20, 1955, ABDA Papers.

110. *Ibid.*

111. Kerr to Itschner, April 14, 1955; Itschner to Kerr, April 26, 1955; General Sturgis to Cannon, Sturgis to Chaves (identical to Cannon letter), March 31, 1955; George H. Roderick to Kerr, March 26, 1955, Kerr Papers. For details of the settlement, see Settle, Ms.

112. Kerr, *Land, Wood and Water*, pp. 350–51. Also see U.S. President, Arkansas-White-Red Basin Inter-Agency Committee, *A Report on the Conservation and Development of Water and Land Resources.* 23 vols. (Washington: Government Printing Office, 1955).

113. Graham to Kerr, April 20, 1955, ABDA Papers.

114. In the House, the ratio was 232 Democrats to 203 Republicans. In the Senate, there were 48 Democrats, 47 Republicans, and one independent, Wayne Morse. See *Congress and the Nation*, p. 21.

115. See Eisenhower, "Annual Budget Message to the Congress: Fiscal Year 1956," January 17, 1955, *Public Papers, 1955*, p. 159.

116. See U.S. Congress, Senate, Committee on Appropriations, *Report to Accompany H.R. 4386*, Senate Report No. 631, 82nd Congress, 1st Session, August 10, 1952 (Washington: Government Printing Office, 1952).

117. For the debate see *Congressional Record*, 82nd Congress, 1st Session, pp. 10023–31; *Tulsa World*, August 16, 1951.

118. The full House had already eliminated $36 million from the President's original budget for water projects.

119. *Tulsa World*, June 4, 1971.

120. U.S. Congress, House, Committee on Appropriations, *Public Works Appropriations Bill for Fiscal Year 1956, House Report on H.R. 6766*, Report No. 747, 84th Congress, 1st Session, June 10, 1955 (Washington: Government Printing Office, 1955).

121. *Congressional Record*, 84th Congress, 1st Session, pp. 8512, 8513, 8519. In 1971, recalling the maneuver in the House, Edmondson said, "Only one man recognized what was involved. He was a Congressman from Massachusetts and he said, 'Hey, isn't this a $1 billion project?' No one else seemed to realize it." See Henderson, "The Men Who Built the Waterways," 35.

122. House Report No. 747 recommended $1,285,746,242 and the House passed bill contained $1,372,122,800.

123. Quote is from McBride Interview. See U.S. Congress, Senate, Committee on Appropriations, *Hearings on H.R. 6766, Public Works Appropriations for 1956*, Pts. 1 and 2, 84th Congress, 1st Session (Washington: Government Printing

Office, 1955). For Kerr's testimony see Part 1, pp. 936–43 and Part 2, pp. 2237–44. Also see U.S. Congress, Senate, Committee on Appropriations, *Public Works Appropriations Bill 1956, Report to Accompany H.R. 6766*, Senate Report No. 700, 84th Congress, 1st Session, July 1, 1955 (Washington: Government Printing Office, 1955), p. 24. For the debate see *Congressional Record*, 84th Congress, 1st Session, pp. 9877–78, 9882.

124. *Congressional Record*, 84th Congress, 1st Session, p. 9877.

125. *Ibid.*, p. 9878.

126. Ellender quoted in Cox, "Senator Robert S. Kerr and the Arkansas River Navigation Project," p. 51.

127. "Senator Kerr Says," July 13, 1955; Kerr to Wilson, July 18, 1955, Kerr Papers.

128. See Eisenhower, *Public Papers, 1957*, July 17, 1955, p. 696; *Oklahoma City Times*, July 16, 1955.

129. "Senator Kerr Says," November 17, 1955, Kerr Papers.

130. Kerr to Graham, July 19, 1955, Kerr Papers.

131. McBride to Kerr, December 1, 1955, Kerr Papers; directive from the President to the Cabinet cited in "Senator Kerr Says," September 6, 1955. Also see Settle, Ms.

132. *New York Times*, September 3, 1955.

133. See Eisenhower, "Annual Budget Message to Congress for Fiscal Year 1957," *Public Papers, 1956*, p. 143.

134. "Senator Kerr Says," January 26, 1956, Kerr Papers.

135. *Ibid.*

136. *Ibid.*

137. Graham urged Kerr to "close down on all new authorizations until more *Now* authorized projects are nearer completion." See Graham to Kerr, January 20, 1956, ABDA Papers.

138. On corps' opposition during the Truman years, see Settle, Ms.; *Tulsa World*, July 18, 1952.

139. Kerr to Ellender, March 26, 1956, Kerr Papers.

140. See U.S. Congress, Senate, Committee on Appropriations, *Hearings Held Before the Public Works Appropriations Committee*, 84th Congress, 2nd Session, April 16, 1956 (Washington: Government Printing Office, 1959), pp. 1044–46.

141. "ABDA Newsletter," December 14, 1955, ABDA Papers.

142. Belcher quoted in Cox, "Senator Robert S. Kerr and the Arkansas Navigation Project," p. 149.

143. *Ibid.*

144. *Ibid.*, p. 150.

145. See Robert E. Merriam to Belcher, July 19, 1956, Page Belcher Papers, Western History Collection, Bizzell Memorial Library, University of Oklahoma, Norman, Oklahoma. Also see *Tulsa Tribune*, July 19, 1956. According to Cox, p. 151, Rowland Hughes, director of the Bureau of the Budget sent a similar letter to the Corps of Engineers.

146. Norman (Okla.), *Transcript* July 1956, Kerr Papers.

147. H.R. 11319, Public Law 84–641 signed on July 2, 1956. See *Congressional*

Record, 84th Congress, 2nd Session, p. 8225.

148. "Senator Kerr Says," April 5, 1956, Kerr Papers.

149. Kerr to Rayburn, June 22, 1956, Kerr Papers.

150. "Report from Senator Kerr in Washington," August 1956; also see Kerr to Eisenhower, July 30, 1956, Kerr Papers.

151. Kerr and Judge Sam Rosenman of New York worked out the compromise plan between public and private power on the Niagara project. See Frank E. Smith, *The Politics of Conservation* (New York: Pantheon Books, 1966), p. 281; *New York Times,* April 11 and 12, 1957, May 29, 1957. For a discussion of the TVA financing controversy and Kerr's role see *Congressional Quarterly Almanac—1959,* p. 261; *New York Times,* May 1, 1957; and *Congressional Quarterly Almanac—1957,* p. 629. Also see Gore, *Memorial Addresses,* p. 53.

152. Cox, "Senator Robert S. Kerr and the Arkansas Navigation Project," p. 207.

153. *Ibid.,* pp. 195–96.

154. Johnson to Kerr, April 16, 1959, Kerr Papers.

155. "During the Eisenhower Administrations, I consistently opposed authorizations and appropriations for foreign aid because I felt that we were not getting our money's worth out of the program." Kerr to Ben F. Kelley, April 20, 1961, Kerr Papers. Also see Kerr, *Land, Wood and Water,* p. 247; *Tulsa Tribune,* October 17, 1959.

156. "The members were genuinely fond of each other, a rare warmth in the Senate where friendship is neither constant nor deep." Charles Bartlett, *Chattanooga Times,* August 11, 1957, Kerr Papers.

157. Kerr to Rayburn, February 12, 1960, Kerr Papers.

158. McBride Interview.

159. Bousquet Interview.

160. Kirwan quoted in Kerr, *Land, Wood and Water,* p. 133.

161. McBride Interview. For Kerr's role in the Lake Michigan Waterway Division debate in 1959, see *Congressional Record,* 86th Congress, 1st Session, pp. 17005–11, 17524 and *Congressional Quarterly Almanac—1959,* p. 272. On the Illinois Waterway problem see *Congress and the Nation,* pp. 968–69 for a summary.

162. McBride Interview. Also see Bill Harmon, *Daily Oklahoman,* August 6, 1960; Toby La Farge, *Tulsa World,* November 2, 1959; *Tulsa Tribune,* November 3, 1959; and Kerr to Wilson, September 12, 1959, Kerr Papers.

163. For quote see Cromley, *Daily Oklahoman,* April 10, 1961. Majority Leader Carl Albert summed up the delegation's years of work in an ABC-TV special filmed for the opening of the Arkansas navigation system in June 1971. "We traded everything we had in our hip pocket, in our pocket book, and so forth. And we finally got it!" Carl Albert, ABC-TV special "The Arkansas River Navigation System," June 4, 1971, transcript in Kerr Papers.

164. *New York Times,* August 11, 1965.

165. *Ibid.*

166. *Congressional Quarterly Almanac—1956,* p. 574; *Wall Street Journal,* August 11, 1956.

167. *New York Times,* August 11, 1956.

168. McBride to John D. McCall, August 21, 1956, Kerr Papers.

169. See *Budget of U.S. Government for Fiscal Year 1958* (Washington: Gov-

ernment Printing Office, 1957), p. 598. The budget was presented to Congress, January 16, 1957. See Eisenhower, "Annual Budget Message to Congress for Fiscal Year 1958," *Public Papers, 1957,* pp. 38–59.

170. U.S. Congress, Senate, Committee on Appropriations, *Public Works Appropriations Bill, 1958, Report to Accompany H.R. 8090,* Senate Report No. 609, 85th Congress, 1st Session, July 12, 1957 (Washington: Government Printing Office, 1957), pp. 8 and 15. For the Senate debate see *Congressional Record,* 85th Congress, 1st Session, p. 11443. The Conference Report on H.R. 8090, House Report 1049, appears in the *Congressional Record,* 85th Congress, 1st Session, pp. 14573–74. The President signed the bill, Public Law 85–167, on August 26, 1957.

171. *New York Times,* December 13, 1957.

172. "Senator Kerr Says," December 26, 1957, Kerr Papers.

173. "Changing the Senate's Finance Watchdog," *Business Week* (February 22, 1958): 25; "Senator Kerr Says," February 27, 1958, Kerr Papers.

174. *Daily Oklahoman,* March 9, 16, 1958, April 16, 1958; "Senator Kerr Says," March 20, 1958, Kerr Papers.

175. *New York Times,* March 14, 1958.

176. "Senator Kerr Says," February 5, 1959, Kerr Papers.

177. Dwight D. Eisenhower, *The White House Years: Waging Peace, 1956– 1961* (Garden City, N.Y.: Doubleday and Company, Inc., 1965), p. 306; *New York Times,* April 16, 1958. The Senate passed S. 497 on March 28, 1957, but the House did not act until the following March 11, 1958. For the legislative history of the bill see *Congressional Record,* 85th Congress, 1st Session, p. 4663, and 85th Congress, 2nd Session, pp. 4035, 5940, 6060, 6099, and 6107.

178. For the debate in the House see *Congressional Record,* 85th Congress, 2nd Session, pp. 6389–91, 6430, 6431, 6525–27, 6673. Democrats on the House Public Works Committee issued a paragraph-by-paragraph rebuttal of the veto message. See *Congressional Record,* 85th Congress, 2nd Session, pp. 7271–76. Congressman Edmondson said the difference of opinion was not between the Democratic party and the President, but between the President and Congress. He warned that if Congress submitted for authorization only items approved by the Bureau of the Budget, "then we might just as well give the President item veto authority . . . and be done with it."

179. Senator Case was a vice-president of the Rivers and Harbors Congress. See Strong, "The Rivers and Harbors Lobby," 14.

180. Cromley, *Daily Oklahoman,* May 17, 1958; *Wall Street Journal,* May 28, 1958.

181. *Congressional Record,* 85th Congress, 2nd Session, p. 11495. Kerr included a breakdown of projects by state, *Ibid.,* pp. 11500–2.

182. See Title III, Water Supply Act of 1958, Public Law 85–500.

183. See *Tulsa World,* February 28, March 12, April 16, May 28, and July 5, 1958. Also see *Daily Oklahoman,* June 5, 6, 25, and 26, 1958. Beginning in 1957 Senator Kerr began to persuade Congress to change the law to include additional factors in calculating the cost/benefit ratio of multipurpose projects. By 1961 he had secured legislation to include the value of stored water for municipal and industrial use, recreational benefits and changed the "estimated useful life" of a project from fifty to one hundred years. In 1962, President Kennedy approved a

new set of criteria, replacing BOB Circular A-47, to be used in determining the feasibility and costs of proposed water projects. See Settle, Ms.; *Congress and the Nation*, pp. 777–78, 856–57, 875–76; McBride to Dean McGee, November 17, 1962, Kerr Papers.

184. See *Congress and the Nation*, p. 847.

185. Humphrey to Kerr, May 9, 1956; Kerr to Humphrey, May 10, 1956, Kerr Papers.

186. Douglas, *In the Fullness of Time*, p. 318.

187. U.S. Congress, House, Committee on Appropriations, *Report to Accompany H.R. 7509, Public Works Appropriations Bill, 1960*, House Report No. 424, 86th Congress, 1st Session, June 2, 1959 (Washington: Government Printing Office, 1959), p. 2.

188. *Congressional Record*, 86th Congress, 1st Session, pp. 10014–65, 10320–23, 13086–97, 15898–910, 15965–78.

189. *Ibid.*, p. 17752; *New York Times*, August 29, 1959, September 3, 1959.

190. There were 282 Democrats and 154 Republicans in the House and 64 Democrats and 34 Republicans in the Senate, see *Congress and the Nation*, p. 30.

191. *Congressional Record*, 86th Congress, 1st Session, p. 6902.

192. *Wall Street Journal*, September 11, 1959.

193. *Ibid.*

194. *Congressional Record*, 86th Congress, 1st Session, pp. 18982–83, 18924–27.

195. *Wall Street Journal, New York Times*, September 11, 1959.

196. At the beginning of 1962, Don McBride totaled the amounts of authorized and appropriated money for the Arkansas navigation project in Oklahoma and Arkansas. "There were $1.4 billions worth in completed costs, of which $843 million was spent in Oklahoma. Congress had actually appropriated $252 million, of which $169 million was money for Oklahoma projects." See *Daily Oklahoman*, January 19, 1962. An article in *U.S. News and World Report* estimated that appropriations for the Arkansas tripled by 1960. At the beginning of 1962, the project was being funded at the rate of more than $100 million a year. See "Seaports for Oklahoma," *U.S. News and World Report*, v. 54 (February 11, 1963): 67. Also see, "ABDA Newsletter," December 1961, ABDA Papers; Altus (Okla.) *Times-Democrat*, October 17, 1962, Kerr Papers.

197. *Tulsa World*, June 4, 1971.

198. "ABDA Minutes," January 23, 1961, ABDA Papers.

199. Bousquet Interview.

200. "Press Release," February 26, 1961, Kerr Papers; "ABDA Newsletter," March 10, 1961, ABDA Papers.

201. In his February 23, 1961, "Special Message to the Congress on Natural Resources," President Kennedy said, "We reject a 'no new starts' policy." See Kennedy, *Public Papers, 1961*, pp. 115–16.

202. William A. Reynolds Interview. May 25, 1974.

203. Roy Stewart, *Daily Oklahoman*; Troy Gordon, *Tulsa World*; Nolen Bullock, *Tulsa Tribune*, September 17, 1958.

204. *Tulsa Tribune*, March 31, 1961.

205. *Daily Oklahoman*, January 30, 1961; Seminole (Okla.) *Producer*, January 31, 1961.

206. *Daily Oklahoman*, October 19, 1962.

207. *Congressional Quarterly Almanac—1962*, p. 461.

208. *Congressional Record*, 87th Congress, 2nd Session, pp. 22167–72.

209. McBride Interview.

210. On predictions for the projects success, see John Lubell, *New York Times*, June 6, 1971. For figures on the projects economic impact, see Howell, *Tulsa Tribune*, March 3 and November 20, 1974. Also see Settle, Ms., Chapter I and Department of the Army, Corps of Engineers, Civil Works Directorate, *Recreation Statistics* (Washington, D.C.: Government Printing Office, 1973), pp. 4–9, 23.

Chapter VII

1. Allen Ellender urged southerners to unite behind Kerr in 1956 because Harriman's racial views were unacceptable, Kefauver was a scalawag, and Stevenson a loser. The plan was to have Kerr rally the Democratic party in a repeat performance of his 1944 keynote address and to emerge as the nominee. Kerr lost the keynoter spot to Governor Frank Clements of Tennessee by one vote in the national committee, although he was a featured speaker at the 1956 convention. See Cromley, *Daily Oklahoman*, March 25, 1956; *Oklahoma City Times*, July 11, 1956; Cromley, *Daily Oklahoman*, June 21, 1956, August 16, 1956; *Rocky Mountain News*, August 13, 1956; *Tulsa World*, April 21, 1956; *New York Times*, January 3, 1955; Cromley, *Daily Oklahoman*, May 15, 1955, and December 7, 1955. Also see Kerr to Fisher Muldrow, June 18, 1956, and Kerr to Mrs. Gertrude Fields, July 3, 1956, Kerr Papers.

Remarking on his availability for the nomination in 1960, Kerr told a reporter, "Old age had kind of approached to that proximity that I was beyond the point where I felt that physically I could undertake the assignment—and realistically, I was aware of the fact that the people had more or less spoken their adverse judgment as to my eligibility." See Cleland, *Tulsa World*, August 12, 1962.

2. Robert T. Elson, "A Question for Democrats: If not Truman, Who?" *Life*, v. 32 (March 24, 1952): 128.

3. McBride stated, "I hope that we can stress our cooperation with Ike and show our genuine willingness to go along with him on his defense, military and natural resources program." McBride to Kerr, August 12, 1953, Kerr Papers. For Clifford's views and advice see Clifford to Kerr, December 29, 1952, Kerr Papers.

4. Quote from Earl E. Emerson to Kerr, May 11, 1953; also see Harry Black to Kerr, May 11, 1953, Kerr Papers.

5. "Senator Kerr Says," January 12, 1956, Kerr Papers.

6. *New York Times*, January 12, 1956.

7. See David Lawrence, "Democratic Sniping at Eisenhower's Heart Reverses GOP," Muskogee (Okla.) *Times-Democrat*, February 18, 1959; "Senator Kerr Says," January 12, 1956; Kerr to Lea M. Nichols, January 25, 1956; Kerr to David

Lawrence, March 28, 1956; Lawrence to Kerr, April 2, 1956; Kerr to Tams Bixby, April 17, 1956; Kerr to John L. Stone, April 25, 1956, Kerr Papers.

8. "Senator Kerr Says," January 1, 1953, Kerr Papers. Author's italics.

9. S. 115 was introduced January 1, 1953. See *Congressional Record*, 83rd Congress, 1st Session, p. 154.

10. *Daily Oklahoman*, February 11, 1953.

11. For Benson's speech see *New York Times*, February 11, 1953. For Kerr's reaction, see *Congressional Record*, 83rd Congress, 1st Session, pp. 1091–96.

12. "Senator Kerr Says," April 23, 1953, Kerr Papers. *Daily Oklahoman*, October 23, 28, 1953.

13. Norman (Okla.) *Transcript*, March 5, 1954, Kerr Papers. Also see *Daily Oklahoman*, March 5, 1954.

14. Sullivant, "Rich Man's Race," *Nation*, v. 178 (June 26, 1954): 542.

15. Seth S. King, *New York Times*, June 13, 1954; *Tulsa World*, March 5, 1954.

16. King, *New York Times*, June 13, 1954; David, *Presidential Nominating Politics*, III, p. 303.

17. Gourley, Henryetta (Okla.) *Daily Free-Lance*, February 2, 1954, Kerr Papers. Also see *Daily Oklahoman*, February 2, 1954.

18. Turner refused to include repeal in his legislative program, but the drys felt betrayed when an initiative petition brought the issue to the voters in spite of his action. See Gibson, *Oklahoma*, p. 399.

19. *Daily Oklahoman*, April 18, 1954.

20. See "Press Release," no date, Kerr for Senate Headquarters; Kerr to Milton Plumb, July 19, 1954, Kerr Papers. COPE's research showed that Kerr had voted against labor's wishes fifty-six out of seventy-two times during his first term. See Jim Reid, "CIO Faction Pulls up Stakes on Kerr," no paper, June 8, 1954, Kerr Papers.

21. Durant (Okla.) *Daily Democrat*, April 14, 1954, Kerr Papers. See *Tulsa World*, *New York Times*, and *Daily Oklahoman*, April 14, 1954.

22. *Tulsa World*, April 14, 1954.

23. Brown to Kerr, May 28, 1954, circulated in Kerr to Dear Oil Man, no date, Kerr Papers. Also see John E. McClure to Frank H. Dunn, July 12, 1954, Kerr Papers.

24. Dunkin to Jenkins Lloyd Jones, June 24, 1954, ABDA Papers; Howell, *Tulsa Tribune*, June 22, 1954.

25. Altus (Okla.) *Times-Democrat*, March 26, 1954, Kerr Papers. Also see editorial, "Bob Kerr Deserves Oklahoma's Best," Frederick (Okla.) *Daily Leader*, November 1, 1954, Kerr Papers.

26. Altus (Okla.) *Times-Democrat*, March 16, 1954, Kerr Papers.

27. *Ibid.*

28. *Daily Oklahoman*, March 4, 1954.

29. See form letter, Farmers of Greer County to City Residents of Mangum, Oklahoma, June 14, 1954, Kerr Papers.

30. Sullivant, "Rich Man's Race," 542. Also see *Tulsa World*, March 5, 1954; *Daily Oklahoman*, February 4, 1954.

31. Fred W. Whetsel to Kerr, June 19, 1953, outlines this strategy for the campaign, Kerr Papers.

32. *Daily Oklahoman*, May 20, 1954.

33. Turner quotation from clipping, no author, no papers, no date, in Kerr Papers. See *Daily Oklahoman*, April 20, 1954.

34. Turner quoted in *New York Times*, July 3, 1954.

35. See "Roy J. Turner Special Edition," Sulphur (Okla.) *Times-Democrat*, no date, Kerr Papers. Also see *Tulsa World*, April 20, June 23, 26, 1954.

36. *Tulsa World*, June 23, 1954.

37. Harold Wilson, "Turner Strategists Get Ready for Slam-Bang Battle with Kerr," no paper, February 17, 1954, Kerr Papers.

38. Ardmore (Okla.) *Daily Ardmoreite*, March 14, 1954, Kerr Papers.

39. *New York Times*, July 3, 1954.

40. See Milton Plumb, *The CIO News*, July 19, 1954, Kerr Papers.

41. John Caustin Curry, *Daily Oklahoma*, April 3, 1962.

42. Fleeson, *Oklahoma City Times*, February 18, 1954; Lawton, (Okla.) *Constitution-Morning Press*, July 13, 1954.

43. See Kirkpatrick, *Oklahoma Voting Patterns*, p. 76. Washington *Evening Star*, July 7, 1954, Kerr Papers.

44. *New York Times*, July 18, 1954; Lawton (Okla.) *Constitution-Morning Press*, July 13, 1954, Kerr Papers.

45. Pawhuska (Okla.) *Journal-Capital*, July 18, 1954, Kerr Papers.

46. Jones, *Oklahoma Politics*, p. 72. Also see Kirkpatrick, *Oklahoma Voting Patterns*, p. 79.

47. *Tulsa World*, August 2, 1954; Sullivant, *Daily Oklahoman*, November 3, 1954.

48. In September 1954, prior to the election, Don McBride wired Kerr at the Pierre Hotel in New York City to tell him of a vacancy on the Senate Appropriations Committee. See McBride to Kerr, September 29, 1954, Kerr Papers. There were actually two vacancies. Burnett Rhett Maybank (D., S.C.), best remembered in the Senate as Robert G. (Bobby) Baker's original sponsor, died September 1. Nevada's Patrick McCarran (D.) also died September 28. If either vacancy had occurred before 1954, Kerr probably would have abandoned his position on the Public Works Committee to become a freshman on Appropriations. But in 1954 events were different. If reelected, he expected to become chairman or the ranking minority member on the Subcommittee on Rivers and Harbors. Either way, he would be entitled to an *ex-officio* seat on Appropriations. If he were not reelected, moving to Appropriations in September 1954 would be pointless when he failed to return to Congress in 1955.

49. Quote from Cromley, *Oklahoma City Times*, November 5, 1954; also see Mary Goddard, *Oklahoma City Times*, November 3, 1954.

50. Cromley, *Oklahoma City Times*, November 5, 1954. Tom Connally retired from Congress in 1953, and Senator George became the ranking Democrat during the two years the Democrats were in the minority. George continued as the ranking Democrat on the Senate Finance Committee until his retirement at the end of the 84th Congress.

51. Although Senator Kerr did not live to succeed Harry Byrd, for a time in 1958 it looked as if he might when Byrd announced his retirement. But pressure from Democratic leaders in Virginia and the business community convinced Byrd to reconsider. For details see William S. White, *New York Times*, February 13,

1958; *Wall Street Journal,* February 13 and 26, 1958; and correspondence in Boxes 256, 257, 258 of Harry F. Byrd, Jr. Collection, Manuscripts Department, Alderman Library, University of Virginia, Charlottesville, Virginia.

52. Riggs, "Lyndon Johnson and Others," in Eric Sevareid, ed., *Candidates, 1960* (New York: Basic Books, Inc., 1959), p. 297.

53. Evans and Novak, *Lyndon B. Johnson,* pp. 43, 52–54.

54. *Ibid.,* p. 67.

55. Cromley, *Daily Oklahoman,* December 30, 1962.

56. Hays Interview.

57. McBride Interview.

58. Charges of voting fraud clouded Johnson's 1948 election to the Senate, and Kerr was accused of falsifying campaign expenditures reports and spending more than the law permitted. On Johnson, see Steinberg, *Sam Johnson's Boy,* pp. 235–72; Evans and Novak, *Lyndon B. Johnson,* p. 39. On Kerr's election problems, see Chapter I.

59. Hawks Interview. See Evans and Novak, *Lyndon B. Johnson,* p. 29 on the growth of Johnson's investment. Also see Steinberg, *Sam Johnson's Boy,* pp. 220–21.

60. Evans and Novak, *Lyndon B. Johnson,* p. 108.

61. Steinberg, *Sam Johnson's Boy,* p. 406.

62. Quoted from Randall B. Ripley, *Power in the Senate* (New York: St. Martin's Press, 1969), p. 31.

63. Paul Douglas waited eight years for a seat on Senate Finance. Kerr, Long, Frear, Anderson, and Johnson—all elected with Douglas in 1948—and Smathers of the class of '50 preceded him on the committee. See Evans and Novak, *Lyndon B. Johnson,* p. 101; Douglas, *In the Fullness of Time,* pp. 427–28.

64. See Evans and Novak, *Lyndon B. Johnson,* p. 101; Gorman, *Kefauver,* pp. 287–90; Sorensen, *Kennedy,* p. 43. The best single article on Johnson's leadership is Ralph K. Huitt, "Leadership in the Senate," *American Political Science Review,* v. 55 (June 1961): 333–44.

65. Quoted from Gorman, *Kefauver,* p. 290.

66. Johnson refused to make even a private commitment to such prominent Democrats as James H. Rowe and Dean Acheson. Rowe finally turned to Humphrey, and Acheson cast his lot with his old boss, Truman, whose candidate was Stuart Symington. See Evans and Novak, *Lyndon B. Johnson,* pp. 245–46; Theodore H. White, *The Making of the President, 1960* (New York: Atheneum Publishers, 1967), pp. 43–46, 131–35. Cited hereafter as White, *The Making of the President, 1960.*

67. Evans and Novak, *Lyndon B. Johnson,* p. 247.

68. *Ibid.*

69. Harry Culver, Cushing (Okla.) *Daily Citizen,* October 16, 1960, Kerr Papers. Democratic candidates were always listed first on the ballot in Oklahoma. On the ballot separation law see *Session's Laws of Oklahoma* 1943, Chapter 7, Section 1, Title 26, and Scales, "Political History of Oklahoma," pp. 452–53.

70. See Don Bachelder, *Tulsa World,* June 13, 1959.

71. Kerr quoted in Reynolds, "Senator Robert S. Kerr and the Arkansas Navigation Project," p. 31.

72. Anderson, *Outsider in the Senate,* p. 301.

73. White, *The Making of the President, 1960,* p. 89.

74. Anderson, *Outsider in the Senate,* p. 301.

75. See *Idaho Daily Statesman,* October 13, 1959, Kerr Papers.

76. Evans and Novak, *Lyndon B. Johnson,* pp. 253–56.

77. Pierre Salinger, *With Kennedy* (Garden City, N.Y.: Doubleday & Company, Inc., 1966), p. 337. Cited hereafter as Salinger, *With Kennedy.*

78. Hawks Interview. Also see Evans and Novak, *Lyndon B. Johnson,* p. 281.

79. Clinton Anderson, Texas Governor Price Daniel, Senator George Smathers, and Ed Weisel all agreed Johnson would be foolish to accept.

80. Evans and Novak, *Lyndon B. Johnson,* p. 282; White, *The Making of the President,* 1960, pp. 172–77.

81. Evans and Novak, *Lyndon B. Johnson,* p. 282. Also see Sorensen, *Kennedy,* pp. 162–67.

82. Hawks Interview.

83. Ralph Sewell, *Daily Oklahoman,* July 15, 1960. Also see *Daily Oklahoman,* November 23, 1963.

William Kerr told the author that he was present when Lyndon Johnson, while visiting the Kerr ranch in the 1960's, gave a different account of how the vice-presidential nomination came about. According to Johnson, prior to the 1960 Democratic convention, Sam Rayburn held a strategy session at which Kerr, Russell, Johnson, and Senate Republican Leader Everett M. Dirksen were present. Close personal friends, these men considered that they had actually been running the country for most of the 1950's. Although a Republican, Dirksen shared this group's antipathy toward Nixon, both as a Senate colleague and as a potential president. Johnson's race for the 1960 Democratic nomination was designed for two possible scenarios. First, his candidacy was essential to slow the Kennedy boom, which threatened the existing power structure of the Democratic party, and to prevent the nomination of a Catholic, which they believed would result in defeat. If his bid for the top spot failed, Johnson's strong showing would force the Kennedy people to accept him as the vice-presidential candidate. This maneuver would give the Democratic ticket geographical as well as religious balance and improve the party's chances for a November victory. William Kerr Interview.

84. Evans and Novak, *Lyndon B. Johnson,* p. 264.

85. *Tulsa Tribune,* November 21, 1949, Kerr Papers.

86. See *Congressional Record,* 84th Congress, 2nd Session, p. 9385; Kerr to Dr. Porter Routh, August 21, 1954; "Kerr Press Release," February 2, 1956, p. 3; Kerr to Dr. Douglas L. Rippeto, February 7, 1956, Kerr Papers.

87. See Anderson, *Outsider in the Senate,* pp. 263–64. Also see *Congressional Record,* 84th Congress, 2nd Session, pp. 12814, 12866, 12994, 13022, 13061–67, 13069, 13081–85. Also see George Meany to Kerr, July 18, 1956, Kerr Papers.

88. See Wilbur Cohen, "The Social Security Amendments of 1960: An Analysis of the Provisions of the Legislation and Its Potentialities" (Ann Arbor: University of Michigan School of Social Work, October 1960), pp. 3–4. Copy in Kerr Papers. Also see *Congressional Record,* 86th Congress, 2nd Session, pp. 1142, 17226–27, 17843–54.

89. The so-called Forand bill, an AFL-CIO proposal introduced in 1957,

was typical of this approach. It provided a maximum of 120 days of combined hospital and nursing home care, plus necessary surgery for aged OASI beneficiaries. See *Congress and the Nation*, p. 1153.

90. President Eisenhower proposed a reinsurance plan in January 1954, but the legislation was recommitted after debate in the House. The administration sent a similar plan to Congress in 1956, but Congress still refused to act. See *Congress and the Nation*, p. 1153; also see Richard Harris, *A Sacred Trust* (Baltimore: Penguin Books, Inc., 1969), pp. 1–86. Cited hereafter as Harris, *A Sacred Trust*. Also see Theodore R. Marmor, *The Politics of Medicare* (Chicago: Aldine Publishing Company, 1973). Cited hereafter as Marmor, *The Politics of Medicare*.

91. Kennedy and Philip Hart (D., Mich.) introduced a medical care bill, S. 2915, on January 26, 1960. See *Congressional Record*, 86th Congress, 2nd Session, p. 1238. The bill was more limited in benefits than the Forand proposal and did not create much interest. For details, see *Congressional Quarterly Weekly Report* January 29, 1960): 179.

92. Harris, *A Sacred Trust*, p. 89.

93. On internal debate within the administration see *Wall Street Journal*, March 21, 24, 31, April 6, 7, 8, and May 3, 1960. On the administration's plan see *Wall Street Journal*, May 5, 9, 10, 12, 17, 19, 1960. Also see Anderson, *Outsider in the Senate*, p. 265; Harris, *A Sacred Trust*, pp. 103–107.

94. *Wall Street Journal*, May 5, 1960.

95. Harris, *A Sacred Trust*, p. 108; Reynolds, "Social Security Transcript," p. 18.

96. See Alfred T. Baker to Kerr, June 25, 1959, Kerr Papers.

97. Reynolds, "Social Security Transcript," p. 20.

98. *Ibid.*

99. Harris, *A Sacred Trust*, p. 110.

100. See Rader to Cohen, March 11, 1959; Cohen to Reynolds, March 14, 1959, Kerr Papers. Wilbur Cohen Interview and Rader Interview.

101. Reynolds, "Social Security Transcript," p. 15.

102. In April, Mills had discussed a curious proposal which used the Social Security mechanism to raise funds for health care costs, but allowed potential recipients to choose increased monthly payments rather than medical benefits. See *Wall Street Journal*, April 21, 1960.

103. See *Wall Street Journal*, May 19, 1960; *Congressional Quarterly Weekly Report* (May 20, 1960): 912.

104. Harris, *A Sacred Trust*, p. 110.

105. Cohen Interview; Marmor, *The Politics of Medicare*, p. 30.

106. Reynolds, "Social Security Transcript," p. 14.

107. *Ibid.*, p. 12.

108. *Ibid.*, p. 13.

109. Quote from Anderson, *Outsider in the Senate*, p. 266; also see *New York Times*, July 31, 1960.

110. The House passed the Social Security amendments, H.R. 12580, on June 23. See *Congressional Record*, 86th Congress, 2nd Session, p. 14054. The Mills plan, a program of federal-state matching grant programs, which was included, was modeled on the administration's May 4 plan. The Mills version allowed the

states greater discretion over the scope of their programs. See *Congressional Quarterly Weekly Report* (May 20, 1960): 912 for details. Also see *Wall Street Journal*, May 19, 1960.

111. Cohen Interview.

112. *Ibid.*; Rader Interview; Harris, *A Sacred Trust*, p. 110.

113. Anderson, *Outsider in the Senate*, p. 264.

114. HEW Secretary Flemming told House Ways and Means that Eisenhower would veto any health plan tied to Social Security. See *Wall Street Journal*, May 16, 1960.

115. *Wall Street Journal*, August 22, 1960.

116. For details see *Congress and the Nation*, p. 1154; Anderson, *Outsider in the Senate*, p. 267. Also see copy of Kerr plan in Kerr Papers.

117. *Congressional Quarterly Weekly Report* (August 19, 1960): 1457. The vote in Senate Finance was 12–5.

118. See Chapter I on Mrs. Kerr decorating Anderson's Connecticut home. Also see *Wall Street Journal*, August 15, 1960; *Tulsa Tribune*, August 17, 1960.

119. *Tulsa Tribune*, August 17, 1960, quoting an article in the *Wall Street Journal*, August 15, 1960. Wilbur Cohen was not aware of any role Anderson may have played in drafting the legislation. See Cohen Interview.

120. *Daily Oklahoman*, August 14, 1960.

121. For the text of Eisenhower's press conference, see *Congressional Quarterly Weekly Report* (August 19, 1960): 1470. Also see Cromley, *Daily Oklahoman*, August 17, 1960.

122. Harris, *A Sacred Trust*, p. 111; Cohen Interview.

123. *Congressional Record*, 86th Congress, 2nd Session, p. 16426.

124. *Ibid.*, pp. 16425–34; *New York Times*, August 14, 1960; Cromley, *Daily Oklahoman*, August 16, 1960; *Wall Street Journal*, August 15, 1960. Paul Douglas and Albert Gore were present. They had fought Kerr in the Senate Finance Committee, but neither took him on. Douglas later told reporters that Kerr was a traitor to the Democratic platform, and Gore held his remarks until Kerr left the floor.

125. *Wall Street Journal*, August 17, 1960.

126. *Ibid.*, August 19, 1960.

127. The Javits amendment was a revised edition of the earlier, May 4 administration proposal and provided more liberal benefits than the Kerr-Mills proposal. It was no more than an eleventh-hour response from the Republicans and, as such, was spurned. See *Congressional Record*, 86th Congress, 2nd Session, pp. 16905, 17176; *Wall Street Journal*, August 22, 1960; *Congress and the Nation*, p. 1154.

128. *New York Times*, August 24, 1960; also see Harris, *A Sacred Trust*, pp. 113–14.

129. The final vote was 44–51 (Democrats: 43–19; Republicans: 1–32). See *Congressional Record*, 86th Congress, 2nd Session, p. 17220.

130. Harris, *A Sacred Trust*, p. 114.

131. Douglas, *In the Fullness of Time*, p. 393.

132. The final vote was 91–2 with Barry Goldwater (R., Ariz.) and Strom Thurmond (D., S.C.) in the negative. See *Congressional Record*, 86th Congress, 2nd Session, p. 17235.

133. Cohen Interview; Harris, *A Sacred Trust*, p. 111.

134. Reynolds, "Social Security Transcript," pp. 28–29.

135. Kerr to Delbert Davis, September 26, 1960, Kerr Papers.

136. *Congressional Record*, 86th Congress, 2nd Session, p. 18096.

137. James L. Sundquist, *Politics and Policy: The Eisenhower, Kennedy and Johnson Years* (Washington, D.C.: The Brookings Institution, 1968), p. 307. Cited hereafter as Sundquist, *Politics and Policy*. Also see, *Congressional Quarterly Almanac— 1960*, p. 161.

138. Rader Interview.

139. William McGoffin, "Dixie Block Behind Kerr Victory," no paper, no date, Kerr Papers; *Congressional Quarterly Almanac— 1960*, p. 161.

140. See "Press Release on Kerr-Mills," August 31, 1960, Kerr Papers.

141. Reynolds, "Social Security Transcript," p. 44.

142. Harris, *A Sacred Trust*, p. 117.

Chapter VIII

1. Confidential source.

2. Dr. Thomas C. Dunn, a Midwest City dentist, and D. R. Condo, a Keoto rancher, were Kerr's opponents in the primary. Condo ran on a platform of preserving segregation, while Dunn concentrated on ending deficit spending. See *Daily Oklahoman*, May 30, 1960.

3. See Jones, *Oklahoma Politics*, p. 211; *Daily Oklahoman*, March 13, April 29, 30 and May 2, 1958.

4. Quoted in Gibson, *Oklahoma*, p. 418.

5. In the primary, Edmondson defeated W. P. "Bill" Atkinson, a Midwest City developer, 363,742 to 158,780. He received 399,533 votes to Republican Phil Ferguson's 107,497 votes in the general election—74.1 per cent of the votes cast. See Kirkpatrick, *Oklahoma Voting Patterns*, pp. 41, 42. Also see *Daily Oklahoman*, November 5, 6, 9, 1958.

6. *Daily Oklahoman*, May 10, 1959; also see J. I. Pitchford to Kerr, July 29, 1958, Kerr Papers.

7. Pearson, *Washington Post*, June 3, 1959; Cromley, *Daily Oklahoman*, June 4, 1959; B. J. Stafford to Kerr, April 28, 1959, Kerr Papers. Stafford feared that the Edmondsons would unite with Kerr's old enemy, Roy J. Turner, who was the head of the Oklahoma Highway Department. This combination would be capable of raising large funds from contractors to defeat Kerr.

8. *Daily Oklahoman*, January 18, June 5, 1959.

9. See Chapter VI.

10. *Oklahoma City Times*, February 17, 1962. In response to a letter from John Kilpatrick, president of the Oklahoma City Chamber of Commerce, Kerr wrote, "Mike is the aviation expert on this team here, and I hope that you have written the same letter to him . . . because of Mike's position, he will be able to do more about it than I can." See Kerr to Kilpatrick, August 3, 1961, Kerr Papers.

11. Hays Interview; Cromley, *Daily Oklahoman*, February 12, 1961. On the initial disagreement, see Roy P. Stewart, *Daily Oklahoman*, May 27, 1952.

12. See F. R. Neely, "Winner of the Collier Trophy," *Collier's Magazine*, v. 116 (December 22, 1945): 24.

13. See James A. Robinson, *The Monroney Resolution, Congressional Initiative in Foreign Policy Making* (New York: Henry Holt & Co., 1959).

14. Reynolds Interview. Also see Cromley, *Daily Oklahoman*, July 3, 1960.

15. Seligman, "Senator Bob Kerr," 138.

16. Reynolds Interview. Republican Henry Bellmon defeated Monroney in 1968 on charges that the junior Senator had grown away from Oklahoma. See *Daily Oklahoman*, September 19, October 26, November 6, 1968.

17. Cromley, *Daily Oklahoman*, January 18, 1959.

18. Cromley, *Daily Oklahoman*, January 26, 1958, and June 18, 1959.

19. See Robert W. Kellough to Kerr, August 12, 1959, Kerr Papers.

20. Purcell (Okla.) *Register*, February 4, 1960, Kerr Papers; *Daily Oklahoman*, May 24, 27 and July 10, 11, 1960.

21. Jim Munroe, *Daily Oklahoman*, February 14, 21, 22, 1960; Jones, *Oklahoma Politics*, pp. 219–20.

22. *Daily Oklahoman*, February 23, December 3, 1960.

23. Jones, *Oklahoma Politics*, p. 220; *Daily Oklahoman*, March 20, May 1, 1960.

24. *New York Times*, July 14, 1960; *Daily Oklahoman*, July 14, 1960, November 23, 1963. Also see Carl Albert, "Oral History Interview," pp. 11–13, John F. Kennedy Library, Waltham, Mass. Cited hereafter as Kennedy Papers.

25. *Daily Oklahoman*, October 12, 13, 1960; *Oklahoma City Times*, October 28, 1960.

26. For Kerr's financial help to selected House members in 1960, see "List of Democratic members needing help in 1960 House Campaigns" in Rayburn Papers and Rayburn to Martha Griffiths, October 15, 1960, Rayburn Papers.

27. *Daily Oklahoman*, August 6, 1960.

28. Claire Conley, *Daily Oklahoman*, August 6, 1960.

29. See *Oklahoma City Times*, October 11, 1960. "It is my opinion that with Lyndon Johnson as Vice President, Sam Rayburn as Speaker of the House and myself in the Senate, along with a very considerable number of other men here whose records on this issue are clear, the oil and gas industry would be fully and equitably treated." See Kerr to Humber Dye, August 20, 1960, Kerr Papers.

30. *Oklahoma City Times*, October 11, 1960.

31. See Frederick (Okla.) *Leader*, April 27, 1960, Kerr Papers. In 1962 Oklahoma oil money supported Republican Hayden Crawford, Kerr's opponent in 1960, over Monroney, who was considered unreliable on the depletion allowance.

32. National Council of the Churches of Christ in the U.S.A., Bureau of Research and Survey, *Churches and Church Membership in the United States* (New York, 1957). Also see Jones, *Oklahoma Politics*, p. 144.

33. *Ibid.*, pp. 138–40.

34. Kerr to Scantlan, July 19, 1960, Kerr Papers.

35. See Kerr to Tim Adair, September 15, 1960, Kerr Papers.

36. See Jones, *Oklahoma Politics*, p. 175.

37. White, *The Making of the President, 1960*, p. 321.

38. Sullivant, *Daily Oklahoman*, November 4, 1960; also see *New York Times*, November 4, 1960.

39. Reynolds, "Social Security Transcript," p. 31.

40. *Daily Oklahoman*, November 7, 1960.

41. Reynolds, "Social Security Transcript," p. 32.

42. See Cromley, *Daily Oklahoman*, February 21, 1960; "Crawford Blasts Kerr," Stillwater (Okla.) *News Press*, no date, Kerr Papers.

43. "No reason appears for questioning Senator Kerr's good faith in the matter. He just happens to be one of the biggest [uranium and helium] suppliers." See *Tulsa Tribune*, October 26, 1960. For a discussion of editorial policy in the campaign, see "State Political Trapeze Keeps Audience Enthralled," Cushing (Okla.) *Daily Citizen*, October 28, 1960, Kerr Papers. The *Tulsa Tribune* had been antagonistic to Crawford for his role as federal district attorney in prosecuting a *Tribune* reporter involved in a liquor conspiracy case some years earlier. In 1962 the *Tribune* remained neutral when Crawford carried Tulsa County against Monroney by 10,000 votes. See Jones, *Oklahoma Politics*, p. 188.

44. Nabors, "Robert S. Kerr, Baptist Layman," p. 83. Reynolds says Kerr should have won by 300,000 votes; see "Social Security Transcript," p. 31.

45. *Ibid.*, p. 32. See Chapter VII for Kerr's disgust with the medical profession in the election.

46. *Ibid.*

47. *Ibid.*, p. 33. Also see Cromley, *Daily Oklahoman*, September 26, 1961.

48. See *Wall Street Journal*, December 19, 1960; *New York Times*, December 20, 1960; *Washington Post*, December 20, 1960; Sorensen, *Kennedy*, pp. 340–42.

49. Sorensen says that for Kennedy the space issue "symbolized the nation's lack of initiative, ingenuity and vitality under Republican rule." See *Kennedy*, p. 524.

50. Hugo Young, Bryan Silcock, and Peter Dunn, *Journey to Tranquility* (Garden City, N.Y.: Doubleday & Company, Inc., 1970), pp. 50–51. Cited hereafter as Young, *Journey to Tranquility*. Also see Evans and Novak, *Lyndon B. Johnson*, pp. 189–94, 222.

51. *Ibid.*, p. 316; John M. Logsdon, *The Decision to go to the Moon*, (Cambridge; The MIT Press, 1970), pp. 67–71. Cited hereafter as Logsdon, *The Decision to Go to the Moon*. The Space Council created during the Eisenhower Administration to shape overall space policy and mediate disputes between military and civilian leaders had never been very influential. Sorensen and Feldman had decided to recommend that Kennedy abandon it, but Johnson persuaded the President-elect to let him assume leadership. After the December meetings in Palm Beach, Kennedy asked that the legislation be revised to make Johnson chairman of the Space Council as well as a member.

52. See Charles L. Markmann and Mark Sherwin, *John F. Kennedy: A Sense of Purpose* (New York: St. Martin's Press, 1961), p. 68. Cited hereafter as Markmann and Sherwin, *John F. Kennedy*.

53. For Kerr's role as a critic of the Eisenhower fiscal policy see "Brain Storm," *Time*, v. 70 (July 29, 1957): 11; "Taking Over Money Probe," *Business Week* (April 20, 1957): 47; "Oklahoma's Kerr—The Man Who Really Runs the U.S. Senate," *Newsweek*, v. 60 (August 6, 1962): 15–17; Seligman, "Senator Bob

Kerr," 136–38. Also see *Congress and the Nation*, p. 367; Carroll Kilpatrick, *Washington Post*, July 16, 1957; Arthur Edwin, *Washington Post*, July 17, 1957; *New York Times*, June 22, 26, July 2, 16, 17, 1957; Cromley, *Daily Oklahoman*, June 26, July 16, 1957; *Oklahoma City Times*, November 16, 1957; and *Daily Oklahoman*, April 14, 1959.

54. See James Free, "Kerr Most Important Senator of All," no paper, no date, Kerr Papers; Henryetta (Okla.) *Daily Free-Lance*, December 15, 1960, Kerr Papers; *Wall Street Journal*, August 24, 1959; Markmann and Sherwin, *John F. Kennedy*, p. 68.

55. Hugh Sidey, *John F. Kennedy, President* (New York: Atheneum, 1964), p. 24. Cited hereafter as Sidey, *John F. Kennedy*. Markmann and Sherwin, *John F. Kennedy* also mention Rooney's presence but offer no explanation.

56. *Tulsa Tribune*, January 13, 1961.

57. Steinberg, *Sam Johnson's Boy*, p. 528.

58. McPherson, *A Political Education*, p. 190.

59. *Ibid.*, p. 184.

60. *Ibid.*, p. 45. Also see *Wall Street Journal*, January 3, 1961. On Mansfield as leader, see William S. White, "Three Scouts Heading West," *Harper's Magazine*, v. 222 (March 1961): 105–6; F. W. Collins, "How to be a Leader Without Leading," *New York Times Magazine* (July 30, 1961): 9, 46, 50; and Douglas Cater, "Contentious Lords of the Senate," *Reporter*, v. 27 (August 16, 1962): 27–28, 29.

61. In the Senate there were 65 Democrats and 35 Republicans. In the House there were 263 Democrats and 174 Republicans as of January 3, 1961. See *Congress and the Nation*, p. 41.

62. *Wall Street Journal*, January 4, 1961. Also see Robert Leon Lester, "Developments in Presidential-Congressional Relations: FDR-JFK," Ph.D. dissertation, University of Virginia, 1969, p. 108 and Helen Fuller, *Year of Trial* (New York: Harcourt, Brace and World, Inc., 1962), pp. 70–71.

63. Tom Wicker, *JFK and LBJ: The Influence of Personality upon Politics* (New York: William Morrow & Company, Inc. 1967), p. 86. Cited hereafter as Wicker, *JFK and LBJ*.

64. "Shift in Men-Shift in Policy," *U.S. News and World Report* (February 21, 1958): 91.

65. Wicker, *JFK and LBJ*, p. 90.

66. Cabell Phillips, *New York Times*, September 27, 1962.

67. Reynolds, "Social Security Transcript," p. 34.

68. Saul Pett, Lawton (Okla.) *Constitution-Morning Press*, September 23, 1962, Kerr Papers.

69. McBride Interview.

70. Hays Interview. Healdton (Okla.) *Herald*, January 19, 1961; Wicker, *JFK and LBJ*, pp. 90–91.

71. See *Wall Street Journal*, January 2, 1963; *New York Times*, January 2, 1963; *Washington Post*, January 2, 1963; St. Louis (Mo.), *Globe-Democrat*, January 4, 1963; "Death of a Senator," *Time*, v. 81, no. 2 (January 11, 1963): 23.

72. McBride Interview.

73. Cromley, *Daily Oklahoman*, October 25, 1970.

74. Young, *Journey to Tranquility*, p. 81. Webb was a founder of the Okla-

homa Frontiers of Science Foundation to promote scientific inquiry and president of a Washington-based group called Education Services connected to MIT. He also served as director of McDonnell Aircraft Corporation of St. Louis and as vice-president and treasurer of Sperry Gyroscope, Co. See *Tulsa World*, May 26, 1961, and Webb Interview.

75. Richard S. Lewis, *Appointment on the Moon: The Inside Story of America's Space Venture* (New York: The Viking Press, 1968), pp. 162–63, 170. Cited hereafter as Lewis, *Appointment on the Moon*. Also see Young, *Journey to Tranquility*, pp. 81–83; Evans and Novak, *Lyndon B. Johnson*, p. 337; Cleland, *Tulsa World*, January 31, 1961; *Wall Street Journal*, January 31, 1961; *Washington Post*, February 3, 1961. On Kerr's early relationship with Webb, see Bill Benton to Kerr, July 28, 1954, Kerr Papers; Webb to Kerr, August 22, 1957, Truman Papers; and Webb Interview.

76. See Wiesner to Dean McGee, January 17, 1961, Kerr Papers.

77. Assistant Secretary of the Air Force Eugene M. Zuckert was a close associate of Harold Stuart of Tulsa, who served with him in the Truman Administration. Stuart worked closely with Kerr and Webb to encourage space industries to locate in Oklahoma. In addition, the public information officer for NASA, O. B. Lloyd, Jr., was a native Oklahoman. See Bradley to F. J. Deering, November 20, 1962, Kerr Papers; *Tulsa Tribune*, December 27, 1960.

78. McBride Interview. As an employee on the official Public Works Committee payroll, McBride was entitled to attend all executive sessions in Kerr's absence.

79. *Daily Oklahoman*, January 19, 1961; Stillwater (Okla.) *News-Press*, January 19, 1961, Kerr Papers.

80. *Tulsa Tribune*, February 25, 1961; Cromley, *Daily Oklahoman*, March 1, 1961; Bradley to Robert H. Bennyhoff, February 7, 1961; Stephenson to Bradley, March 10, 1961; Bradley to Stephenson, May 11, 1961, Kerr Papers.

81. "Washington Roundup," *Aviation Week* (February 11, 1961), no page, Kerr Papers. Also see Zell ? to Bob ?, June 14, 1961, "Memo #42 re: making list for Space Committee publications;" Kerr to E. M. Deckerman, June 14, 1961, Kerr Papers. Mr. Deckerman was the director of sales, services, and contracts for the Allison Division of General Motors.

82. Cromley, *Oklahoma City Times*, April 13, 1961.

83. On the Weisner report see, Logsdon, *The Decision to Go to the Moon*, pp. 71–72; John G. Norris, *Washington Post*, January 11, 1961; *Washington Post*, January 12, 1961.

84. *New York Times*, January 17, 1961; *Daily Oklahoman*, January 17, 1961.

85. Logsdon, *The Decision to Go to the Moon*, p. 69. On Johnson and the Democratic caucus, see Anderson, *Outsider in the Senate*, p. 309; McPherson, *A Political Education*, p. 184; Gore, *Let the Glory Out*, p. 148; Robert Albright, *Washington Post*, January 4, 1961; Pearson, *Washington Post*, January 8, 1961.

86. Evans and Novak, *Lyndon B. Johnson*, p. 350; Anderson, *Outsider in the Senate*, p. 309. Johnson and Kerr remained close personal friends. They frequently had dinner together after late evening Senate sessions during 1961 and 1962, and Johnson occasionally visited at Kerr's ranch. William Kerr Interview.

87. On April 20, 1961, Congress approved the plan to make the Vice-President chairman of the National Space Council. See *Congressional Record*, 87th

Congress, 1st Session, p. 6891. In this capacity, Kennedy asked Johnson to review the entire space program. See Young *Journey to Tranquility*, pp. 85–86; Logsdon, *The Decision to Go to the Moon*, p. 71. Also see Kennedy to Johnson, September 30, 1961, Kennedy Papers.

88. Cromley, *Oklahoma City Times*, November 29, 1961; McPherson, *A Political Education*, pp. 69–70; Logsdon, *The Decision to Go to the Moon*, p. 120.

89. *Daily Oklahoman*, John Finney, *New York Times*, and *Washington Post*, May 10, 1961.

90. See Kennedy, "Special Message on Urgent National Needs, May 25, 1961," *Public Papers, 1961*, pp. 396–406. On Kerr's speech, see *Daily Oklahoman*, May 10, 1961 and draft of remarks "To the National Convention of Radio and TV Broadcasters," Kerr papers.

91. Kennedy had already asked for an increase of $125,670,000 for development of the Saturn C-2 launch vehicle system. See *New York Times*, March 29, 1961.

92. *Congressional Record*, 87th Congress, 1st Session, p. 8828 gives the House vote. For Senate Report 475 on H.R. 6874, see *Congressional Record*, 87th Congress, 1st Session, p. 11355.

93. Young, *Journey to Tranquility*, p. 92. Gordon Allott (R., Colo.) was the only Senate dissenter. "I do not believe in engaging in a useless contest with the Russians." He suggested, instead, the development of a manned, weapons carrying orbital space vehicle. See *Congressional Record*, 87th Congress, 1st Session, pp. 11627–28.

94. Hugo Young, Bryan Silcock, and Peter Dunn, "Why We Went to the Moon: From the Bay of Pigs to the Sea of Tranquility," *The Washington Monthly*, v. 2, no. 2 (April 1970): 29; Young, *Journey to Tranquility*, p. 2; *Wall Street Journal*, August 1, 8, 1961.

95. See Press release, "First National Conference on the Peaceful Uses of Space," April 12, 1961: Kerr to Kennedy, April 12, 1961, Kerr Papers.

96. Quoted in *Daily Oklahoman*, May 26, 1961. Also see Checotah (Okla.) *McIntosh County Democrat*, April 27, 1961; *Tulsa Tribune*, May 25, 26, 27, 1961; Enid (Okla.) *Daily Eagle*, May 31, 1961.

97. The President sent telephone greetings. See "Remarks by Telephone to the Conference on Peaceful Uses of Space Meeting in Tulsa, May 26, 1961," Kennedy, *Public Papers, 1961*, pp. 406–7.

98. Letter in article, "Webb Lauds Space Meet," no paper, June 10, 1961, Kerr Papers. On origins of the conference, see *Daily Oklahoman*, May 26, 1961, *Tulsa World*, May 26, 1961.

99. Webb Interview.

100. North American Aviation bought 300 acres adjacent to the port site at Catoosa, Oklahoma, and planned to employ over 11,000 persons there. See *Daily Oklahoman*, October 10, 1961. See also Perry M. Hoisington II, Department of the Air Force, to Kerr, July 31, 1961, confirming a $10 million contract on the B-47, Kerr Papers. On North American interests in Oklahoma, also see, "Seaports for Oklahoma," *U.S. News and World Report*, v. 54 (February 11, 1963): 67. On other industries related to space, see *Daily Oklahoman*, October 10, 1961.

101. On Kerr's desire to supplant California as the leading state in producing

materials for the space industry, see Hays Interview and Hawks Interview. Webb doubted that Kerr had this in mind. See Webb Interview. Figures reported in *Daily Oklahoman*, November 4, 1962, showed that in that year Oklahoma received $2.1 million in new space-related contracts. California received over $1 billion, Florida $843.2 million, Alabama $708.3 million and Virginia $380.1 million. While California was still the leading contractor, Oklahoma was gaining.

102. *Tulsa Tribune*, January 24, 1961.

103. See Lawton (Okla.) *News Review*, November 9, 1961; *Daily Oklahoman*, September 21, December 24, 1961, January 27, 1962. In August 1961 Kennedy asked Congress to approve supplemental federal grants of more than $6 million for two eastern Oklahoma watershed projects. See *Tulsa Tribune*, August 14, 1961.

104. Quoted in Ada (Okla.) *Evening News*, October 27, 1961, Kerr Papers. For a discussion of Kerr's resistance to federal water pollution controls in the 1950's, see Kent Jennings, "Legislative Politics and Water Pollution Control, 1956–1961," Frederic N. Cleaveland, ed., *Congress and Urban Problems* (Washington: The Brookings Institution, 1969), pp. 72–109.

Senator Kerr became so enthusiastic about pollution control in the 1960's that he spoke of the "hydronauts of the New Frontier" and even designed an antipollution symbol—a mermaid with a broom, inspired by Smoky the Bear. He toyed with the idea of a national contest to name the lady. "Polly d'Pollute," "Bea Kleen," "Miss C'leen Sweep," and "Cherokee Princess Clear Water" were among the suggestions he favored before dropping the idea. See *New York Times*, April 18, June 1, 1961; Betty Beale, Washington *Evening Star*, June 23, 1961.

105. See Kerr to David C. Matthews, May 17, 1961, Kerr Papers.

106. See Kerr to A. E. Pearson, August 10, 1961, Kerr Papers. Also see Cromley, *Daily Oklahoman*, July 16, 1961.

107. *Congressional Quarterly Almanac—1961*, p. 375. The standing committee was composed of one representative from each of the federal court districts.

108. Hays Interview.

109. Cromley, *Daily Oklahoman*, July 26, 1961. It seems likely that Kerr spoke with the President about the Bohanon appointment because on July 5, 1961, Kennedy dictated a note to Mrs. Lincoln to remind him to "speak to Bobby about Senator Kerr's judgeship." See "Notes Dictated by the President," July 5, 1961, President's Office Files, Staff Memos—Evelyn Lincoln, Kennedy Papers.

110. Hays Interview. Also see Mary Jo Nelson, *Oklahoma City Times*, August 4, 1961.

111. Cromley, *Daily Oklahoman*, August 9, 1961.

112. Hawks Interview. There is no record of the meeting in the President's appointment book, but impromptu meetings were seldom entered in the official log.

113. "Bohanon Press Release," Thursday, August 17, 1961, Kennedy Papers. Cromley, *Oklahoma City Times*, August 17, 1962.

114. Hawks Interview.

115. See *Congressional Quarterly Almanac—1961*, pp. 293–310.

116. *New York Times*, July 22, July 30, August 17, 1961; Cromley, *Daily Oklahoman*, August 12, 13, 1961. The Bohanon appointment was not one of the 74 new federal judgeships created early in 1961.

117. Quoted in Cromley, *Daily Oklahoman*, August 12, 1961.

118. See Kerr to Ben F. Kelley, April 20, 1961. Kerr to Mrs. Mae Dorothy, May 24, 1961, Kerr Papers.

119. Hays Interview. William Kerr believed that his father might have withdrawn the Bohanon nomination rather than risk a confrontation with the President had he not given Aubrey his word that he would see the nomination through. William Kerr Interview. An incident that Robert Kerr, Jr., recounted to the author seems to confirm this judgment. When Robert, Jr., and Breene were small they got into a fight while waiting for their mother to pick them up from school. When she found the boys exchanging blows she warned them that she was going to report the incident to their father. That night Kerr gave the boys a rare spanking and a lesson they never forgot. He told them, "You may disagree in private, but never fight your own brother in public!" Robert S. Kerr, Jr. Interview, May 4, 1976.

120. See Kerr to Kennedy, August 21, 1961, Kennedy Papers. *Daily Oklahoman*, September 29, October 15, 18, 30, 31, 1961; *New York Times*, October 30, 31, 1961.

121. The President reminded Edmondson of Kerr's committee memberships saying "he has more control over my legislative program than any other person in Congress." Edmondson told the story to William Reynolds. See Reynolds Interview.

122. "Senator Kerr Says," August 21, 1961, Kerr Papers.

123. *Tulsa Tribune*, October 19, 1961. On the two residents of Big Cedar, Mr. W. W. McBride, an 81 year old farmer, and Nat Croly, 73, owner of the gas station/country store, see Ada (Okla.) *Evening News*, October 25, 1961, Kerr Papers.

124. Quoted in *Tulsa Tribune*, October 30, 1961; also see Lawton (Okla.) *News-Review*, November 9, 1961, Kerr Papers.

125. See "Remarks at Big Cedar, Oklahoma, October 30, 1961," Kennedy Papers. Several small newspapers in the area of Big Cedar ran articles on the general theme, "my trip to see President Kennedy." See Leedey (Okla.) *Star*, selected clippings in the Kerr Papers and the Atoka (Okla.) *County Times*, November 2, 1961, Kerr Papers.

126. Hawks Interview. On the house, see Bill Butler, *Tulsa World*, October 25, 1956; Cromley, Elviretta Walker, *Daily Oklahoman*, August 27, 1961.

127. McBride Interview.

128. Enid (Okla.) *Morning News*, November 5, 1961, Kerr Papers.

129. Cromley, *Daily Oklahoman*, December 30, 1962.

130. Pett, Lawton (Okla.) *Constitution-Morning Press*, September 23, 1962, Kerr Papers.

131. See Novak, *Wall Street Journal*, July 31, 1962. Also see Childs, *Washington Post*, October 12, 1962.

132. When the administration's literacy test bill, S. 2750 was referred to Senate Judiciary, the traditional southern burial ground for civil rights legislation, Majority Leader Mansfield promised that if the bill were not reported by April, he would call it up by other means. On April 24, he offered the bill as an amendment to a pending House measure, H.R. 1316, a private bill involving a Texas farmer. When the southern filibuster began, Mansfield refused to keep the

Senate in round-the-clock sessions as Johnson had done. The Majority Leader's handling of the vote of closure was so clumsy that it actually permitted a senator to "have it both ways." He announced that a vote on a motion to table the literacy bill would follow the vote on cloture. That meant a senator could support the tradition of unlimited Senate debate by opposing cloture and then cast a pro-civil rights vote by voting against the motion to table. This strategy also allowed Republicans from states where civil rights was not an important issue to impede the Democratic legislative program. The cloture vote should have been the equivalent of a vote for or against civil rights. In Mansfield's hands, it was neither. See *Congressional Quarterly Almanac—1962*, pp. 371–77.

133. Novak, *Wall Street Journal*, July 31, 1962.

134. See James Reston, *New York Times*, January 3, 1962; *Washington Post*, January 3, 1962.

135. See Pearson, *Washington Post*, December 2, 1961; William S. White, "Kerr Best Hope for JFK?" no paper, February 12, 1962, Kerr Papers. Kerr attributed Albert's advancement from whip to majority leader to Kennedy's kind words, "which reverberated not only through the mountains of Southeast Oklahoma and the third congressional district, but reached the halls of Congress." See *Tulsa Tribune*, January 24, 1962. On Albert's election as continuing the historic concept of office, see Krock, *New York Times*, January 5, 1962.

136. *New York Times*, January 27, 1962.

137. See *Wall Street Journal*, June 28, 1962.

138. *Ibid.*, August 16, 1961.

139. *Ibid.*, June 28, 1962.

140. Executive Order 11062, 27 *Federal Register* (November 20, 1962): 11527.

141. *Wall Street Journal*, June 28, 1962.

142. *Ibid.*, January 12, 1962. The *New York Times* predicted that only tax, trade, and medicare would pass in a form satisfactory to the administration. See *New York Times*, January 12, 1962.

143. Chalmers M. Roberts, *Washington Post*, June 8, 1962; Cromley, *Oklahoma City Times*, June 8, 1962. Cromley said that Kerr's Senate staff was unaware of the meeting. Cromley Interview. Also see Joseph Alsop, *Washington Post*, June 15, 1962.

144. Byrd was not entirely at fault in delaying the President's program. Secretary of the Treasury Dillon tarried six weeks before sending the administration's response to the House version of the tax proposal to Senate Finance. And Mansfield's morning Senate sessions interferred with committee hearings when Republicans refused to agree to unanimous consent motions to permit committees to hold meetings while the Senate was in session. See *Wall Street Journal*, May 1, 1962.

145. Cromley, *Daily Oklahoman*, January 14, 1962.

146. *Wall Street Journal*, May 4, 1962.

147. *Ibid.*, May 22, 1962; Clayton Knowles, *New York Times*, May 21, 1962.

148. Sorensen, *Kennedy*, p. 343; Harris, *A Sacred Trust*, p. 142.

149. *New York Times*, May 22, 1962.

150. See Anderson, *Outsider in the Senate*, p. 272; Sorensen, *Kennedy*, p. 343; *Wall Street Journal*, May 5, 1962.

151. *Wall Street Journal*, February 27, 1962.

152. Reynolds, "Social Security Transcript," p. 58.

153. *Ibid.* They discussed a medicare program tied to Social Security for future retirees.

154. *New York Times*, January 5, 1962.

155. For details see, *Congressional Quarterly Almanac—1962*, pp. 212–18.

156. *New York Times*, June 30, 1962. The Anderson-Javits amendment was not printed in the *Record* at the time it was introduced. See *Congressional Record*, 87th Congress, 2nd Session, pp. 14628–29.

157. *Wall Street Journal*, July 2, 1962.

158. Reynolds, "Social Security Transcript," p. 55.

159. *Ibid.*

160. Mrs. Smith commended Kerr for keeping her advised of every aspect of business before the Space Committee. "In fact, no committee chairman ever kept me so currently informed, so constantly sought my reaction and so completely extended consideration and courtesy to me as did Bob Kerr." See Smith to Mr. Marshall McNeil, January 23, 1963, quoted in *Memorial Addresses*, p. 174.

161. Reynolds, "Social Security Transcript," pp. 37–38.

162. See tally sheet on medicare vote, Kerr Papers.

163. The eighty-four-year-old chairman of the Senate Appropriations Committee was facing a difficult reelection challenge from a Republican, and medicare was an unpopular issue in Arizona. Hayden was also sensitive to charges that he was "a rubber stamp for Kennedy," so he had let it be known that unless his "nay" was crucial, he would vote as his constituency wanted. See handwritten notes on Anderson-Javits amendment in Carl Hayden Papers, Manuscripts Collection, Arizona State University, Tempe, Arizona. On Mundt, see Harris, *A Sacred Trust*, p. 148; Cromley, *Daily Oklahoman*, July 18, 1962.

164. *Congressional Record*, 87th Congress, 2nd Session, p. 13871.

165. Sorensen said at the beginning of the roll call there were 48 solid votes for medicare. "If Randolph supported it, Carl Hayden should support it out of party loyalty; and fifty votes, with Vice President Johnson breaking any tie, would pass the bill." See Sorensen, *Kennedy*, p. 344.

166. For Randolph's explanation of his vote, see *Congressional Record*, 87th Congress, 2nd Session, p. 13871. Also see *Wall Street Journal*, July 18, 1962; *Washington Post*, July 18, 1962; *Congressional Quarterly Almanac—1962*, p. 195.

167. Hays Interview. On Kerr's appearance at Salem College see the Clarksburg (W. Va.) *Exponent*, June 9, 1962, Kerr Papers. Also see *Wall Street Journal*, July 18, 1962.

168. Sundquist, *Politics and Policy*, p. 313; Lawrence F. O'Brien, *No Final Victories* (New York: Doubleday & Company, Inc., 1974), pp. 134–35. Cited hereafter as O'Brien, *No Final Victories*. Harris, *A Sacred Trust*, p. 147.

169. O'Brien, *No Final Victories*, pp. 134–35.

170. For the text of the amendment, see *Congressional Quarterly Almanac—1962*, p. 217 and *Congressional Record*, 87th Congress, 2nd Session, p. 12668.

171. Sorensen, *Kennedy*, p. 344; O'Brien, *No Final Victories*, p. 135.

172. *Congressional Quarterly Almanac—1962*, p. 195.

173. Sorensen, *Kennedy*, p. 176.

174. Only four southern Democrats—Gore and Kefauver of Tennessee, Johnston of South Carolina, and Yarborough of Texas—voted with the administration.

175. *Wall Street Journal*, July 18, 1962.

176. Kraft, "King of the U.S. Senate," 26.

177. Cromley, *Oklahoma City Times*, July 17, 1962.

178. Reynolds, "Social Security Transcript," p. 36.

179. Cromley, *Oklahoma City Times*, July 24, 1962.

180. See Transcript of NBC's "Meet the Press," August 19, 1962, Kerr Papers. Also see New York *Herald Tribune*, August 20, 1962, Kerr Papers.

181. Kraft, "King of the U.S. Senate," 27.

182. Hays Interview.

183. For a detailed discussion of the tax bill in both houses of Congress, see David James Stern, "Congress, Politics and Taxes: A Case Study of the Revenue Act of 1962," Ph.D. dissertation, Claremont Graduate School and University Center, 1965. Also see *Congressional Quarterly Almanac—1962*, pp. 478–96; *Congress and the Nation*, I, pp. 429–30. On the Trade Expansion Act of 1962, see Raymond A. Bauer, Ithiel de Sola Pool, and Lewis Anthony Dexter, *American Business and Public Policy: The Politics of Foreign Trade* (New York: Atherton Press, 1963); John F. Manley, *The Politics of Finance: The House Committee on Ways and Means* (Boston: Little, Brown and Company, 1970); *Congressional Quarterly Almanac—1962*, pp. 249–90.

184. Kraft, "King of the U.S. Senate," 27.

185. Bruce Ian Oppenheimer, *Oil and the Congressional Process: The Limits of Symbolic Politics* (Lexington, Mass.: Lexington Books, D. C. Heath and Company, 1974), p. 106.

186. McPherson recorded this anecdote as "a good story" he heard, but it is essentially correct. Confidential source. See McPherson, *A Political Education*, p. 197. The story also appeared in Elizabeth Drew, "Dam Outrage: The Story of the Army Engineers," *The Atlantic*, v. 225, no. 4 (April 1970): 51–62.

187. See Myer Feldman to Kennedy, "Memo on Program for the Oil Industry," June 25, 1962, Kennedy Papers; Novak, *Wall Street Journal*, January 2, 1963.

188. "Kerr Switches Sides to Push Trade Bill," *Business Week* (July 28, 1962): 86. Myer Feldman drafted Kerr's October 29, 1962 speech to the Independent Petroleum Producers Association meeting in Dallas concerning the administration's policy on oil imports. See Feldman to Kerr, October 24, 1962, Kennedy Papers and copy of draft in Kerr Papers. Also see Cromley, *Daily Oklahoman*, January 9, March 20, 29, 1962; Joseph Huttlinger, *Oklahoma City Times*, April 1, August 5, 1962; Albright, *Washington Post*, September 20, 1962.

189. Quote in *Tulsa Tribune*, January 2, 1963. On the communications satellite bill, see Ronald Chesney Moe, "Tele-communications Policy: The Legislative History of the Communications Satellite Act of 1962," Ph.D. dissertation, Columbia University, 1968.

190. Stern, "Congress, Politics and Taxes," pp. 380–83.

191. Gore, *Let the Glory Out*, p. 157.

192. For Byrd's views on the tax bill, see *New York Times*, April 1, 1962, and *Wall Street Journal*, May 22, 1962.

193. Stern, "Congress, Politics and Taxes," p. 389.

194. Novak, *Wall Street Journal*, May 7, 1962.

195. *Ibid.*, July 31, 1962.

196. Anderson, *Outsider in the Senate*, p. 280.

197. Jones, *Oklahoma Politics*, p. 242.

198. William Kerr Interview. For another view see *Ibid.*

199. *Oklahoma City Times*, October 26, 1962.

200. *Daily Oklahoman*, January 26, 1958.

201. Albright, *Washington Post*, October 13, 1962.

202. The implication was that Kerr wanted his eldest son to succeed him if he did not live to finish his term. Hawks Interview.

203. Cleland, *Tulsa World*, December 19, 1962; Lawton (Okla.) *Constitution-Morning Press*, December 20, 1962; *New York Times*, December 20, 1962; *Washington Post*, December 19, 1962. Breene Kerr Interview.

204. See Baker to Mansfield, Memo, "Legislative Problems of the 88th Congress," December 27, 1962, copy in Kennedy Papers.

205. Cromley, *Daily Oklahoman*, January 2, 1963.

206. *Ibid.*, January 7, 1963. Johnson wanted to punish Edmondson for refusing to support him in 1960 and for seconding Kennedy's nomination. Hawks Interview.

207. Gibson, *Oklahoma*, p. 422.

208. Fred R. Harris was elected to Kerr's seat in 1964 and served one term.

209. Kenneth Crawford, "The Senate's Way," *Newsweek*, v. 61, no. 2 (January 14, 1962): 2.

210. Editorial in the Duncan (Okla.) *Daily Banner*, reprinted in the Ada (Okla.) *Evening News*, January 3, 1963, Kerr Papers.

Epilogue

1. Richard L. Strout, *Wall Street Journal*, January 3, 1963.

2. *Ibid.*

3. Kraft, "King of the U. S. Senate," 27.

4. Cushing (Okla.) *Daily Citizen*, January 4, 1963, Kerr Papers.

BIBLIOGRAPHICAL ESSAY

BIBLIOGRAPHICAL ESSAY

Manuscript Collections

This study was based primarily on the Robert Samuel Kerr Papers in the Western History Collection, Bizzell Memorial Library at the University of Oklahoma, Norman, Oklahoma. The collection consists of 949 letter cases of public and private papers dating from 1943 to 1963. There are also fifteen scrapbooks and several hundred tapes and photographs. The bulk of the papers was deposited in 1963 following Senator Kerr's death, but they were not open to scholars until the early 1970's. A detailed guide, indexing the papers by subject headings and then in chronological order, was completed in 1974.

The majority of the collection relates to Kerr's Senate career with only 105 boxes on the gubernatorial years. Under statute, the official papers of the Kerr Administration are deposited in the Oklahoma State Archives in Oklahoma City.

There are some personal letters from Mrs. Kerr and the children in the part of the collection that pertains to the gubernatorial years, but the family removed later private correspondence. There is only scattered correspondence relating to Kerr-McGee Industries in the collection. While the company has carefully preserved records, they have commissioned a history of the corporation; and all such material, except for the clipping files of the Public Relations Department, is restricted for that use.

The Kerr Papers are excellent on the development of water

resources, particularly the Arkansas River Navigation Project and the natural gas controversy in 1949–1950. The Papers also are very complete on Kerr's various election campaigns, but they are disappointing as a source on national Democratic party politics.

The collection is also deficient in material on such areas as Kerr's activities on Social Security legislation, health care, and the development of the space program. Some of this material is in the files of the Senate Finance Committee and the Senate Aeronautical and Space Sciences Committee, which are not yet available to scholars. Information on these subjects was gleaned from newspapers, federal documents, the *Congressional Record*, and interviews.

The Senator's personal correspondence is disappointing. Like most politicians of the twentieth century, Robert Kerr used the telephone whenever possible. Not only was it faster and more direct than a letter, but he savored the intrigue of innuendo and the nuances of inflection that were absent in correspondence. Kerr also preferred the flexibility that a conversation afforded. For these reasons, his own letters are seldom more revealing than the public record.

The newspaper clipping files, seventeen letter cases in the Kerr Papers, were a significant lode of information and the historian's delight. An avid newspaper reader, Kerr subscribed to several clipping services and the collection contains an excellent sample of small-town Oklahoma papers, both dailies and weeklies, and a representative cross section of the national press. In anticipation of the 1952 try for the presidential nomination, Kerr expanded his subscription to concentrate on western and southern papers. These clipping files were arranged by subject and year, and they gave the collection an unexpected scope and depth of insight into the development of Oklahoma politics within the context of national issues. There were also some useful items in the replica of Kerr's Senate office at the Kerr Museum in Poteau, Oklahoma.

The papers of other political figures in the Western History Collection were helpful. The Elmer Thomas Papers were useful on the Arkansas River Project, Kerr's early years in the Senate, and the Kerr-Monroney relationship. The Page Belcher Papers contained important information on Belcher's role as the Oklahoma delegation's link with the Eisenhower Administration on the Arkansas River project, but their use is still severely restricted. The Johnston Murray Papers were helpful on Democratic party politics in Oklahoma in 1952. The Leon C. Phillips Papers are good on Oklahoma politics in the 1930's and 1940's and Phillips' feud with the federal government over the Grand River dam. In addition to a large number of newspaper clippings, the collection contains a substantial amount of correspondence between Phillips and James Farley. The George Schwabe Papers and the Wilburn Cartwright Papers contain little that relates to Senator Kerr, although they are of some help in understanding development in Oklahoma in the early post–World War II period. The Harrington Wimberly Papers contain no personal correspondence. They are primarily materials relating to the natural gas investigation of 1947. The Carl Albert Papers, the A. S. "Mike" Monroney Papers, and the J. Howard Edmondson Papers in the Western History Collection should prove a useful complement to the Kerr Papers when they are opened.

The papers of Kerr's contemporaries in the Senate were disappointing. The Paul Douglas Papers at the Chicago Historical Society were incomplete. Senator Douglas retained most of the significant material for use in his autobiography, *In the Fullness of Time*, and it will not be deposited until his death. The Sam Rayburn Papers at the Rayburn Library in Bonham, Texas, were unrewarding. The Carl Hayden Papers at Arizona State University, Tempe, Arizona, were good on Hayden's decision to vote against the administration on medicare in 1962. The Harry Byrd Papers at the Alderman Library at the University of Virginia, Charlottesville, Virginia, contained a great deal of correspondence on Byrd's proposed retirement and the possibility of Kerr's succeeding him as chairman of Senate Finance. But they were very weak on the Kennedy legislative program in the Finance Committee for 1961 and 1962. The Lyndon Johnson Papers at the Johnson Library at Austin, Texas, the Richard Russell Papers at the University of Georgia, Athens, Georgia, and the Allen Ellender Papers at Tulane University, New Orleans, Louisiana, are not yet open to scholars. The Clinton Anderson Papers dealing with the congressional career at the Library of Congress technically have been open for years, but Anderson has not permitted any scholar to examine them. The Dennis Chavez Papers at Albuquerque University, as well as copies at Yale University, were open for a time, but the family has recently requested that they be closed for twenty-five years from the date of his death in 1962.

The papers of the Arkansas Basin Development Association of Tulsa were excellent on the Arkansas Navigation Project. Most of Newton Graham's correspondence with Kerr and Don McBride was missing from the Kerr Papers, so this collection was essential for a complete understanding of the state and national politics involved in water development.

The Kerr-Truman correspondence in the Truman Papers at the Harry S. Truman Library in Independence, Missouri, was useful in gauging the close relationship between the President and the Senator. The material on the natural gas controversy bill veto was also very enlightening. The James E. Webb Papers at the Truman Library shed some light on Webb's association with Kerr in the 1950's, but those portions pertaining to Webb's role as head of NASA remain closed. The portions of the John F. Kennedy Papers at the Kennedy Library in Waltham, Massachusetts, open thus far contained little on the Kerr-Kennedy relationship. While Senator Kerr's views were mentioned frequently in legislative memoranda in the President's Office Files and the White House Staff Files of Myer Feldman, Theodore Sorensen and Lee White, the extent of Kerr's involvement in the administration's legislative planning will not be clear until the Larry O'Brien and Michael Manatos files on congressional liaison are available to scholars.

The Eisenhower Papers at the Dwight D. Eisenhower Library in Abilene, Kansas, were unrevealing. The Laurence Spivak Papers at the Library of Congress contained several folders of viewers' comments on Kerr's various appearances on "Meet the Press." The Harold Ickes Papers at the Library of Congress failed to illuminate Ickes' role in the Leland Olds episode, and Olds' papers recently opened at the Franklin Delano Roosevelt Library at Hyde

Park, New York, added nothing of value.

Interviews

I attempted to interview the most-prominent persons closely associated with Senator Kerr who are still living. His former staff
members were anxious to talk about him and were very candid.
In several instances they followed up an interview with phone
calls to correct a detail in their account of an event or to suggest
new sources of information. While the interviews did not really
provide any striking new information, they were useful in confirming what I knew and in helping me form a more vivid impression of the man and the period. Although I conducted most interviews in person, several individuals preferred a written interview.
Of those, Dean McGee, president of Kerr-McGee Industries, and
Clark Clifford failed to respond upon seeing the questions. Neither
answered any followup correspondence. Senator Allen Frear
agreed to a written interview, then said he could not put anything
on paper, but he graciously flew to Washington to talk with me in
March, 1975. While his comments were not particularly revealing,
his eagerness to "set the record straight on Kerr" was as generous
as it was flattering. A list of persons interviewed follows:

Carter Bradley	Allan Cromley	Eileen Galloway
Kenneth J. Bousquet	Paul Douglas	Rex Hawks
Wilbur Cohen	J. Allen Frear	Harrington Wimberly
Burl Hays	William Reynolds	Robert S. Kerr, Jr.
Don McBride	Theodore Schad	William Kerr
Lloyd E. Rader	James E. Webb	Breene Kerr
	Kay Kerr Clark	

Newspapers

As indicated earlier, the clipping files in the Kerr Papers were very
useful. In addition, the *Daily Oklahoman,* the *Oklahoma City*

Times, the *Tulsa Tribune*, and the *Tulsa World* were consulted from 1940 to 1963. Although national coverage of Senator Kerr was cursory until the 1960's, the *Washington Post*, the *New York Times*, and the *Wall Street Journal* were examined from 1949 to January 31, 1963. The *Wall Street Journal*'s coverage was the most complete and the most analytical. Robert Novak was the *Journal*'s Washington correspondent for the early 1960's, and his interest in Congress plus the paper's concern with tax, trade, and Social Security legislation were the perfect focus for material on Kerr.

Public Documents

The most important federal documents used in this study were the hearings and reports of Senate committees—the Public Works Committee, the Finance Committee, the Interior Committee, the Aeronautical and Space Sciences Committee, and the Appropriations Committee. The hearings and reports of the House Public Works Committee, the House Ways and Means Committee, and the House Appropriations Committee were also useful. Specific hearings consulted appear in the footnotes.

The *Congressional Record* was consulted from 1949–1962 for details on important debates. The *Public Papers* of Presidents Truman, Eisenhower, and Kennedy were also useful.

Materials on Congress

The publications of the Congressional Quarterly Service, Inc., *Congressional Quarterly Weekly Report*, *Congressional Quarterly Almanac*, and *Congress and the Nation, 1945–1964* are indispensable to the serious student of the Congress. The various studies on the Senate, memoirs and biographies of Kerr's contemporaries, and books on specific committees of Congress are listed in the bibliography.

Oral History Transcripts

Most of the transcripts of oral history interviews read in connection with this study were not revealing. The exception was

William A. Reynolds' interview in the Social Security Administration Project at the Columbia University Oral History Project. Reynolds' comments on Kerr's relationship with Wilbur Cohen and his account of the defeat of medicare in 1962 were exceptionally helpful.

The Carl Albert transcript at the Kennedy Library was good on the Kerr-Howard Edmondson relationship. Other oral history transcripts consulted at the Kennedy Library were by Paul Douglas, Michael Mansfield, Wilbur Mills, Myer Feldman, Jacob Javits, Luther Hodges, and Wilbur Cohen.

Unpublished Materials

Dr. William A. Settle, Jr.'s manuscript on the history of the Tulsa Conservation District of the Army Corps of Engineers was the most useful single source on the Arkansas River Navigation Project and the perfect complement to materials in the Kerr Papers and the Arkansas Basin Development Association Papers. John Robert Ferrell, "Water Resource Development in the Arkansas Valley: A History of Public Policy to 1950," Ph.D. dissertation, University of Oklahoma, 1968, was good on the debate surrounding public- versus private-power development. Thomas L. Reynolds, "Senator Robert S. Kerr and the Arkansas Navigation Project," M.A. thesis, Oklahoma State University, 1964, and J. David Cox, "Senator Robert S. Kerr and the Arkansas River Navigation Project: A Study in Legislative Leadership," Ph.D. dissertation, University of Oklahoma, 1972, were also helpful.

James Ralph Scales, "The Political History of Oklahoma, 1907–1949," Ph.D. dissertation, University of Oklahoma, 1949, is virtually a primary source. On Kerr's early life and political career, Claude R. Thorpe, "Robert S. Kerr's 1948 Senatorial Campaign," M.A. thesis, University of Oklahoma, 1967, and John Huddleston Nabors, "Robert S. Kerr, Baptist Layman: A Study of the Impact of Religion and Politics on the Life of an Oklahoma Leader," M.A. thesis, University of Oklahoma, 1964, are adequate.

There are two studies on Kerr as a speaker by William Baker English, "An Analysis of Modes of Proof in Robert S. Kerr's Senate

Speeches on Conservation," M.A. thesis, University of Oklahoma, 1964, and "Robert S. Kerr: A Study in Ethos," Ph.D. dissertation, University of Oklahoma, 1966.

An unpublished manuscript in the Kerr Papers was excellent on the historical development of the natural gas controversy. It was Burton N. Behling, "Federal Regulation of the Natural Gas Industry," a paper presented at the December 29, 1949, session of the American Economic Association meeting in New York City.

Two case studies of legislative issues helped illuminate Kerr's role in the Eighty-seventh Congress. They were David James Stern, "Congress, Politics and Taxes: A Case Study of the Revenue Act of 1962," Ph.D. dissertation, Claremont Graduate School and University Center, 1965, and Ronald Chesney Moe, "Tele-communications Policy: The Legislative History of the Communications Satellite Act of 1962," Ph.D. dissertation, Columbia University, 1968.

On the 1952 presidential race, Jack R. Yakey, "Prelude to Defeat: Alben Barkley's Quest for the 1952 Democratic Presidential Nomination," M.A. thesis, Central Missouri State University, 1973, was helpful. Robert Leon Lester, "Developments in Presidential-Congressional Relations: FDR–JFK," Ph.D. dissertation, University of Virginia, 1969, was also consulted.

BIBLIOGRAPHY OF SECONDARY SOURCES

BIBLIOGRAPHY OF SECONDARY SOURCES

Books

Abell, Tyler, ed. *Drew Pearson's Diaries, 1949–1959*. New York: Holt, Rinehart and Winston, 1974.

Allen, Robert S., and Shannon, William V. *The Truman Merry-Go-Around*. New York: Vanguard Press, Inc., 1950.

Anderson, Clinton P., with Viorst, Milton. *Outsider in the Senate: Senator Clinton Anderson's Memoirs*. New York: The World Publishing Company, 1970.

Anderson, Jack. *Washington Exposé*. Washington: Public Affairs Press, 1967.
────── and Pearson, Drew. *The Case Against Congress*. New York: Simon and Schuster, 1968.

Anderson, Odin W. *The Uneasy Equilibrium, Private and Public Financing of Health Services in the United States, 1875–1965*. New Haven: College and University Press, 1968.

Bailey, Stephen K., and Samuel, Howard D. *Congress at Work*. New York: Henry Holt and Company, 1952.

Barrett, Major General Charles F. *Oklahoma After Fifty Years*. 4 vols. Oklahoma City: The Historical Record Association, 1941.

Bauer, Raymond A.; Pool, Ithiel de Sola; and Dexter, Lewis Anthony. *American Business and Public Policy: The Politics of Foreign Trade*. New York: Atherton Press, 1963.

Benson, Oliver and others. *Oklahoma Votes, 1907–1962*. Norman: University of Oklahoma Press, 1964.

Blachly, Frederick F., and Oatman, Miriam E. *Natural Gas and the Public Interest*. Washington: Granite Press, 1947.

Blum, John Morton, ed. *The Price of Vision: the Diary of Henry A. Wallace, 1942–1946*. Boston: Houghton Mifflin Company, 1973.

Bryant, Keith L., Jr. *Alfalfa Bill Murray*. Norman: University of Oklahoma Press, 1968.

Campbell, Anson B., with Hoheisel, H. Paul, ed. *Stalwart Sooners*. Oklahoma City: Paul and Paul, 1949.

Cary, William. *Politics and the Regulatory Agencies*. New York: McGraw-Hill

Book Company, 1967.

Chamberlain, Hope. *A Minority of Members: Women in the U.S. Congress*. New York: Praeger Publishers, 1973.

Childs, Marquis. *Eisenhower: Captive Hero*. New York: Harcourt, Brace & World, Inc., 1958.

Cleaveland, Frederic N., ed. *Congress and Urban Problems*. Washington: The Brookings Institution, 1969.

Cochran, Bert. *Adlai Stevenson, Patrician Among the Politicians*. New York: Funk and Wagnalls, 1969.

David, Paul T.; Moos, Malcolm; and Goldman, Ralph M. *Presidential Nominating Politics in 1952*. 5 vols. Baltimore: The Johns Hopkins Press, 1954.

Democratic National Committee. *Official Report of the Proceedings of the Democratic National Convention, 1952*. Washington: Democratic National Committee, 1952.

Divine, Robert A. *Foreign Policy and U.S. Presidential Elections*. New York: New Viewpoints, a Division of Franklin Watts, Inc., 1974.

Dorough, C. Dwight. *Mr. Sam*. New York: Random House, 1962.

Douglas, Paul H. *In the Fullness of Time, The Memoirs of Paul H. Douglas*. New York: Harcourt, Brace Jovanovich, Inc., 1971.

Eisenhower, Dwight D. *The White House Years: Mandate for Change, 1953–1956*. Garden City, N.Y.: Doubleday & Company, Inc., 1963.

————. *The White House Years: Waging Peace, 1956–1961*. Garden City, N.Y.: Doubleday & Company, 1965.

Engler, Robert. *The Politics of Oil: A Study of Private Power and Democratic Direction*. New York: The Macmillan Company, 1961.

Evans, Rowland, and Novak, Robert. *Lyndon B. Johnson: The Exercise of Power*. New York: The New American Library, 1968.

Feingold, Eugene. *Medicare: Policy and Politics, A Case Study and Policy Analysis*. San Francisco: Chandler Publishing Company, 1966.

Fenno, Richard F. Jr. *The Power of the Purse: Appropriations Politics in Congress*. Boston: Little, Brown and Company, 1966.

Ferejohn, John A. *Pork Barrel Politics: Rivers and Harbors Legislation, 1947–1968*. Stanford: Stanford University Press, 1974.

Foreman, Grant. *A History of Oklahoma*. Norman: University of Oklahoma Press, 1945.

Fox, Irving K., and Picken, Isabel. *The Upstream-Downstream Controversy in the Arkansas-White-Red Basins Survey*. University, Alabama: University of Alabama Press, 1960. (ICP Case Series: Number 55.)

Fuller, Helen. *Year of Trial*. New York: Harcourt, Brace and World, Inc., 1962.

Gibson, Arrell M. *Oklahoma: A History of Five Centuries*. Norman, Oklahoma: Harlow Publishing Corporation, 1965.

Gore, Albert. *Let the Glory Out: My South and Its Politics*. New York: Viking Press, 1972.

Gorman, Joseph Bruce. *Kefauver: A Political Biography*. New York: Oxford University Press, 1971.

Greenfield, Margaret. *Health Insurance for the Aged: The 1965 Program for Medicare, Its History and a Summary of Other Provisions of P.L. 89–97*. Berkeley: Institute of Governmental Studies, University of California, 1966.

Griffith, Alison. *The National Aeronautics and Space Act: A Study of the Development of Public Policy.* Washington, D.C.: Public Affairs Press, 1962.

Griffith, Winthrop. *Humphrey: A Candid Biography.* New York: William Morrow & Company, 1965.

Gunther, John. *Inside U.S.A.* (rev. ed.). New York: Harper & Row Publishers, 1951.

Hamby, Alonzo L. *Beyond the New Deal: Harry S Truman and American Liberalism.* New York: Columbia University Press, 1973.

Harlow, Rex Francis (comp.). *Makers of Government in Oklahoma.* Oklahoma City: Harlow Publishing Company, 1930.

Harris, Richard. *A Sacred Trust.* Baltimore: Penguin Books, Inc., 1969.

Haveman, Robert H. *Water Resource Investment and the Public Interest: An Analysis of Federal Expenditures in Ten Southern States.* Nashville: Vanderbilt University Press, 1965.

Haynes, George H. *The Senate of the United States, Its History and Practice.* 2 vols. Boston: Houghton Mifflin Company, 1938.

Holmes, Jay. *America on the Moon: The Enterprise of the Sixties.* Philadelphia: J. B. Lippincott Company, 1962.

Horn, Stephen. *Unused Power: The Work of the Senate Committee on Appropriations.* Washington, D.C.: The Brookings Institution, 1970.

Huitt, Ralph K., and Peabody, Robert L. *Congress: Two Decades of Analysis.* New York: Harper & Row, Publishers, 1969.

Ickes, Harold L. *The Secret Diary of Harold L. Ickes: The Lowering Clouds, 1939–1941.* v. 3. New York: Simon and Schuster, 1954.

Jones, Stephen. *Oklahoma Politics in State and Nation, 1907–1962.* v. 1. Enid, Oklahoma: The Haymaker Press, Inc., 1974.

Joseph, Peter. *Good Times, An Oral History of America in the Nineteen-Sixties.* New York: William Morrow & Company, 1974.

Kearns, Doris. *Lyndon Johnson and the American Dream.* New York: Harper & Row, Publishers, 1976.

Kerr, Robert S. *Land, Wood and Water* (edited by Malvina Stephenson and Tris Coffin). New York: Fleet Publishing Corporation, 1960.

Kirkpatrick, Samuel A., and Morgan, David R. *Oklahoma Voting Patterns: Presidential, Gubernatorial and Senatorial Elections.* Norman, Oklahoma: Bureau of Government Research, 1970.

———; ———; and Edwards, Larry G. *Oklahoma Voting Patterns, Congressional Elections.* Norman, Oklahoma: Bureau of Government Research, 1970.

Kohlmeier, Louis M., Jr. *The Regulators: Watchdog Agencies and the Public Interest.* New York: Harper & Row, 1969.

Krutilla, John V., and Eckstein, Otto. *Multiple Purpose River Development.* Baltimore: Johns Hopkins Press, 1958.

Kuntz, Eugene O. *A Treatise on the Law of Oil and Gas.* Cincinnati: W. H. Anderson Company, 1962.

Lewis, Richard S. *Appointment on the Moon: The Inside Story of America's Space Venture.* New York: The Viking Press, 1968.

Logsdon, John M. *The Decision to Go to the Moon: Project Apollo and the National Interest.* Cambridge: The MIT Press, 1970.

Long, Luman H., ed. *World Almanac, 1968*. New York: Doubleday and Company, Inc., 1968.

Maas, Arthur. *Muddy Waters: The Army Engineers and the Nation's Rivers.* Cambridge: Harvard University Press, 1951.

MacAvoy, Paul W. *Price Formation in Natural Gas Fields: A Study of Competition, Monopoly, and Regulation.* New Haven: Yale University Press, 1962.

———, ed. *The Crisis of the Regulatory Commissions: An Introduction to a Current Issue of Public Policy.* New York: W. W. Norton & Company, Inc., 1970.

McKie, James. *The Regulation of Natural Gas.* Washington, D.C.: American Enterprise Association, Inc., 1957.

MacNeil, Neil. *Dirksen: Portrait of a Public Man.* New York: The World Publishing Company, 1970.

McPherson, Harry. *A Political Education.* Boston: Little, Brown and Company, 1972.

McReynolds, Edwin C. *Oklahoma: A History of the Sooner State.* Norman: University of Oklahoma Press, 1954.

———; Marriott, Alice; and Faulconer, Estelle. *Oklahoma: The Story of Its Past and Present* (rev. ed.). Norman: University of Oklahoma Press, 1968.

Manley, John F. *The Politics of Finance: The House Committee on Ways and Means.* Boston: Little, Brown and Company, 1970.

Markmann, Charles L., and Sherwin, Mark. *John F. Kennedy: A Sense of Purpose.* New York: St. Martin's Press, 1961.

Marmor, Theodore R. *The Politics of Medicare.* Chicago: Aldine Publishing Company, 1973.

Matthews, Donald R. *The Social Background of Political Decision-Makers.* Garden City, N.Y.: Doubleday & Company, Inc., Doubleday Short Studies on Political Science, 1954.

———. *U.S. Senators and Their World.* Chapel Hill: The University of North Carolina Press, 1960.

Mooney, Booth. *The Politicians: 1945–1960.* New York: J. B. Lippincott Company, 1970.

Moore, William Howard. *The Kefauver Committee and the Politics of Crime, 1950–1952.* Columbia: University of Missouri Press, 1974.

Morgan, Robert J. *Governing Soil Conservation: Thirty Years of the New Decentralization.* Baltimore: Johns Hopkins Press, 1965.

Nash, Gerald D. *United States Oil Policy, 1890–1964: Business and Government in Twentieth Century America.* Pittsburgh: University of Pittsburgh, 1968.

Neuner, Edward J. *The Natural Gas Industry: Monopoly and Competition in Field Markets.* Norman: University of Oklahoma Press, 1960.

O'Brien, Lawrence F. *No Final Victories.* New York: Doubleday & Company, Inc., 1974.

Oppenheimer, Bruce Ian. *Oil and the Congressional Process: The Limits of Symbolic Politics.* Lexington, Mass.: Lexington Books, D. C. Heath and Company, 1974.

Parmet, Herbert S. *Eisenhower and the American Crusades.* New York: The Macmillan Company, 1972.

Patterson, James T. *Mr. Republican.* Boston: Houghton Mifflin Company, 1972.

Pealy, Robert H. *Comprehensive River Basin Planning: The Arkansas-White-*

Red Basins Interagency Committee Experience. Ann Arbor: University of Michigan, 1959.

Peterson, Elmer T. *Big Dam Foolishness: The Problem of Modern Flood Control and Water Shortage*. New York: The Devin-Adair Company, 1954.

Polsby, Nelson W. *Congress and the Presidency*. 2nd ed. Englewood Cliffs, N.J.: Prentice-Hall, Inc., 1971.

Pressman, Jeffrey L. *House vs. Senate: Conflict in the Appropriations Process*. New Haven: Yale University Press, 1966.

Presthus, Robert. *Men at the Top: A Study in Community Power*. New York: Oxford University Press, 1964.

Provence, Harry. *Lyndon B. Johnson*. New York: Fleet Publishing Company, 1964.

Rayback, Elton. *Professional Power and American Medicine: The Economics of the AMA*. Cleveland: The World Publishing Company, 1967.

Redford, Emmette S., ed. *Public Administration and Policy Formation*. Austin: University of Texas Press, 1956.

Richardson, Elmo. *Dams, Parks and Politics*. Lexington: The University Press of Kentucky, 1973.

Ripley, Randall B. *Power in the Senate*. New York: St. Martin's Press, 1969.

Rogers, Lindsay. *The American Senate*. New York: Alfred A. Knopf, 1926.

Roseboom, Eugene H. *A History of Presidential Elections*. New York: The Macmillan Company, 1970.

Ross, Irwin. *The Loneliest Campaign: The Truman Victory of 1948*. New York: The New American Library, 1968.

Salinger, Pierre. *With Kennedy*. Garden City, N.Y.: Doubleday & Company, Inc., 1966.

Salter, J. T., ed. *Public Men In and Out of Office*. Chapel Hill: The University of North Carolina Press, 1946.

Schlesinger, Arthur M. Jr., and Israel, Fred, eds. *History of American Presidential Elections, 1789–1968*. v. 4. New York: Chelsea House, 1971.

Settle, William A., Jr. *The Dawning, a New Day for the Southwest: A History of the Tulsa District Corps of Engineers 1939–1971*. Tulsa: U.S. Army Corps of Engineers, Tulsa District, 1975. (This is the published version of the Settle manuscript referred to in the notes and in the essay on sources.)

Sevareid, Eric, ed. *Candidates 1960*. New York: Basic Books, Inc., 1959.

Sidey, Hugh. *John F. Kennedy, President*. New York: Atheneum, 1964.

Smith, Frank E. *The Politics of Conservation*. New York: Pantheon Books, 1966.

Sorensen, Theodore C. *Kennedy*. New York: Harper & Row, Publishers, 1965.

Steinberg, Alfred. *Sam Johnson's Boy: A Close-up of the President from Texas*. New York: The Macmillan Company, 1968.

Stevens, Rosemary. *American Medicine and the Public Interest*. New Haven: Yale University Press, 1971.

Stromer, Marvin E. *The Making of a Political Leader: Kenneth S. Wherry and the U.S. Senate*. Lincoln: University of Nebraska Press, 1969.

Sundquist, James L. *Politics and Policy: The Eisenhower, Kennedy, and Johnson Years*. Washington, D.C.: The Brookings Institution, 1968.

Sykes, Jay G. *Proxmire*. Washington, D.C.: Robert B. Luce, Inc., 1972.

Truman, Harry S. *Year of Decisions*. v. 1. Garden City, N.Y.: Doubleday & Company, Inc., 1955.
———. *Years of Trial and Hope*, v. 2. Garden City, N.Y.: Doubleday & Company, Inc., 1955.
Truman, Margaret. *Harry S Truman*. New York: William Morrow & Company, Inc., 1973.
Van Dyke, Vernon. *Pride and Power: The Rationale of the Space Program*. Urbana: University of Illinois Press, 1964.
Vawter, Wallace R. "Case Study of the Arkansas-White-Red Basin Interagency Committee," in U.S. Commission on Organization of the Executive Branch of the Government. *Task Force Report on Water Resources and Power*. v. 3. Washington: Government Printing Office, June 1955.
Wellman, Paul I. *Stuart Symington: Portrait of a Man with a Mission*. Garden City, N.Y.: Doubleday & Company, Inc., 1960.
White, Theodore H. *The Making of the President, 1960*. New York: Atheneum Publishers, 1967.
White, William S. *Citadel: The Story of the U.S. Senate*. New York: Harper & Brothers, 1956.
———. *The Professional, Lyndon B. Johnson*. Boston: Houghton Mifflin Company, 1964.
———. *The Taft Story*. New York: Harper & Brothers, Publishers, 1954.
Wicker, Tom. *JFK and LBJ: The Influence of Personality Upon Politics*. New York: William Morrow & Company, Inc., 1968.
Yarnell, Allen. *Democrats and Progressives: The 1948 Presidential Election as a Test of Postwar Liberalism*. Berkeley: University of California Press, 1974.
Young, Hugo; Silcock, Bryan; and Dunn, Peter. *Journey to Tranquility*. Garden City, N.Y.: Doubleday & Company, Inc., 1970.

Periodicals

Ames, Glen R. "Bound for Oklahoma—The Frontier Dream of a Navigational Arkansas River Will Soon Become a Reality," *American Scene*, v. 4, no. 1 (Spring 1961): 3–4.
"Another Coal Settlement," *Commonweal*, v. 51 (March 17, 1950): 595–99.
Bendiner, Robert. "The Raid on the Gas Fields," *The Nation*, v. 170 (March 11, 1950): 217–19.
Berger, Raoul, and Krash, Abe. "The Status of Independent Producers Under the Natural Gas Act," *Texas Law Review*, v. 30 (1951): 29–61.
"Brain Storm," *Time*, v. 70 (July 29, 1957): 11.
Buck, Solon J. "The Settlement of Oklahoma," *Transactions of the Wisconsin Academy of Science, Arts and Letters*, v. 15, pt. 2 (1907): 325–80.
Cater, Douglas. "Contentious Lords of the Senate," *Reporter*, v. 27 (August 16, 1962): 27–28, 29.
"Changing the Senate's Finance Watchdog," *Business Week* (February 22, 1958): 24–25.

Childs, Marquis. "The Big Boom From Oklahoma," *Saturday Evening Post*, v. 221, no. 41 (April 9, 1949): 22–23, 118–20.

Collins, F. W. "How to Be a Leader Without Leading," *New York Times Magazine* (July 30, 1961): 9, 46, 50.

Crawford, Kenneth. "The Senate's Ways," *Newsweek*, v. 61, no. 2 (January 14, 1963): 27.

Crenshaw, Charles E. "The Regulation of Natural Gas," *Law and Contemporary Problems*, v. 19 (1954): 325–41.

"Curse or Blessing," *Time*, v. 50 (April 17, 1950): 100–101.

Dahlgren, E. G. "Ty". "Robert S. Kerr: Staunch Champion of Oil Industry in the U.S. Senate," *Oil* (September 1960): 9–12.

"Death of a Senator," *Time*, v. 81 (January 11, 1963): 23.

"Democratic Prodders Take the Field," *USNWR*, v. 34 (February 20, 1953): 58–61.

"The Democrats and Ike," *USNWR*, v. 35 (July 24, 1953): 30–31.

DeRoose, Robert, and Maas, Arthur A. "The Lobby that Can't Be Licked," *Harper's Magazine*, v. 199 (August 1949): 21–30.

"Dollar Derby," *Newsweek*, v. 43 (May 24, 1954): 26–27.

Drew, Elizabeth. "Dam Outrage: The Story of the Army Engineers," *The Atlantic*, v. 225, no. 4 (April 1970): 51–62.

"Duff Carrying the Ball," *Newsweek*, v. 36 (October 23, 1950): 30.

Dugger, Ronnie. "Oil and Politics," *The Atlantic*, v. 224, no. 3 (September 1969): 67–90.

"Election Issues Grow Hot," *USNWR*, v. 29 (October 23, 1950): 20.

Elson, Robert T. "A Question for Democrats: If Not Truman, Who?" *Life*, v. 32 (March 24, 1952): 118–120, 122, 125, 126, 128, 130, 133.

"A Friend in Need," *Newsweek*, v. 69 (January 30, 1967): 29–30.

Hardwicke, Robert E. "Some Consequences of Fears by Independent Producers of Gas of Federal Regulation," *Law and Contemporary Problems*, v. 19 (1954): 342–60.

Harris, Joseph P. "The Senatorial Rejection of Leland Olds: A Case Study," *American Political Science Review*, v. 45, no. 3 (September 1951): 674–92.

Henderson, Jim. "The Men Who Built the Waterways," *Tulsa*, v. 48 (May 27, 1971): 26–29, 32–33.

"High Ride for Gas," *Time*, v. 55 (April 10, 1950): 20.

"High v. Low," *Time*, v. 59 (March 31, 1952): 21.

"The Housewife's Friend," *New Republic*, v. 122 (April 10, 1950): 11.

Huitt, Ralph K. "Leadership in the Senate," *American Political Science Review*, v. 55 (June 1961): 333–44.

Ickes, Harold L. "Kerr's Asphyziation Bill," *New Republic*, v. 122 (April 17, 1950): 25.

"The Inflation Row Turns into a Three Ring Rumpus," *Business Week* (June 29, 1957): 44–45.

"Kefauver Knocks Out Kerr," *Life*, v. 32 (April 14, 1952): 40–41.

Kerr, Robert S. "Tax Loopholes," *Look*, v. 26 (March 13, 1962): 92, 95, 96.

"Kerr Switches Sides to Push Trade Bill," *Business Week* (July 28, 1962): 84–86.

Kraft, Joseph. "Kennedy's Working Staff," *Harper's Magazine*, v. 225 (December 1962): 29–36.

———. "King of the U.S. Senate," *Saturday Evening Post*, v. 236, no. 1 (January

5, 1963): 26–27.

McConaughty, James L. Jr. "The World's Most Exclusive Clubmen," *Life*, v. 36 (April 19, 1954): 110–11.

"Natural-Gas Blow Off," *Newsweek*, v. 35 (April 3, 1950): 17–18.

Neely, F. R. "Winner of the Collier Trophy," *Colliers*, v. 116 (December 22, 1945): 24, 80.

"Oklahoma Politics," *Life*, v. 13, no. 2 (July 13, 1942): 21–27.

"Oklahoma's Kerr, Man of Confidence," *Time*, v. 80 (July 27, 1962): 10.

"Oklahoma's Kerr—The Man Who Really Runs the U.S. Senate," *Newsweek*, v. 60 (August 6, 1962): 15–17.

"People of the Week," *USNWR*, v. 37 (July 16, 1954): 16.

Rothchild, John H. "The Great Helium Bubble," *The Washington Monthly*, v. 2, no. 4 (June 1970): 22–29.

"Seaports for Oklahoma," *USNWR*, v. 54 (February 11, 1963): 66–69.

Seligman, Daniel. "Senator Bob Kerr, the Oklahoma Gusher," *Fortune*, v. 59 (March 1959): 136–38, 179–88.

"Senator Kerr Talks About Conflict of Interest," *USNWR*, v. 53 (September 3, 1962): 86.

Shannon, Charles V. "Effect of Recent Supreme Court Decisions on the Production and Conservation of Natural Gas," *Interstate Oil Compact Quarterly Bulletin* (1945): 41–42.

"Shift in Men-Shift in Policy," *USNWR*, v. 44, no. 8 (February 21, 1958): 90–92.

Strong, Benton J. "The Rivers and Harbors Lobby," *New Republic*, v. 121 (October 10, 1949): 13–15.

Sullivant, Otis. "Rich Man's Race," *The Nation*, v. 178 (June 26, 1954): 542–43.

"Taking Over Money Probe," *Business Week* (April 20, 1957): 47.

"Uranium: Boom with a Bang," *Time*, v. 68 (July 30, 1956): 68.

"Votes before Dollars," *New Republic*, v. 122 (April 24, 1950): 7.

Wallace, Robert. "New Gouge for Consumers," *New Republic*, v. 122 (March 13, 1950): 11–13.

"Where the Death of Senator Kerr Will Be Felt," *USNWR*, v. 54 (January 14, 1963): 34.

White, William S. "Democrats' 'Board of Directors,'" *New York Times Magazine* (July 10, 1955): 10–11.

———. "Three Scouts Heading West," *Harper's Magazine*, v. 222 (March 1961): 105–106.

"Wildcatter," *Time*, v. 59 (February 25, 1952): 24–25.

Wright, Muriel H. "Early Navigation and Commerce Along the Arkansas and Red Rivers in Oklahoma," *Chronicles of Oklahoma*, v. 8, no. 1 (March, 1930): 65–88.

Young, Hugo; Silcock, Bryan; and Dunn, Peter. "Why We Went to the Moon: From the Bay of Pigs to the Sea of Tranquility," *The Washington Monthly*, v. 2, no. 2 (April 1970): 28–58.

INDEX

DATE DUE

JOSTEN'S 30 508